7*3

VITAL RECORDS

OF

NEWBURY

MASSACHUSETTS

• TO THE END OF THE YEAR 1849
1850
VOLUME II.
MARRIAGES AND DEATHS

v.2., pt 1

PUBLISHED BY
THE ESSEX INSTITUTE
SALEM, MASS.
1911

1897440

NEWCOMB & GAUSS
Printers
Salem, Massachusetts

ABBREVIATIONS

a.—age.
abt.—about.
b.—born.
bef.—before.
bet.—between.
bp.—baptized.
bur.—buried.
c. c.—copy made by Joshua Coffin.
c. R. 1.—church record, First Congregational Church.
c. R. 2.—church record, Second Church, now First of West Newbury.
c. R. 3.—church record, Third Church, now First Religious Society (Unitarian), of Newburyport.
c. R. 4.—church record, Fourth Church, now Second of West Newbury.
c. R. 5.—church record, Byfield Church.
c. R. 6.—church record, Amesbury Monthly Meeting of Friends.
c. R. 7.—church record, Queen Anne's Chapel (Episcopal).
c. R. 8.—church record, St. Paul's Church (Episcopal), of Newburyport.
c. R. 9.—church record, First Presbyterian Church, Old South, of Newburyport.
c. R. 10.—church record, Belleville Congregational Church, Newburyport.
c. R. 11.—church record, Purchase Street Methodist Church, Newburyport.
ch.—child.
chn.—children.
Co.—county.
cr. F.—court files, Essex Co. Quarterly Court.
cr. R.—court record, Essex Co. Quarterly Court.
d.—daughter; day; died.
Dea.—Deacon.
dup.—duplicate entry.
g. R. 1.—gravestone record, private burial ground on Joseph Ilsley's farm, Oldtown.

G. R. 2.—gravestone record, Oldtown Cemetery.

G. R. 3.—gravestone record, Newbury Neck Cemetery.

G. R. 4.—gravestone record, Queen Anne's Churchyard, Belleville, Newburyport.

G. R. 5.—gravestone record, St. Paul's Churchyard, Newburyport.

G. R. 6.—gravestone record, Walnut Hill Cemetery, West Newbury.

O. R. 7.—gravestone record, Bridge Street Cemetery, West Newbury.

G. R. 8.—gravestone record, Merrimac Cemetery, West Newbury.

G. R. 9.—gravestone record, Crane Neck Hill Cemetery, West Newbury.

G. R. 10.—gravestone record, Friends' Burying Ground, Turkey Hill road, West Newbury.

G. R. 11.—gravestone record, private burial ground, C. W. Ordway farm, West Newbury.

G. R. 12.—gravestone record, Lower Green Cemetery, Oldtown.

G. R. 13.—gravestone record, Highland Cemetery, Newburyport.

G. R. 14.—gravestone record, Byfield Cemetery.

G. R. 15.—gravestone record, Sawyer's Hill Cemetery, Newburyport.

G. R. 16.—gravestone record, Old Burying Hill, Newburyport.

h.—husband ; hour.

inf.—infant.

int.—intention of marriage.

jr.—junior.

m.—male ; married ; month.

P. R. 1.—Short's sexton's book, now in possession of Miss Ruth Short.

P. R. 2.—Record of deaths from selectmen's books.

P. R. 3.—Interleaved almanacs of Capt. Joseph O'Brien, now in possession of the Essex Institute.

P. R. 4.—Bible record now in possession of James L. Odiorne of West Newbury.

P. R. 5.—Bible record now in possession of Alonzo Jaques of West Newbury.

P. R. 6.—Bible record now in possession of the heirs of John Greenleaf Plummer of Newburyport.

P. R. 7.—Bible record now in possession of Mrs. Catherine Pearson of Newburyport.

P. R. 8.—Manuscript of Rev. Moses Parsons now in possession of the heirs of Mrs. Susan E. Parsons Forbes of Byfield.

P. R. 9.—Bible record now in possession of Edward A. Hale of Newburyport.

P. R. 10.—Bible record now in possession of the heirs of Maj. E. F. Bartlett.

P. R. 11.—Bible record now in possession of Charles F. Smith of Newburyport.

P. R. 12.—Diary of Samuel Tappan now in possession of the heirs of Mrs. Abbie Smith Nickerson.

P. R. 13.—Family record now in possession of Frank Thurlo.

P. R. 14.—Bible record now in possession of Miss Ruth Short.

P. R. 15.—Bible record now in possession of Mrs. Phebe Plumer Todd of Newburyport.

P. R. 16.—Sampler now in possession of Miss Eleanor Jones of Newburyport.

P. R. 17.—Bible record now in possession of Miss Lizzie Jaques.

P. R. 18.—Ancient book of accounts and records kept by Stephen Emery now in possession of Rev. Rufus Emery, D. D., of West Newbury.

P. R. 19.—Bible record now in possession of Miss Emily A. Bailey of West Newbury.

P. R. 20.—Copy book now in possession of Mrs. J. Appleton Brown of West Newbury.

P. R. 21.—Family record now in possession of Miss Harriet N. Hills of Newburyport.

P. R. 22.—Bible record now in possession of Miss Mary Russell Curzon of Newburyport.

P. R. 23.—Bible record now in possession of Daniel M. Davis.

P. R. 24.—Bible record now in possession of Stephen P. Hale.

P. R. 25.—Family register now in possession of Leonard Smith of Haverhill.

P. R. 26.—Family register now in possession of Leonard Smith of Haverhill.

P. R. 27.—Family register now in possession of Leonard Smith of Haverhill.

P. R. 28.—Bible record now in possession of Mrs. Harriet A. Menut.

P. R. 29.—Bible record now in possession of Mrs. Margaret M. Coffin.

P. R. 30.—Bible record now in possession of Edwin S. Jaques.

P. R. 31.—Diary kept by Dudley and Thomas Stickney, formerly in possession of Matthew Stickney of Salem.

P. R. 32.—Bible record now in possession of Edward A. Hale.

P. R. 33.—Stephen Jaques' Journal printed in the Essex Institute Historical Collections.

P. R. 34.—Family register now in possession of Miss Lizzie Jaques.

P. R. 35.—Records kept by Rev. Moses Hale now in possession of Rev. Rufus Emery, D. D.

P. R. 36.—Records kept by Moody Emery now in possession of Rev. Rufus Emery, D. D.

P. R. 37.—Records kept by Stephen Hale now in possession of Rev. Rufus Emery, D. D.

P. R. 38.—Family records now in possession of Rev. Rufus Emery, D. D.

P. R. 39.—Vital records kept by Eunice M. Emery now in possession of Rev. Rufus Emery, D. D.

P. R. 40.—Bible record now in possession of Mrs. J. A. Brown.

P. R. 41.—Bible record now in possession of Miss Charlotte Smith.

rec.—recorded.

s.—son.

S. dup.—copy of vital records made by Henry Short about 1690.

sr.—senior.

T. c.—town copy.

unm.—unmarried.

w.—wife ; week.

wid.—widow.

widr.—widower.

y.—year.

7 *br.*—September.

8 *br.*—October.

9 *br.*—November.

x br.—December.

NEWBURY MARRIAGES

ABBOT (see also Abbott), Catharine, of Newburyport, and
Richard Mayer Tilburn, int. Nov. 29, 1806.
Elizabeth, of Newburyport, and William Fitts of South
Hampton, Apr. 2, 1826.
Francis H., and Emily Dodge, Dec. 18, 1820.*
Francis H., and Mary Wade of Ipswich, int. Mar. 25, 1826.
Hannah, and Daniel Pilsbury, jr., Mar. 28, 1816.*
Jacob, and Abigail Frazer, Jan. 7, 1716.
Phebe, and John Chase, 3d, int. Mar. 24, 1780.
Phebe, and Gideon Rogers, int. May 8, 1812.
Sam[ue]ll, and Mary Coker, Feb. 14, 1757.*
Sarah, and Robert Cary, both of Rowley, June 18, 1804. c. r.
5.

ABBOTT (see also Abbot), Eb[enezer], and Eliz[abeth]
Tucker, both of Amesbury, —— 26, 1716. c. r. 7.

ABERDEEN, Mary, and Gilbert Affleck, both of Boston,
Dec. 18, 1729. c. r. 7.

ACREMAN (see also Akerman), Steven, and Sarah Stickney,
Dec. 17, 1664. [1684?]

ACRES (see also Akers), Henry, and Hannah Silver, Mar. 13,
1673-4.
Katharine, and Ephraim Hunt of Bridgewater, int. Oct. 8,
1698.
Martha, and Joseph Flood, int. Jan. 5, 1704-5.

*Intention also recorded.

7

ADAMS (see also Addams), Abigail P., and Tallack Bronbeck, of Newburyport, Jan. 6, 1831.*
Abraham, and Mary Pettingall, Nov. 16, 1670.
Abraham, jr., and Mrs. Anne Longfellow, int. Nov. 13, 1703.
Abraham [jr. int.], and Abigail Peirce, Dec. 6, 1716.*
Abraham [4th. int.], and Mary Coleman, Nov. 18, 1737.*
Abraham [3d. int.], and Mary Adams, Mar. 14, 1737-8.*
Abraham, 4th, and Mary Bricket, Nov. 18, 1768.*
Abraham, jr., and Judith Little, July 12, 1774.*
Alice [of Newburyport. int.], and Thomas Stickney, Sept. 24, 1798. c. r. 1.*
Alice, and Enoch Bointon, Apr. 25, 1799.*
Ann, and Robert Stuard of Rowley, Dec. 11, 1727.*
Anne, and John Knap of Newburyport, Apr. 28, 1767.
Archelaus, and Sarah March [wid. int.], Mar. 18, 1697-8.*
Archelaus, and Mrs. Dorothy Clement, Aug. 26, 1741.*
Archelaus, and Mrs. Mary Pearson, Apr. 20, 1742.*
Asa, and Dolly [Dorothy. int.] Morse, July 1, 1795.*
Asa, and Nancy Little, Nov. 20, 1826.*
Benjamin, jr., and Judith Adams of Rowley, at Rowley, Dec. 7, 1772.*
Betsey, and Ezra Adams, Jan. 14, 1796.*
Charles, and Rebeckah Adams, Jan. 25, 1753.*
Charles, and Mary Hills, Dec. 18, 1760.*
Charlottee, and James Johnson of Newburyport, int. Jan. 16, 1808.
Clarissa, and Wade Ilsley, Nov. 8, 1821.*
Daniel, and Ednah Noyes, Oct. 26, 1758.*
Daniel, and Elisabeth Colly of Newburyport. Dec. 25, 1777.*
Daniel, jr., and Hannah Poor, May 24, 1779.*
Daniel, and Jane Somerby, int. May 15, 1784.
Daniel, and Mary Lord of Ipswich, at Ipswich, Jan. 14, 1787.*
Daniel [jr. int.], and Edna Noyes, Nov. 26, 1788.*
Daniel [jr. int.], and Sarah Peirce, 2d w. [of Newburyport. int.], Jan. 18, 1800. c. r. 1. [int. May 1, 1800.]*
Daniel, Capt., 3d, and Polly Adams, Apr. 20, 1813.*
David, and Hannah Jackman, both of Rowley, Sept. 29, 1742.
David, and Mary Woodman, Sept. 22, 1778.*
David, and Lydia Whealer of Rowley, Mar. 1, 1798.*
David J., and Sarah C. Pettingell of Newburyport, ——, 1842. [Feb. 12. int.]*
Deborah, of Rowley, and William T. Winchester of Wiscasset, Feb. 10, 1812.

*Intention also recorded.

ADAMS, Deborah, and Rev. John Pike of Rowley, Aug. —, 1841.*

Eben, and Eliza I. Adams of Derry, N. H., int. Nov. 9, 1845.

Ebenezer, and Ednah Adams, Sept. 18, 1798.*

Edmund, and Hannah Thirston, Nov. 22, 1764.*

Edna [wid. int.], and John Noyes, jr., May 4, 1777.*

Ednah, and Ebenezer Adams, Sept. 18, 1798.*

Eleanor, and Capt. Jeremiah Jewett of Rowley, Apr. 21, 1832.*

Eliphalet, of Ipswich, and Anne Morss, Apr. 16, 1730.*

Elisabeth, and Samuell Swett, jr., Aug. 5, 1730.*

Elisabeth, and Jacob Freeze, Dec. 17, 1761.*

Elisabeth, and Paul Thurla, Feb. 19, 1789.*

Eliza, and James Young, Oct. 1, 1810.*

Eliza, and Ebenezer Little, Dec. 30, 1822.*

Eliza, of West Newbury, and Moody Adams, jr., int. Apr. 14, 1832.

Eliza, of Derry, N. H., and Nehemiah A. Bray, int Jan. 1, 1834.

Eliza I., of Derry, N. H., and Eben Adams, int. Nov. 9, 1845.

Elizabeth, of Rowley, and Israel Adams, jr., int. July 29, 1775.

Elizabeth, and Nathaniel Brown of Londonderry, N. H., int. May 19, 1781.

Elizabeth, and Maj. John Rowe of Gloucester, Apr. 7, 1791. c. R. 2.*

Elizabeth, and George Adams, Oct. 27, 1792.*

Elizabeth, and [Lt. c. R. 10.] Gibbins Adams, Sept. 25, 1817.*

Elizabeth, of Limerick, Me., and Moses N. Adams, int. Dec. 29, 1845.

Elvira, and Moses Plummer, Dec. 6, 1831.*

Enoch, and Sarah Jackman, July 28, 1747.*

Enoch, and Sarah Bragg of Andover, at Andover, Aug. 6, 1778.*

Enoch, and Elisabeth Russell, May 11, 1781.*

Enoch, of East Andover, and Lydia Moody, Jan. 30, 1803.*

Esther, and Moses Goodwin, July 19, 1797.*

Eunice, and Broadstreet Tyler of Boxford, Sept. 18, 1788.*

Eunice, and Nathan Longfellow, Feb. 24, 1814.*

Ezra, and Betsey Adams, Jan. 14, 1796.*

Freeborn, and Ruth Adams of West Newbury, int. Oct. 17, 1828.

George, and Elizabeth Adams, Oct. 27, 1792.*

*Intention also recorded.

ADAMS, George, jr., and Judith Dole, Dec. 22, 1823.*

George, and Hannah Thurlow, int. Dec. 1, 1838.

George W., a. 30 y., farmer, s. Gibbins and Elizabeth, and Mary Tyler Thurlow of West Newbury, a. 26 y., b. West Newbury, d. William and Miriam, of West Newbury, Nov. 14, 1848.*

Gibbins [Lt. c. R. 10.], and Elizabeth Adams, Sept. 25, 1817.*

Giles A., a. 26 y., carpenter, s. Richard, jr. and Abigail, and Sarah E. Jackman [of Newburyport. int.], a. 22 y., d. Moses B. and Harriet, Jan. 13, 1848.*

Hannah, and William Warham, Feb. 10, 1681.

Hannah, and Daniel Chute of Rowley, at Rowley, Apr. 20, 1743.*

Hannah, of Rowley, and John Woodman, Dec. 12, 1751.*

Hannah, of Rowley, and Noyes Pearson, at Rowley, Aug. 28, 1764.*

Hannah, and Paul Lunt, Feb. 5, 1789.*

Hannah, and Silas Moulton, May 7, 1791.*

Hannah, and Paul Thurla, Feb. 17, 1795.*

Hannah, and Joseph Russel [jr. c. R. 1.; at Haverhill. dup.], Oct. 19, 1797.*

Hannah, and John Carey, Nov. 1, 1798. c. R. 5.

Hannah, and Ebenezer Plumer of Newburyport, June 16, 1831.*

Hannah L., and George J. Poor of Rowley, Apr. 24, 1832.*

Harriet, and Joseph Adams, jr., Dec. 29, 1820. [Dec. 28. c. R. 1.]*

Henry, and Sarah Emery, Nov. 20, 1746.*

Henry, jr., and Sarah Dole, int. Nov. 7, 1767.

Henry, and Catherine Gerrish, Mar. 2, 1768.*

Henry, and Sarah Pulsepher of Ipswich, at Ipswich, Nov. 30, 1786.*

Henry, of Newburyport, and Sarah Jaques Pearson, Dec. 27, 1798.*

Henry, and Hannah Severance of Kingstown, int. Mar. 25, 1799.

Isaac, and Sarah Adams, int. Oct. 15, 1774.

Isaac, and Hannah H. Plumer, Apr. 7, 1835.*

Isaac, and Hannah O. Kent, int. Oct. 12, 1839..

Isanna, and Joseph Tappen of Newburyport, int. Nov. 9, 1838.

Israel, and Rebecca Atkinson, Oct. 15, 1714.*

Israel, and Deborah Sarl, both of Rowley, Oct. 16, 1740.

*Intention also recorded.

ADAMS, Israel, jr., and Elizabeth Adams of Rowley, int. July 29, 1775.

Israel, Capt., and Deborah Jaques, Nov. 11, 1779.*

Jacob, and Anna Ellen, Apr. 7, 1677.

Jacob, and Mary Hills, Aug. 31, 1742.*

Jacob, and Elisabeth Hidden, int. Oct. 3, 1789.

Jacob, and Hannah Bartlet, Dec. 4, 1817.*

James, of Washington, D. C., and Caroline Hunt, May 26, 1828.*

Jane, of Rowley, and John Sawyer Blaisdel, at Rowley, Dec. 13, 1781.*

Jesse, and Elizabeth Kent, int. Nov. 16, 1835.

Jesse, and Sarah Ann Knapp of Conway, N. H., int. Sept. 22, 1849.

Joann, and John Adams of Londonderry, N. H., int. Jan. 12, 1836.

Joannah, and Joseph Lunt, Dec. 4, 1708.

Joel, and Irena Felch of Newburyport, July —, 1832.*

Johane, and Lancelt Granger, Jan. 4, 1653.

John, and Elizabeth Noyes, Jan. 22, 1707.*

John, and Sarah Person, Nov. 17, 1713.*

John, and Elisabeth Morss, Nov. 2, 1730.*

John, and Elisabeth Thorla, Dec. 22, 1761.*

John [jr. c. R. 1.], and Margaret Lunt, June 22, 1800.*

John, 3d, and Rebeckah Atkinson, Nov. 26, 1801.*

John, of Londonderry, N. H., and Joann Adams, int. Jan. 12, 1836.

John C., and Sarah Jane Noyes, June 20, 1838.*

John J., and Lucy Ilsley, Nov. 20, 1832.*

John P[rentiss. int.], of Dover, N. H., and Ruth W[ade. int.] Dodge, Mar. 29, 1824.*

John Q., and Eliza Ann Hager, int. Dec. 31, 1847.

Joseph, of Stratham, N. H., and "Ms." Mary Greenlef, int. Nov. 29, 1746.

Joseph, and Elisabeth Atkinson, int. Jan. 16, 1768.

Joseph, jr., and Abigail Thorla, Feb. 22, 1770.*

Joseph, jr., and Mary Carlton, Jan. 6, 1774.*

Joseph, and Rachel Boynton, Dec 14, 1807.*

Joseph, jr., and Harriet Adams, Dec. 29, 1820. [Dec. 28. c. R. 1.]*

Judeth, and Edmund Little, Mar. 18, 1735-6.*

Judith, of Rowley, and Benjamin Adams, jr., at Rowley, Dec. 7, 1772.*

*Intention also recorded.

ADAMS, Judith, and Enoch Eastman, Nov. 21, 1808.*
Katharine, and Benjamin Poor, Dec. 4, 1777.*
Liphe, and Mary Boynton, Mar. 14, 1775.*
Lois, and Harrison W. Dearborn, Jan. 22, 1839.*
Love, and Stephen Pettengill, int. Nov. 15, 1800.
Lucy, and Thomas Cook of Newburyport, Nov. 24, 1807.*
Lucy, and Daniel Dodge of Newburyport, int. Oct. 15, 1814.
Lydia, and Eliphalit Jaques, Jan. 3, 1737-8.*
Lydia S., and Henry Lander of Newburyport, June 18, 1820.*
Margaret, and Elisha Bean of Newburyport, Nov. 25, 1823.*
Maria, and Josiah Titcomb, int. Oct. 24, 1818.
Martha, and Obadiah Short of Newburyport, int. Oct. 5, 1805.
Mary, and Jeremy Goodridg, Nov. 15, 1660.
Mary, and George Thurloe, Nov. 26, 1694. CT. R.
Mary, and James Merrill, Nov. 23, 1714.*
Mary, and Thomas Poor of Andover, Sept. 30, 1728.*
Mary, of Boston, and George Ledain, ——, 1729. C. R. 7.
Mary, of Falmouth, and David Stickne, int. Aug. 10, 1734.
Mary, and Abraham Adams [3d. int.], Mar. 14, 1737-8.*
Mary, and Nathaniel Clement [resident in Newbury. int.], Mar. 27, 1751.*
Mary, and Jeremiah Pearson [jr. int.], Jan. 20, 1756.*
Mary, and Abraham Weed, Oct. 14, 1756.*
Mary, of Rowley, and Benjamin Jaques, at Rowley, Mar. 25, 1760.*
Mary, and Jonathan Ilsley, Nov. 24, 1778.*
Mary, and Robert Morse of Newburyport, int. Mar. 29, 1806.
Mary, and Gilman Sargent of Amesbury, Apr. 27, 1819.*
Mary, and Gideon R. Lucy, May 5, 1831.*
Mary, and George W. Dennis, int. Aug. 20, 1831.
Mary H., of Newburyport, and William Coker, int. Mar. 19, 1836.
Mary L., a. 23 y., d. Richard, jr. and Abigail, and Joseph N. Rolfe, a. 25 y., farmer, s. Moses and Sarah, Apr. 8, 1847.*
Matthew, and Sarah Knight, Apr. 4, 1707.*
Matthew, jr., and Sarah Bartlet, May 2, 1734.*
Matthew, see Ordway, Matthew.
Mehetabel, and John Knight, July 21, 1763. C. R. 9.*
Molly, and Anthony Morss of Newburyport, int. Jan. 1, 1768

*Intention also recorded.

ADAMS, Moody, jr., and Eliza Adams of West Newbury, int.
　Apr. 14, 1832.
Moses, and Ruth Palmer, Feb. 6, 1760.*
Moses, and Pheby Jewit of Rowley, May 16, 1793.*
Moses, jr., and Mrs. Marcy Lunt, Dec. 26, 1811.*
Moses N., and Elizabeth Adams of Limerick, Me., int. Dec.
　29, 1845.
Nancy, and Ezra Hale, Jan. 1, 1800.*
Nancy, and Josiah B. Tilton of Deerfield, N. H., int. Oct. 15,
　1822.
Nathan [Capt. int.], and Mary Trumbal of Charlestown, at
　Charlestown, Feb. 17, 1757.*
Nathan, and Louisa Knowles of Newburyport, Apr. 6, 1826.*
Nath[anie]l, Lt., and Mary Pearson, Nov. 9, 1784.*
Paul, and Hannah Ilsley, Apr. 30, 1785.*
Paul, s. Richard, deceased, and Hannah, and Hannah G. Ken-
　iston, d. Moses and Dolly of Amesbury, 28 : 4 m: 1803.
　C. R. 6.
Paul, and Harriet N. Lanford, both of Newburyport, Nov.
　27, 1838.
Phebe, and Nathaniel Currier, int. Apr. 18, 1795.
Phebe, and Benjamin J. Tenney of Rowley, Dec. 22, 1811.*
Philip D., and Ruth Coffin, Dec. 30, 1841.*
Polly, and Capt. Daniel Adams, 3d, Apr. 20, 1813.*
Prudence, and John Bricket, Apr. 17, 1760.*
Rebecca [jr. int.], and [Ens. int.] Joseph Hilton of Exeter,
　Oct. 10, 1716.*
Rebecca, and Joseph Mors [3d. int.], Dec. 22, 1721.*
Rebecca, and Samuel Davis of Newburyport, int. Oct. 14,
　1797.
Rebecca B., and Benja[min] C. Perkins, Nov. 20, 1832.*
Rebecca P., of Derry, N. H., and Ezra Hale, jr., int. Apr. 14,
　1839.
Rebeckah, and Charles Adams, Jan. 25, 1753.*
Rebeckah [of Reading. int.], and Capt. Stephen Adams, May
　5, 1801.*
Richard, jr., and Sarah Noyes, Jan. 21, 1755.*
Richard, and Mary Cook of Newburyport, int. Apr. 3, 1818.
Richard, jr., and Abigail Little, Apr. 30, 1821.*
Robert, and Sarah Short, Feb. 6, 1677.
Robert, and Rebekah Knigt, d. John, int. July 13, 1695.
Robert, jr., and Ann Jaques, Oct. 29, 1725.*
Robert, 3d, and Love Jaques, Sept. 7, 1738.*

*Intention also recorded.

ADAMS, Robert, jr., and Eunice Little, July 12, 1774.*
Robert, and Susannah Little, Oct. 10, 1799.*
Robert, and Hannah Little, June 12, 1808.*
Robert, and Sarah Poor of Georgetown, Aug. 10, 1843.*
Ruth, and Joseph Thorla, Mar. 25, 1783.*
Ruth, of West Newbury, and Freeborn Adams, int. Oct. 17,
    1828.
Samuel, and Mary Brown of Rowley, at Rowley, Nov. 26,
    1747.*
Samuel, Esq., of Rowley, and Ann Wheelwright, July 7,
    1818.*
Sarah, and John Hutchinson of Andover, Jan. 28, 1714-15.*
Sarah, and Samuel Sommerby, Sept. 29, 1735.*
Sarah, and Joseph Bartlet, Jan. 5, 1735-6.*
Sarah, and Benjamin Scott, int. Jan. 4, 1739-40.
Sarah, and Parker Jaques, jr., Dec. 1, 1767.*
Sarah, and Isaac Adams, int. Oct. 15, 1774.
Sarah and Benjamin Plumer, jr., May 15, 1777.*
Sarah, and Stephen Adams, jr., Dec. 25, 1783.*
Sarah, and Dudly Brown of Kensington, Jan. 13, 1795.*
Sarah, and Moses Kent of Newburyport, Feb. 18, 1795.*
Sarah, and Samuel Blake, Dec. 26, 1799.*
Sarah J., of Derry, N. H., a. 23 y., b. Derry, d. Sewall and
    Sarah, and Charles H. [W. dup.] Hale, a. 26 y.,
    carpenter, s. Ezra and Anna, May 5, 1846.*
Seneca, and Sarah B. Rolf, Oct. 23, 1839.*
Sewell, of Londonderry, N. H., and Sarah Ilsley, Dec. 7,
    1820.*
Silas, Capt., and Lucy Underwood, Sept. 8, 1779.*
Simeon, and Salla Little, Apr. 13, 1790.*
Simon, and Sarah Lunt, Oct. 17, 1799.*
Smith, and Hannah Bray of Newburyport, int. Aug. 2, 1794.
Stephen, and Sarah Bartlet, Dec. 8, 1761.*
Stephen, jr., and Sarah Adams, Dec. 25, 1783.*
Stephen, Capt., and Rebeckah Adams [of Reading. int.],
    May 5, 1801.*
Stephen, jr., and Mary Jaques, Jan. 27, 1814.*
Stephen, jr., and Mary Ann Longfellow, Jan. 16, 1822.*
Susanna, and Stephen Dole, Mar. 15, 1768.*
Susanna, and Thomas Warthen, Feb. 11, 1786.*
Susanna, and John Coker, int. Dec. 14, 1805.
Susanna, and David Longfellow, June 29, 1809.*

*Intention also recorded.

ADAMS, Susannah, and Jonathan Merrill, jr. of Methuen,, Mar. 29, 1800.*

Thomas, and Mary Leach, June 5, 1805.*

Thomas, and Sally Saunders of Haverhill, int. Sept. 18, 1813.

Thomas H[all. int.], and Mary Jane Jennings, Dec. 2, 1838.*

Washington, of Newburyport, a. 30 y., merchant, s. Moses and Marcy, and Susan B. Coffin, a. 29 y., d. Edmund and Lucy, May 10, 1846.*

William, and Mary Osgood of Amesbury, int. Apr. 3, 1843.

Williams, of Rowley, and Elisabeth Noyes, Apr. 22, 1728.*

ADDAMS (see also Adams), Richard, and Susannah Pike, Dec. 12, 1717.

AFFLECK, Gilbert, and Mary Aberdeen, both of Boston, Dec. 18, 1729. C. R. 7.

AIMS (see also Ames), Hannah [Ames. int.], and Samuel Ruggs of Lancaster, Nov. 8, 1716.*

AIRES (see also Ayres), Mary, and Sam[ue]ll Jackman, Dec. 14, 1737. C. R. 7.

AIRS (see also Ayres), Elizabeth, and Thomas Safford of Ipswich, July 7, 1737. C. R. 7.*

AKERMAN (see also Acreman), John, jr., of Newburyport, and Elizabeth Foot, int. July 21, 1821.

Oliver M., of Newburyport, widr., a. 40 y., butcher, s. John, of Newburyport, and Mary J. Bradbury, wid., a. 26 y., d. John Longfellow, July 25, 1844.*

Sarah, and William Salmon, Oct. —, 1729. [He takes her without any of her former husband's estate. int.]*

Stephen, and [wid. int.] Sarah Wheeller, Feb. 12, 1711.*

William, and Jane Johnson, both of Newburyport, ——, 1832.

AKERS (see also Acres),. Abigail, and Richard Jackman, jr., int. July 9, 1785.

Daniel, and Sarah Worcester, int. Apr. 3, 1736.

Francis, and Rebecka Danford, Apr. 18, 1718.

Hannah, and Moses Knight, Nov. 29, 1737.*

Hannah, and Joseph Davis of Newburyport, July 10, 1774.*

*Intention also recorded.

AKERS, John, and Esther Buck, Aug. 1, 1771.*
Lydia, and Benjamin Fellows, May 4, 1758.*
Mary, and William Samson, Nov. 5, 1734.*
Mary, and William Elder of Falmouth, Nov. 21, 1751.*
Rebecca, and Joseph Russell, jr., May 12, 1761.*
Rebeccah, and John French, Jan. 31, 1739-40.*
Samuel, and Tab**ha Kenney, int. Jan. 21, 1715-16.

AKINS, Mary Ann, and Holbrook Burroughs, int. Dec. 2, 1839.

ALDEN, Thomas, and Jane Whippe, both of Boston, Jan. 3, 1726-7. C. R. 7.

ALEXANDER, William, of Londonderry, and Eunice Plumer, June 3, 1771.*
William, and Hannah Pearson, Jan. 20, 1818.*

ALGREEN (see also Allgreen), Mary, of Newburyport, and Edward Bass, int. July 2, 1829.

ALLE (see also Ally), Sarah, and Daniel Pilsbury, Jan. 18, 1703-4.*

ALLEN (see also Allin, Alline), Abigail, and Josiah Lunt, Nov. 21, 1751.*
Daniel, and Sarah Brown, May 18, 1718. C. R. 7.
Elizabeth, and William Fanning, Mar. 24, 1667-8.
Frances, of Boston, and William Cromartie of London, Oct. 5, 1762. C. R. 8.
George O., of Lowell, and Margaret Smith, July 2, 1843.*
Gilman P., of Essex, and Elizabeth Collins, Mar. 5, 1840.*
Hannah, of Newburyport, and Moses Chase, int. Jan. 20, 1821.
Henry, of Boston, and Jane Swett, July 4, 1734.*
Isaac, and Mary Jane Green, int. Apr. 26, 1845.
James, and Mary Chace, int. Dec. 15, 1827.
Jeremiah, jr., and [Mrs. C. R. 7.] Abigail Woldo, both of Boston, Mar. 21, 1727-8.
Joanna, and Henry Somerby, Nov. 4, 1764.*
Joanna, and James Tompson, int. Dec. 7, 1805.

*Intention also recorded.

ALLEN, Mark [Capt. int.], of Gloucester, and Hannah Floyd, Dec. 13, 1807.*

Mary J., a. 19 y., d. Joseph and Abigail, and Stephen H. March, a. 34 y., ship carpenter, s. Ichabod and Mary, Oct. 5, 1845.*

Nathan, and Joanna Cheny, Sept. 24, 1754.*

Samuel, of Gloucester, and Mary March, Jan. 26, 1726-7.*

Samuel, and Hannah Godfry, Sept. 25, 1735.*

Sarah, Mrs., of Newburyport, and Capt. Jeremiah Blanchard, Jan. 14, 1810.*

Sarah, and Timothy Richardson of Boston, int. Dec. 1, 1810.

William, Capt., of Salisbury, and Mrs. Elisabeth Giles, int. Sept. 21, 1745.

ALLGREEN (see also Algreen), Mary, Mrs., and James Fudge, Nov. 9, 1816.*

Mary Ann, and Charles Martin, int. Aug. 17, 1816.

ALLIN (see also Allen), Charls, and Joanah Scott, int. Aug. 21, 1703.

Daniel, of Boston, and Sarah Coker, Dec. 8, 1720.*

Elizbeth, Mrs., of Salisbury [Hampton. int.], and Joshua Moodey, at Salisbury, June 23, 1715.*

Margeret, Mrs., and William Mackhard, Dec. 15, 1743.*

ALLINE (see also Allen), Judith, and Nathaniel Bricket, jr., June 11, 1783.*

Margeret, of Reading, and John Ordeway, at Reading, Aug. 18, 1726.

Nathan, and Abigail Homans, Aug. 25, 1784.*

ALLY (see also Alle), Thomas, and Sara Silver, Feb. 9, 1670.

ALTER, John [Altex. int.], of Philadelphia. Pa., a. 38 y., merchant, b. Pennsylvania, s. Jacob and Elizabeth, and Sarah J. Hardy, wid., a. 35 y., d. Nicholas and Jane, May 3, 1846.

AMBROSE, Mary, of Salisbury, and Francis George, int. Nov. 9, 1754.

Samuel Goodhue, and Mrs. Sally Phalan, Nov. 8, 1812.*

*Intention also recorded.

AMES (see also Aims), Hepzibah, of Wilmington, and Joseph
  East of Dracut, Feb. 3, 1732-3. c. r. 7.
Joseph [resident in Newbury. int.], and Elisabeth Noyes,
  Mar. 5, 1765.*
Joseph, and Elisabeth Noyes, int. Aug. 10, 1765.
Joseph, and Nancy Tenny, Feb. 24, 1303.*
Lydia, of Bradford, and John Kelly, sr., Mar. 15, 1715-16.*
Mary, and Benja[mi]n Taylor of Ware, Nov. 27, 1800.*
Nancy, and Daniel Tuksbury, ——, 1809. [Feb. 1, 1810.
  int.]*
Nathan, and Margaret Sweet of Bradford, int. July 27, 1805.

ANDERSON, James, a. 22 y., caulker, s. Robert and Jane, and
  Lydia [A. int.] Flanders, a. 18 y., d. John and Ruth,
  June 2, 1849.*
Margaret, of Brunswick, and John Pease, int. Oct. 27, 1809.
Philander, and Elizabeth Crockett, int. May 26, 1832.
William, 3d, of Londonderry, N. H., and Mary Dana, int.
  Sept. 25, 1830.

ANDERTON, Elizabeth, and Robert Savory of Bradford, Jan.
  10, 1717-18.
James, jr., and Rachel Stanwood, Nov. 22, 1733.*
Rachel, Mrs., and William Mireck, Oct. 31, 1745.*
Sarah, and Henry Lunt, 4th, Mar. 24, 1724.*
William, and Elisabeth Holeman, Oct. 28, 1725.*
William, and Mary Peirse of Salem, at Salem, Feb. 28, 1737.*

ANDREWS, Eliz[abeth], of Marblehead, and Ben[jamin]
  Short of Enon, Great Britain, Nov. 13, 1717. c. r. 7.
Mary J[ane. int.], Mrs., and Obadiah S. Davis, Aug. 28,
  1843.*
Rebekah, wid., and John Horton, both of Marblehead, Sept.
  30, 1734. c. r. 7.
Sally, Mrs., and Abraham Shaw of Kensington, N. H., Feb.
  29, 1808.*

ANGER (see also Angier), Sybil, Mrs., of Cambridge, and
  Daniel Farnam, resident in Newbury, int. June 21, 1740.

ANGIER (see also Anger), Mary, Mrs., of Reading [Water-
  town. int.], and John March, at Reading, Dec. 11, 1700.*
Sarah, Mrs., of Watertown, and Christopher Tappan, int.
  Nov. 19, 1698.

*Intention also recorded.

ANNIS, Abigail, Mrs., and Robert Coffrin, Dec. 7, 1727.*
Abraham, jr., and Abigail Sawyer, Dec. 11, 1735.*
Charls, and Mary Morrison, Oct. 18, 1716.*
Christopher, and Ruth Merryl, Dec. 3, 1730. c. r. 7.
Curmac, alias Charls, and Sara Chase, May 15, 1666.
Daniel, and Catherine Thomas, Aug. 1, 1732.*
Dorothy, and Nathan Ordway, July 12, 1768.*
Eliner, and Robert Long, May 19, 1724.*
Hannah, and Benjamin Rawlins, Nov. 20, 1716.*
Hannah, and Thomas Eastman, Nov. 2, 1732. c. r. 7.
[John. int.], and Abigail Rolfe of Bradford, Dec. 16, 1724.*
Keziah, and Nathaniel Chaney, Oct. 25, 1733.*
Priscilla, and Peter Merryl, Mar. 10, 1730-1. c. r. 7.
Priscilla, and Daniel Mace, July 1, 1735.*
Rebecca, and Shimuel Griffin. Nov. 6, 1716.*
Rolfe, of Bradford, and Sarah Rawlings, Sept. 1, 1757.*
Ruth, and Samuel Davis, Oct. 28, 1756.*
Ruth, and Samuel Emery, Nov. 25, 1760.*
Sarah, and Ens. Orlando Bagley of Amesbury, int. Mar. 24,
    1703-4.
Tabitha, and Daniel Woodman, Mar. 9. 1737-8.*

APLETON (see also Appleton), Elizabeth, Mrs., and Rich-
    ard Dumer, Nov. 2, 1673.
Samuel, and Mary Oliver, Dec. 8, 1656.

APPLETON (see also Apleton), Caroline, of Newburyport,
    and John Haskell Tenney of Boston, May 8, 1839.
Robert, of Boston, and Rebecca Wentworth Means, int. Dec.
    14, 1846.

ARBUCKLE, Abigail, of Beverly, and Thomas L. Laskey, int.
    Dec. 27, 1834.

ARDWAY (see also Ordway), James, and Anne Emery, Nov.
    25, 1648.

ARNALL (see also Arnold), Joseph, of Boston, and Mrs.
    Rachal Sergant, Dec. 24, 1717.

*Intention also recorded.

ARNOLD (see also Arnall), Ann S., of Providence, R. I., and Capt. Charles Tyng, int. Oct. 24, 1826.

Hannah C., of Newburyport, and Hiram Huse, int. July 11, 1841.

Joseph, and Rebekah Woodman, Aug. 21, 1751.*

Thomas, and Anne Eaton of Salisbury, at Salisbury, Nov. 10, 1747.*

William, and Elisabeth Colby, Apr. 27, 1750.*

ASH, George, and Elizabeth Dutton of Newburyport, Oct. 11, 1835.*

Martha Ann, and Benjamin Dutton, both of Newburyport, Oct. 9, 1836.

Sarah, and Millet Smith of Newfield, Me., int. May 23, 1835.

ASHLEY, Esther, Mrs., of Braintree, and Dr. Joshua Bayley, 3d, int. Nov. 18, 1708.

ASLET, John, and Rebecca Ayres, Oct. 8, 1648.

ATHORN, John B., ship carpenter, s. ——, of Berwick, and Sophronia B. Chase, d. Jacob and Betsey, Sept. 22, 1844.*

ATKIN (see also Atkins), Mary, and Richard Lowell, Jan. 16, 1752.*

ATKINS (see also Atkin), Catharine, and Samuel Eliot of Boston, int. Apr. 21, 1786.

Dudley, and Mrs. Sarah Kent, May 7, 1752.*

John [Attkinson. CT R.], and Sara Mirricke, Apr. 27, 1664.

Joseph, Esq., and Dame Mary Wainwright of Boston, Apr. 7, 1730.*

Joseph, Capt., and Mrs. Ruth Doliber of Marblehead, Nov. 18, 1734. C. R. 7.

Rebekah, and Thomas Francis, Nov. 3, 1776.*

Sarah, and John Dean of Salem, Sept. 1, 1763. C. R. 8.

William, and Mrs. Abigail Beck, Aug. 15, 1737. C. R. 7.

ATKINSON (see also Atkison), Abigael, d. John, sr., and Jonathan Woodman, int. Jan. 1, 1695-6.

Abigail, and Joshua Moodey, jr., Apr. 8, 1725.*

Abigail, a. 18 y., and Abner Little, a. 20 y., cordwainer, Apr. 30, 1771.

*Intention also recorded.

ATKINSON, Abigail, and Benj[ami]n Currier, Nov. 25, 1802.*
Amos, Lt., and Anna Bayley of Amesbury, int. Oct. 17, 1778.
Amos, Lt., and Anna Knowlton of Newburyport, int. June 12, 1784.
Amos, of Boston, and Anna Greenleaf Sawyer, Apr. 28, 1818.*
Ann, and John Stanwood, Sept. 11, 1746.*
Anna, and Stephen Little, June 2, 1795.*
Benjamin Lunt, and Eliza Ann Knight, July 26, 1821.*
Elisabeth, and Samuel Pilsbury, Feb. 19, 1735-6.*
Elisabeth, and Moses Pettingill, Nov. 9, 1738.*
Elisabeth, and Mychael Toppan, Dec. 27, 1750.*
Elisabeth, and Joseph Adams, int. Jan. 16, 1768.
Eliza R., Mrs., of Newburyport, and Oliver S. Gordon of Boston, June 9, 1829.
Eliza Smith, and Mark Staples of Newburyport, int. Mar. 22, 1828.
Elizabeth, and Thomas Lovet of Hampton, N. H., int. Jan. 4, 1703-4.
Elizabeth E., and George K. W. Gallishan of Andover, Apr. 3, 1831.*
Elizabeth G[reenleaf. c. R. 2.], and Thomas Pettingall, Mar. 18, 1793.*
Eunice, and Joshua Little, Jan. 5, 1775.*
Eunice, and Moses C. Currier, Sept. 15, 1835.*
Eunice L., and James Horton of Newburyport, Dec. 5, 1826.*
Hannah, and Joseph Clement, Mar. 4, 1730-31.*
Humphery, and Mrs. Sarah Hale, Aug. 25, 1743.*
Ichabod, and Priscilla Bailey, Nov. 6, 1733. c. R. 7.*
Jacob, and Elizabeth Little, Oct. 5, 1825.*
Jane, and Phillip Dealane, int. Oct. 26, 1695.
Joanna C., and David Woodwell, Dec. 30, 1819.*
John [sr. int.], and Hannah Cheny [wid. Peter. int.], June 3, 1700.*
John, jr., and Judeth Worth, Nov. 23, 1721.*
John, and Lydia Little, Oct. 4, 1770.*
John, and Sarah Crooker of Minot, Me., int. Sept. 12, 1824.
John, and Sarah Ann Jenness of Haverhill, int. Jan. 8, 1831.
Jonathan, Rev., and Betsy Petengil, Feb. 6, 1794.*
Joseph, and Ann Wyat, both of Newbury, July 15, 1731. c. R. 7.
Joseph, and Hannah Hale, Jan. 23, 1744-5.*
Joseph, of Exeter, N. H., and Hannah Courser, Dec. 9, 1756.*

*Intention also recorded.

ATKINSON, Joseph A., and Frances G. Denny of Warner, N.
   H., Nov. 24, 1825.*

Joseph A., and Mary C. Brackett of Newburyport, int. Mar.
   27, 1830.

Josiah L., and Elizabeth Toppan of Newburyport, May 10,
   1821.*

Judith, Mrs., and Silas Pearson, Nov. 22, 1744.*

Judith, and Cutting Pettingill, jr., Jan. 13, 1746-7.*

Lois, and Joseph B. Brookings, Nov. 4, 1838.*

Lydia, and Richard Stickny, Oct. 24, 1751.*

Lydia, and Joseph Muzzey, jr., May 26, 1756.*

Lydia, and Charles Moody, Nov. 24, 1802.*

Lydia, and Elbridge G. Rogers of West Newbury, June 12,
   1824.*

Lydia E., a. 18 y., d. Jacob and Elizabeth, and Augustus K.
   Cole, a. 20 y., victualer, s. N. W. and Sarah S., Aug.
   5, 1849.*

Margarit, and Elias Jackman, Apr. 19, 1737.*

Mary, and George Frees, Apr. 19, 1737.*

Mary, and Moses Coffin, Feb. 14, 1765.*

Mary, and John Stockman of Amesbury, Dec. 12, 1827.*

Mary C., and Henry Somerby, jr., June 22, 1829.*

Matthias, and Abigail Bayley, Apr. 10, 1766.*

Michael, and Joanna Lunt, Apr. 17, 1794.*

Michael, jr., and Emeline Currier of Newburyport, int. Oct.
   3, 1835.

Miriam, and Ralph Cross, jr., Sept. 21, 1757. [Sept. 24.
   c. R. 9.]*

Molly, and Henry Gale of Kingston, Aug. 10, 1795.*

Moses, and Mary Merrill of Rowley, at Rowley, May 19,
   1757.*

Moses, and Sarah Hale of Hampstead, N. H., int. Aug. 4,
   1781.

Moses, 3d, and Charlotte Dutch of Exeter, int. May 22, 1808.

Moses L., and Catharine M. Bartlett of Newburyport, int.
   Apr. 19, 1845.

Nancy, and Alfred Johnson, jr. of Belfast, Me., Oct. 25,
   1817.*

Nathaniel, jr., and Elisabeth Greenleaf, Nov. 30, 1738.*

Nathaniell, and Deborah Knight, Jan. 22, 1707.*

Nath[anie]ll, and Sarah Morss, Apr. 1, 1756.*

Rebecca, and Israel Adams, Oct. 15, 1714.*

Rebeckah, and John Adams, 3d, Nov. 26, 1801.*

*Intention also recorded.

ATKINSON, Sara, and Steven Coffin, Oct. 8, 1685.

Sarah, and David Stickne, May 13, 1730.*

Sarah, and Joseph Clement [jr. int.] of Newburyport, Jan. 17, 1765.*

Sarah, and Stephen Atkinson, Feb. 27, 1794.*

Sarah J[ane. c. r. 10.], and Daniel Lakeman, Apr. 3, 1831. c. r. 10.*

Stephen, and Mercy Clark of Newburyport, int.. Dec. 15, 1770.

Stephen, and Sarah Atkinson, Feb. 27, 1794.*

Susanna, Mrs., and Robert Cole, Nov. 11, 1742.*

Theodore, and Mary Noyes, Feb. 13, 1796.*

Thomas, and Mary Pike of Salisbury, at Salisbury, Aug. 25, 1719.

William, widr., mariner, and Elizabeth Stratton, both of Boston, Nov. 18, 1725. c. r. 7.

William, and Anna Little, Apr. 10, 1804.*

William, and Jane Watt, Sept. 16, 1838.*

ATKISON (see also Atkinson), Theodore, and Lydia Stickny, Jan. 30, 1752.*

ATWOOD, Job and Elsy Chase, Nov. 27, 1814.*

Samuel, of Bradford, and Mary Uran, Aug. 15, 1751.*

AUBIN, George W., and Ursula S. Smith, Feb. 14, 1839.*

John, and Martha Ball, July 4, 1831.*

Mary, of Newburyport, and David Carey, int. Dec. 9, 1820.

Monroe, a. 27 y., seaman, s. John and Mary, and Sarah A. B. Richardson, a. 21 y., d. James and Hannah, Aug. 14, 1846.*

Nathaniel, and Bettee Carr of Salisbury, int. Nov. 8, 1760.

Samuel, and Jane Cole, Jan. 17, 1732-3.*

Thomas, and Phebe Peterson, June —, 1837. [Sept. 9. int.]*

AUSTIN, Mehitable, of Methuen, and Peter Rogers [jr. int.], at Methuen, Mar. 21, 1771.*

AVERY, Mary, of Newburyport, and Nathaniel Pettengill, int. Oct. 16, 1802.

*Intention also recorded.

AYER (see also Ayres), Hannah, of Haverhill, and Samuel
Lull of Byfield, at Haverhill, July 28, 1729.

Hannah, and Jonathan Lowel of Amesbury, Nov. 14, 1734.
c. R. 7.*

John, of Haverhill, and Sarah Perkins, Sept. 26, 1759.*

John, Capt., of Haverhill, and Susanna Hills, Dec. 8, 1818.*

Moses, and Lydia Hale, int. Oct. 2, 1804.

Ruth, of Haverhill, and Stephen Noyes, int. Feb. 7, 1818.

Susanna Woodbridge, of New Milford, and Charles Coffin,
jr., Oct. 19, 1802.*

Susannah, of Haverhill, and John Lull of Byfield, at Haverhill, Feb. 8, 1727-8.

Timothy, of Haverhill, and Huldah Chase, at Haverhill
[bef. 1784].

AYERS (see also Ayres), Charles W., of Portsmouth, N. H.,
and Martha Goodwin, int. Jan. 20, 1837.

Ebenezer, and Dorcas Gatchell of Salisbury, at Salisbury,
Oct. 5, 1710.*

Jabes, and Rebecca Kymbal, Dec. 8, 1718.*

John, and Elisabeth Boynton, Jan. 1, 1712-13.

Martha, and John L. Knight, int. Oct. 2, 1847.

Timothy, and Huldah Chase, Oct. 15, 1795.*

AYRE (see also Ayres), John, and Ruth Browne, Oct. 31,
1698.

John, of Haverhill, and Elisabeth Hale [at Haverhill. dup.],
Jan. 27, 1746-7.*

AYRES (see also Aires, Airs, Ayer, Ayers, Ayre), Rebecca,
and John Aslet, Oct. 8, 1648.

BABB, Daniel, and Belinda S. Brown, Mar. 29, 1825.*

BABBIDGE, Elisabeth, and James McGray, Nov. 28, 1753.
c. R. 8.

BABSON (see also Bapson), Lydia, of Newburyport, and
Abraham Somerby, int. Nov. 10, 1804.

BACHELDER (see also Batchelder), Josiah, of Kingston, and
Sarah Morss, Jan. 18, 1737-8.*

*Intention also recorded.

BACHELER (see also Batchelder), Sarah, of Reading, and Joseph Titcom, at Reading, Dec. 19, 1715.

BACHELLOR (see also Batchelder), William, Dr., of Haverhill, and Lydia Chase, at Haverhill [int. Feb. 20, 1771.].*

BACHELOUR (see also Batchelder), John, of Reading, and Sarah Poer [d. John. int.], Nov. 10, 1696.*

BACON, Susanna, and Samuel Long, Nov. 20, 1733.*

BADGE, Ann, of Charlestown, and John Lothrop of Rhode Island, goldsmith, Aug. 20, 1730. c. r. 7.

BADGER, Abigail, and Samuel Parmer, June 23, 1785.*
Benjamin, and Susannah Putman, May —, 1729.*
Elisabeth, and Samuel Blake of Hampton, Dec. 11, 1718.*
Elizabeth, wid., and Richard Browne, Feb. 1-, 164[7?].
Hannah, see Bodge, Hannah.
John, and Hannah Swet, Feb. 23, 1670.
John, and Rebecca Browne, Oct. 5, 1691.
John [s. John. int.], and Elizabeth Harris, Dec. 29, 1713.*
John Philip, and Mary Elizabeth Young, Sept. 2, 1841.*
Joseph, and Hannah Peaslee [of Haverhill. dup.], at Haverhill, Nov. 3, 1721.*
Judeth, and William Samson, July 8, 1730.*
Mary, and John Wyatt, Dec. 15, 1700.
Mary, and Samuel Macclure, Dec. 27, 1733.*
Nathaniel, and Mary Lunt, Mar. 27, 1693.
Rebecca, and Frederick Gray, Mar. 17, 1814.*
Ruth, and Thomas Jewill, Feb. 17, 1701.*
Sara, and Joseph Wheeler, Dec. 24, 1685.
Stephen, and Hannah Whittier of Haverhill, at Haverhill, Nov. 25, 1725.
Susanna, and Daniel Cheeney, jr., Feb. 18, 1790.*
William, and Anstis Emerson of Ipswich, int. Oct. 3, 1751.
William, widr., a. 57 y., farmer, s. Thomas and Abigail, and Lydia Piper, wid., a. 53 y., d. Robert and Ruth Long, Sept. 17, 1848.*
William James, and Sophia Ann Plumer, int. July 20, 1833.

*Intention also recorded.

BAGLEY, Isaac, of Amesbury, and Mehetable Bartlet, int. Dec. 16, 1780.

Orlando, Ens., of Amesbury, and Sarah Annis, int. Mar. 24, 1703-4.

BAILEY (see also Baily, Bayley, Bayly), Abigail, and Jonathan Hills, int. Oct. 10, 1748. (Abigail Bayle forbids proceeding.)

Abigail, and Joseph Ordway, Sept. 4, 1796.*

Abigail, and David Bartlet, jr., Jan. 14, 1813.*

Abner [3d. int.], and Sarah Bradbury, Mar. 29, 1803.*

Abner, 3d, and Sally Hardy of Bradford, int. Dec. 26, 1818.

Almira T., of Haverhill, and Benj[ami]n B. Littlefield, Oct. 7, 1838.*

Betsy, and Eliphalet Flanders, int. Apr. 13, 1807.

Beulah, of Bradford, and Daniel Griffin, int. Jan. 31, 1735-6.

Charles, and Marcia Lunt, Apr. 4, 1822.*

Charles M., of Haverhill, and Lydia Ann Smith, June 4, 1840.*

Christopher Toppan, and Hepzibah Pettingell, Apr. 16, 1820.*

Daniel [jr. int.], and Elizabeth Willit, Oct. 12, 1736. C. R. 7.*

Daniel, jr., and Sarah Noyes, Sept. 17, 1806.*

Dan[ie]ll, and Elisabeth Dennen of Glo[u]cester, May 23, 1750. C. R. 9.*

David, and Experience Putman, Nov. 11, 1713.*

David, and Elizabeth Dole, Feb. 22, 1738-9.*

Edmund, and Mary Parkhurst of Weston, at Weston, Aug. 20, 1731.

Edmund, and Abigail Bartlet, May 22, 1739.*

Elisabeth, and Stephen Merrill, Nov. 4, 1731.*

Elizabeth, of Rowley, and Daniel Tenne, Jan. 2, 1721-2.

Elizabeth, of Roxbury, and Lt. Joseph Bennet of Lancaster, Oct. 21, 1730. C. R. 7.

Hannah, and James Merril, Oct. 2, 1733. C. R. 7.*

Hannah, and Tappan Bailey, Feb. 18, 1812.*

Isaac [jr. int.], and Abigail Hills, Apr. 15, 1731.*

James A., and Mary Christa, ——, 1809. [Aug. 5. int.]*

John, and wid. Sarah Giddins of Chebacco, int. Oct. 6, 1711.

John, and Rachel Leadiary of Marblehead, Nov. 14, 1721.

John, and Mrs. Sarah Greeley, Oct. ——, 1833.

John, and Pamela England, Mar. 4, 1837.*

Joseph, and Deborah Hudson, Nov. 17, 1726.*

*Intention also recorded.

BAILEY, Joseph, and Myra Danforth, Nov. 23, 1826.*
Joshua [3d. int.], and Elizebeth Johnson, Apr. 25, 1715.*
Joshua, jr., and Elisabeth Chase, Sept. 4, 1734.*
Joshua, and Abigail Morse, Apr. 23, 1812.*
Joshua, jr., and Sally Chase, Aug. 25, 1812.*
Joshua, and Elizabeth Chase Carr, Feb. 8, 1817.*
Judeth, and James Ordway [3d. int.], Nov. 28, 1711.*
Judith, and Isaac Short, ——, 1808. [May 6. int.]*
Judith, and John Follansbee, int. Nov. 11, 1809.
Laura, and Enoch Chase, Dec. 4, 1817.*
Lydia, and Daniel Rutter [Retter. int.], May 13, 1715.*
Margaret, and John Caswell, int. Mar. 16, 1822.
Martha, and John Whittier of Haverhill, at Haverhill [bef.
    1784.].
Mary, and Abraham Dayes of Bradford, Jan. 25, 1737-8.*
Moses, and Gartret [Carteret. int.] Sawyer of Amesbury, at
    Amesbury, Oct. 28, 1792.*
Nancy, and Josiah Parker, Nov. 25, 1802.*
Nathaniel, of Rowley, and Mary Worster, July 25, 1726.
Parker, and Pamelia Minot, int. Nov. 10, 1832.
Priscilla, and Ichabod Atkinson, Nov. 6, 1733. C. R. 7.*
Rebecca, and Parker Noyes, int. Aug. 8, 1807.
Robert, jr., and Abigail Pettingell, Feb. 25, 1808.*
Samuel, and Jane Wyatt, Feb. 7, 1733-4.*
Samuel, and Mrs. Elizabeth Todd, Oct. 20, 1741.*
Samuel [jr. int.], and Anne Noyes, Mar. 19, 1748.*
Sarah [wid. C. R. 2.], and Richard Bartlet [2d. int.; widr.
    C. R. 2.], Sept. 27, 1727.*
Sarah, and John Rawlins, May 25, 1738.*
Sarah, of Newburyport, and Daniel Flanders, jr., int. Dec.
    3, 1807.
Sarah, and Joseph Head of Concord, Oct. 31, 1817.*
Sarah M., and Wyatt Osgood of Salisbury, July 29, 1832.*
Stephen, and Hannah Kelley, May 13, 1729.*
Stephen, and Mary Look, int. Jan. 24, 1735-6.
Stephen, of Bradford, and Sarah Church, June 14, 1737.*
Stephen, jr., and Rebeccah Chase of Andover, at Andover,
    Nov. 22, 1798.*
Stephen, jr., and Mary Greenleaf, ——, 1811. [July 30. int.]*
Tappan, and Hannah Bailey, Feb. 18, 1812.*
Thomas, and Eunice Stickney, May 24, 1806.*
Uriah, and Julia Gage of Bradford, int. Oct. 24, 1818.
Walter, and Mary Pilsbury Noyes, July 10, 1816.*

*Intention also recorded.

BAILEY, William, and Anne Lowell [of Amesbury. int.], at
     Amesbury, Nov. 25, 1742.*
William, and Hitty Hamilton of Rowley, at Rowley, June
     17, 1786.
W[illia]m, and Mary Cheeney, Nov. 25, 1813.*
William, and Margaret Colby, Oct. 24, 1815.*

BAILY (see also Bailey), Ann, of Rowley, and Thomas Wi-
     com, Apr. 1, 1728.*
Isaac, and Sarah Emery, June 13, 1683.
James, and Mrs. Mary Car, Sept. 17, 1672.
Rachell, and Samuel Poore, jr., Feb. 16, 1679.
Rebecca, and Isaac Brown, Aug. 22, 1661.
Sara, and Daniel Cheny, Oct. 8, 1665.

BAKER, Abigail, of Beverly, and Daniel Massey of Salem,
     May 21, 1734. C. R. 7.
Anna, and Tristram Thurla, Jan. 31, 1787.*
Deborah, and Samuel Cheney, both of Rowley, July 3, 1825.
Elisabeth, and Joseph Wallingford, both of Rowley, Sept. 5,
     1751.
Gideon, and Sarah Barnard Kelley, int. Aug. 23, 1809.
Josiah, of Falmouth [in Casco Bay. int.], and Lydia Mer-
     rill, Nov. 7, 1768.*
Lucretia, of Manchester, and Gideon Woodwell, jr., int. Dec.
     15, 1821.
Martha, and Moses Noyes, both of Rowley, Mar. 14, 1816.
     C. R. 5.
Polly [Mary. int.], of Topsfield, and Jacob Brown, at Tops-
     field, Apr. 11, 1793.*
Sarah, and Forbes Little, both of Marshfield, Nov. 30, 1733.
     C. R. 7.
Susan, of Salisbury, and William Goodwin, int. Dec. 11,
     1828.
Zachariah, of Falmouth, and Abigail Merrill, Feb. 23, 1778.*

BALCH, Benjamin, of Newburyport, and Hannah Pattin,
     Sept. 8, 1786.*
Daniel, and Hannah Clement, Aug. 19, 1756.*
Daniel, of Newburyport, and Judith Thurston, Mar. 24,
     1784.*
Eunice, and Enoch Moody of Hallowell, Nov. —, 1816.*

*Intention also recorded.

BALCH, Hannah, of Bradford, and Ezekiel Hale, int. Feb. 6, 1752.

Hannah, and Ebenezer Dole of Hallowell, Nov. 14, 1814.*

John, and Eunice Bartlett, Mar. 1, 1783.*

Lucy, and Charles French of Boston, Oct. —, 1821.*

Lydia P[ilsbury. int.], and Jeremiah P[earson. int.] Toppan of Newburyport, Apr. 15, 1822.*

Mary, and Hon. Jeremiah Nelson, Apr. 11, 1831.*

Phineas C., of Bradford, and Jane Merrill, May 17, 1820.*

Sarah, of Newburyport, and Rev. Isaac Braman of Rowley, Mar. 22, 1837.

Sophronia, and Josiah Little of Newbury, Vt., Jan. 24, 1814.*

BALDMAN, Rachel, of Newburyport, and Isaac Carpenter, Dec. 7, 1832.

BALL, James, and Elisabeth Dressor, Feb. 6, 1789.*

James, jr., and Nancy Battis, Mar. 6, 1812.*

John, and Nancy Bradbury, Nov. 2, 1788.*

Martha, and John Aubin, July 4, 1831.*

Nancy, Mrs., and William Jackman [jr. int.], Nov. 18, 1816.*

Phebe, and Cornelius Peterson, Oct. 28, 1806.*

BALLARD, Daniel, and Phebe Mitchel, both of Boston, Apr. 27, 1727. C. R. 7.

Dorothy, of Andover, and Benjamin Smith, at Andover, Aug. 16, 1734.*

William Samuel, of Boston, and Mrs. Hannah Hudson, Aug. 2, 1738. C. R. 7.

BAMFORD, Elizabeth Haskell, of Newburyport, and Samuel Smith, May 10, 1821.*

Joseph, and Tammey Haskel, June 9, 1796.*

BANCRAFT (see also Bancroft), Thomas, of Reading, and Lydiah Deane, Oct. 31, 1717.

BANCROFT (see also Bancraft), Elisabeth, and Sam[ue]ll Woodman, Mar. 25, 1756.*

Lidia, of Reading, and Jonathan Noice, at Reading, Aug. 24, 1742.*

Mary, of Reading, and Thomas Follingsby, at Reading, Feb. 18, 1734-5.*

Susanna, and Joseph Chase, jr., Aug. 27, 1751.*

*Intention also recorded.

BANISTER (see also Bannister), Thomas, and Rebeckar Green, both of Bradford, Dec. 15, 1724. c. r. 7.

BANKS, John E., of Portsmouth, N. H., and Eliza Ann Leibby, int. Oct. 13, 1849.
Samuell, of York, and Sarah Webster, Dec. 22, 1728.*

BANNISTER (see also Banister), Cypriam, and Mahala Worcester of Tyngsboro, int. Oct. 21, 1810.
Sarah White, of Newburyport, and Dr. Ebenezer Hale, at Newburyport, June 13, 1844.*

BAPSON (see also Babson), Betsy, and Joseph Putnam of Newburyport, May 26, 1783.*

BARBAR (see also Barbour), Thomas, and Anne Chase, Apr. 27, 1671.

BARBOUR (see also Barbar), Jerusha, of Bridgport, Vt., and Martin Root, M. D., Mar. 2, 1829.*

BARETUE, Elisabeth, and Amos Osiliway, at Amesbury, Jan. 5, 1737-8.*

BARK, Thomas, and Eunice Stickney, int. Aug. 5, 1803.

BARKER, Daniel, of Bradford, and Mary Sergent, int. Dec. 2, 1743.
Elizabeth, and Jonathan Farnem, both of Andover, Oct. 16, 1708.
Ezra, of Tyngsboro, and Mary [Sarah. int.] Pitman, at Tyngsboro, Dec. 7, 1795.*
Hannah, and Jacob Chase, int. Dec. 30, 1805.
James, of Bradford, and Elizabeth Brown of Byfield-Rowley, Feb. 22, 1781.
John, of Methuen, and Sarah Roberts, Nov. 11, 1742.*
John, of Bradford, and Mary Jackman of Byfield-Rowley, Mar. 27, 1781.
Jonathan, of Greenland, and Rachel Lunt, Sept. 26, 1734. c. r. 7.*
Lydia, and Joseph Langdon Whitten [Whittemore. c. r. 10.], Dec. 30, 1809.*

*Intention also recorded.

BARKER, Martha, and Christopher Carlton, both of Andover, July 6, 1715.
Parker, and Abigail Rogers, Mar. 6, 1801.*
Samuel, and Sarah Gage, both of Andover, Oct. 16, 1708.
Samuel, and Betsy Rogers, Sept. 28, 1783.*
Susanna, Mrs., of Boxford [Andover. int.], and Moses Tupenden [Fessenden. int.], at Boxford, Nov. 30, 1777.*
William [Nathan. int.], of Andover, and Mary Merrill, May 13, 1742.*

BARNARD (see also Bernard), Abigail [of Amesbury. int.], and Abraham Mace, Mar. 21, 1733-4.*
Elionar, and Georg Little, July 19, 1681.
Elisabeth, and Nathaniel Plummer, jr., int. Feb. 25, 1786.
Elisha, and Eunice Colman, int. June 20, 1806.
Elizabeth, of Amesbury, and Stephen Bartlet, int. July 20, 1776.
Mary, and Anthony Morse, Nov. 10, 1669.
Sally, of Amesbury, and Jeremiah Waterhouse, Jan. 1, 1821.*
Samuel, of Amesbury, and Mary Kingsbury, Mar. 1, 1759.*
Sarah, Mrs., of Andover, and [Rev. int.] John Tucker, at Andover, Aug. 27, 1747.*
Sarah S., and Ralph C. Huse of Newburyport, int. Sept. 7, 1839.
Thomas, and Mrs. Mary Woodbridge, Apr. 9, 1741.*
Thomas, of Amesbury, and Martha Robinson, int. Sept. 13, 1782.

BARRET (see also Barrett), Alexander, and Alice Landrigan, June 3, 1756. c. r. 8.

BARRETT (see also Barret), Betsy, and William Bartlett, Feb. 26, 1817.*
Elisabeth, and Jonathan Moulton, Nov. 29, 1759. c. r. 8.
Joseph Edmonds, and Nancy Norwood, Feb. 2, 9 or 16, 1812.*
Robert, and Tirzah Brown, Mar. 5, 1732-3. c. r. 7.

BARSTOW, Mary, and William Silvester, both of Hanover, May 12, 1736. c. r. 7.

BARTELL (see also Battelle), Thomas, and Sarah Webster of Salisbury, at Salisbury, Feb. 14, 1710.

· *Intention also recorded.

BARTLET (see also Bartlett), Abigael, jr., d. Samuel, and Abraham Merrill, jr., int. Oct. 7, 1696.

Abig[ail], Mrs., and Sam[uel] Goodhue, Nov. 6, 1717. C. R. 7.

Abigail, and Thomas Merrill, June 19, 1729.*

Abigail, and Edmund Bailey, May 22, 1739.*

Abigail, Mrs., and James Pettingill, May 15, 1744.*

Abigail, and William Ordway, Nov. 8, 1801.*

Abigail, of Salisbury, and John Brewster, Nov. 22, 1814.*

Abigel, and John Emery [sr. int.], May 27, 1700.*

Alice, and Benjamin Chase, jr., int. Oct. 17, 1781.

Anna, and Elijah Pilsbury, Mar. 18, 1762.*

Anne, and Edward Richardson, Oct. 28, 1673.

Apphia, and Joseph Bayley of Tewksbury, Oct. 21, 1755.*

Betsey, and Azariah Boody, int. June 15, 1803.

Betsy, and John Whicher, int. Mar. 7, 1803.

Betty, and Joshua Tyler of Bradford, Apr. 24, 1800.*

Caroline, and William Tapley of Salisbury, int. Feb. 1, 1834.

Christopher, and ——, Apr. 17, 1645.

Christopher, and Mary Hoyt, Dec. 17, 1663.

Christopher, and Deborah [Weed. c. c.], Nov. 29, 1677.

Christopher, and Esther Kelle, Mar. 8, 1724-5.*

Cutting, and Anne Moulton, Aug. 27, 1745.*

Cutting, and Hannah Brown, Nov. 17, 1763.*

Daniel, and Priscilla Merrill, May 31, 1770.*

Daniel, and Jemima Smith, Apr. 10, 1806. [Apr. 14. dup.]*

David, and Priscilla Hulgate, Jan. 31, 1754.*

David [jr. c. R. 2.], and Susanna Folansbe, Sept. 10, 1785.*

David, jr., and Abigail Bailey, Jan. 14, 1813.*

Dorothy, and John Ropes of Salem, June 6, 1707.*

Dorothy, and Cutting Moody, Dec. [15. c. R. 7.], 1737.

Dorothy, and Nathaniel Pearly, Nov. 24, 1801.*

Edmund, and Mrs. Hannah Hall. Oct. 3, 1745.*

Ehud, of Amesbury, and Elizabeth Lunt, Nov. 14, 1734. C. R. 7.

Elisabeth, and Josiah Bartlet. Apr. 13, 1725.*

Elisabeth, and Seth Chase, May 31, 1738.

Elisabeth, and Thomas Morss, June 30, 1747.*

Eliza, of Newburyport, and Moses C. Knight, Apr. 28, 1831.*

Elizabeth, of Newburyport. and Jonathan Cone of Campton, N. H., Jan. 26, 1773.

Enoch, of Haverhill and [Mrs. dup.] Catharine Dummer [at Haverhill. dup.], Aug. 21, 1755.*

*Intention also recorded.

BARTLET, Enos, and Mary Ordway, Jan. 28, 1730.*

Enos, jr., and Sarah Bricket, int. May 14, 1768.

Enos, and Rebecca Durgin [of Durham. int.], Feb. 16, 1815.*

Ezekiel, and Abigail Kent, Mar. 6, 1788.*

Fanny, of Newburyport, and David Dunlap, int. Jan. 17, 1824.

Francis, and Mary Eliot, both of Amesbury, Sept. 9, 1741. C. R. 7.

Francis, and Eliza Stevens of Woolwich, int. Dec. 8, 1797.

Frederick, and Sarah P. Merrill, int. June 9, 1838.

George, and Betsey C. Merrill, int. Aug. 16, 1837.

Gideon, and Abigail Emery, Dec. 16, 1725.*

Hannah, and John Ordway, jr., Dec. 18, 1706.*

Hannah, and Richard Kelly, jr., Dec. 16, 1725.*

Hannah, and Benjamin Merryl, Feb. 23, 1729-30. C. R. 7.

Hannah, Mrs., and Nathaniel Brown of Wenham, Jan. 1, 1732-3. C. R. 7.

Hannah, Mrs., and James Chase, Sept. 18, 1739.*

Hannah, and Thomas Bartlet, Dec. 21, 1763.*

Hannah, and Charles Chase, Nov. 3, 1796.*

Hannah, and Jacob Adams, Dec. 4, 1817.*

Harriet F., of Newburyport, and William Collins, jr., int. Feb. 25, 1837.

Humphry, and Abigail Jackman, July 4, 1786.*

Isaac, and Rebekah Sarjant of Haverhill, int. Dec. 6, 1776.

Isaac, jr., and Abigail Mores, int. Aug. 16, 1804.

Israel, and Hannah Lowell of Salisbury, int. May 11, 1805.

Jacob, and Eleanor Hagget of Andover, at Andover, Mar. 9, 1762.*

Jacob, and Hannah Sargeant of Bradford, int. Jan. 19, 1771.

Jacob, of Salisbury, and Mary True, int. July 28, 1810.

Jane, and Will[iam] Bolton, Jan. 16, 1654.

Jemima, and Silas Rogers [jr. int.], Jan. 21, 1802.*

John, and Sara Knight, Mar. 6, 1659-60.

John, and Mary Rust, Sept. 29, 1680.

John, 3d, and Mary Ordway, Nov. 18, 1702.*

John, 4th [3d. int.], and Prudence Merrill [d. Dea. Abraham. int.], Nov. 25, 1702.*

John, sr., and Mrs. Dorcas Phillips of Rowley, int. Sept. 30, 1710.

John, and Hephzibah Stevens, Jan. 18, 1763.*

John, and Sarah Souther of Ipswich, int. Apr. 6, 1782.

John, and Jane Carr of Newburyport, int. Mar. 17, 1792.

*Intention also recorded.

BARTLET, John Emery, of Newburyport, and Judith Dole, int. May 8, 1807.

Jonas, and Hannah Plummer Dole, May 18, 1800.*

Jona[than], and Mary Jones, Oct. 12, 1749.*

Jonathan, and Sarah Shute of Newburyport, int. Nov. 28, 1840.

Joseph, and Sarah Adams, Jan. 5, 1735-6.*

Joseph, and Isabella Hebron, Feb. 20, 1760.*

Joseph, 3d, and Sarah Morss, Oct. 12, 1762.*

Joseph, 3d, and Mary Currier, Jan. 4, 1797. c. r. 2.*

Joseph, and Nancy Brown, May 23, 1822.*

Josiah, and Elisabeth Bartlet, Apr. 13, 1725.*

Josiah, and Lydia Hale, June 19, 1744.*

Josiah, and Affia Dole, Aug. 18, 1767.*

Josiah, jr., and Prudence Ordway, June 1, 1773.*

Josiah, and Salley Moody, Apr. 23, 1801.*

Judeth, and Moses Chase, 3d, Dec. 9, 1736.*

Judith, Mrs., and Samuel Cook, Feb. 18, 1745-6.*

Judith, and Ichabod Coffin, Aug. 21, 1775.*

Judith, and Moses March, Jan. 6, 1777.*

Judith, and Edmund Little, jr., Aug. 2, 1789.*

Julia A., of Brentwood, N. H., a. 21 y., b. Brentwood, d. Aaron and Matilda, of Brentwood, and Daniel Lunt, a. 23 y., cordwainer, s. Daniel A. and Elizabeth, Nov. 27, 1849.*

Loruhamah Collins, and Moses Merrill of Salisbury, June 24, 1811.*

Love, and Joshua Lunt, Mar. 4, 1756. c. r. 8.

Lydia, Mrs., and Matthias Plant, "minister of ye church of England," Dec. 27, 1722.

Lydia, and Jacob Gidins, Dec. 6, 1737.*

Lydia, and Nathaniel Chaney, Aug. 19, 1741.*

Lydia, and Samuel Gregg of New Boston, int. Feb. 24, 1804.

Lydia, and Edmund Greenleaf of Canterbury, N. H., ——, 1810 or 11. [Jan. 26, 1811. int.]*

Lydia, of Newburyport, and William Jaques, int. Mar. 11, 1815.

Margaret, and Benjamin Morss, 3d, Oct. 3, 1726.*

Margaret, and Isaac Platts of Bradford, Mar. 10, 1735-6.*

Martha, and Thomas Stevens, Apr. 15, 1671.

Martha, and Nathaniel Ordway, Nov. 27, 1800.*

Mary [d. John, jr. int.], and John Bayley, July 2, 1700.*

Mary, and Josiah Hills, Sept. 30, 171[8. c. r. 2.].*

*Intention also recorded.

BARTLET, Mary, and Joseph Jacobs of Ipswich, Apr. 29, 1723.
C. R. 7.

Mary, and Samuel Tompson, Sept. 7, 1727. C. R. 7.

Mary, and Henry Hale, May 21, 1730.*

Mary, and Daniel Somerby, Aug. 8, 1751.*   1897440

Mary, and John Plumer, 3d, Nov. 25, 1761.*

Mary, of Amesbury, and Timothy Pilsbury, int. Feb. 19,
1770.

Mary, and Joseph Gerrish of Boscawen, N. H., int. Sept. 11,
1779.

Mary, and Oliver Pilsbury, May 18, 1797.*

Mary, and Joseph Brickett of Newburyport, Dec. 28, 1815.*

Mary Smith, and John Burrill of Newburyport, Jan. 13,
1791. C. R. 2.*

Mehetable, and Isaac Bagley of Amesbury, int. Dec. 16, 1780.

Mehitabel, of Weare, N. H., and James Tewksbury, int. Dec.
26, 1817.

Melinda, and Nicholas Felch of Newburyport, int. Sept. 28,
1839.

Molly, and Isaac Bayley, Dec. 25, 1788.*

Moses, and Judith Rogers, May 17, 1744.*

Moses, and Lydia Carnes [Cone. int.], Apr. 25, 1803.*

Moses, and Judith C[lark. int.] Dole, June 13, 1822.*

Nathan, and Joanna Flanders of Salisbury, at Salisbury, Mar.
5, 1740-41.*

Nathaniel, and Mrs. Meribah Littlefield of Kittery, int. Sept.
22, 1705.

Nathaniel, and Mary Woodman, Sept. 25, 1760.*

Nathaniel, and Hannah Hills, Jan. 12, 1773.*

Nehemiah, and Abigail Moulton, Jan. 7, 1791.*

Rebeca, and Isaac Bayley, Sept. 5, 1700.*

Rebecca, and Daniel Coffin, July 15, 1725.*

Rebecca, and Benjamin Kelly of Amesbury, Oct. 7, 1736.*

Rebecca, of Campton, N. H., and Nathaniel Moody, int.
Mar. 25, 1831.

Rebeckah, and Moses Morse, Nov. 6, 1800.*

Richard, and Hanna Emery, Nov. 18, 1673.

Richard [jr. int.], and Margeret Woodman, Apr. 12, 1699.*

Richard, 4th, and Sarah Chase, Dec. 5, 1723.*

Richard [2d. int.: widr. C. R. 2.], and [wid. C. R. 2.] Sarah
Bailey, Sept. 27, 1727.*

Richard, and Anna Moody, Sept. 25, 1787.*

Ruth, and Ebenezer Farrington, int. Oct. 8, 1803.

*Intention also recorded.

BARTLET, Ruth, and Ruben Currier of Southampton, int. Sept. 28, 1804.

Ruth, and William Moulton, jr., Dec. 25, 1817.*

Samuel [3d. int.], and Judeth Coffin, Jan. 2, 1716-17.*

Samuel, 3d, and Elisabeth Brown, Jan. 17, 1736-7.*

Samuel, and Rachel Coffin, Sept. 30, 1756.*

Samuel, of Newburyport, and Ruth Pilsbury, Aug. 29, 1799.*

Samuel, of Amesbury, and Rebecca Blanchard, int. Aug. 26, 1815.

Samuell, and Elizabeth Titcomb, May 23, 1671.

Sarah, and Joseph Fowler of Ipswich, Dec. —, 1707.*

Sarah, and Matthew Adams, jr., May 2, 1734.*

Sarah, Mrs., "belonging to New Hampshire government, bordering on ye line in dispute," and Gideon Sawyer, Dec. 25, 1746. C. R. 7.

Sarah, and Sergeant Smith, Feb. 7, 1754.*

Sarah, and Joshua Coffin, Jan. 21, 1755.*

Sarah, and Stephen Adams, Dec. 8, 1761.*

Sarah, and Frederick Lewis [of Deerfield, N. H. int.], Sept. 22, 1777.*

Sarah, and Stephen Emery, jr., int. Apr. 22, 1780.

Sarah, and Samuel Rameck, int. Sept. 29, 1783.

Seth, and Sarah Merryl, Nov. 19, 1728. C. R. 7.

Seth, and Rebecah Ordway, Jan. 22, 1754.

Shuah, and Dr. Edmund Coffin, both of Kittery, at Kittery, Nov. 15, 1732.

Stephen, and Hannah Webster of Salisbury, at Salisbury, Dec. 18, 1712.*

Stephen, and Elizabeth Barnard of Amesbury, int. July 20, 1776.

Stephen, of Newburyport, and Betty Little, June 9, 1796.*

Stephen A., of West Northwood, N. H., and Susan G. Chase, June 1, 1842.*

Susanna, and John Pilsbury, Feb. 8, 1762.*

Susanna, and John Emery, jr., int. Oct. 19, 1781.

Thomas, and Tirza Titcomb, Nov. 24, 1685.

Thomas, and Sarah Webster of Salisbury, int. Jan. 13, 1710.

Thomas, and Hannah Moodey, Nov. —, 1718.*

Thomas [jr. int.], and Hannah Bartlet, Dec. 21, 1763.*

Tirza, and Josiah Sawyer, Jan. 22, 1707.*

Tirza, and Hawthorn Coker, Dec. 17, 1708.*

BARTLETT (see also Bartlet), Abba M., and Charles H. Chase, int. Mar. 14, 1849.

*Intention also recorded.

BARTLETT, Abigail, Mrs., and Joseph Rogers of Amesbury,
Dec. 7, 1738. c. R. 7.*

Benjamin, and Jemima Parkhurst of Weston, at Weston, Apr.
20, 1738.*

Catharine M., of Newburyport, and Moses L. Atkinson, int.
Apr. 19, 1845.

Charles, and Mrs. Hannah Milton, Apr. 15, 1827.*

Charles, and Elisabeth Kilborn of Newburyport, int. Sept.
13, 1845.

Daniel, and Sarah Tuexbury of Amesbury, at Amesbury, Nov.
8, 1760. [int. Nov. 15, 1760.]*

Dorcas, Mrs., of Amesbury, and Mark Batchlour of Wenham,
June 6, 1738. c. R. 7.

Edmund, and Mary Marsh of Haverhill, at Haverhill, Oct.
2, 1754.*

Elizabeth, and John Moulton, jr., Dec. 2, 1833.*

Enoch, and Mrs. Anna Bayley of Haverhill, at Haverhill,
Apr. 27, 1749.*

Eunice, and John Balch, Mar. 1, 1783.*

Hannah, of Bradford, and John Martin of Andover, May 7,
1729. c. R. 7.

Hannah [Mrs. int.], and Jabez Bradbury, Nov. 3, 1785.*

Hannah L., of Newburyport, and Joseph C. Rundlett, of
Andover, Jan. 24, 1839.

Israel T., a. 33 y., shoemaker, s. Israel and Hannah, and
Charlotte H. Wigglesworth, a. 32 y., d. William and
Sarah, Dec. 19, 1847.*

Joseph, and Joanna Jackman, Nov. 3, 1825.*

Lydia, and Samuel Coffin, June 17, 1777.*

Lydia, and Ebenezer Moody, Nov. 6, 1784.*

Lydia C., and George W. Jackman, July 16, 1834.*

Mary, of Marblehead, and Thomas Ewell of Ramsgate, Kent,
Eng., now of Marblehead, July 5, 1735. c. R. 7.

Mary, and James Delpratt, Apr. 9, 1778.*

Mary, and Stephen Jaques, July 6, 1783.*

Michael W., a. 29 y., school teacher, b. West Newbury, s.
John E. and Nancy, of West Newbury, and Mary Colby,
a. 31 y., d. Joseph L. and Hannah, Aug. 20, 1846.

Moses C., a. 23 y., shoemaker, b. Amesbury, s. Samuel and
Rebecca, of Amesbury, and Margaret Ryan, a. 18 y., b.
Bangor, Me., d. Daniel and Margaret, of Bangor, Nov.
15, 1849.*

Nancy, and Robert Griffis of Newburyport, May 6, 1817.*

*Intention also recorded.

BARTLETT, Priscilla, and John Davis, Apr. 18, 1784.*
Prudence, and Samuel Hills, int. June 22, 1807.
Rebecca B., of Newburyport, a. 25 y., b. Newburyport, d.
Samuel and Rebecca, of Newburyport, and Hazen L. Fol-
lansbee, of Newburyport, a. 23 y., trader, b. Newbury-
port, s. Nathan and Catherine, of Newburyport, July 3,
1846.
Rebekah, and Eliphalet Ordway of Sanbornton, N. H., June
18, 1822.*
Richard, and Abigail Ropes of Salem, at Salem, Nov. 21,
1706.
Richard, widr., and wid. Abihail Diamond of Amesbury, at
Amesbury, Nov. 11, 1718.
Samuel, jr., and Abigail Wells of Amesbury, at Amesbury,
Feb. 6, 1704-5.
Samuel B., and Elizabeth A. Hussey of North Berwick, Me.,
int. Jan. 6, 1849.
Sarah, and Emery Coffin, both of Newburyport, Jan. 1, 1828.
Susan C., and James Marrow of Newburyport, int. Sept. 12,
1846.
Thomas [3d. int.], and Dolly Blasdell of Amesbury, at Ames-
bury, June 19, 1760.*
William, and Betsy Barrett, Feb. 26, 1817.*

BARTLEY, John M. C., Rev., of Hampstead, N. H., and Susan Dana, int. Jan. 12, 1837.

BARTON, Anne [wid. int.], and Walter Penuel, Apr. 15,
1700.*
Ebenezer, and Esther Flood, May 5, 1710.*
Ebenezer, and Margeret Hunt, June 23, 1741.*
Henry, Capt., and wid. Rachel Winter, both of Boston, June
3, 1730. C. R. 7.
Marcy, and James Thirston, Feb. 24, 1735-6.*
Rufus [Baston. int.], and Mary Donnell, Dec. 18, 1832.*
Sarah, and Daniel Rawlins, June 10, 1708.*
Sarah, and Nathaniel Chase, June 15, 1732.*

BASS, Edward, Rev., and Sarah Beck, Sept. 19, 1754. C. R. 8.
Edward, and Mary Algreen of Newburyport, int. July 2, 1829.
Edward, and Rhoda Winn of Newburyport, int. Sept. 25,
1830.

*Intention also recorded.

BASSET (see also Bassett), Nehemiah, of Lynn, and Mary Griffin of Charlestown, Feb. 3, 1731-2. c. r. 7.

BASSETT (see also Basset), John, of Lynn, and Lovey Sawyer, int. Feb. 23, 1806.

BASTON, Mary, and William Hale, int. Sept. 11, 1847.
Rufus, see Barton, Rufus.

BATCHELDER (see also Bachelder, Bacheler, Bachellor, Bachelour, Batcheldor, Batchlour), Augustus, of Danvers, and Esther Carr, Sept. 15, 1836.*
Daniel C., and Mary T. Randall, int. July 11, 1835.
David S., of Haverhill, and Sarah Hodges of Rowley, June 2, 1808. c. r. 5.
Ebenezer Damon, of Reading, and Rebecca Longfellow, Jan. 23, 1823.*
John, and Hannah Hobson of Rowley, int. Mar. 21, 1809.
Martha, of Newburyport, and William Porter of Rowley, Oct. 16, 1831.
Samuel K., and Mehitabel Smith, Jan. 8, 1822.*
Samuell [of Hampton. int.], and Elizabeth Davise, May 14, 1707.*

BATCHELDOR (see also Batchelder), David, of Hampton Falls, N. H., and Mary Emery, Jan. 1, 1771.*

BATCHLOUR (see also Batchelder), Mark, of Wenham, and Mrs. Dorcas Bartlett of Amesbury, June 6, 1738. c. r. 7.

BATES, James, and Sarah D. Boynton, June 25, 1829.*

BATT, Anne, and John Webster, June 13, 1653.
Jane, and [Pet. c. c. and ct. r.]er Tappin, Apr. 3, 1661.

BATTELLE (see also Bartell), Thomas, of Boston, and Sarah C[offin. c. r. 10.] Peirce, Nov. 6, 1815.*

BATTERS, Lydia, and Thomas Chase, int. May 20, 1804.

*Intention also recorded.

BATTES (see also Battis), Joseph J., and Edna A. Thurlow, July —, 1839. [Nov. 3. int.]*

BATTIS (see also Battes, Bettis, Bettys), Hannah, and Amos Floyd, July 5. 1809.*
Joseph Boughdon, and Olive Pierce Jackman, Dec. 29, 1811.*
Mary E., and Tristram Hobson of Rowley, int. Feb. 1, 1845.
Matilda A., and Varnum Rogers of Rowley, Nov. 15, 1844.*
Nancy, and James Ball, jr., Mar. 6, 1812.*
Olive Ann, a. 25 y., d. Joseph and Olive, and Charles Henderson of Newburyport, a. 29 y., carpenter, b. Newburyport, s. Samuel and Rhoda, of Newburyport, May 24, 1846.*

BAXTER, Samuel F., of New York City, and Harriet A. Chase of Newburyport, Aug. 20, 1837.

BAYARD, Mehitabel, of Boston, and Capt. Frederick Porter of the Royal American Regt., in New Hampshire, Mar. 17, 1759. c. R. 8.
Sarah, and John Elliott, of the Royal Scots, in New Hampshire, July 17, 1761. c. R. 8.

BAYLEY (see also Bailey), Abigail, and Moses Little, jr., June 5, 1743.*
Abigail, and James Chase [jr. int.], Mar. 25, 1746.*
Abigail, and Jacob Kent of Plaistow, N. H., Dec. 26, 1752.*
Abigail, and Enoch Long, Dec. 2, 1755.*
Abigail [Mrs. c. R. 2.], and Caleb Moody, jr., June 3, 1756.*
Abigail, and Matthias Atkinson, Apr. 10, 1766.*
Abigail, and Joseph Noyes, jr., June 12, 1766.*
Abigail, and David Morss, Sept. 3, 1770.*
Abner, and Abigail Cheney, May 24, 1758.*
Abner, Dea., and [Mrs. int.] Judith Kindrick, Apr. 7, 1785.*
Abner, jr., and Mary Kindrick, Sept. 26, 1788.*
Abraham, and Ruth Harris, July 29, 1762.*
Almira D., a. 18 y., d. Joseph and Almira, and John H. Marshall, a. 18 y., shoemaker, May 20, 1849.*
Anna, Mrs., of Haverhill, and Enoch Bartlett, at Haverhill, Apr. 27, 1749.*
Anna, of Tewksbury, and Stephen Merrill, int. July 13, 1777.
Anna, of Amesbury, and Lt. Amos Atkinson, int. Oct. 17, 1778.

*Intention also recorded.

BAYLEY, Anna, and Samuel Currier, int. Dec. 10, 1791.

Asa, and Abigail Chase, Nov. 26, 1767.*

Daniel, jr., of Newburyport, and Elizabeth Jackman, int. Oct. 10, 1777.

Daniel, and Mary Merrill, Oct. 31, 1779.*

Ebenezer, and Sarah Bayley, June 6, 1786.*

Edmund, Dea., and Mrs. Prudence Morss, Jan. 4, 1758.*

Edmund, jr., and Abigail West, int. Dec. 27, 1769.

Elisabeth, and William Mireck, Oct. 24, 1765.*

Elizabeth, and Samuel Titcomb, jr. of Newburyport, Nov. 17, 1774.*

Elizabeth, and Stephen England, Sept. 21, 1775.*

Elizabeth Ann, and John L. Huntington, int. Oct. 5, 1849.

Enoch, and Esther Sawyer of Amesbury, int. Aug. 10, 1765.

Enoch, and Elisabeth Morse of Haverhill, N. H., int. May 21, 1796.

Ephraim, and Sarah Low, Dec. 6, 1781.*

Eunice, and Simeon Chase [jr. int.], Apr. 15, 1787.*

Ezekiel, and Sarah Green of Haverhill, at Haverhill, June 17, 1746.*

Hannah, and John Flanders, Mar. 31, 1777.*

Hannah, and Josiah Hills, July 23, 1786.*

Hannah, and Benjamin Russell, int. Oct. 8, 1843.

Hannah L. H., of West Newbury, and Joseph E. Hodgkins, int. Nov. 6, 1835.

Hepzibah, and John Beal, Mar. 1, 1744-5.*

Isaac, and Rebeca Bartlet, Sept. 5, 1700.*

Isaac, and Sarah Titcomb, May 18, 1708.*

Isaac, and Mary March, Aug. 23, 1764.*

Isaac, and Molly Bartlet, Dec. 25, 1788.*

Jacob, and Prudence Noyes, Oct. 16, 1745.*

Jacob, and Betsy Woodman, June 5, 1790.*

Jedediah, of Rowley, and Martha Thorla, June 1, 1756.*

John, and Mary Bartlet [d. John, jr. int.], July 2, 1700.*

John, and Anna Chase, Nov. 9, 1752.*

John, jr., of Rowley, and Mary Holeman, Nov. 4, 1756.*

John, and Sarah Emery, Nov. 16, 1786.*

John, jr., and Mary Currier of Newton, N. H., int. Sept. 8, 1787.

John, and Martha Johnson of Salem, int. Dec. 11, 1802.

Joseph, sr., and wid. Sarah Sawyer, Nov. 27, 1707.*

Joseph, and Martha Boynton of Rowley, at Rowley, Mar. 15, 1733.

*Intention also recorded.

BAYLEY, Joseph, of Tewksbury, and Apphia Bartlet, Oct. 21, 1755.*

Joseph, and Deborah Hardy of Bradford, int. Dec. 25, 1756.

Joseph, and Mary Chase, Oct. 5, 1775.*

Joseph, and Anna Niles, Nov. 2, 1800.*

Joshua [jr. int.], and Sarah Coffin, Feb. 4, 1706.*

Joshua, Dr., 3d, and Mrs. Esther Ashley of Braintree, int. Nov. 18, 1708.

Joshua, jr., and Sally Chase, Mar. 18, 1780.*

Josiah, and Ruth Poor, Nov. 27, 1788.*

Judith, and Stephen Little, June 5, 1743.*

Judith, and James Kinreck, int. Dec. 17, 1763.

Judith, and Daniel Pilsbury, jr., Feb. 25, 1768.*

Judith, and John Brown, 3d of Newburyport, Oct. 12, 1784.*

Lydia, and Joshua Brewster, May 26, 1772.*

Martha, and Ezra Pilsbury, jr., Nov. 29, 1759.*

Martha, Mrs., and Timothy Morss, Sept. 27, 1769.*

Mary, and Peter Merryl, Feb. 8, 1725-6. c. R. 7.

Mary, and Joseph Goodridge, Mar. 17, 1763.*

Moses, and Mary Ordway, July 10, 1739.*

Moses, and Ruth March, int. July 25, 1761.

Moses, and Hittey Chase, Apr. 26, 1798.*

Moses, jr., and Sarah Merrill, int. Feb. 18, 1803.

Moses, and Priscilla Chase, int. Feb. 21, 1805.

Nancy, and John Plummer, Dec. 20, 1792.*

Nathan, and Sarah Pilsbury, Feb. 8, 1757.*

Nathaniel, and Mary Davis of Gloucester, int. June 20, 1747.

Nathaniel, and Martha Emery, Aug. 6, 1761.*

Nathaniel, of Newburyport, and Abigail Pilsbury, int. Jan. 26, 1793.

Paul, and Eunice [Emma. c. R. 2.] Carr, Feb. 19, 1787.*

Prudence, see Rogers Prudence.

Rhoda, and Jonathan Emerson of Salem, N. H., int. Dec. 13, 1780.

Robert, of Newburyport, and Dorothy March, July 5, 1772.*

Ruth, and Lt. Nathaniel Parker of Bradford, Sept. 22, 1782.*

Salley, of Bradford, and William Little, int. Feb. 11, 1797.

Samuel, jr., and Hannah Chase, int. Oct. 26, 1791.

Sarah, and Edward Toppan, Sept. 7, 1743.*

Sarah, and Micah Carlton, Apr. 12, 1753.*

Sarah, and Benjamin Emery of Rumford, N. H., [Pennacook. c. R. 2.], Mar. 12, 1761.*

Sarah, and Eleazer Johnson, Sept. 28, 1762.*

*Intention also recorded.

BAYLEY, Sarah, and Isaac Rogers of Amesbury, Apr. 13, 1779.*
Sarah, and Moses Clements [jr. dup.] of Haverhill [at Haverhill. dup.], May 16, 1780. [May 17. dup.]*
Sarah, and Samuel Smith, Sept. 16, 1784.*
Sarah, and Ebenezer Bayley, June 6, 1786.*
Stephen, and Anna Westcom of Haverhill, int. May 10, 1754.
Stephen, jr., and Sarah Pilsbury, Oct. 3, 1759.*
Stephen, and Anna Carr, int. Oct. 27, 1787.
Stephen, and Jane Robinson of Newburyport, int. Nov. 4, 1848.
Susanna, and Joseph Brown, Nov. 21, 1752.*
Susannah, and Joseph Sawyer, Nov. 26, 1778.*
Thomas, and Elizabeth Kimball, int. Oct. 8, 1774.
Webster, and Mary Noyes, Aug. 24, 1773.*
William, a. 26 y., shoemaker, s. William, and Eliza A. Wilson of Amesbury, a. 18 y., d. John and Harriet, of Amesbury, May 1, 1845.*

BAYLY (see also Bailey), Sarah, and Benjamin Chase, May 20, 1718.*

BEACHAM (see also Bechem), Abigail, and Ephraim Hoyt, June 25, 1761.*
Abigail, and Samuel Goodwin, int. Aug. 29, 1763.
Edward, and Mary Dow, int. Nov. 15, 1755.
Edward, and Abigail Stickney, May 11, 1758.*
Samuel, and Mary Currier, June 5, 1754.*
Susanna, and David Downing, Mar. 7, 1762.*

BEAL (see also Beals, Beel), Elisabeth, and Jacob [John. c. R. 9.] Hidden, Nov. 20, 1760.*
Hannah, of Newmarket, and Benjamin Knight, int. Dec. 13, 1791.
Joanna, and Asa Herriman, Mar. 5, 1761.*
John, and Hepzibah Bayley, Mar. 1, 1744-5.*
John, and Elisabeth Symmes, Mar. 18, 1750.*
Katharine [wid. int.], and Robinson Hidden of Gloucester, Nov. 21, 1775. [He takes said Katharine naked without any estate. int.]*
Mercy, and Joseph Lunt, 3d [4th. int.], Oct. 31, 1751.*
Nabby, and Paul Knight, int. Nov. 5, 1791.
Zachariah, of York, and Ruth Stickney, Mar. 11, 1735-6.*

*Intention also recorded.

BEAL, Zechariah, jr., and Hannah Elsworth of Rowley, at Rowley, Apr. 10, 1766.*

BEALS (see also Beal), Eunice, of Boston, and John Smith, at Boston, Oct. 22, 1772.

BEAN, Castor, of Haverhill, a. 32 y., barber, s. James and Lydia, of Haverhill, and Mary Ann Francis, a. 29 y., d. John and Dorcas, May 18, 1845.
Elisha, of Newburyport, and Margaret Adams, Nov. 25, 1823.*
Elisha, jr., a. 23 y., shoemaker, s. Elisha and Margaret, and Louisa Noyes, a. 20 y., d. John and Sarah, June 28, 1848.*
Eliza, of Kingston, N. H., and Benja[min] Kimball, Aug. 16, 1827.*
Hannah, of York, and Capt. W[illia]m Wilkins of London, July 13, 1730. c. r. 7.
James, and Abigail Goodridge, July 4, 1734.*

BEARD, John, of Wilmington, and Hannah Knight, Apr. 10, 1744.*

BECHEM (see also Beacham), George, and Abigail Hodgkins [Haskins. int.], Mar. 30, 1726.*

BECK, Abigail, Mrs., and William Atkins, Aug. 15, 1737. c. r. 7.
Abigail, and William Parsons of Gloucester, Feb. 8, 1753.*
Hannah, and Stephen Cross, Nov. 20, 1759. c. r. 9.*
Jonathan, and Mrs. Joanna Hodge of Salisbury, at Salisbury, Aug. 2, 1743.*
Joshua, of Portsmouth, and Abigail Daniel, Apr. 20, 1716.*
Mary, Mrs., and Nathaniel Carter, Sept. 21, 1742.*
Sarah, and Rev. Edward Bass, Sept. 19, 1754. c. r. 8.

BECKET (see also Beckett, Beckit), Betsy, and Isaac Crocket, Feb. 4, 1798.*
Elisabeth, of Gloucester, and Timothy Condre, int. Aug. 28, 1756.
Robert [jr. int.], of Gloucester, and Sarah Mitchel, Dec. 16, 1756.*
Salley, and Eleazer Pettengil, June 6, 1795.*
Sarah, and John Lunt, Sept. 20, 1769.*

*Intention also recorded.

BECKETT (see also Becket), Mary, and James Collins, both of Salem, Oct. 8, 1730. c. R. 7.

Sarah [of Gloucester. int.], and Jonathan Coats, at Gloucester, June 18, 1752.

BECKFORD, see Bickford.

BECKIT (see also Becket), Dorothy, and Thomas Brookins, Nov. 4, 1802.*

BEEL (see also Beal), Benjamin, and Katharine Noyes, June 7, 1772.*

Hannah, and John Woodbridge, int. Oct. 4, 1783.

BEETLE, Elizabeth, and John Davis, jr. of Amesbury, June 28, 1708.

BEHONY, Bridget, and Jonathan Lovewell, both of Dunstable, Oct. 16, 1734. c. R. 7.

BELCHER, Mary, and Robert Sharp, abt. 1727. c. R. 7.

Sam[ue]l, of Stockbridge, Vt., and Anna G. Caldwell of Weare, N. H., Oct. 10, 1818. c. R. 10.

Sarah [Mrs., of Boston. int.], and Abner Dole, at Boston, Jan. 5, 1698. [int. Dec. 10, 1698.]*

BELCONG[ER], John, and Mary [Kelly. c. c. and cT. R.], Apr. 12, 1666.

BELKNAP, Abel, and Moly Richardson of Woburn, at Woburn, Oct. 6, 1765.

BELL, David, and Marcy Betton, Nov. 29, 1710.*

John, of Newburyport. a. 24 y., manufacturer, s. John and Hannah, and Phoebe A. Pettingell, a. 21 y., d. Benjamin and Joanna, Nov. 15, 1847.*

Mercy, and Benjamin Mors, 3d, Jan. 22, 1712-13.*

BELLAMEE, Elisabeth, and Enos Bishop, of Contocook [N. H. int.], Nov. 21, 1749.*

*Intention also recorded.

BENINGTON, Ann, and Joseph Gutridge, mariner, both of Boston, Nov. 19, 1726. c. r. 7.

BENJY, Mary, and Windsor Goulding, Feb. 5, 1735-6.*

BENNET (see also Bennett), Joanna, of Newburyport, and Enoch Gerrish, int. Oct. 15, 1780.
Joseph, Lt., of Lancaster, and Elizabeth Bailey of Roxbury, Oct. 21, 1730. c. r. 7.
Moses, of Newburyport, and Betty Hale, Nov. 5, 1787.*
Sarah, and Thomas Noyes, 4th, Jan. 20, 1784.*
Tho[ma]s, and Sarah Gee, both of Boston, Oct. 12, 1734. c. r. 7.

BENNETT (see also Bennet), Elizabeth, and Henry Chapman of Newburyport, int. Sept. 7, 1811.
Emanuel J., of New York, a. 23 y., cigar maker, b. New York City, s. John and Mary, of New York, and Harriet M. Floyd, a. 23 y., d. John and Abigail, Apr. 24, 1848.*
Mary, and Nathaniel L. Ordway, int. Mar. 10, 1823.
Roxanna H., of Guilford, Me., and William O. Toppan, int. Sept. 10, 1842.

BERDGE, Samuel, and Rhoda Boynton, Nov. 22, 1812.*
Samuel S., and Sally Eaton of Salisbury, int. Oct. 20, 1811.

BERNARD (see also Barnard), Jonathan, and Tabitha Coleby, both of Amesbury, Oct. 6, 1726. c. r. 7.

BERRY (see also Berrye), Ambros, and Mrs. Sarah Emery, June 3, 1728.*
Elisabeth, and Thomas Browne, int. Aug. 31, 1695.
Eunice G., of Newburyport, a. 23 y., b. Sheffield, Vt., d. John and Polly, of Sheffield, and Samuel Russell, a. 29 y., shoemaker, s. Samuel P. and Eliza, Dec. 2, 1849.*
Hannah, and Isaac Chace, Oct. 29, 1710.*
John, and Mary Little, Jan. 22, 1740-41.*

BERRYE (see also Berry), Ambros, and Hannah Kingsbury, Jan. 10, 1716-17.

*Intention also recorded.

BETTIS (see also Battis), Anna Mary, and Henry Rogers, Aug. 29, 1821.*

Elizabeth, of Georgetown, and Stephen Rogers, int. Feb. 26, 1840.

Maria, of Georgetown, and Uriah Pilsbury, int. Nov. 2, 1839.

BETTON, Marcy, and David Bell, Nov. 29, 1710.*

BETTYS (see also Battis), Andrew, and Martha Pierce, both of Rowley, Jan. 10, 1822.

BEVERLY, Samuel, of St. Johns, N. F., and Ruth Conner, Nov. 11, 1776.*

BIAS, Mary Jane, and William B. Cheeney, int. June 24, 1836.

BICKFORD (see also Bigford), Betsey, and John Dow, int. Mar. 7, 1835.

John, of Newburyport, and Joanna Pettingall, Dec. 28, 1784.⁺

John, and Lydia Proctor, Nov. 24, 1808.*

BIGFORD (see also Bickford), Joseph [of Newburyport. int.], and Doritha Cheney, Mar. 22, 1770.*

BINGLY, Elizabeth, and John Chase, May 23, 1677.

William, and Elizabeth Preston, Feb. 27, 1659.

BISBEE, Mary, and John Keen, jr., both of Pembroke, Oct. 28, 1727. c. r. 7.

BISHOP, Arabella A., of Lowell, a. 22 y., housekeeper, d. Nathan and Martha, of Lowell, and Joseph [H. int.] Smith, a. 23 y., mason, s. Samuel and Elizabeth, Dec. 14, 1844.*

Benjamin, and Lydia Goodwin, Mar. 18, 1739-40.*

Benjamin, and Hannah Bishop, int. Nov. 6, 1762.

Bethia, and Jonathan Moors, jr., Oct. 16, 1741.*

Elisabeth, and Daniel Goodwin, int. Oct. 5, 1734.

Enos, of Contocook [N. H. int.], and Elisabeth Bellamee, Nov. 21, 1749.*

Hannah, and George Jackman, at Rowley, Aug. 27, 1728.

*Intention also recorded.

BISHOP, Hannah, and Benjamin Bishop, int. Nov. 6, 1762.
Jemima, and Bezaleel Knight, Sept. 16, 1754.*
John, and wid. Rebecca S[cullerd. T. C.], Oct. 3, 164[7. T. C.].
Lydia, and Joseph Willet, at Rowley, Dec. 4, 1728.
Lydia, and Joshua Norton, Jan. 14, 1752.*

BIXBY, see Bisbee.

BLACK, John, and Susannah Davis, both of Haverhill, Jan.
1, 1729-30. C. R. 7.
Mehitable, of York, and Michal Dalton, Nov. 23, 1730.*

BLACKENBURY (see also Brackenbury), Sam[ue]ll [Brack-
enbury. int.], and Anne Smith, Mar. 13, 1758.*

BLACKLEACH, Dorcas, and Hugh March, May 29, 1676.

BLAIR, Mary Ann, a. 20 y., d. Alexander and Betsey, and Jeremiah K. Chase, a. 24 y., seaman, s. Moses and Hannah,
Nov. 9, 1845.*

BLAISDEL (see also Blaisdell), Eliphalet, and Alice George
of Haverhill, int. Oct. 23, 1812.
John Sawyer, and Jane Adams of Rowley, at Rowley, Dec. 13,
1781.*

BLAISDELL (see also Blaisdel, Blasdel, Blasdell, Blasdil,
Blasdill), Levi D., of Danville, N. H., and Harriet M.
Wells, int. Aug. 11, 1838.
Moses, and Elizabeth Manley, int. Jan. 26, 1821.
Thomas C., of Danville, N. H., and Lydia B. Stoddard of
Salem, July 26, 1840.

BLAKE, Amos, s. Aaron and Martha, of Hampton, and Lydia
Coker, d. Harthorn and Terza, Jan. 26, 1742-3. C. R. 6.
Harriet P., of Newburyport, and Robinson N. Shuff, int. Feb.
17, 1844.
Joanna, of Salisbury, and Skipper Eliot, int. May 23, 1752.
Jonathan, and Mary Ordway, May 18, 1721.*
Jonathan, and Joanna Fosdick, Jan. 16, 1727-8.*
Jonathan, jr., and Hannah Thompson of Newburyport, int.
Feb. 19, 1842.

*Intention also recorded.

BLAKE, Judith, Mrs., and James Mackmilion, Dec. 30, 1745.*

Lydia, and Allen Smith Rich of Lynn, Sept. 30, 1804.*

Lydia E., of Hampton, N. H.. and Samuel Fisk, jr. of Newburyport, Nov. 20, 1834.*

Mary, Mrs., of Newburyport, and William Lunt, jr., int. Nov.
10, 1849.

Nathan B., and Eunice B. Bragdon of Newburyport, int. Nov.
26, 1831.

Samuel, of Hampton, and Elisabeth Badger, Dec. 11, 1718.*

Samuel, and Sarah Adams, Dec. 26, 1799.*

Sarah, of Newburyport, and Charles Lunt [jr. int.], Aug. 7,
1838.*

BLAKELY, Hester, and John Bonde, Aug. 15, 1649.

BLANCHARD (see also Blancherd), Jeremiah, and Susanna
Pearson, int. Nov. 20, 1784.

Jeremiah, Capt., and Mrs. Sarah Allen of Newburyport, Jan.
14, 1810.*

Josiah, and Lydia Perkins, June —, 1838.*

Lois Pearson, and Capt. Jeremiah Lunt, Oct. 22, 1812.*

Mary, of Littleton, and Jonathan Dows of Charlestown, Mar.
26, 1734. C. R. 7.

Rebecca, and Samuel Bartlet of Amesbury, int. Aug. 26,
1815.

Samuel, of Andover, and Ruth Tenny, May 25, 1748.

BLANCHERD (see also Blanchard), Polly, and Moses Chase
[3d. int.], Oct. 6, 1805.*

BLANE, Jane, and Nathaniel French, Nov. 1, 1750.*

BLASDEL (see also Blaisdell), Abigail, of Amesbury, and
Richard Jackman, int. July 22, 1803.

Jacob, and Jemima Hook, both of Amesbury, Oct. 19, 1727.
C. R. 7.

BLASDELL (see also Blaisdell), Deborah, wid., and George
Warthen, widr., Oct. 24, 1732. C. R. 7.

Dolly, of Amesbury, and Thomas Bartlett [3d. int.], at Amesbury, June 19, 1760.*

Dolly E., of Salisbury, and Moses A. Currier, int. Oct. 19,
1844.

*Intention also recorded.

BLASDELL, William H., of Salisbury, a. 26 y., tailor, s. David, of Salisbury, and Charlotte A. Varnum, a. 22 y., tailoress, d. Samuel, Sept. 5, 1844.*

BLASDIL (see also Blaisdell), Nathaniel, and Mary Blay, Jan. 14, 1744-5.*

BLASDILL (see also Blaisdell), John, of Chelmsford, and Mary Sawyer, Aug. 5, 1756.*
Stephen, of Hopkinton, N. H., and Mehetable Cheney, Oct. 11, 1770.*

BLAY (see also Blye), Abigail, and Noah West, Oct. 16, 1745.*
Mary, and Nathaniel Blasdil, Jan. 14, 1744-5.*
[William. int.], of Haverhill, and Lydia Chase, Nov. 5, 1724.*

BLEIGH (see also Blye), Ann, and Ambrose Vincent, both of Boston, June 5, 1736. c. r. 7.

BLOOD, George, and Mary Ann Kimball, both of Worcester, May —, 1839.

BLUMPEY, Betsy, and Capt. James Cook, both of Newburyport, Oct. 14, 1838.
Philip H., of Newburyport, and Ann M. Gerrish, int. Apr. 18, 1846.

BLUNT, William, of Portsmouth, N. H., and Elisabeth March, int. Sept. 9, 1769.

BLYDENBURGH, John, M. A., and Hannah Moody, Feb. 26, 1779.*

BLYE (see also Blay, Bleigh), James, and Joanna Hadly of Amesbury, at Amesbury, Apr. 2, 1731.

BOADEN, Lydia Ann, of Newburyport, and Felix D. Colby, Nov. 6, 1834.*

*Intention also recorded.

BOARDMAN (see also Boarman), Ann, and Wadleigh Noyes, Dec. 30, 1809.*

Anna, and Joseph Moulton, Sept. 5, 1754.*

Elisabeth, and John Pearson [3d. int.], May 5, 1748.*

Eunice, of Newburyport, and Daniel Moody, int. Mar. 19, 1807.

Isaac H., of Newburyport, and Elizabeth Ann Pike, int. Nov. 7, 1843.

John, and Judith Marsh of Haverhill, at Haverhill, Nov. 9, 1752.*

Jonathan, and Rebecca Moody, Mar. 12, 1761.*

Jonathan, of Newburyport, and Sally Noyes, Feb. 15, 1820.*

Judith, and Offin Boardman, jr., int. Dec. 31, 1802.

Martha H., and Joseph B. Morss, both of Newburyport, Jan. 6, 1840.

Mary, of Newburyport, and Richard Pike, int. Nov. 18, 1809.

Nathaniel, and Hannah Penson, int. Dec. 28, 1820.

Offin, of Salisbury, and Mrs. Judith Moss, at Salisbury, Apr. 24, 1740.*

Offin, and Hannah Carr, Oct. 21, 1746.*

Offin, jr., and Judith Boardman, int. Dec. 31, 1802.

Orphan [jr. int.], and Sarah Woodman, Jan. 17, 1722-3.*

Sarah, and Stephen Coffin, jr., Aug. 16, 1722.*

Sarah, and Stephen Wyatt, Nov. 17,1737.*

Susan Greenleaf, and John Odiorne of Newburyport, ——, 1810. [Sept. 21. int.]*

Thomas, and Anne Pearson, May 9, 1749.*

William, jr., of Newburyport, and Esther Wigglesworth Toppan, Mar. 12, 1815.*

BOARMAN (see also Boardman), Nathaniell, of Topsfield, and Abigail Rolfe, June 28, 1710.*

BODDILY, Mary C., and Joshua J. Danforth, Nov. 21, 1833.*

BODGE, Hannah [Badger. c. r. 2.], and Amos Currier, Dec. 22, 1793.*

BODWELL, Hannah, of Haverhill, and Henry Hills, at Haverhill. Sept. 3, 1715.*

Henry, and Bithia Emery, May 4, 1681.

James, of Methuen, and Elisebeth Roberts, June 13, 1734.*

*Intention also recorded.

BODWELL, Lydia, of Methuen, and Robert Chase, at Methuen,
Dec. 7, 1780.*
Ruth, of Haverhill, and Israel Huse, Aug. —, 1716.*
Ruth, and Moses Emery, jr., Dec. 15, 1768.*

BOGAN, Walter, and Mary Pressey, int. Aug. 3, 1810.

BOINTON (see also Boynton), Abigail, and Ralph White-
head, June 3, 1810.*
Enoch, and Alice Adams, Apr. 25, 1799.*
Martha, and Richard Jackman, int. Sept. 5, 1840.
Methuselah, and Amelia Dodge, Aug. 17, 1806.*
Sally, of Bradford, and Thomas Knight, Mar. 27, 1791.*

BOLEY (see also Bowley), Mary, and Aquila Chase, Feb. 13,
1738-9. C. R. 7.

BOLLMAN, Philip [M. int.], of Newburyport, and Mary S.
Lunt, Aug. 2, 1827.*

BOLTON, Ann, and Nathaniel Ordway, both of West New-
bury, Aug. 25, 1825.
Will[iam], and Jane Bartlet, Jan. 16, 1654.
William, and Mary Denison, Nov. 22, 1659.

BOND (see also Bonde), Eliza Jane, and Anthony Ilsley,
June 19, 1842.*
Sarah, wid., of Salisbury, and Dea. Abraham Merrill, int. Aug.
15, 1713.

BONDE (see also Bond), John, and Hester Blakely, Aug. 15,
1649.

BOODY, Azariah, and Betsey Bartlet, int. June 15, 1803.

BOOTH, John, and Abigail Wood, both of Sudbury, Sept. 18,
1734. C. R. 7.

BOOTMAN (see also Butman), Jonathan [Bodman. C. R. 3.],
of Gloucester, and Judeth Hudson, Dec. 27, 1733.*
Joseph [Butman. int.], of Beverly, and Margarett Wise, Jan.
12, 1730-31.*

*Intention also recorded.

BORROW (see also Burroughs), George [Capt. int.], and
Mary Fosdick of Charlestown, at Charlestown, Aug. 12,
1789.*

BOUCHER, Mary [Goucher, of Boston. int.], and Richard
Greenleaf, at Boston, May 19, 1747.*

BOUER (see also Bowers), Eliza Jane [Bowers. int.], and
Amos Jackman, Feb. 26, 1809.*

BOULTER, Mary, of Kensington, and Lemuel Fowler, May
10, 1757.*

BOWEN, Martha, and Joseph Wheeler, both of Boston, July
26, 1734. c. r. 7.

BOWERS (see also Bouer), Elizabeth, of Newburyport, and
William Jewett, jr., int. July 2, 1819.

BOWKER, Joel, of Salem, and Eunice Pearson, Dec. 23,
1802.*

BOWLE (see also Bowley), James, and Martha Sergeant,
Aug. 11, 1763.*
John [jr. int.], and Elesabeth Courser, Dec. 7, 1744.*
Oliver, and Anna Weed of Amesbury, int. Feb. 7, 1744-5.

BOWLES, Sarah J[ane. int.], Mrs., and Holbrook Burroughs, Nov. 14, 1841.*

BOWLEY (see also Boley, Bowle), Abigail, and Daniel
Cross, int. July 20, 1804.
Sarah, of Methuen, and Samuel Chase, at Methuen, July 6,
1769.*
William, and Abigail Goodridge, Mar. 13, 1791. c. r. 2.*

BOYD, James, and Susanna Coffin, Aug. 11, 1757.*

BOYENTON (see also Boynton), William, and Joanna Stevens of Salisbury, at Salisbury, Nov. —, 1713.*

*Intention also recorded.

BOYINTON (see also Boynton), Zacheriah, and Sarah Wicom, Nov. 15, 1715.*

BOYLE, James, and Abigail Plumer, int. Sept. 29, 1744.

BOYLSTON, Abigail, of Charlestown, and Dr. Francis Mooers of Cambridge, Jan. 1, 1733-4. c. r. 7.

BOYNTON (see also Bointon, Boyenton, Boyinton), Amelia, Mrs., and Joshua Mace, Mar. 22, 1824.*
Caleb, and Mary Moores, June 24, 1672.
Caleb, and Mary Shackford, Aug. 30, 1762.*
David, and Mary Stickne, resident in Newbury, int. Aug. 31, 1738.
David, and Susanna Richardson, Feb. 8, 1783.*
Ebenezer, and Sarah Wheeler, May 25, 1711.
Edmund, and Mary [Polly. int.] Heard of Ipswich, at Ipswich, Mar. 22, 1792.*
Elisabeth, and John Ayers, Jan. 1, 1712-13.
Elizabeth, and James Williams of Newburyport, int. Oct. 26, 1811.
Ephraim, and Abigail Emery, Feb. 19, 1756.*
Hannah, and John Dickson [Dreser. int.] of Rowley, Apr. 2, 1724.*
Hannah, and Francis Worcestor of Sandwich, Oct. 28, 1741.*
Hannah, and Thomas Tenney, Feb. 3, 1745-6.*
Hannah, and Jacob Lurvey [of Newburyport. int.], Feb. 26, 1782.*
Hephsibah, and Judah Colman, June 12, 1711.
Joshua, and Sara Br[owne. c. c.]. Apr. [7. c. r. 7.], 1678.
Joshua, and Hannah Burnet, Apr. 9, 1678.
Joshua, and Mary Dole, int. Apr. 30, 1708.
Joshua, jr., and Martha Stickne of Rowley, Apr. 14, 1743.*
Love, of Bradford, and Bartholomew Pearson, May 25, 1737.*
Lydia, and Abraham Thorla, int. May 20, 1763.
Lydia, and Theodore Staple, Oct. 21, 1810.*
Martha, of Rowley, and Joseph Bayley, at Rowley, Mar. 15, 1733.
Mary, Mrs., and Jonathan Leighton of Rowley, Apr. 25, 1739.*
Mary, and Moses Hardy of Bradford, Dec. 3, 1760.*
Mary, and Liphe Adams, Mar. 14, 1775.*
Mary, and Richard Smith, Nov. 5, 1810.*

*Intention also recorded.

BOYNTON, Moses, and Abigail Goodridge, May 13, 1742.*
Moses, and Meribah Chesemor, Sept. 24, 1744.*
Rachel, and Joseph Adams, Dec. 14, 1807.*
Rhoda, and Samuel Berdge, Nov. 22, 1812.*
Samuel, and Apphia Duty, May 14, 1766.*
Sarah, and Moses Call, jr. of Boscawen, N. H., Oct. 26, 1779.*
Sarah D., and James Bates, June 25, 1829.*
Susanna, and Charles Welch, resident in Newbury, Oct. 29, 1776.*

BRACKENBURY (see also Blackenbury), William, and Abigail Heard, both of Ipswich, Sept. 3, 1707.

BRACKET (see also Brackett), Zachariah, of Hampton, and Hannah Rolfe, Dec. 1, 1707.*

BRACKETT (see also Bracket), Mary C., of Newburyport, and Joseph A. Atkinson, int. Mar. 27, 1830.

BRADBURY, Ann, and Samuel Greenleaf, May 17, 1749.*
Barnabas, of Haverhill, and Meriam Mors, Jan. 26, 1742-3.*
Dorothy, Mrs., and Rev. Ammi Ruhamah Cutler, both of North Yarmouth, Aug. 14, 1734. c. R. 7.
Elisabeth, and Samuel Nelson, Oct. 28, 1762.*
Harriet, and Benjamin Pettingell, jr., Nov. 26, 1817.*
Jabez, and Mary Marril, May 16, 1749.*
Jabez, and [Mrs. int.] Hannah Bartlett, Nov. 3, 1785.*
James, of Haverhill, and Sarah Coffin, Nov. 6, 1783.*
Jane, of Kensington, N. H., and John Gould, int. Nov. 5, 1807.
Jonathan, and Abigail Smith, Dec. 21, 1758.*
Joseph S., of New York, and Mary M. Lunt, May 27, 1838.*
Judith, and Caleb Moodey, Nov. 9, 1665.
Mary, and Sam[ue]ll Noyes [jr. int.], Nov. 17, 1757.*
Mary J., wid., a. 26 y., d. John Longfellow, and Oliver M. Akerman of Newburyport, widr., a. 40 y., butcher, s. John, of Newburyport, July 25, 1844.*
Molly, of Salisbury, and John Burbank, int. Aug. 31, 1781.
Nancy, and John Ball, Nov. 2, 1788.*

*Intention also recorded.

BRADBURY, Olive J., a. 22 y., d. David and Sarah, and Freder-
ick Marsh, a. 34 y., seaman, s. Joseph and Betscy, of New-
buryport, Mar. 1, 1846.*
Rowland, and Mary Greenleaf, Nov. 15, 1723.*
Sarah, and Abner Bailey [3d. int.], Mar. 29, 1803.*
Theophilus, of Salisbury, and Ann Woodman, Aug. 4, 1730.*
Theophilus, and Mrs. Judeth Moodey, Mar. 28, 1744.*
Theophilus, 3d, of Newburyport, and Lois Pilsbury, Oct. 3,
1792.*
William, of Milford, and Sarah Mitchel, int. Jan. 16, 1805.

BRADFORD, Dorcas, and Silas Noyes, at Boston, Feb. 4,
1790.

BRADING, James, and Hannah Rock, Oct. 11, 1657.

BRADLEY, Benjamin, of Canterbury, and Judith Morse
[Mace. int.], Dec. 26, 1799.*
Henry, and [wid. int.] Judith Davis, Jan. 7, 1695-6.*
Henry, and wid Hannah Hendrick of Haverhill, at Haverhill,
Apr. 17, 1729.
Joseph [Dea. dup.], of Haverhill, and [Mrs. dup.] Sarah
French, Sept. 20, 1748.*

BRADSHAW, Anna [Hannah. int.], and David Ingersoll of
Gloucester, Apr. 12, 1756.*
Ruth, of Charlestown, and Jacob March, at Charlestown, June
24, 1747.*

BRADSTREET (see also Broadstreat), Anne, and Benjamin
Moodey, Nov. 7, 1728.*
Benjamin, and Mrs. Sarah Greenleaf, Nov. 9, 1726.*
Betty, Mrs., and Rev. William Johnson [jr. int.], Aug. 30,
1731.*
Charles, of Newburyport, and Sarah Ann Noyes, Mar. 17,
1830.*
Elisabeth, of Ipswich, and Samuel Plumer, at Rowley, May
31, 1764.*
John, of Ipswich, and Judith Hale, Feb. 14, 1771.*
Moses, and Mrs. Mary Sayward, at Gloucester, Feb. 16, 1731.

*Intention also recorded.

BRADSTREET, Moses B., of Rowley, a. 27 y., shoemaker, s.
Nathaniel, of Rowley, and Susan M. Scott, a. 25 y., d.
John, Sept. 3, 1844.*

Samuel N., of Rowley, a. 26 y., shoemaker, b. Rowley, s.
Nathaniel and Charlotte, of Rowley, and Elizabeth W.
Rogers, a. 18 y., d. John, Sept. 6, 1846.*

Sarah, Mrs., and John Tufts, Nov. 9, 1714.*

Sarah, Mrs., and Capt. Edward Sergent, June 9, 1719.*

Sarah, and Henry Brookins, Dec. 14, 1766.*

BRAGDEN (see also Bragdon), Mehitable, of York, and Benjamin Mitchil, int. Jan. 22, 1736-7.

BRAGDON (see also Bragden), Ellen C., a. 19 y., b. York,
d. James and Alice, of York, Me., and Benjamin
H. Noyes, a. 24 y., trader, s. Amos and Nancy, Oct. 2,
1845.*

Eunice B., of Newburyport, and Nathan B. Blake, int. Nov.
26, 1831.

Joanna, of York, and Samuel Hunt, int. Nov. 26, 1808.

Joseph, of York, and Sarah Stickne, Nov. 26, 1719.*

Sarah, and Manus Rooney, Feb. 18, 1838.*

BRAGG, Sarah, of Andover, and Enoch Adams, at Andover,
Aug. 6, 1778.*

BRAMAN, Isaac, Rev., of Rowley, and Sarah Balch of Newburyport, Mar. 22, 1837.

Isaac G., Dr., of Georgetown, and Ann M. Moody, int. Mar.
5, 1839.

BRAMBLE, Elisabeth, wid., and John Longland, mariner,
both of Boston, Mar. 6, 1732-3. c. r. 7.

BRAY, Amos, of Gloucester, and Sarah T. Currier, Nov. 27,
1826.*

Eben[eze]r, and Mary Short, July 8, 1818.*

George W., and Lavina Mace, Nov. 21, 1842.*

Hannah, of Newburyport, and Smith Adams, int. Aug. 2,
1794.

*Intention also recorded.

BRAY, Isaac [of Newburyport. int.], and Sarah Dole Poor,
    Oct. 6, 1808. c. r. 1.*
James, and Nancy Day, of Gloucester, int. Oct. 5, 1816.
Nehemiah A., and Eliza Adams of Derry, N. H., int. Jan. 1,
    1834.
Sarah Dole, Mrs., and Thomas Moody of Newburyport, July
    21, 1817.*
Stephen P., and Elizabeth Wood, both of Newburyport, Oct.
    3, 1839.

BREED, Mary, of Boston, and Jeremiah Bumstead, int. Feb.
    28, 1756.

BRETT (see also Britt), John, Capt., and Mrs. Mary Mood-
    ey, Sept. 10, 1747.*

BREWER (see also Bruer), Polly, and Michael Wormsted,
    Jan. 2, 1794.*

BREWSTER, Elizabeth, of Newburyport, and John Coffin, jr.,
    int Apr. 19, 1823.
John, and Abigail Bartlet of Salisbury, Nov. 22, 1814.*
Joshua, and Lydia Bayley, May 26, 1772.*
Mary, Mrs., and Capt. Robert Way, b. Penn., both of Bos-
    ton, Oct. 23, 1733. c. r. 7.

BRIANT (see also Bryant), Deborah, and Nehemiah Ward,
    both of Hingham, July 30, 1728. c. r. 7.

BRICKET (see also Brickett), Abigail, and Thomas Neck
    of Dover, Nov. 5, 1705.
Amos, and Abigail Thurla, Apr. 18, 1793.*
Elisabeth, and Stephen Moody Little, Oct 9, 1794.*
James, Dr. [3d. int.], and Ednar Merrill, Oct. 8, 1760.*
James, and Lucy Woods of Princetown, int. June 13, 1801.
John, and Prudence Adams, Apr. 17, 1760.*
Lydia, and Nathaniel Hastings of Salem, N. H., Nov. 23,
    1818.*
Mary, and Stephen Merrill, Sept. 25, 1756.*
Mary, and Abraham Adams, 4th, Nov. 18, 1768.*
Mary, and Enoch Little, jr., Sept. 15, 1796.*
Moses, and Sarah Chase, Oct. 5, 1768.*

*Intention also recorded.

BRICKET, Nathaniel, and Anna Woodman, Nov. 13, 1750.*
Nathaniel, jr., and Judith Alline, June 11, 1783.*
Sally, and Abiel Swett, Oct. 13, 1792.*
Sarah, and Henry Lunt [3d. int.], Jan. 1, 1701.*
Sarah, and Enos Bartlet, jr., int. May 14, 1768.
Susanna, and Charles Haddock of Haverhill [at Haverhill.
  dup.], Oct. 22, 1767.*
Susanna, and John Woodman, Dec. 13, 1773.*
Thomas, and Mary Noyes, Aug. 27, 1766.*

BRICKETT (see also Bricket, Brickit), Anna, and Benjamin
  Hills, jr., Sept. 27, 1774.*
Barnard, and Deborah Town of Topsfield, int. Nov. 14, 1772.
James, and Anna Wheeler of Salem, N. H., int. Feb. 14, 1786.
Joseph, of Newburyport, and Mary Bartlet, Dec. 28, 1815.*
Judith, and Caleb Titcomb, int. Dec. 25, 1784.
Moody, and Elizabeth [G. c. R. 1.] Titcomb, Nov. 9, 1815.*
Susanna, and Stephen Coffin, May 23, 1776.*

BRICKIT (see also Brickett), Barnerd, and Sarah Hale, Dec.
  21, 1737.*
Hannah, and John Feavor, June 28, 1716.*
James, jr., and Susannah Pilsbury, Aug. 7, 1729.*
Mary, and Solomon Holman, May 23, 1722.*
Sarah, and Abel Chase, May 14, 1728.*
Sarah, and Moses Morss, Oct. 25, 1759.*

BRICKWOOD, Grace, and Thomas Dudding, both of Boston, ——, 1729. C. R. 7.

BRIDGES, Anna, of Rowley, and Samuel Poor, at Rowley,
  Oct. 21, 1784.*
James, of Andover, and Ellenor Moodey, Dec. 28, 1721.*
John, widr., of Georgetown, a. 63 y., shoemaker, s. John, and
  Mary Rogers, wid., d. Samuel Rogers, Mar. 30, 1845.*
Samuel, and Sarah Stickney of Mangerville, Sunbury Co., N.
  S., at Rowley, Dec. 18, 1776.
Sarah, and Nathan Frye, both of Andover, July 6, 1715.
Stephen, of Newburyport, and Sarah Lul, Feb. 2, 1786.*

BRIGGHAM, Charles, and Mrs. Mary Peters, both of Marlboro, Mar. 30, 1732. C. R. 7.

*Intention also recorded.

BRIGGS, Luther, and Mrs. Mercy O. Magoun, both of Pembroke, Aug. 3, 1834.

BRIGHT, Fanny, and Nathan Tayler, Apr. 22, 1806.*
Joseph, of Watertown, and Eliz[abeth] Eliot of Newtown, June 5, 1750. c. r. 7.
Sarah [of Newburyport. int.], and Richard Lunt [jr. int.], ——, 1796 or 97. c. r. 1. [int. July 16, 1796.]*

BRIGHTWELL, Elizabeth, of Suffolk, Eng., and Capt. Edward Knight of Dusley, Gloucestershire, Eng., Aug. 13, 1731. c. r. 7.

BRINDLEY, Katharine, Mrs., of Roxbury, and Godfrey Malbone of Newport, R. I., Aug. 9, 1748. c. r. 7.

BRITT (see also Brett), Hannah, Mrs., and Dr. Joseph Hills [jr. int.], Sept. 10, 1730.*

BROADSTREAT (see also Bradstreet), Dor[othy], Mrs., and Nathaniell Sargent, Oct. 16, 1710.*

BROCAS, John, of Boston, and Abigail Coker, June 17, 1731.

BROCK, Benjamin, and Mary Roberts, Oct. 27, 1743.*

BROCKLEBANK (see also Broklbanck, Broklebank), Jane, and Abiel Somerby, Jan. 26, 1692-3.
Martha, of Rowley, and Jonathan Thorla, Mar. 24, 1728-9.*
Phebe, of Rowley, and Thomas Pike, at Rowley, Mar. 17, 1763.*
Sarah, and Henry Dole, Nov. 3, 1686. ct. r.
Sarah, of Rowley, and Daniel Emery, at Rowley, Feb. 28, 1757.*

BROCKWAY, Maria J., of Newburyport, and George Little, Nov. 17, 1839.*

BRODERIC, Jeremiah E., and Lucy A. Robbins, int. Dec. 1, 1849.

*Intention also recorded.

BRODWALL, Christian, and Arthur Stoakes, both of Salem, July 31, 1728. C. R. 7.

BROKLBANCK (see also Brocklebank), Mary, and William Dole, Oct. 13, 1684.

BROKLEBANK (see also Brocklebank), Hannah, and Rich- and Dole, sr., Mar. 4, 1678.

BRONBECK, Tallack, of Newburyport, and Abigail P. Adams, Jan. 6, 1831.*

BROOKINGS (see also Brookins), Albert, and Mary S[om-erby. C. R. 10.] Merrill, Apr. 17, 1830.*
Betsey, and Josiah Thing of Newburyport, int. July 9, 1796.
Elizabeth, and George W. Manning of Ipswich, Dec. 26, 1833.*
Emily, and Robert H. Knapp of Newburyport, int. Mar. 11, 1831.
Eunice M., and Moses E. Cook, Aug. 11, 1844.*
Joseph B., and Lois Atkinson, Nov. 4, 1838.*
Joseph B., and Sophia Toppan of Newburyport, int. Mar. 14, 1840.
Mary, and Henry Toppan of Newburyport, Mar. 26, 1821.*
Philip B[agley. int.], and Hannah L. Stevens, Mar. 5, 1826.*
Sally B., and Joseph Toppan, jr., Nov. 23, 1819.*
Samuel, jr., and Elizabeth Little, Mar. 11, 1823.*
Tho[ma]s, jr., and Mary Jane Burroughs, Oct. 3, 1829.*

BROOKINS (see also Brookings), Henry, and Sarah Brad-street, Dec. 14, 1766.*
Henry, and Anna March, Mar. 19, 1772.*
Jane, and Capt Enoch Lunt, int. Oct. 10, 1789.
John, and Elisabeth Williams of Newburyport, int. Oct. 11, 1805.
Johnson, and Sarah Ford of Newburyport, int. Nov. 24, 1770.
Joseph, and Jane Perkins, int. Nov. 27, 1773.
Lydia, and Hugh Felton [a sea faring man. int.], Nov. 27, 1781.*
Samuel, and Mrs. Mary Lunt, June 16, 1741.*
Samuel, jr., and Elisabeth Mighill, int. Apr. 5, 1772.

*Intention also recorded.

BROOKINS, Samuel, and Abigail Clerk, Apr. 19, 1790.*
Samuel, and Eunice McIntire of Portsmouth, Apr. 4, 1799.*
Sarah, and Moses Whittier of Newburyport, Jan. 18, 1774.*
Sarah, and Daniel Ely of Newburyport, Nov. 6, 1774.*
Thomas, and Dorothy Beckit, Nov. 4, 1802.*

BROOKS, Anna, and Hale Knight, Jan. 1, 1797. c. r. 1.
Frances Loisa, and Samuel Drowne of Newburyport, ——,
    1811. [Mar. 9. int.]*
Mary Ann, and Lewis Cessimir, July 26, 1840.*
Samuel, a. 27 y., mariner, s. Samuel and Rebecca, and Sarah
    Piper of Newburyport, a. 21 y., b. Newburyport, d. Eben-
    ezer and Deborah, of Newburyport, Oct. 29, 1846.*
Sarah, of Ipswich, and Philip Coolidge, Oct. 14, 1726.*
Susanna, of Methuen, and Peter Waters, at Methuen, Mar.
    21, 1771.

BROUGHTON, Joseph, and Sally Jackson, int. Oct. 26, 1808.
Sarah, and Moses Cheeney, jr., Sept. 5, 1824.*
Sarah M., of Newburyport, and Bard P. Roberts, Sept. 17,
    1839.

BROWN (see also Browne), Abby H., of Lowell, and Thomas
    Hoyt of Manchester, Dec. 19, 1839.
Abigail, and Moses Peirce, Apr. 17, 1740.*
Abigail, and Amos Rogers, int. Oct. 14, 1748.
Abigail, of Rowley, and Paul Pearson, int. Apr. 24, 1755.
Abigail, and Simeon Pearson [of Newburyport. int.], Jan. 17,
    1784.*
Abigail, d. Stephen and Meriam, and Chivey Chase of Weare,
    N. H., s. John and Sarah, 20: 8 m: 1808. c. r. 6.
Abner, of Salisbury, and Mary Mors, Sept. 23, 1713.*
Abraham, and Hannah Pilsbury, June 18, 1793.*
Achsah, of Rowley, and Dudley Heath, Mar. 28, 1811.*
Ann B., of Newburyport, and John L. Robinson, Sept. 15,
    1833.*
Anna [Bruer. int.], of Danvers, and Abel Coffin, at Danvers,
    Sept. 2, 1765.*
Anna, and Jonathan Plummer [jr. int. and c. r. 1.], July 15,
    1773.*
Anna, d. Stephen, late of Newbury, and Sarah, and Edward
    Gove of Seabrook, N. H., Nov. 1, 1775. c. r. 6.

*Intention also recorded.

Brown, Anna, and Edward Hogan, int. Feb. 26, 1803.

Anne, and Benjamin Coleman, July 5, 1743.*

Anne, and Moses Toppan, Apr. 19, 1759. c. r. 9.*

Anne, and Edmund Noyes of Newburyport, int. Sept. 22, 1770.

Bartholomew, of Newburyport, and Rhoda Condry, int. Nov. 3, 1804.

Belinda S., and Daniel Babb, Mar. 29, 1825.*

Ben[jamin], s. John, and Mary Colins, wid. Jonathan, of Hampton, d. John Green of Hampton, 28: 10 m: 1727-8. c. r. 6.

Benjamin, of Rowley, and Sarah Pilsbury, Nov. 13, 1768.*

Benjamin, and Prudence Kelley, Feb. 2, 1776.*

Benjamin, and Lucy [H. int.] Folansbee, Oct. 25, 1806.*

Betsey, and Isaac Williams, both of Salem, ——, 1781.

Betsey, and John Carr, Jan. 3, 1796.*

Betsey, and Nath[anie]l Kelley, Nov. 30, 1797.*

Betsey, of Newburyport, and Moses Moody, jr., int. Apr. 4, 1806.

Betsy, of Newburyport, and Daniel Whitmore, int. Sept. 30, 1809.

Betty, and Enoch Pike of Newburyport, int. May —, 1772.

Betty, and William Collins, resident in Newbury, Feb. 22, 1778.*

Charles, of Newburyport, and Elizabeth C. Hunt, int. Feb. 26, 1819.

Charles, of Newburyport, and Lydia Flanders, int. Oct. 22, 1823.

Cornelia, and Moses C. Toppan, int. Dec. 24, 1827.

Daniel, Capt., of Exeter, Eng., and Mrs. Sarah Jackson of Marblehead, Nov. 12, 1730. c. r. 7.

Daniel, and Betsey Stickney, May 3, 1801.*

Daniel, of Newburyport, and Philippi Pettingell, int. Feb. 25, 1804.

Daniel, and Elizabeth Donnell, Apr. 6, 1823.*

David, a. 23 y., ship carpenter, s. James and Lucy, and Sarah C. Currier, a. 20 y., d. William, Oct. 22, 1846.*

Dolly C., and Charles W. Piper, int. Oct. 11, 1845.

Dorothy, and Joseph Sawyer, Dec. 1, 1729. c. r. 7.

Dudly, of Kensington, and Sarah Adams, Jan. 13, 1795.*

Ebenezer, and Elisabeth England, Sept. 18, 1785.*

Elisabeth, and W[illia]m Timmons, Feb. 14, 1718-19. c. r. 7.

*Intention also recorded.

BROWN, Elisabeth, and Daniel Ring of Salisbury, June 18, 1722. [May 24. C. R. 7.]

Elisabeth, and Samuel Bartlet, 3d, Jan. 17, 1736-7.*

Elisabeth, and Moses Brown, int. Oct. 15, 1748.

Eliza H., and Joseph L. Colby, jr., May 23, 1824.*

Elizabeth, and John Car of Salisbury, Mar. 29, 1727. C. R. 7.

Elizabeth, of Southampton, and Simeon Cooper, int. May 11, 1776.

Elizabeth, of Byfield-Rowley, and James Barker of Bradford, Feb. 22, 1781.

Elizabeth, wid. John, of Newbury, and Peter Morrill of Berwick, s. John and Hannah, both deceased, Dec. 21, 1782. C. R. 6.

Elizabeth, and Joseph Hutchins of Newburyport, June 8. 1812.*

Elizabeth, and Person Kenney, both of Rowley, Jan. 12, 1814. C. R. 5.

Elizabeth, and Phillips Clark, Jan. 21, 1821.*

Elizabeth, a. 18 y., d. Daniel and Betsey, and James Noyes, a. 21 y., farmer, s. Noah J. and Mehitable, June 7, 1845.*

Elizabeth L., Mrs., of Salisbury, and Edward Hale of Newbury, Vt., Jan. 30, 1837.

Enoch, of Haverhill, and Mary Morse of Methuen, Jan. 16, 1734-5. C. R. 7.

Esther, of Newburyport, and Jacob Tucker, int. Aug. 12, 1798.

Eunice Wells, of Seabrook, N. H., and William Brown Woodman, int. Nov. 15, 1834.

Francis, and Sarah Pettingal, Dec. 15, 1715.*

Francis, and Mary [Mercy. int.] Lowell, May 5, 1741.*

Francis, and Hannah Chase, int. Aug. 17, 1804.

George, of Concord, and Harriet Colby, int. Aug. 9, 1834.

Hannah, and John Goodridge [jr. int.], Jan. 13, 1707.*

Hannah, and Geog Sintclear, Aug. 1, 1722.*

Hannah, and Jonathan Rogers, Dec. 2, 1724.*

Hannah, and Cutting Bartlet, Nov. 17, 1763.*

Hannah, of Newburyport, and Amos Coffin, int. Aug. 21, 1779.

Hannah, and Jonathan Chase [3d. C. R. 1.], Nov. 30, 1797.*

Hannah, Mrs., and Capt. William Colman of Boscawen, June 12, 1816.*

*Intention also recorded.

Brown, Hannah M., and Phillips White of South Hampton, N. H., int. Apr. 25, 1838.

Harriet C., wid., a. 37 y., d. Joseph L. and Sarah Colby, and William H. Ladd, widr., of Newburyport, a. 38 y., mariner, b. Newburyport, s. Daniel and Elizabeth, Feb. 13, 1848.*

Isaac, and Rebecca Baily, Aug. 22, 1661.

Isaac, of Salisbury, and Lovedee Rogers, June 26, 1739.*

Jacob, and Mary Woodman, Sept. 25, 1717.*

Jacob, jr., cordwainer, a. 22 y., and Mercy Quarles, a. 18 y., both of Ipswich Hamlet, Feb. 13, 1727-8. c. r. 7.

Jacob, and Polly [Mary. int.] Baker of Topsfield, at Topsfield, Apr. 11, 1793.*

James, Capt., of Waterford, Ire., and Mary Orange of Boston, Nov. 19, 1725. c. r. 7.

James [jr. int.], and Jane Kelly of Haverhill, at Haverhill, Apr. 13, 1737.*

James, jr., and Elisabeth Worth, Dec. 18, 1770.*

Jane, and Sewal Short, Dec. 11, 1760.*

Jane L., and Henry P. Moody, int. Oct. 31, 1846.

John, and Ruth Huse, Aug. 27, 1683.

John, jr., and Elisabeth Dole, Jan. 20, 1712-13.*

John, s. Stephen, and Elisabeth Sawyer, d. Stephen and Sarah, 17: 6 m: 1748. c. r. 6.

John, Esq., and Elisabeth Clement, Jan. 14, 1762.*

John, 3d, and Abigail Rowe, Nov. 28, 1762.*

John, 3d, of Newburyport, and Judith Bayley, Oct. 12, 1784.*

John, and Sally Noyes, Sept. 5, 1795.*

John, jr., and Mary Mitchel, Oct. 15, 1795.*

John, and Mary Pilsbury of Scarborough, int. Oct. 2, 1818.

John Ordway Webster, and Mary Sumner of Newburyport, int. Oct. 19, 1815.

John Wood, of Newburyport, and Mary Richards, July 13, 1775.*

Joseph, 3d, and Sarah Po[or. int.], Dec. 11, 1707.*

Joseph [3d. int.], and Abigail Person, Nov. 11, 1714.*

Joseph, 3d, and Abigaill Hills, Dec. 26, 1723.*

Joseph, and Sarah Herrick, both of Salem, Nov. 2, 1733. c. r. 7.

Joseph, and Susanna Bayley, Nov. 21. 1752.*

Joseph, of Rowley, and Lydia Poor, at Rowley, Apr. 19, 1770:*

BROWN, Joseph, Capt., and Abigail Dean, Dec. 2, 1777.*
Joshua, and Sarah Roberts of Somersworth, N. H., int. Oct.
10, 1772.
Joshua, Lt., and Elizabeth Stephens of Newburyport, int. Dec.
7, 1778.
Joshua, Lt., and Dolly Moody, July 25, 1799.*
Josiah, and Sarah Rogers, Jan. 20, 1731-2.*
Josiah, and Sarah Keizer, Nov. 28, 1762.*
Judith, and Zachary Davis, Feb. 4, 1680-81.
Judith, d. John, deceased, and Obadiah Johnson, s. Edmon[d],
of Hampton, 28: 11 m: 1729-30. c. r. 6.
Judith, and Jonathan Morss of Newburyport, Feb. 18, 1779.*
Judith, and Capt. Benjamin Young of Salisbury, int. Sept.
21, 1793.
Katharine, Mrs., of Reading, and Joseph Gerrish, at Read-
ing, Feb. 16, 1731-2.
Katherine, Mrs., and Stephen Mitchel, Jan. 4, 1774.*
[Said Stephen takes said Katherine naked and so will
not be obliged to pay any of her former husband's debts.
int.]*
Lois W., of Newburyport, and Nathaniel Goodwin, int. Oct.
22, 1843.
Lucy M., and Francis Hardy of Newburyport, int. Sept. 3,
1831.
Lydia, and Edmund Greenleaf, jr., Mar. 12, 1718-19.*
Lydia, and Joseph Mireck, Jan. 6, 1735-6.*
Lydia, and John Longfellow, both of Rowley, Sept. 4, 1803.
c. r. 5.
Martha, Mrs., and John March, Esq., Mar. 4, 1741-2.*
Martha, and Joseph Jaques, Mar. 4, 1756.*
Mary, and William P tridg, Dec. —, 1680.
Ma[ry], of Salisbury, and Phillip Morse, Dec. 11, 1707.*
Mary, and Jacob Marston of Andover [at Andover. dup.],
Dec. 11, 1718.*
Mary, and Johnnathan Phillips of Lynn, int. 16: 6 m: 1722.
c. r. 6 .
Mary, of Salisbury, and John King, at Salisbury, Nov. 23,
1725.
Mary, and William Huse, jr., Feb. 17, 1731-2.*
Mary, wid John, and William Hall of North Kingston, R. I.,
18: 8 m: 1734. c. r. 6.
Mary, and Samuel Peirce, Mar 8, 1738-9.*
Mary, Mrs., and Capt. Daniel Marquand, Mar. 13, 1739-40.*

*Intention also recorded.

BROWN, Mary, of Rowley, and Samuel Adams at Rowley, Nov. 26, 1747.*

Mary, and William Gerrish, jr., Oct.31, 1751.*

Mary, and John Perry, June 5, 1754.*

Mary, of Rowley, and Joseph Pettengell, int. Aug. 23, 1765.

Mary, d. Stephen, deceased, and Sarah, and Nathan Paige, s. Theophilus and Hannah, of Kensington, N. H., Oct. 23, 1765. C. R. 6.

Mary, and Abiel Rogers, Feb. 26, 1784.*

Mary, and Thomas Noyes, ——, 1812. [Oct. 10. int.]*

Mary, and Emerson Gardiner, both of West Newbury, May 11, 1826.

Mary, a. 18 y., b. Greenland, N. H., d. Nutter and Margaret, of Greenland, and James Wilkinson, a. 22 y., farmer, b. Sanford, Me., s. James and Sarah, of Sanford, Mar. 13, 1847.*

Mary Jane, and Isaac Marston of Newburyport, int. Apr. 5, 1834.

Mary L., Mrs., of Newburyport, and James M. Woodman, of South Hampton, N. H., ——, 1837.

Mary Little, and Moses Brown of Newburyport, int. Aug. 5, 1827.

Mary P., and Charles Goodwin, int. Oct. 27, 1829.

Mary W[hite. int.], and Gideon W[oodwell. int.] Hunt, Feb. 5, 1834.*

Mehitable, and Samuel Danford, Jan. 13, 1736-7.*

Mercy [Eunice. int.], and Jacob Hale [of Newburyport. int.], Nov. 16, 1769.*

Micaijah, and Miriam Sawyer, Nov. 26, 1803.*

Miriam, d. Stephen and Miriam, and Elijah Sawyer, s. Humphrey and Hannah, 25: 5 m: 1803. C. R. 6.

Molly, and Abraham Somerby of Newburyport, Apr. 23, 1765.*

Moses, of North Yarmouth, and Susanna Morss, int. July 19, 1746.

Moses, and Elisabeth Brown, int. Oct. 15, 1748.

Moses, jr., and Sarah Coffin, int. Nov. 12, 1763.

Moses, and Polly Kimbal, Nov. 20, 1794.*

Moses, jr., and Sarah Chase, Sept. 7, 1815.*

Moses, of Newburyport, and Mary Little Brown, int. Aug. 5, 1827.

Nancy, and Joseph H. Chase, Dec. 11, 1817.*

Nancy, and Joseph Bartlet, May 23, 1822.*

*Intention also recorded.

Brown, Nancy H., of Newburyport, and Daniel Hall of Barrington, Nov. 13, 1825.

Nathan, and Rebeca Morss, Dec. 24, 1736.*

Nathaniel, of Wenham, and Mrs. Hannah Bartlet, Jan. 1, 1732-3. c. r. 7.

Nathaniel, and Ann Stewart of Rowley, June 13, 1737.*

Nathaniel, of Londonderry, N. H., and Elizabeth Adams, int. May 19, 1781.

Nicholas, Capt., jr., of Newburyport, and Jane Little, Feb. 27, 1808.*

Nicholas R., and Hannah P. Kilborn of Newburyport, int. May 6, 1843.

Obadiah, of Rowley, and Cynthia Thornton, int. Aug. 6, 1836.

Patty Horton, and William Noyes, Nov. 22, 1809.*

Pearson, of Newburyport, and Jane Gerrish, int. Apr. 27, 1793.

Phillis, wid., and Ruben Griffin, int. June 14, 1783.

Polly, of Rowley, and Ephraim Noyes, jr., int. Aug. 9, 1792.

Priscilla, of Haverhill, and Daniel Hale, int. June 8, 1765.

Rachel, and Timothy Remeck of Kittery, Dec. 18, 1729.*

Rebecca, and Ezekiel Hoyt of Amesbury, Dec. 25, 1735.*

Rebecca, and Moses Sweat, int. Apr. 1, 1758.

Reuben, and Elizabeth Greenleaf, June —, 1810.*

Richard, and Mary Jaques, May 7, 1674. [1675. ct. r.]

Richard, jr., and Mrs. Martha Whipple [of Ipswich. dup.], at Ipswich, Apr. 22, 1703.

Richard, Capt., and Mrs. Mary Hudson, June 19, 1726. c. r. 7.

Roxanna, of Newburyport, and Jonathan Knight, int. Feb. 6, 1830.

Ruth, and Thomas Rogers, May 18, 1677.

Ruth, and Benjamin Davis, Nov. 19, 1728. c. r. 7.

Ruth, and Joseph Emerson, Jan. 6,1735-6.*

Ruth, and Phillips White, May —, 1749. c. r. 2.*

Ruth, and Joseph Coffin, jr., Apr. 14, 1767.*

Ruth, and Lemuel Coffin, June 29, 1789.*

Sally, of Rowley, and Asa Low, Jan. 1, 1793.*

Sally, and Ezekiel Whicher, both of Rowley, June 2, 1803. c. r. 5.

Samuel, and Mrs. Dorothy Woodbridge, int. Mar. 28, 1712.

Samuel, and Hannah Pike, Apr. 27, 1736.*

Samuel, and Mrs. Sarah Brown, Apr. 11, 1738. c. r. 7.

*Intention also recorded.

BROWN, Samuel, and Mrs. Abigail Harvey, Jan. 3, 1743-4.*

Samuel, and Anne Carr, Mar. 1, 1759.*

Samuel, and Molly Hidden, at Gloucester, Dec. 7, 176-.

Samuel, and Sarah Gould of Nottingham West, int. Jan. 24, 1778.

Sara, and Benaiah Titcomb, Dec. 24, 1678.

Sara, and Hugh Pike, June 17, 1685.

Sarah, and John Weed, Dec. 2, 1717.

Sarah, and Daniel Allen, May 18, 1718. C. R. 7.

Sarah, and Nathan Ordway, Mar. —, 1726-7.*

Sarah, Mrs., and Samuel Brown, Apr. 11, 1738. C. R. 7.

Sarah, Mrs., and Samuel White [jr. int.] of Haverhill [at Haverhill. dup.], Nov. 15, 1744.*

Sarah, and Nathan Ordway, Dec. 29, 1748.*

Sarah, and John Goodridge, Nov. 28, 1754.*

Sarah, of Salem, and [Ens. int.] Lemuel Noyes, at Salem, Nov. 3, 1781.*

Sarah [Mrs. C. R. 2.], of Hamilton, and Joseph Goodridge, Aug. 28, 1796.

Sarah, and Joseph Knight, May 31, 1809.*

Sarah, and Stephen Sawyer, ——, 1810 or 11. [Sept. 22, 1810. int.]*

Sarah [Mrs. C. R. 10.], of West Newbury, and Daniel Chamberlain of Salem, June 10, 1826.

Sarah Ann, and Ebenezer Burnham, both of West Newbury, Nov. 28, 1839.

Sarah Jane, and Capt. John [C. int.] Hardy of Newburyport, Dec. 19, 1828.*

Sarah Jane, of Newburyport, and Abel L. Goodwin, int. Oct. 14, 1831.

Simeon, Dr., of Amesbury, and Hannah Young of Salisbury, Mar. 13, 1728-9. C. R. 7.

Simon, of Derry, N. H., and Eunice W. Pilsbury, Dec. 2, 1828.*

Stephen, and Sarah Mors, Feb. 26, 1721-2.*

Stephen, s. Stephen, late of Newbury, and Sarah, and Miriam Challis, wid. Thomas, late of Amesbury, Oct. 30, 1765. C. R. 6.

Stephen, jr., and Molley Pearson, July 23, 1803.*

Susan Moody, and William Searle Wheeler of Rowley, May 30, 1816.*

Susanna, and Thomas Greanleaf, Mar. 9, 1762.*

Susanna, and Moses Sargent Moody, May 15, 1783.*

*Intention also recorded.

BROWN, Susannah, and Bradstreet Johnson, June 19, 1760.*
Thomas, of Hampton, and Dorcas Fannin, Dec. 13, 1710.*
Thomas [jr. int.], and [wid. int.] Ann Chaney, Dec. 3, 1712.*
Thomas, and Deborah Merryl, Nov. 14, 1727. c. r. 7.
Thomas, and Hannah Merrill, June 8, 1769.*
Thomas, and Salley Currier, Nov. 11, 1797.*
Tirzah, and Robert Barrett, Mar. 5, 1732-3. c. r. 7.
Tristam, and Hannah Curier, Oct. 28, 1799. c. r. 5.
True, jr., of Deerfield, N. H., and Deborah Jaques, Feb. 5, 1824.*
William, and Anne Poor, June 23, 1730.*
William [jr. int.], and Eunice Peirce, July 8, 1760.*
William, and Mary Plummer of Ipswich, int. July 5, 1806.
Woodbridge, of Abington, and Ann Emery, Nov. —, 1736.*
Zaccheus, of Hampton, N. H., and Sarah L. Noyes, int. Nov. 6, 1842.
———, and Amos Rogers, Nov. 22, 1748. c. r. 2.

BROWNE (see also Brown), Elisabeth, and Skiper Lunt, July 18, 1704.*
Elisabeth, and Ebenez[er] Little, Apr. 5, 1737.*
Elizabeth, and Israel Webster, Jan. 3, 1665.
Eliza[beth], and William Hodgekin, Nov. 11, 1687. ct. r.
Francis, and Mary Johnson, Nov. 21, 1653.
Francis, and Mary Mors, Dec. 31, 1679.
James, jr., and Mary Edwards, Apr. 28, 1694.
James, and Mary Edwards, Apr. 8, 1695.
James, jr., and Rebecca Kelly, Jan. 2, 1701.
John, and Mary Woodman, Feb. 20, 1659.
John, jr., and Mrs. Sarah Putnam of Salem, int. Dec. 1, 1733.
Joseph, and Lydia Emery, d. Sergt. John, deceased, int. May 23, 1696.
Joshua, and Sara Sawyer, Jan. 15, 1668.
Mary, and Peter Godfry, May 13, 1656.
Mary, and Nathan Parker, Dec. 15, 1675.
Rebecca, and John Badger, Oct. 5, 1691.
Rebecca, and John Doggett [Dagett of Marshfield. int.], June 22, 1697.*
Richard, and wid. Elizabeth Badger, Feb. 1-, 164[7?].
Ruth, and John Ayre, Oct. 31, 1698.

*Intention also recorded.

BROWNE, Sara, and Joshua Boynton, Apr. [7. c. c.], 1678.
Sarah, and William Wright, Oct. 5, 1692. CT. R.
Sarah, and Richard Lowle, Apr. 8, 1695.
Sarah, and Thomas Wells, May 14, 1696.*
Thomas, and Elisabeth Berry, int. Aug. 31, 1695.
Thomas [jr. int.], and Mary Pilsbury [d. Abel, deceased. int.],
    Oct. 6, 1697.*

BRUER, Anna, see Brown, Anna.

BRYANT (see also Briant), John, and Margaret Caswell, int.
    Apr. 9, 1825.
Patience, of Newburyport, and Nathan Lunt, int. Oct. 14,
    1784.
William, of Reading, and Sarah Huse, Mar. 17, 1736-7.*

BRYER, Richard, and Ellinar Wright, Dec. 21, 1665.

BUCK, Esther, and John Akers, Aug. 1, 1771.*
Jonathan, of Haverhill, and Lydia Morss [at Haverhill. dup.],
    Oct. 19, 1742.*
Phebe, of Haverhill, and Benjamin Chase, at Haverhill [int.
    May 13. 1781.].*
Samuel, of Sutton, and Sarah Lull of Byfield-Rowley, Nov.
    23, 1775.
William, and Phillis Hooper, int. Sept. 20, 1783.

BUCKLEY, John, of Haverhill, and Rebeckah Danforth,
    Sept. 30, 1800.*

BUCKMAN (see also Butman), Mary, of Salem, and Phile-
    mon Casady, int. Jan. 20, 1766.
Sam[ue]ll, and Mary Parker, Nov. 25, 171[7. c. R. 2.].
Sarah, and Abraham Colby of Rowley, Nov. 21, 1712.*

BUFFUM, David B., of Amesbury, and Mrs. Jemima Morrill
    of Salisbury, Oct. 30, 1839.

BULLARD, Francis, mariner, and Hannah Orange, both of
    Boston, July 4, 1733. c. R. 7.
Jonathan, and Sarah Hill, both of Sherburn, Dec. 8, 1733.
    c. R. 7.

*Intention also recorded.

BULLOCK, Joseph, of Haverhill, N. H., and Sarah Worth, Jan. 30, 1812.*

BUMSTEAD, Jeremiah, and Mary Breed of Boston, int. Feb. 28, 1756.

BURBANK, Abigail, and Jonathan Pearson, 3d, Oct. 30, 1759.*
Abigail, wid., and Capt. Jacob Morrill of Salisbury, Apr. 9, 1771.*
Abigail, and William Moody, June 1, 1773.*
Benjamin, and Mary Coffin, Apr. 16, 1780.*
Benjamin, and Sally Carr, Oct. 20, 1795.*
Caleb, of Bradford, and Margeret Wheeller, Aug. 17, 1732.*
Gershom, and Anna Pearson, Nov. 26, 1760.*
Jane, and Timothy Kelly, May 19, 1808.*
John, and Susanna Merrill, Oct. 15, 1663.
John, and Mary Johnson of Rowley, int. Apr. 4, 1777.
John, and Molly Bradbury of Salisbury, int. Aug. 31, 1781.
Margaret, and Jonathan Hopkinson, int. Mar. 4, 1737-8.
Martha, and Eliphalet Danford of Rowley, Nov. 23, 1738.*
Molly, of Bradford, and Timothy Jackman, 3d of Byfield-Rowley, Oct. 19, 1768.
Nathan, and Abigail Goodridge, Oct. 18, 1742.*
Sally, of Boscawen, and Caleb Colman, int. Sept. 12, 1795.
Sarah, and Samuel Woodman, May 11, 1807.*

BURBECK, William, and Jerusha Plummer, Oct. —, 1833.

BURDITT, Elisabeth, of Malden, and Dea. John Currier, int. June 1, 1802.
Elizabeth, and Jacob Chase, Oct. 6, 1811.*
Stephen, of Newburyport, and Susanna Woodwell, int. Oct. 8, 1808.

BURK, Richard Sanders, and Mary Goddard, both of Boston, Apr. 23, 1728. c. r. 7.

BURLEIGH, Josiah, jr., of Newmarket, N. H., and Margaret M[uzzey. int.] Newcomb, Jan. 13, 1813.*

BURNAM (see also Burnham), Lucy, and Daniel Jackson, int. Nov. 13, 1754.
Mary, of Ipswich, and Joseph Grinleaf, Jan. 9, 1735-6. c. r. 7.

*Intention also recorded.

BURNAP, Samuel, of Reading, and Ruth Huse, Dec. 1, 1726.*

BURNET, Hannah, and Joshua Boynton, Apr. 9, 1678.

BURNHAM (see also Burnam), Ebenezer, and Sarah Ann Brown, both of West Newbury, Nov. 28, 1839.
James, Esq., of Newburyport, and Mrs. Hannah Sawyer, July 3, 1806.*
James, and Lucy Varina of Newburyport, Jan. 13, 1831.*
Moses, and Elizebeth Merrill, Mar. 30, 1815.*
Moses P., a. 27 y., farmer, s. Ezekiel and Mary, and Mary Tibbetts, a. 21 y., d. Hezekiah and Rachel, Nov. 4, 1846.*
Olive B., of Lowell, and John A. Rideout, int. Dec. 9, 1848.

BURNS, Margaret D., of Newburyport, and Enoch Colby, int. Nov. 1, 1834.
Sarah E., a. 20 y., d. John and Loretta, and Jeremiah S. Moody [of Newburyport. int.], a. 26 y., house carpenter, s. Daniel and Jemima, of Newburyport, May 4, 1848.*

BURPE, Ebenezer, of Rowley, and Merriam Person, Dec. 15, 1721.*
Hannah, of Rowley, and John Plumer, Dec. 25, 1728.*
Mehitable, of Rowley, and Samuel Searl, jr. of Byfield-Rowley, Dec. 14, 1780.
Sarah, of Rowley, and Benjamin Thirston, Nov. 24, 1731.*

BURRELL (see also Burrill), Abigail, and William Turner, Mar. 1, 1763.*
Jacob, and Miriam Weed of Amesbury, int. Feb. 16, 1760.
Samuel, and Mary Pearson, Mar. 3, 1736.*
Sam[ue]ll, and Sarah Steward, Dec. 23, 1755.*

BURRIL (see also Burrill), Jacob, jr., and Sarah Chase of Deerfield, int. Nov. 6, 1801.
William, and Martha Wedg, int. Oct. 27, 1787.

BURRILL (see also Burrell, Burril), Abigail, and William Perkins of South Hampton, N. H., Jan. 9, 1809.*
Abigail, of West Newbury, and Amos Downer, Sept. 11, 1828.*
Anthony, and Betsey Pritchard, int. Nov. 17, 1821.

*Intention also recorded.

BURRILL, Anthony, and Abigail Cary, June 10, 1824.*
Caleb, of Rowley, a. 31 y., shoemaker, s. James and Mary, of
    Rowley, and Sarah Chase of Rowley, a. 22 y., d. Silas and
    Mary, of Rowley, ——, 1844.
Charles, of Newburyport, and Charlotte Toppan, May 17,
    1824.*
Charlotte M., and John Parsons, int. July 3, 1839.
Elisabeth, and Jacob Rogers, int. June 15, 1792.
Elizabeth G., of Newburyport, and Stephen Jackman, jr., Oct.
    27, 1828.*
James, and Mary Pilsbury, ——, 1809. [Sept. 29. int.]*
Jeremiah, and Jerusha Rogers, Nov. 5, 1812.*
John, of Newburyport, and Mary Smith Bartlet, Jan. 13, 1791.
    C. R. 2.*
John, and Mary Toppan, both of Newburyport, Sept. 28,
    1825.
Joseph, and Mrs. Hannah Easterbrook, Feb. 9, 1743-4.*
Levi D., and Elmira Keily of Pittston, Me., int. Sept. 3, 1848.
Martha, see Burroughs, Martha.
Mary, of Ipswich, and Amos Stickne, Nov. 7, 1739.*
Nancy, d. Jonathan and Mary, and Sam[uel] C. Chase, a. 24
    y., shoemaker, s. Joseph and Ruth, Sept. 10, 1848.*
Patience Evans, and John Huddle, int. Dec. 6, 1823.
Patrick, and Elizabeth Davis, Dec. 7, 1813.*
Samuel, and Anna Rogers, Feb. 21, 1838.*
William, and Lydia Flood, int. Oct. 28, 1786.
William, and Sarah Evens Flood, Feb. 16, 1789.*

BURROUGH (see also Burroughs), Chandler, and Hannah
    Horton of Newburyport, int. Sept. 25, 1790.
Hannah, and John Wood, jr. of Newburyport, Nov. 21, 1790.*
Holbrook, and Mrs. Sarah J[ane. int.] Bowles, Nov. 14,
    1841.*

BURROUGHS (see also Borrow, Burrough, Burrows), Emely,
    and Asa Pearl of Plaistow, N. H., int. Oct. 27, 1838.
George, and Bridget Wood of Rowley, at Rowley, Nov. 23,
    1758.*
Holbrook, and Mary Elizabeth Cyer, int. June 2, 1838.
Holbrook, and Mary Ann Akins, int. Dec. 2, 1839.
James Manly, and [Mary. int.] Elizabeth Cyers, July —,
    1838.*

*Intention also recorded.

Burroughs, Martha [Mrs. Burrill. c. r. 2.], and John Knight,
June 28, 1792. ("The s'd John Knight declared before
several witnesses that he took s'd Martha Burroughs
naked, i. e., without any of her own earnings or without
anything that was her former husband's." c. r. 2.)*
Mary Jane, and Tho[ma]s Brookings, jr., Oct. 3, 1829.*
Webster, of Newburyport, and Mary Tone, Apr. 8, 1810.*
William, of Newburyport, and Polly Chase Huse, May 25,
1806.*

BURROWS (see also Burroughs), Will[ia]m, late of Jamaica, widr., and Eliz[abeth] Ingersoll of Salem, Apr. 16,
1728. c. r. 7.

BURT (see also Burtt), Zeubah, and Phineas Farnsworth, both
of Groton, Feb. 12, 1729-30. c. r. 7.

BURTT (see also Burt), Samuel, of Boston, and Elisabeth
Kent, Dec 7, 1749.*

BUSSELL (see also Buswell), Jane, of Boston, b. Amesbury,
and George Perrey of Fenington, Eng., seafaring man,
Nov. 11, 1729. c. k. 7.
Mary, of Salisbury, and John Sawyer, int. Nov. 22, 1752.

BUSWELL (see also Bussell, Buzzel, Buzzell), David, and
Clarissa Follansbee, Feb. 28, 1809.*
Hannah, of Kingston, N. H., and Stephen Rogers, int. Feb.
20, 1808.
James, and Molly Coleby, Aug. 6, 1761.*
Sarah T. [Jane. c. r. 10.], and Ebenezer Hoyt, both of New-
buryport, Aug. 14, 1824.

BUTLER, Elisabeth, and Ezekiel Eldridge, Apr. 5, 1750.
("This man convicted of and branded in ye hand for Po-
lygamy after this marriage." c .r. 3.)*
George, and Dorothy Gooding, Nov. 4, 1712.*
George, and Tabitha Pettingill, July 17, 1732.*
Joan, and John Cromwell, Nov. 2, 1662.
John, and Hannah Herd of Ipswich, int. Aug. 27, 1748.
John, and Mary Morgaridge of Salisbury, int. Aug. 20, 1757.
John, 3d, of Newburyport, and Sarah Poor, Feb. 26, 1782.*

*Intention also recorded.

BUTLER, Mary, Mrs., and Richard Small, Mar. 25, 1741.*
Philip, and Mary Tucker, Mar. 22, 1726.*
Philip, of Newburyport, and Ruth Dole, Sept. 18, 1782.*
Sally, and Henry Dole, jr. of Limerick, Feb. 21, 1808.*
Sarah, Mrs., and Ebenezer Knaps, Nov. 15, 1743.*
Susanna, and John Pearson [jr. int.], Oct. 29, 1747.*
Susanna, and Benjamin Cooper, Oct. 23, 1754.*

BUTMAN (see also Bootman, Buckman), John, of Newbury-
port, and wid. Anna Stickney, int. Aug. 4, 1781.
Richard S., and Eliza B. Perkins, Jan. 1, 1841.*
Thomas [jr. c. R. 1.], and Sarah Pierce, Aug. 26, 1784.*

BUTTERFIELD, Samuel, and Mary Lancaster, Nov. 23,
_ 1785.*

BUTTON, Mary, Mrs., and Nathaniel Gifford, both of Boston, Nov. 18, 1732. c. R. 7.

BUZZEL (see also Buswell), Sally, of West Newbury, and
Isaiah Southwick, Nov. 23, 1823.*

BUZZELL (see also Buswell), Mary, and Moses Hoit, Feb. 5,
1740-41.*

CALDWELL, Abner, of Newburyport, and Lydia Story, Dec.
19, 1809.*
Anna, Mrs., and Enoch Waymouth, Mar. 31, 1808.*
Anna G., of Weare, N. H., and Sam[ue]l Belcher of Stock-
bridge, Vt., Oct. 10, 1818. c. R. 10.
David S., of Dunbarton, N. H., and Abigail Newman, Dec. 5,
1827.*
John B., of Newburyport, and Harriet M. Questron, Nov. 12,
1821.*
Maria, and William Swain, both of Newburyport, Jan. 3,
1830.
Mary Ann, and Samuel Somerby, Apr. 12, 1815.*
Miriam, and Merrill Chase, Apr. 29, 1819.*
Rebeckah, Mrs., of Ipswich, and Stephen Little, jr., at Ips-
wich, Apr. 3, 1797.*
Ruth, and John Page of Newburyport, int. Feb. 4, 1809.
Stephen, of Newburyport, and Mary Lunt, int. Jan. 21, 1819.
William, and Lydia Lull, both of Ipswich, Nov. 29, 1729.
    c. R. 7.

*Intention also recorded.

CALEF (see also Calf, Calfe), Ann, and Thomas Green, both
of Boston, Jan. 11, 1725-6. c. r. 7.
James, and Abigail Jewett of Rowley, Jan. 2, 1734-5.*
John, and Deborah King of Boston, int. May 23, 1702.
Joseph, of Boston, and Hannah Jordon, Nov. 9, 1718.*
Martha, Mrs., of Boston, and Soloman Hewes, int. June 19,
1700.
William, and Sarah Chaney, Nov. 5, 1728.*
William, and Lois Sawyer, Nov. —, 1736.*

CALF (see also Calef), John, and Naomi Elliot [of Amesbury. int.], at Amesbury, Oct. 31, 1739.*
Sarah, and Henry Tuxbary of Amesbury, int. Mar. 20, 1764.

CALFE (see also Calef), Margaret, and Jasper Star, both of
Boston, Nov. 7, 1729. c. r. 7.

CALL (see also Caul, Coll), Alice, and Samuel Dowse, both
Charlestown, Oct. 2, 1733. c. r. 7.
Jonathan, and Phillippe French [of Boston. int.], at Boston,
June 18, 1745.*
Moses, jr., of Boscawen, N. H., and Sarah Boynton, Oct. 26,
1779.*

CALLEY, Elizabeth, Mrs., and Edmund Hall, Feb. 21, 1813.*
John, of Newburyport, and Elizabeth Condry, Dec. 21, 1806.*

CAMBEL (see also Campbell), Hannah, and Francis Follansbe, Nov. 20, 1777.*

CAME, George Washington, and Sally Warner, Jan. 26,
1808.*

CAMEL (see also Campbell), Hannah, and Abel Chase, Apr.
2, 1761.*

CAMPBEL (see also Campbell), Elexander, and Elisabeth
Fowler, Sept. 21, 1786.*
George, Capt., and Sarrah Popkins, 2d w., July —, 1819.
c. r. 1.

*Intention also recorded.

CAMPBELL (see also Cambel, Camel, Campbel), George,
Capt., of Newburyport, and Mary March, Mar. 9, 1813.*
John, and Hannah Morss, Dec. 5, 1754.*
Margaret, of Newburyport, and Nathaniel Gerrish, int. Jan.
1, 1803.
Margaret A., of Newburyport, and Benjamin P. Dow, int.
Nov. 30, 1838.
Randolph, Rev., and Elizabeth Perkins, both of Newburyport,
July —, 1839.

CANDIS, Joseph [Candish. int.], of Boston, and Seusanna
Trunde, May 17, 1714.*

CANE, Eliza, and Robert Mingo, Sept. 27, 1687. CT. R.

CANN, Eliza, of Newburyport, and William P. Plumer, int.
Oct. —, 1849.

CANNEY (see also Kenney), Hiram, of Newburyport, and
Mary Poor, int. July 3, 1841.
Oliver, and Catharine Dummer, Aug. 14, 1826.*

CANNON, Newton, and Rebecca Knowlton, Dec. 3, 1761.*

CANTERBURY, Beatrix, and Francis Plumer, Nov. 29, 1665.

CAR (see also Carr), John, of Salisbury, and Elizabeth
Brown, Mar. 29, 1727. C. R. 7.
Katharine, and Sam[ue]ll Marston of Hampton, Mar. 17,
1709.*
Mary, Mrs., and James Baily, Sept. 17, 1672.

CAREY (see also Cary), David, and Mary Aubin of New-
buryport, int. Dec. 9, 1820.
Elizabeth, and Thomas Fudge, int. Sept. 7, 1811.
James, and Hannah Poor, Nov. 17, 1808.*
John, and Hannah Adams, Nov. 1, 1798. C. R. 5.
Susan, and Henry Johnson of Newburyport, int. Nov. 13,
1812.

CARIO, William, and Mary Ann Pollard, both of Boston,
Sept. 5, 1735. C. R. 7.

*Intention also recorded.

CARKIN, Luther, of Newburyport, and Jane Crockett, int.
Apr. 19, 1828.
Mary E., and William R. Fox, both of Newburyport, June 20,
1833.
Sybil, and Charles J. Fox of Newburyport, Dec. 3, 1835.*

CARLETON (see also Carlton), Benjamin, of Plaistow, N.
H., and Minor Thurston, June 27, 1785.*
Hannah, of St. Johnsbury, Vt., and James Dole, int. June 2,
1815.
Jonathan, and Hannah Rowel of Amesbury, Aug. 9, 1736.*
Stephen, of Bradford, and Judith Chase, July 30, 1793.*
Thomas, and Lucinda Noyes, Jan. 31, 1811.*

CARLTON (see also Carleton), Aaron, and Prudence Gage,
both of Bradford, Apr. 21, 1735. c. r. 7.
Amos, and Sarah Dole, Oct. 3, 1780.*
Betsey, and John Chase, 4th, Nov. 16, 1803.*
Christopher, and Martha Barker, both of Andover, July 6,
1715.
Daniel, and Louis Pearson, May 5, 1786.*
Ebenezer, and Elis[abeth] Kimball, both of Bradford, Aug.
18, 1729. c. r. 7.
Hannah, of Andover, and Moody Moss, at Andover, May 27,
1741.*
Hannah, and Bayley Day of Bradford, May 5, 1787.*
John, of Newburyport, and Nabby Somerby, int. Jan. 7, 1791.
John, Capt., and Nabby Follensbe, Jan. 27, 1791. c. r. 2.
John, of Bradford, and Mary Chisemore, int. June 10, 1797.
Jonathan, and Abigail Ordway, Jan. 3, 1784.*
Jonathan, and Eunice Lufkin, Sept. 25, 1786.*
Joseph, of Bradford, and Mary Goodridge, Oct. 12, 1742.*
Joseph, and Polly Hills, int. Feb. 6, 1806.
Mary, and John Wooster, June 5, 1727.*
Mary, and John Holmes of Rowley, Mar. 18, 1755.*
Mary, and Joseph Adams, jr., Jan. 6, 1774.*
Micah, and Sarah Bayley, Apr. 12, 1753.*
Nabby, and Oliver Dole, Nov. 24, 1790.*
Patty, and Moses Day of Bradford, int. Oct. 18, 1785.
Sally, and Daniel Dougherty of Newburyport, int. June 11,
1785.

· *Intention also recorded.

CARLY, Job, and Sarah Glesen, both of Marlboro, Apr. 18, 1733. c. r. 7.

CARNES, Hephzibah, of Boston, and Dr. Charles Coffin, July 1, 1773.*
Lydia [Cone. int.], and Moses Bartlet, Apr. 25, 1803.*

CARPENTER, Hannah, and Edmund Chaney, jr., int. Dec. 30, 1738. ("Forbidden by Mr. Carpenter, the father.")
Isaac, and Rachel Baldman of Newburyport, Dec. 7, 1832.
Mary, and Daniel Chase, Jan. 22, 1722-3.*
William, and Jane March, Feb. 12, 1756.*

CARR (see also Car), Abigail, of Salisbury, and Stephen Sweett, int. Apr. 27, 1753.
Anna, and Thomas Perrin [jr. int.] of Ipswich, July 28, 1729.*
Anna, and Stephen Bayley, int. Oct. 27, 1787.
Anne, and Samuel Brown, Mar. 1, 1759.*
Anny, and Thomas Kimbal, Oct. 23, 1794.*
Bettee, of Salisbury, and Nathaniel Aubin, int. Nov. 8, 1760.
Bradbury, of York, and Anna Richardson, Dec. 5, 1734.*
Caleb Moody, resident in Newbury, and Mary Marshall of Ipswich, int. Oct. 30, 1750.
Clarissa, and John Currier, jr., int. Nov. 19, 1830.
Daniel, and Betty Chase, July 19, 1757.*
Daniel, and Elisabeth Chase, Oct. 19, 1772.*
Daniel, jr., and Elizabeth Worth, Nov. 19, 1795.*
Daniel, of Newburyport, and Patience Noyes, int. Oct. 28, 1825.
Elisabeth, and Joseph Serjant of Amesbury, Nov. 17, 1715.*
Elisabeth, of South Hampton, N. H., and Nathan Rogers, int. Aug. 18, 1744.
Elisabeth, and Daniel Pike, Apr. 29, 1755.*
Elisabeth, and John Chase, jr., July 11, 1771.*
Elisabeth, and William Wigglesworth of Newburyport,, Mar. 20, 1783.*
Elisabeth, of Newburyport, and Jonathan Pettengill, Dec. 10, 1804.*
Elizabeth Chase, and Joshua Bailey, Feb. 8, 1817.*
Esther, and Augustus Batchelder of Danvers, Sept. 15, 1836.*
Eunice [Emma. c. r. 2.], and Paul Bayley, Feb. 19, 1787.*

*Intention also recorded.

CARR, Hanna, and Symon Maston of Hampton, N. H., int.
Jan. 26, 1705-6.
Hannah, and Offin Boardman, Oct. 21, 1746.*
Hannah, of Salisbury, and Jacob Whitmore, int. Aug. 6, 1785.
Hannah, and Caleb Chase, Nov. 5, 1800.*
Hannah, and Robert Pearson of Newburyport, int. May 19,
1804.
Harriet, and Moses B. Jackman, Apr. 22, 1821.*
Hepzibah, and Charls Chase, July 15, 1714.*
James, and Mary [Sears. C. C. and CT. R.], Nov. 14, 1677.
James, jr., and Ruth Moodey, Apr. 25, 1712.*
James, and Sarah Follensbe, Oct. 5, 1749.*
James, and Anna [Hannah. int.] Poor, Jan. 3, 1760.*
James, of Newburyport, and Love Merrill, May 7, 1796.*
Jane, of Newburyport, and John Bartlet, int. Mar. 17, 1792.
Jeremiah, of Poplin, and Ruth Chase, Mar. 10, 1802.*
John, and Elizabeth Chace, Dec. 14, 1708.*
John, jr., and Ann Moody, July 28, 1738.*
John, and Abigail Morss, Nov. 23, 1758.*
John, jr., and Ruth Morss, May 5, 1763.*
John, 3d, and Sarah Rowe, Nov. 13, 1763.*
John, of Salisbury, and Elizabeth Little, Nov. 24, 1774.*
John, and Betsey Brown, Jan. 3, 1796.*
John, jr., and Abigail Williams, Dec. 15, 1796.*
John, and Hannah Worth, Nov. 20, 1800.*
John, and Rhoda Ranlet of Epping, int. Feb. 24, 1801.
John, of Poland, and Hannah Whitmore, Sept. 13, 1801.*
Joseph, and Sarah Smith, July 23, 1741.*
Joseph, of Chester, and Hannah Lull of Byfield, Rowley, Oct.
25, 1764.
Josiah, and Anna Danforth, Mar. 11, 1792.*
Judeth, and Stephen Morss, jr., Oct. 5, 1749.*
Judith, and James Jeffers, Nov. 15, 1803.*
Levi, and Mary Ireland, June 1, 1843.*
Martha, of Salisbury, and Benjamin Willit, int. Sept. 3, 1748.
Mary, and Zacheriah Nowell, Nov. 27, 1735.*
Mary, and John Rawlins, Nov. 23, 1742.*
Mary, of Newburyport, and Nathan Merrill, 3d, int. Nov. 7,
1797.
Mary, and Enoch Chase, June 12, 1806.*
Mary, and Daniel Norton of Newburyport, int. Feb. 16, 1822.
Miriam, and Josiah Worster, Dec. 13, 1748.*
Moses, jr., and Abigail Noyes, Oct. 23, 1800.*

*Intention also recorded.

CARR, Polly, and William Pilsbery, Apr. 19, 1787.*

Rebecca, of South Hampton, and Benjamin Ordway, int. Oct. 3, 1746.

Richard, of Salisbury, and Judith [Lydia. int.] Coffin, Nov. 18, 1715.*

Richard, jr., of Salisbury [widr. c. r. 2.], and wid. Sarah Chase, June 13, 1720.

Richard, and Sarah Couch, Apr. 16, 1746.*

Richard, jr., of Salisbury, and Joanna Noyes, Nov. 16, 1770.*

Richard, of Salisbury, and Abigail Coffin, May 17, 1778.*

Robert, and Polly Chase, Jan. 20, 1813.*

Sally, and Benjamin Burbank, Oct. 20, 1795.*

Samuel, and Emme Chace, Dec. 23, 1762.*

Samuel, of Amesbury, and Sarah Carr, Nov. 2, 1784.*

Samuel [jr. c. r. 1.], and Elisabeth Chase, June 29, 1797.*

Sarah, and Richard Taylor of Hampton, N. H., int. Dec. 23, 1704.

Sarah, and Francis Roberts of Somersworth [Dover. int.], N. H., Sept. 19, 1745.*

Sarah, and John Sweet, Jan. 10, 1754.*

Sarah, and Barnard Goodridge, Sept. 28, 1768.*

Sarah, and Samuel Carr of Amesbury, Nov. 2, 1784.*

Sarah E., a. 19 y., d. Dudly and Sarah Ann, and Jacob Haskell, a. 26 y., school-teacher, s. Jacob and Eunice, Mar. 9, 1847.*

Susan H., of Newburyport, and Stephen Ilsley, Jan. 29, 1833.*

William, and Mary Greenleaf, int. Jan. 11, 1805.

William, and Lydia Kelley, int. Dec. 30, 1809.

CARRELL (see also Carroll), Mary, and Moses Stevens, Oct. 5, 1811.*

CARROLL (see also Carrell), Mary, and Will[ia]m Ramsdel, Nov. 27, 1799.*

CARTER, Abi, and James Worcester of Georgetown, int. Mar. 14, 1841.

Elizabeth Margaret, of Newburyport, and William Belcher Reynolds of Boston, Apr. 24, 1821.

Hannah, Mrs., of Charlestown, and Richard Kent, Esq., at Charlestown, Sept. 8, 1724.

Hannah, Mrs., and Capt. Patrick Tracy, Jan. 25, 1742-3.*

*Intention also recorded.

CARTER, Jeremiah, and Sally Woodman of Newburyport, int. Oct. 26, 1827.

Jeremiah, and Mrs. Mary Young, both of Newburyport, Mar. 17, 1839.

Judeth, of Kingstown, and William Cooper, jr., int. Jan. 19, 1748-9.

Mary, and William Chandler, Apr. 16, 1677.

Mary, and George Wheelwright of Arundel, Dec. 24, 1816.*

Nathaniel, and Mrs. Mary Beck, Sept. 21, 1742.*

Sara, and John Davis, Apr. 8, 1681.

Thomas, of Leominster, and Rebeckah Cooper, Aug. 12, 1800.*

Thomas, Capt., and Mrs. Mehitabel Hackett, Oct. 9, 1809.*

CARY (see also Carey), Abigail, and Anthony Burrill, June 10, 1824.*

Alice, and Edward A. Cilley, int. Nov. 7, 1835.

David E., and Mary (should be Sarah) Nichols of Newburyport, int. July 31, 1847.

Elizabeth, and Samuel H. Green, int. May 9, 1835.

Hannah, and Richard Tenney, Oct. 3, 1827.*

James, jr., and Sarah S. Wheeler of Newburyport, int. Jan. 5, 1839.

Nancy, and Ebenezer Flood, int. Oct. 13, 1803.

Robert, and Sarah Abbot, both of Rowley, June 18, 1804. C. R. 5.

Sophronia, and Richard Tenny, Dec. 23, 1824.*

Susan, and Pethuel Stockbridge, Nov. 9, 1815.*

CASADY (see also Casida, Cassadey, Cassody), Philemon, and Mary Buckman of Salem, int. Jan. 20, 1766.

CASIDA (see also Casady), Mary, and Nathaniel Mason of Newburyport, int. Aug. 16, 1766.

CASSADEY (see also Casady), Elisabeth, and Samuel Lecount of Newburyport, int. July 2, 1772.

CASSODY (see also Casady), Susanna, and Zebulon Roe, July 22, 1777.*

*Intention also recorded.

CASWELL, Eliza, and Robert Willey, Aug. 16, 1818.*

Eliza Ann, and George Wallace of Newburyport, int. May 3, 1817.

Hannah, and Edmund Mountfort, Nov. 1, 1753.*

John, and Margaret Bailey, int. Mar. 16, 1822.

Lydia, Mrs., of Newburyport, and Benjamin Howard, July 27, 1816.*

Lydia L., a. 23 y., b. Gosport, and Moses Stevens, jr., a. 30 y., seaman, s. Moses and Mary, Jan. 10, 1848.*

Margaret, and John Bryant, int. Apr. 9, 1825.

Samuel, and Mrs. Nancy Smith, Nov. 28, 1828.*

Thomas, and Susan S. Harris, Nov. 2, 1836.*

Thomas, widr., of Newburyport, a. 30 y., ropemaker, s. Samuel and Lydia, and Clarissa Green, wid., of Newburyport, a. 30. y., d. Jacob and Tabitha, Feb. 24, 1846.

CATER, Samuel, of Danvers, and Abigail Noyes, Nov. 12, 1836.*

CAUL (see also Call), Jonathan [Call. int.], and Sarah Payson of Rowley, at Rowley, May 26, 1761.*

CAULEY (see also Cawley), Richard, of Stratham, and Sarah Palmer of Bradford, July 15, 1728. c. r. 7.

CAVALEY, Clarinda, and John H. P. McQuillin, int. Sept. 18, 1847.

CAVENDER, Anna, and John Townsend, Mar. 22, 1794.*

Hannah, and Thomas Downs, Sept. 5, 1800.*

James, and Polly Murry, May 17, 1790.*

CAWLEY (see also Cauley), Samuel, and Elizabeth G[age. c. r. 10.] Cole, Aug. 24, 1816.*

CESSIMIR, Lewis, and Mary Ann Brooks, July 26, 1840.*

CHACE (see also Chase), Abigail, and Joseph Robertson of Exeter, int. Sept. 26, 1710.

Aquila, and Eunice Plumer of Newburyport, int. Apr. 21, 1827.

Daniel [jr. int.], and Sarah March, Jan. 2, 1706.*

*Intention also recorded.

CHACE, Eliza B., and John Floyd, jr., int. Mar. 19, 1826.
Elizabeth, and John Carr, Dec. 14, 1708.*
Emme, and Samuel Carr, Dec. 23, 1762.*
Hannah, and Joseph Hoyt, Dec. 22, 1707.*
Isaac, and Hannah Berry, Oct. 29, 1710.*
James, and Martha Rolfe, Dec. 17, 1707.*
Jonathan, and Joanna Palmer of Bradford, int. July 11, 1702.
Joseph, and Abigael Thirston, Nov. 8, 1699.*
Mary, and James Allen, int. Dec. 15, 1827.
Sarah, of Sandown, and Samuel Sawyer, int. Oct. 29, 1803.

CHADDOCK, Thomas, and Sara Woollcutt, Apr. 6, 1674.

CHADWICK, Betsey, of Bradford, and Thomas Hills, at Bradford, Apr. —, 1783.*

CHAFFIN, Moses A., of Louisville, Ky., and Emeline Titcomb of Newburyport, Mar. 31, 1840.

CHALLIS, Hannah, of Amesbury, and Nicholas Chase, int. May 19, 1781.
Mary, of Kingstown, N. H., and Daniel Morss, int. June 6, 1779.
Miriam, wid. Thomas, late of Amesbury, and Stephen Brown, s. Stephen, late of Newbury, and Sarah, Oct. 30, 1765. c. r. 6.

CHAMBERLAIN (see also Chamberlin), Daniel, of Salem, and [Mrs. c. r. 10.] Sarah Brown of West Newbury, June 10, 1826.
Henry, and Elizabeth Tyng of Newburyport, Jan. 6, 1833.

.CHAMBERLIN (see also Chamberlain), Asa, and Elizabeth Swasey Hickey of Newburyport, int. Sept. 3, 1813.
Ch[arles] P., of Newburyport, a. 23 y., tinman, b. Newburyport, s. Henry and Mary, of Newburyport, and Sarah D. Winder, a. 23 y., d. Thomas and Nancy, Sept. 24, 1848.*
James, of Andover, and Mrs. Olive Tuttle, July 29, 1839.*
Polly Philips, and Jacob Rice George, both of Newburyport, June 15, 1808. c. r. 10.

*Intention also recorded.

CHAMPNEY, Tho[ma]s, and Jane Hubbard, both of Cambridge, Sept. 18, 1730. c. r. 7.

CHANDELER (see also Chandler), James, Rev., of Rowley, and Mrs. Mary Hale [at Rowley. dup.], Dec. 14, 1736.*

CHANDLER (see also Chandeler), Joseph, and Mary Hall [Hale. int.], Feb. 10, 1699-1700.*
Joseph, of Atkinson, N. H., and Elizabeth Cook, Jan. 7, 1768.
Josiah, and Sarah Parker, wid., both of Andover, July 1, 1735. c. r. 7.
Mary, and Percival Lowle, Sept. 7, 1664.
Mary [d. William. int.], and Jonathan Sampson, Nov. 16, 1695.*
Phebe, and John Turner, Apr. 24, 1762.*
Sara, and Richard Smith, Oct. 17, 1666.
William, and Mary Lord, Feb. 26, 1666.
William, and Mary Carter, Apr. 16, 1677.
William, jr., and Hanah Huntington, Nov. 29, 1692.
William, and Jane Nelson, of Rowley, at Rowley, Feb. 11, 1752.*

CHANEY (see also Cheney), Abigail, and Francis Harde, of Bradford, int. Nov. 16, 1738.
Ann [wid. int.], and Thomas Brown [jr. int.], Dec. 3, 1712.*
Edmund, and Mary Plummer [of Rowley. int.], Nov. 18, 1714.*
Edmund, jr., and Hannah Carpenter, int. Dec. 30, 1738. ("Forbidden by Mr. Carpenter, the father.")
Hannah, and John Coffin, jr., Apr. 28, 1726.*
Joanna, and Nathan Chase, Dec. 30, 1740.*
John, jr., and Joannah Pike, July 27, 1732.*
Martha, Mrs., and Tristram Coffin [jr. int.], Nov. 17, 1715.*
Martha, and Amos Poor, Aug. 22, 1745.*
Mary, and Joseph Homan, 3d of Marblehead, Dec. 20, 1734.*
Mary, and Amos Harde of Bradford, Feb. 22, 1738-9.*
Nathaniel, and Keziah Annis, Oct. 25, 1733.*
Nathaniel, and Lydia Bartlet, Aug. 19, 1741.*
Sarah, and William Calef, Nov. 5, 1728.*

*Intention also recorded.

CHANY (see also Cheney), Edmund [jr. int.], and Susanah Midleton, Oct. 9, 1740.*

CHAPLAIN (see also Chaplin), Jeremiah, Rev., of Danvers, and Marcia S. Obrine, Apr. 16, 1806.*

CHAPLIN (see also Chaplain), Charles, of Rowley, and Marcy Fisk, Apr. 10, 1832.*
Ebenezer, of Rowley, and Rebecca Poor, at Rowley, Jan. 5, 1744. [int. May 26, 1744.]*
Jeremiah, and Eunice Stickney, both of Rowley, Oct. 6, 1801. c. r. 5.
John, of Rowley, and Sarah Stickney, of Byfield Rowley, June 16, 1772.
Martha, of Rowley, and Samuel Longfellow, int. Jan. 1, 1780. (1790?)

CHAPMAN, Debby, and George How of Rowley, June 9, 1798.*
Dorothy, and Lt. Archelaus Woodman, Nov. 13, 1678.
Eliphaz, "a lay preacher," of Rowley, and Hannah Jackman of Byfield Rowley, Aug. 18, 1772.
Henry, of Newburyport, and Elizabeth Bennett, int. Sept. 7, 1811.
Jane, and Bartholomew R[ussell. c. r. 1.] Lunt, Jan. 25, 1823.*
William, and Jemima Knight, Dec. 11, 1799. c. r. 1.

CHASE (see also Chace, Chass), Abel, and Sarah Brickit, May 14, 1728.*
Abel, and Sarah Holmon, Mar. 23, 1730-31.*
Abel, and Hannah Camel, Apr. 2, 1761.*
Abigail, and David Emery, Jan. 27, 1731-2.*
Abigail, and Asa Bayley, Nov. 26, 1767.*
Abigail, and Jeremiah Dole, Nov. 11, 1773.*
Abigail, and Benjamin Pettingall, Dec. 21, 1780.*
Abigail, and Moses Harrington of Cornish, N. H., Oct. 22, 1795.*
Abigail, and Caleb Lamson, July 15, 1802.*
Abigail, and Nathaniel Colburn, of Leominster, Dec. 1, 1803.*
Abraham, and Ruth Mors, Nov. 16, 1716.*

*Intention also recorded.

CHASE, Abraham, and Abigail Redford Cogswell of Haverhill, int. Aug. 23, 1794.

Amos, and Eunice Merrill, Aug. 2, 1787.*

Amos [jr. C. R. 2.], and Judith Little, Sept. 24, 1794.*

Amos, jr., and Lydia Drew of Peeling, N. H., int. Oct. 19, 1816.

Ann, Mrs., of Haverhill, and Daniel Noyes [3d. int.], at Haverhill, Oct. 3, 1745.*

Ann, and Isaiah Plumer, Dec. 31, 1823.*

Anna, and Amos Pilsbury, Oct. 16, 1745.*

Anna, and John Bayley, Nov. 9, 1752.*

Anna, of Haverhill, and John Chase, 3d, at Haverhill, Dec. 18, 1777.*

Anna, and Thomas Knight, int. Nov. 8, 1786.

Anna, and Moses Little, jr., Nov. 15, 1800.*

Anna, and John Ordway, Mar. 25, 1807.*

Anna W., of Philadelphia, Pa., and Joshua Coffin, at Philadelphia, Apr. 28, 1835.

Anne, and Thomas Barbar, Apr. 27, 1671.

Anne, sr., and Daniel Missilloway, June 14, 1672.

Anne, and Abraham Foulsom of Exeter, Oct. 27, 1703.*

Anthony, and Abigail Woodman, June 29, 1758.*

Aquila, jr., and Mary Smith of Ipswich, int. May 31, 1712.

Aquila, and Hannah Davis of Haverhill, int. Mar. 12, 1736.

Aquila, and Mary Boley, Feb. 13, 1738-9. C. R. 7.

Aquila, jr., and Anna Moulton, July 9, 1780.*

Benjamin, and Sarah Bayly, May 20, 1718.*

Benjamin, and Phebe Buck of Haverhill, at Haverhill [int. May 13. 1781.].*

Benjamin, jr., and Alice Bartlet, int. Oct. 17, 1781.

Bennoni, and Mary Rodgers, Sept. 4, 1728.*

Bethia [Abiah. int.], and Samuel Hopson of Rowley, Jan. 19, 1793.*

Betsey, and Aaron Tibbits, June 15, 1815.*

Betty, and Daniel Carr, July 19, 1757.*

Betty, and Stephen Noyes, jr., Mar. 23, 1758.*

Caleb, and Hannah Carr, Nov. 5, 1800.*

Caroline B., and Capt. George Lunt, both of Newburyport, July 10, 1833.

Charles, and Hannah Bartlet, Nov. 3, 1796.*

Charles, "alias Aquila," and Hannah Wyatt, int. Dec. 7, 1816.

Charles, and Mary Jane Coffin, int. June 27, 1823.

*Intention also recorded.

CHASE, Charles, and Hannah Frost of Marblehead, int. Nov. 23, 1828.

Charles H., and Abba M. Bartlett, int. Mar. 14, 1849.

Charls, and Hepzibah Carr, July 15, 1714.*

Chivey, of Weare, N. H., s. John and Sarah, and Abigail Brown, d. Stephen and Meriam, 20: 8 m: 1808. c. R. 6.

Daniel, and Martha Kimble, Aug. 25, 1683.

Daniel, and Mary Carpenter, Jan. 22, 1722-3.*

Daniel, and Hannah Somerby, Oct. 19, 1748.*

Daniel, and [wid. int.] Elizabeth England, May 7, 1777.*

Daniel, and Mary Whitcher of Newburyport, int. July 10, 1784.

Daniel, jr., and Abigail Currier of Haverhill, int. Feb. 16, 1793.

David, and Sarah Emery, Nov. 24, 1729.*

David, jr., and Sarah Johnson, Mar. 20, 1755.*

Ebenezer, and Dorothy Foot, May 18, 1741.*

Edmund, and Esther Merrill, Nov. 30, 1769.*

Edwin T., Esq., of Philadelphia, Pa., and Lucia T. Coffin, at Philadelphia, June 14, 1841.

Eleanor P., a. 19 y., d. Jacob, and John C. Stevens, a. 25 y., mariner, s. Moses and Mary, Dec. 8, 1847.*

Elisabeth, and Joshua Bailey, jr., Sept. 4, 1734.*

Elisabeth, and Thomas Chase, jr., July 13, 1758.*

Elisabeth, and Daniel Horton, Nov. 15, 1759.*

Elisabeth, and Enoch Thirston, Apr. 14, 1762.*

Elisabeth, and Daniel Carr, Oct. 19, 1772.*

Elisabeth, and Lt. Moses Chase, Oct. 13, 1796.*

Elisabeth, and Samuel Carr [jr. c. R. 1.], June 29, 1797.*

Eliza B., and Jeremiah Hanson, int. Apr. 14, 1824.

Eliza B., and John Harmon, Aug. 30, 1826.*

Eliza Jane, and Ruben Page of Newburyport, Mar. 22, 1804.*

Elizabeth, and Will[ia]m Russell, both of Hampton, Mar. 28, 1726. c. R. 7.

Elizabeth, and Jonathan Eastman of Salisbury, May 21, 1812.*

Elizabeth, and John Janvrin, Oct. 24, 1842.*

Elizabeth L., and John A. Hills of Wells, Me., Oct. 24, 1839.*

Elizabeth S., and John Ordway, jr., Nov. 21, 1831.*

Elsy, and Job Atwood, Nov. 27, 1814.*

Emery, and Mehittabel Moar of Andover, at Andover, July 25, 1768.*

Emma, and Joseph Chase, 3d., Dec. —, 1785.*

*Intention also recorded.

CHASE, Enoch, and Mary Carr, June 12, 1806.*
Enoch, and Laura Bailey, Dec. 4, 1817.*
Eunice, and Samuel Jaques [jr. int.], Aug. 12, 1779.*
Eunice, and Abbe Severance, resident in Newbury, Oct. 12,
    1781.*
Eunice, and Moses Ordway, May 9, 1822.*
Ezekel, Dr., of Groton, and Priscila Merrill, May 20, 1729.*
Ezra, and Abigail Lowe, Oct. 13, 1743.*
Fanny, and Robert Howell, Nov. 30, 1809.*
Francis, of Hampton Falls, N. H., and Mary Howard Wildes,
    int. Oct. 24, 1840.
George, and Susan A. Chase, both of West Newbury, Aug. 26,
    1841.
Hannah, and Abraham Parker, jr. of Bradford, Dec. 14,
    1738.*
Hannah, and Dea. James Chute of Rowley, int. Oct. 30, 1762.
Hannah, and [Dr. int.] Ebenezer Noyes of Dover, N. H.,
    Nov. 29, 1764.*
Hannah, and George Nowell [Newell. int.], Sept. 14, 1786.*
Hannah, and Samuel Bayley, jr., int. Oct. 26, 1791.
Hannah, and Francis Brown, int. Aug. 17, 1804.
Hannah, and Moses Jaques, jr., int. Oct. 27, 1804.
Hannah, and Henry Merrill, June 10, 1824.*
Hannah, and Henry Dane, jr. of Andover, int. Mar. 19, 1831.
Hannah, of West Newbury, and John Ordway, Mar. 29,
    1837.*
Hannah Morse, and Stephen Poor, jr., Dec. 2, 1813.*
Hannah S., and Charles C. [P. int.] Crockett of Concord,
    N. H., May 11, 1835.*
Harriet A., of Newburyport, and Samuel F. Baxter of New
    York City, Aug. 20, 1837.
Harriet A., a. 24 y., d. Nath[anie]l and Harriet, and Ezra
    Trumbull, a. 26 y., shipwright, b. Boscawen, N. H., s.
    Simon and Sally, Dec. 9, 1847.*
Henry, and Betsey B. Warner of Londonderry, int. Feb. 16,
    1821.
Hephsibah, and Samuel Stocker, May 14, 1789.*
Hittey, and Moses Bayley, Apr. 26, 1798.*
Huldah, and Timothy Ayer of Haverhill, at Haverhill [bef.
    1784.].
Huldah, and Timothy Ayers, Oct. 15, 1795.*
Increase Sumner, and Maria Noyes, May 14, 1818.*

*Intention also recorded.

CHASE, Jacob, and Johanna Davis of Haverhill, Aug. 24, 1716.*

Jacob, jr., and Ellice Hodge of Newburyport, int. Sept. 8, 1803.

Jacob, and Hannah Barker, int. Dec. 30, 1805.

Jacob, and Elizabeth Burditt, Oct. 6, 1811.*

Jacob, jr., and Eleanor A. Hunt of Newburyport, int. Apr. 6, 1833.

Jacob B., a. 23 y., mariner, s. Joseph H. and Nancy, and Hannah J. Thurlow, a. 20 y., July 3, 1844.*

James, of Stratham, and Ann Goodridge, Aug. 10, 1736.*

James, and Elizabeth Peterson, May 21, 1739.*

James, and Mrs. Hannah Bartlet, Sept. 18, 1739.*

James [jr. int.], and Abigail Bayley, Mar. 25, 1746.*

James, and Sarah Hobson of Ipswich, int. May 7, 1819.

Jemima, and Peter Ordway, Nov. 3, 1721.*

Jeremiah, and Hannah Pilsbery, Feb. 2, 1786.*

Jeremiah, jr., and Anna Emerson of Hampstead, N. H., int. May 22, 1789.

Jeremiah K., a. 24 y., seaman, s. Moses and Hannah, and Mary Ann Blair, a. 20 y., d. Alexander and Betsey, Nov. 9, 1845.*

Joanna, and Samuel Rogers, May 15, 1796.*

Joanne, and Joseph Thurla, Nov. 25, 1789.*

John, and Elizabeth Bingly, May 23, 1677.

John, jr., and Hannah Hoite, July 30, 1728.*

John, and Hannah Plumer, Nov. 27, 1753.*

John, and Ruth Hills, Feb. 16, 1762.*

John, jr., and Elisabeth Carr, July 11, 1771.*

John, 3d, and Anna Chase of Haverhill, at Haverhill, Dec. 18, 1777.*

John, 3d, and Phebe Abbot, int. Mar. 24, 1780.

John, jr. [4th. int.], and Molly Emery, Oct. 2, 1781.*

John, 4th, and Betsey Carlton, Nov. 16, 1803.*

John, 3d, and Olive Dame of Barrington, N. H., int. Mar. 8, 1817.

John B., and Susan S. Downs, Oct. 16, 1824.*

Johnson, and Abigail Pike, July 19, 1753.*

Jonathan, and Joanna [Hanna. int.] Morss, Jan. 24, 1744-5.*

Jonathan, of Newburyport, and Hannah Rawlins, int. July 12, 1767.

Jonathan, jr., and Hannah Merrill, Apr. 22, 1773.*

*Intention also recorded.

CHASE, Jonathan [3d. C. R. 1.], and Hannah Brown, Nov. 30,
    1797.*
Jonathan, a. 24 y., farmer, s. Moses and Lorana, and Anna C.
    Thurlow, a. 24 y., d. Samuel and Sarah, Sept. 6, 1849.*
Joseph [jr. int.], and Mary Morss, Sept. 7, 1724.*
Joseph, jr., and Susanna Bancroft, Aug. 27, 1751.*
Joseph, 3d, and Hannah Lakeman, May 29, 1773.*
Joseph, 3d, and Emma Chase, Dec. —, 1785.*
Joseph, and Lydia Sawyer, Feb. 10, 1789.*
Joseph H., and Nancy Brown, Dec. 11, 1817.*
Joseph R., and Jane M. Hoyt of Haverhill, Oct. 20, 1832.
Joshua, Dr., and Polly Shackford of Portsmouth, int. Sept. 7,
    1780.
Joshua, and Molly Stocker of Amesbury, int. Oct. 8, 1785.
Josiah, and Sarah Tufts, Apr. 5, 1743.*
Josiah, and Susanna Thurston, Oct. 11, 1781.*
Josiah, jr., and Sarah L. Woodward, Nov. 25, 1809.*
Josiah, jr., and Esther S. Furnald, Feb. 5, 1817.*
Judeth, and William Currier [jr. C. R. 2.] of Amesbury, Feb.
    19, 1735-6.*
Judeth, and William Greenough, int. Aug. 11, 1749.
Judith, and John Tuttle of Lebanon, Jan. 21, 1713-14.*
Judith, and Enoch Robie of Deerfield, N. H., June 9, 1768.*
Judith, and Stephen Carleton of Bradford, July 30, 1793.*
Judith, and William Hills, jr., Jan. 21, 1802.*
Judith, and George Griffin of Bradford, Feb. 19, 1807.*
Judith, and James Ordway [jr. int.], Apr. 28, 1836.*
Judith S., and Joseph G. Rogers, int. Nov. 22, 1828.
Lizzee, and Benjamin Rogers, Aug. 17, 1732.*
Lois, and Edmund Rogers, Nov. 30, 1768.*
Lydia, and William Evins, Jan. 30, 1715-16.*
Lydia, and [William, int.] Blay of Haverhill, Nov. 5, 1724.*
Lydia, and William Johnson, jr., Mar. 31, 1761.*
Lydia, and —— "married out," bef. 21: 9 m: 1775. C. R. 6.
Lydia, and Dr. William Bachellor of Haverhill, at Haverhill,
    [int. Feb. 20, 1771.].*
Lydia, and William Millar, Feb. 7, 1809.*
Lydia T., and Job Tapley of Brooksville, Me., Nov. —, 1832.*
Margaret C., and Moses L. Chase, int. Aug. 5, 1849.
Margaret L., and Luther Hatch, int. May 31, 1845.
Martha, wid., and Josiah Heth, sr. of Haverhill, int. May 9,
    1713.

*Intention also recorded.

CHASE, Martha, and David Lawson, resident in Newbury, Aug. 3, 1716.*

Martha, and Stephen Gerrish [of Canterbury. int.], July 21, 1738.*

Mary, and John Stevens, Mar. 9, 16€9.

Mary, and Joseph Safford of Ipswich, July 30, 1728.*

Mary, and Ruben Mace, Sept. 20, 1739. C. R. 7.*

Mary, and Joseph Pearson, int. Aug. 15, 1740.

Mary, and Josiah Mors of Chester, Oct. 27, 1743.*

Mary, and William Emery of Contoocook, N. H., int. Aug. 4, 1749.

Mary, and Joseph Bayley, Oct. 5, 1775.*

Mary, and Joshua Ordway, jr., Nov. 25, 1800.*

Mary, and Daniel Morse, July 24, 1806.*

Mary, and Samuel Merrill, jr., Apr. 14, 1813.*

Mary, and Newman Follansbee, Sept. 23, 1814.*

Mary, and Eliphalet Randall, Sept. 25, 1814.*

Mary, and Jonathan Fisk, Nov. 17, 1823.*

Mary, and George Janvrin, Nov. 21, 1839.*

Mary, a. 19 y., d. Nathaniel and Sarah, and William B. Coffin, a. 22 y., shipwright, s. Joseph and Mary C., Sept. 21, 1847.*

Mary E., of Newburyport, a. 20 y., and Isaiah G. Littlefield, of Newburyport, a. 25 y., farmer, s. William and Betsey, Jan. 27, 1846.

Mary E., and Robert A. Smith, int. Jan. 22, 1848.

Mary J., a. 18 y., d. Josiah and Esther, and James A. Davis, a. 22 y., painter, s. Alex J. and Mary, Dec. 12, 1848.*

Mehettebel, and Timothy Osgood of Salisbury, Nov. 29, 1715.*

Mehitabel, and David Poor of Rowley, May 1, 1816.*

Mehitabel B., and Charles Hills of Rowley, Dec. 3, 1818.*

Mercy, and John Presse, jr. of Amesbury, Aug. 16, 1733. C. R. 7.

Merrill, and Salley Tucker, Mar. 3, 1796.*

Merrill, and Miriam Caldwell, Apr. 29, 1819.*

Minah, and Nathaniel Thirston, Jan. 5, 1740-41.*

Molle, and Joseph Huse, Oct. —, 1737.*

Molly, and Stephen Richardson, Aug. 18, 1761.*

Molly, and Moody Smith, Feb. 17, 1774.*

Moody, and Anne Webster of Hampstead, int. June 16, 1768.

Moses, and Anne Follinsby, Nov. 10, 1684.

Moses, jr., and Elisabeth Wells of Amesbury, at Amesbury, Oct. 12, 1709.*

*Intention also recorded.

CHASE, Moses, Ens., and Mrs. Sarah Jacobs of Ipswich, int.
. May 10, 1713.
Moses, 3d, and Judith Bartlet, Dec. 9, 1736.*
Moses, 3d, and Susanna Kelley, June 17, 1760.*
Moses, and Anne Sergeant, June 5, 1766.*
Moses, 3d, and Mary Ordway, Aug. 14, 1777.*
Moses, 3d, and Joanna Lunt, Apr. 21, 1783.*
Moses, 3d, and [wid. int.] Mary Hale, Mar. 9, 1784.*
Moses, of Plaistow, and Mary Noyes, Apr. 17, 1788.*
Moses, Lt., and Elisabeth Chase, Oct. 13, 1796.*
Moses, jr., and Nabby Little of Amesbury, July 10, 1800.*
Moses, jr., and Betsey Pilsbury, int. Aug. 10, 1805.
Moses [3d. int.], and Polly Blancherd, Oct. 6, 1805.*
Moses, and Sally Davis, Nov. 7, 1814.*
Moses, and Hannah Allen of Newburyport, int. Jan. 20, 1821.
Moses, jr., and Emily Stickney of Newburyport, Feb. 17,
    1840.*
Moses L., and Margaret C. Chase, int. Aug. 5, 1849.
Nancy [Mary. int.], and Amos Hills, Apr. 25, 1793.*
Nancy, and Richard Hawes, May 12, 1818.*
Nathan, and Judeth Sawyer, Nov. 29, 1723.*
Nathan, and Joanna Chaney, Dec. 30, 1740.*
Nathan, and Lydia Molton, Nov. 24, 1747. c. R. 2.*
Nathan, and Ruth Davis, June 22, 1763.*
Nathan, jr., and Dorothy Sarjent, May 1, 1776.*
Nathan, jr., and Sarah Pebe of Newburyport, int. May 22,
    1784.
Nathan [jr. int.], and Salley [Mary. int.] Neal of Newbury-
    port, Feb. 18, 1800.
Nathan [4th. int.], and Betsey Warner, Jan. 20, 1806.*
Nathan, 3d, and Judith Rogers, int. Mar. 29, 1807.
Nathaniel, and Sarah Barton, June 15, 1732.*
Nathaniel, and Harriet Doyle, Apr. 18, 1822.*
Nathaniel, and Mrs. Sally Merrill, Feb. 22, 1835.*
Nathaniel Low, and Lydia Dustan, Apr. 8, 1773.*
Nicholas, and Hannah Challis of Amesbury, int. May 19, 1781.
Parker, and Ruth Kelley, Dec. 28, 1774.*
Paul, and Sarah Pike of Salisbury, int. Jan. 27, 1745-6.
Phebe Ann, and Enoch Goodwin, Dec. 9, 1841.*
Philip, and Mary Follinsby, Apr. 17, 1712.*
Polly, and John Ordway, Oct. 2, 1783.*
Polly, and Robert Carr, Jan. 20, 1813.*

*Intention also recorded.

CHASE, Priscila, and Joseph Hills, int. Feb. 26, 1703-4.
Priscilla, and Abell Merrill, Feb. 10, 1670.
Priscilla, and Anthony Whitmore of Newburyport, Jan. 15, 1795.*
Priscilla, and Moses Bayley, int. Feb. 21, 1805.
Priscilla, and Nehemiah Follansbee, June 2, 1808.*
Rachel, of Haverhill, and Joseph Kimbal, int. Dec. 26, 1800.
Rebecca, and Jonathan Moulton, Dec. 5, 1716.*
Rebecca, and Steven Moulton, Dec. 14, 1721.*
Rebecca, and Joseph Nichols of Amesbury, Feb. 1, 1732-33.*
Rebecca, and Samuel Longfellow, Nov. 30, 1768.*
Rebecca B., and Samuel Coffin, jr., Mar. 27, 1832.*
Rebeccah, of Andover, and Stephen Bailey, jr., at Andover, Nov. 22, 1798.*
Rebeckah, and Jonas Lewis, int. Oct. 5, 1805.
Rebekah, and Stephen Ordway, jr., Nov. 29, 1784.*
Robert, and Lydia Bodwell of Methuen, at Methuen, Dec. 7, 1780.*
Roger, and Abigail Morrison, Mar. 16, 1725-6.*
Rufus H., of West Newbury, and Sarah H. Rogers, ——, 1844. [Aug. 27. int.]*
Ruth, and Nathaniel Miller [Millerd. C. R. 2.] of Rehoboth, May 29, 1716.*
Ruth, and Jeremiah Carr of Poplin, Mar. 10, 1802.*
Salley, and Enoch Noyes, jr., June 16, 1803.*
Sally, and Joshua Bayley, jr., Mar. 18, 1780.*
Sally, and Joshua Bailey, jr., Aug. 25, 1812.*
Samuel, and Hannah Emery, Dec. 8, 1713.*
Samuel, and Sarah Steward of Amesbury, int. Nov. 23, 1751.
Samuel, and Mary Conner, int. Aug. —, 1768.
Samuel, and Sarah Bowley of Methuen, at Methuen, July 6, 1769.*
Samuel, and Priscilla Merrill, Nov. 25, 1779.*
Samuel, jr., and Sarah Merrill of Rumney, N. H., int. Jan. 30, 1808.
Samuel, jr., and Mary Doe of Rumney, N. H., int. Sept. 2, 1810.
Sam[ue]l C., a. 24 y., shoemaker, s. Joseph and Ruth, and Nancy Burrill, d. Jonathan and Mary, Sept. 10, 1848.*
Sara, and Curmac, alias Charls Annis, May 15, 1666.
Sarah, and Francis Danford, Nov. 17, 1714.*
Sarah, wid., and Richard Carr, jr. of Salisbury [widr. C .R.2.], June 13, 1720.

*Intention also recorded.

CHASE, Sarah, and Richard Bartlet, 4th, Dec. 5, 1723.*
Sarah, and Moses Mors, jr., Sept. 15, 1743.*
Sarah, and Stevens Merril, Jan. 7, 1752.*
Sarah, and Moses Bricket, Oct. 5, 1768.*
Sarah, and —— "married" out bef. 8th m. 1773. c. r. 6.
Sarah, and Mark Woodman, Feb. 28, 1780.*
Sarah, and Maj. Thomas Noyes, Dec. 9, 1798.*
Sarah, of Deerfield, and Jacob Burril, jr., int. Nov. 6, 1801.
Sarah, and Moses Brown, jr., Sept. 7, 1815.*
Sarah, of Rowley, a. 22 y., d. Silas and Mary, of Rowley, and
    Caleb Burrill, of Rowley, a. 31 y., shoemaker, s. James
    and Mary, of Rowley, ——, 1844.
Sarah Ellen, of Newburyport, and Peter Le Breton, jr., int.
    Oct. 3, 1823.
Sarah L., and Ebenezer Tucker of Gloucester, int. Aug. 4,
    1837.
Sarah W., and George W. Whitmore of Newburyport, Nov. 27,
    1839.*
Seth, and Elisabeth Bartlet, May 31, 1738.*
Simeon, and Hannah Johnson, Sept. 9, 1772.*
Simeon [jr. int.], and Eunice Bayley, Apr. 15, 1787.*
Somersby, and Sarah Jaques, Apr. 16, 1777.*
Sophronia B., d. Jacob and Betsey, and John B. Athorn, ship
    carpenter, s. ——, of Berwick, Sept. 22, 1844.*
Sprague, and Susan Davis Ordway, Nov. 8, 1832.*
Stephen, and Prudence Morss, Aug. 29, 1769.*
Stephen, and Sarah Smith, Dec. 12, 1771.*
Stephen, and Mary Sanborn of Exeter, N. H., int. May 22,
    1773.
Stephen, of Plaistow, N. H., and Sarah Merrill, int. Feb. 5,
    1819.
Susan, of West Newbury, and George Thurlow, June 17,
    1830.*
Susan A., and George Chase, both of West Newbury, Aug. 26,
    1841.
Susan G., and Stephen A. Bartlet of West Northwood, N. H.,
    June 1, 1842.*
Susan O., and James P. L. Wescott, July 3, 1842.*
Susanna, and Stephen Noyes, jr., June 15, 1756.*
Susanna, and Tristram Chase [jr. c. r. 2.], Sept. 29, 1796.*
Thomas, and Rebecca Follinsby, Nov. 22, 1677.
Thomas [sr. int.], and Elisabeth Moers, Aug. 2, 1714.*

*Intention also recorded.

CHASE, Thomas, 3d, and Mary Mooers, Sept. 3, 1724.*
Thomas, 3d, and Emme Kent, Nov. 24, 1726.*
Thomas, jr., and Elisabeth Chase, July 13, 1758.*
Thomas, and Lowis Ordway, June 12, 1800.*
Thomas, and Lydia Batters, int. May 20, 1804.
Thomas Gray, and Patty Noyes, int. Nov. 3, 1807.
Thomasin, and Daniel Merrill, jr., Nov. 1, 1743.*
Thurston S., a. 21 y., carriage builder, s. Josiah and Ester, and
    Sarah L. Goodwin, a. 19 y., d. Nathaniel and Sarah, Sept.
    11, 1845.*
Tristram, and Priscilla Woodman, Dec. 9, 1762.*
Tristram [jr. c. R. 2.], and Susanna Chase, Sept. 24, 1796.*
Wells [of Amesbury. int.], and Martha Morss, Aug. 6, 1734.*
Wells, and Sarah Hovey, Feb. 21, 1760.*
William, and Elisabeth Eaton of Newburyport, int. Feb. 10,
    1798.
William, and Elizabeth Reed, May 5, 1811.*

CHASS (see also Chase), Stephen, and Sarah Hale, Dec. 17,
    171[7. c. R. 2.]

CHEENEY (see also Cheney), Daniel, jr., and Susanna Bad-
    ger, Feb. 18, 1790.*
Mary, and W[illia]m Bailey, Nov. 25, 1813.*
Moses, jr., and Sarah Broughton, Sept. 5, 1824.*
Samuel, and Anna Clark, Feb. 23, 1812.*
William B., and Mary Jane Bias, int. June 24, 1836.

CHEENY (see also Cheney), David, of Plymouth, N. H., and
    Anna Worth, int. Nov. 10, 1792.
Elisabeth, and Ebenezer Kelly, Apr. 29, 1790.*
John, and Mary Waterman, Nov. 25, 1787.*

CHEEVER (see also Chever, Chevers), Albert, and Rebecca
    K. Newman, int. Oct. 5, 1844.
Belinda, of Salem, and Dea. Putnam Perley, int. Feb. 18, 1831.
Benjamin Hale, of Newburyport, and Mary March Dutton, int.
    Apr. 9, 1825.
Eunice, and Benja[min] Pettingell, jr., int. June 21, 1835.
Eunice, and Charles Lavalette, both of Newburyport, Aug. 1,
    1839.
John, of Newburyport, and Sarah Hidden, int. Jan. 16, 1779.

*Intention also recorded.

CHEEVER, John, jr., of Newburyport, and Eunice Moulton, Apr. 19, 1808.*
Molly, and Michael Smith, Dec. 14, 1777.*
Moses, and Rebeckah Hale, Jan. 15, 1770.*
Nancy, of Newburyport, and Stephen H. Fowle, int. Jan. 24, 1829.
Ruth, Mrs., and John Wingate, both of Newburyport, Dec. 12, 1830.
Sarah, and Henry Pettingell of Newburyport, Feb. 1, 1770.*
William, and Jean Hale, Nov. 12, 1772.*

CHENEY (see also Chaney, Chany, Cheeney, Cheeny, Cheny), Abigail, and Abner Bayley, May 24, 1758.*
Abner Moors, and Lois Haniford, July 22, 1800. C. R. 5.
Benja[min], and Judith Holeman, Nov. 6, 1753.*
Daniel, and Elisabeth Davis, Feb. 17, 1757. [1756. C. R. 2.]*
Doritha, and Joseph Bigford [of Newburyport. int.], Mar. 22, 1770.*
Eldad, and Mary Walker, both of Bradford, Dec. 31, 1707.
Elias, and Jane Plumer of Rowley, at Rowley, Sept. 7, 1762.*
Elias, and Ruth Jackman of Byfield Rowley, Mar. 9, 1768.
Elias, and Hannah Pike of Byfield Rowley, June 8, 1774.*
Esther, and John Foss, both of Rowley, Feb. 8, 1814. C. R. 5.
Hannah, and John Holeman of Sutton, Nov. 25, 1755.*
Harriet, and Robert Taylor, Nov. —, 1833.*
Hephsibah, and Thomas Smith, both of Byfield Rowley, Dec. 5, 1776.
Icabod, and Ann Chute [of Rowley. int.], Jan. 5, 1708.*
John, and Susanna Cheney of Bradford, Oct. 16, 1766.*
John C[lark. int.], and Mary S[awyer. int.] Taylor, Mar. 9, 1840.*
Jonathan, jr., of Rowley, and Catharine Floid, int. July 4, 1834.
Joseph, and Sarah Jane Kilborn, Oct. 10, 1838.*
Keziah, and Stephen Thirston, Sept. 1, 1773.*
Lydia, and Jeremy [Jeremiah. int.] Poor [of Rowley. int.], Apr. 27, 1709.*
Mark, and Sarah Tenney, both of Rowley, May 17, 1808. C. R. 5.
Mary B., and John B. Gough, Nov. —, 1838.*
Mehetable, and Stephen Blasdill of Hopkinton, N. H., Oct. 11, 1770.*

*Intention also recorded.

CHENEY, Moses, and Sarah Whitten of Rowley, at Rowley, Oct. 23, 1740.*
Moses, and Sarah Sawyer of Newburyport, int. Oct. 8, 1785.
Nicholas, and Hannah Tenney of Rowley, Dec. 1, 1717.
Samuel, and Abigail Joseph, both of Byfield Rowley, Dec. 9, 1783.
Samuel, and Deborah Baker, both of Rowley, July 3, 1825.
Sarah, and Isaac Remick, May 11, 1757.*
Sarah, and Moses Smith, jr., Mar. 29, 1759.*
Susanna, of Bradford, and John Cheney, Oct. 16, 1766.*
Susanna, and Ephraim Hardy of Bradford, Nov. 17, 1767.*
Susanna, and John [W. int.] Jewett of Rowley, Dec. 2, 1824.*
William, and Elisabeth Sweet, Apr. 14, 1763.*
William A., jr., of Newburyport, a. 21 y., mariner, b. Newburyport, s. Edward and Sarah, of Newburyport, and Sarah T. Silloway, of Newburyport, a. 22 y., b. Newburyport, d. Joseph and Mary, of Newburyport, Nov. 25, 1849.

CHENY (see also Cheney), Anna, and Lyonel Chute of Rowley, int. Nov. 21, 1702.
Daniel, and Sara Baily, Oct. 8, 1665.
Edmund, and Anne Poor, Sept. 16, 1748.*
Eloner [d. Daniel, deceased. int.], and Richard Sachell of Ipswich, Dec. 17, 1696.*
Hanah [d. Daniel, deceased. int.], and Thomas Wisewell of Newtowne [Cambridge. int.], Dec. 17, 1696.*
Hannah, and Richard Smith, Nov. 16, 1659.
Hannah [wid. Peter. int.], and John Atkinson [sr. int.], June 3, 1700.*
Jemima, and Richard Petengall [jr. int.], Oct. 10, 1701. [Nov. 1. int.]*
Joanna, and Nathan Allen, Sept. 24, 1754.*
John, and Mary Plumer, Apr. 20, 1660.
John, and Mary Chute, Mar. 7, 1693-4.
John, and Phebe Russel, Nov. 30, 1797.*
Joseph, and Sarah Wiswell of Newtowne, int. Nov. 14, 1702.
Lydia, and John Kenricke, Nov. 12, 1657.
Peter, and Hanna Noyes, May 14, 1663.
Rebcah, and Daniel Richardson, 3d, Feb. 13, 1755.*
Sara, and Joseph Plumer, Dec. 23, 1652.
Sarah, and John Richards, July 16, 1696.*

*Intention also recorded.

CHESEMOR (see also Chesemore), Meribah, and Moses Boynton, Sept. 24, 1744.*

CHESEMORE (see also Chesemor, Chisemore, Chisimore, Chissemore), Abigail, and Daniel Rogers, Dec. 1, 1721.*
Mary, and John Cornish, resident in Newbury, int. Aug. 11, 1716.

CHESLEY, Betsey, and Harrison Wentworth, both of Ipswich, Mar. 21, 1836.
Elizabeth Ann, of Lee, N. H., and Luther Merrill, int. Sept. 11, 1841.
Hannah F., a. 20 y., b. Gilmanton, d. Timothy and Betsy, of Gilmanton, and David C. Elliot, a. 22 y., b. Dorchester, N. H., s. Isaac and Dorothy, of Dorchester, Nov. 25, 1847.*

CHEVER (see also Cheever), Benjamin Hale, of Newburyport, and Rebeckah Tompson, int. Sept. 18, 1795.

CHEVERS (see also Cheever), William, and Sarah Knight, Mar. 31, 1741.*

CHEWTE (see also Chute), Elisabeth, of Rowley, and Enoch Noyes, Feb. 24, 1746-7.*
Judith, of Byfield Rowley, and Daniel Thurston of Rowley, Feb. 4, 1768.

CHILDS, Lucy E., of Newburyport, a. 23 y., d. James and Eliza, and Ebenezer Perkins, a. 25 y., seaman, s. William and Sarah, Apr. 14, 1846.*

CHIPMAN, Cha[rle]s D., and Naomia P. McQuillen, int. Apr. 5, 1848.
Henry, and Mary Nowell, Feb. 5, 1755.*
Paulina, and Michael Morrison, both of Newburyport, Oct. 20, 1794.

CHISEMORE (see also Chesemore), Daniel, and Abigail Morss [Morse. c. R. 2.], Mar. 7, 1759.*
Mary, and John Carlton of Bradford, int. June 10, 1797.
Susanna, and Stephen Downer, Dec. 9, 1773.*

*Intention also recorded

CHISIMORE (see also Chesemore), Ruth, and Barker Lapham of Bradford, at Bradford, Feb. 10, 1795.*

CHISSEMORE (see also Chesemore), Jacob [jr. int.], and Hannah Turner, Oct. 16, 1770.*

CHOAK (see also Chooke), Mary, and John Mitchil, Sept. 18, 1746.*

CHOAT (see also Choate), Benjamin, and Anna Knap, Aug. 10, 1754.*
John, and Hannah Pearson, Oct. 5, 1789.*

CHOATE (see also Choat), Ebenezer, of Ipswich, and Elisabeth Greenleaf, Sept. 3, 1730.*

CHOOKE (see also Choak), Samuel, and Mary Mireck, Apr. 16, 1714. c. r. 7.*

CHRISTA, Mary, and James A. Bailey, ——, 1809. [Aug. 5. int.]*

CHRISTIAN, James B., of St. John's, and Lydia Dodge of Newburyport, Apr. 5, 1833.

CHURCH, Sarah, and Stephen Bailey of Bradford, June 14, 1737.*

CHUTE (see also Chewte, Shute), Ann [of Rowley. int.], and Icabod Cheney, Jan. 5, 1708.*
Betsy, of Rowley and Daniel Hale, Dec. 8, 1796.*
Daniel, of Rowley, and Hannah Adams, at Rowley, Apr. 20, 1743.*
Daniel, jr., of Byfield Rowley, and Mary Stimpson, Dec. 11, 1781.*
Eunice, of Rowley, and Joseph Hale of Salem, Sept. 18, 1806. c. r. 5.
Hannah, of Rowley, and Timothy Jackman, Apr. 9, 1723.*
James, of Rowley, and Mary Thirston, int. Jan. 14, 1715-16.
James, Dea., of Rowley, and Hannah Chase, int. Oct. 30, 1762.
Lyonel, of Rowley, and Anna Cheny, int. Nov. 21, 1702.
Martha, and Josiah Smith, Apr. 15, 1712.

*Intention also recorded.

CHUTE, Mary, and John Cheny, Mar. 7, 1693-4.
Mary, and Benjamin Colman, jr., June 29, 1780.*
Mary, of Rowley, and Jeremiah Colman of Newburyport, June
    8, 1808. C. R. 5.
Mehitabel [of Rowley. int.], and Jonathan Eliot, Oct. 2,
    1800.*
Richard, of Rowley, and Dorothy Pearson, Oct. 17, 1805.*

CILLEY, Edward A., and Alice Cary, int. Nov. 7, 1835.
Mercy M. J., of Newburyport, and Joseph Gould, int. June 17,
    1848.
Susan, of Newburyport, and Nathan Kilborn, Jan. 9, 1837.*

CIMBAL (see also Kimball), John, and Mara Prese of Ames-
    bury, Feb. 9, 1712-13.

CLANEN, Mary, of Newburyport, and John Hidden, int. Nov.
    29, 1793.

CLARCK (see also Clark), Elizabeth, and Daniell Thing of
    Exeter, Mar. 3, 1717-18.

CLARK (see also Clarck, Clarke, Clerk), Abigail, and Oliver
    Worcester, Dec. 6, 1756.*
Ann P., of Newburyport, a. 24 y., b. Newburyport, d. Amos
    and Rebecca, and Henry A. Lander, a. 27 y., shoemaker,
    s. Henry and Lydia, June 4, 1848.*
Anna, and Samuel Cheeney, Feb. 23, 1812.*
Anne, and Edmund Cottle, Nov. 10, 1726.*
Daniel, and Mehetable Hale, Jan. 28, 1752.*
Ebenezer, and Susanna Perrey [Perring. int.], May 15, 1753.*
Edwin Augustus, of New Orleans, and Henrietta Toppan,
    June 29, 1825.*
Elisabeth, Mrs. [wid., sr. int.], and ·John Hale of Beverly,
    Aug. 8, 1698.*
Elisabeth, and Edward Richardson, Dec. 30, 1731.*
Elisabeth, and Timothy Worcester, Nov. 1, 1743.*
Elisabeth, and Edw[ar]d Pettengell, Mar. 20, 1755.*
Elisabeth, and Stephen Pettengell, jr. of Newburyport, June
    23, 1765.*
Enoch, and Sabrina Thurlo, Feb. 5, 1824.*

*Intention also recorded.

CLARK, Henry, and Mrs. Elisabeth Greenleaf [d. Capt. Stephen. int.], Nov. 7, 1695.*

Henry, and Mary Peirce, Jan. 24, 1723-4.*

Jane, and Joseph G. Flanders, int. May 1, 1847.

John, and Sarah Power, Dec. 6, 1687. CT. R.

John, of Kingston [Hampton. int.], and Rookby Greenleaf, Apr. 21, 1738.*

Jonathan, and Lidia Titcomb, May 15, 1683.

Joseph, and Bathsheba Gales, both of Hingham, July 20, 1731. C. R. 7.

Judith, and Jacob Hidden, Sept. 10, 1812.*

Lucy, of Salem, and Bezaleel Woodbury, resident in Newbury, int. Aug. 8, 1761.

Lydia, and John Morss of Newburyport, int. Nov. 13, 1780.

Margaret M., of Newburyport, and Charles Noyes, int. Nov. 12, 1842.

Mary, of Andover, and Jonathan Morse, at Andover, Feb. 14, 1792.*

Mary Pearson, of Newburyport, and Nathaniel Hunt, jr., int. Mar. 3, 1821.

Mercy, of Newburyport, and Stephen Atkinson, int. Dec. 15, 1770.

Micah, and Abigail Jewell, Apr. 15, 1779.*

Nathaniel, and Elizabeth Somerby, Nov. 23, 1663.

Nathaniel, and Sarah Greenleaf, Mar. 7, 1710.*

Oliver, and Lydia Knight, Jan. 12, 1742-3.*

Parcivall, and Sarah Tompson [jr. int.], Mar. 26, 1712-13.*

Parker, jr., and Judith Lunt, int. July 8, 1769.

Phillips, and Elizabeth Brown, Jan. 21, 1821.*

Richard, of Rowley, and Abigel Wicomb, int. Oct. 24, 1702.

Sarah [d. John. int.], of Rowley, and James Ordway [jr. int.], at Rowley, June 19, 1696.*

Sarah, Mrs., and Nicholas Gilman [of Exeter. int.], June 9, 1697.*

Sarah [wid. int.], and Stephen Webster, Nov. 1, 1698.*

Sarah, and Nathan Noyes, June 3, 1714.*

Sarah, and William Lunt, Dec. 29, 1747.*

Sarah, and Moses Follansbe, jr. of Weare, N. H., Oct. 13, 1778.*

Sarah, and Thomas Smith, int. Jan. 30, 1784.

Somers, and Emme Hills, Nov. 26, 1735.*

Stephen, and Rebeccah Watson, Mar. 26, 1747.*

*Intention also recorded.

CLARK, Susanna, and Edmund Pettingell of Newburyport, int. July 8, 1811.

Thomas, and Mrs. Lidia Moodey, Oct. 17, 1705.*

Thomas, jr., and Elisabeth Perkins of the Isles of Shoals, int. July 12, 1715.

Thomas, of Boston, and Mrs. Jane Greenleaf, Nov. 10, 1747.*

Thomas M[arch. int.], Capt., of Newburyport, and Rebecca Wheelwright, May 28, 1811.*

William, and Bettee Hale, Mar. 24, 1763.*

CLARKE (see also Clark), Ellen W., of Newburyport, a. 27 y., b. Newburyport, d. Samuel and Abby, of Newburyport, and Hosea T. Crofoot of Newburyport, a. 28 y., bookbinder, s. Ira and Betsy, June 28, 1847.

Martha [Mrs. int.], and Joseph Noyes [sr. int.], Nov. 10, 1715.*

Mary, and Jonathan Morse, May 3, 1671.

Nathaniel, and Elizabeth Tappan, Dec. 15, 1685.

Sarah, and Benjamin Dole, Dec. 21, 1731.*

CLARKSON, Eliza A., a. 21 y., d. Jacob and Eliza Ann, and Thomas P. Lord of Amesbury, a. 23 y., harnessmaker, s. Benjamin and Margaret, Nov. 27, 1845.*

Elizabeth, and Eleazer Johnson, Mar. 8, 1809.*

Jacob G., of Amesbury, and Mary Collins, int. Jan. 24, 1846.

James, and Sophia Wheeler of Gloucester, int. Nov. 24, 1810.

CLEAVELAND, John P., Rev., of Salem, and Susan H. Dole, Nov. 6, 1827.*

Nehemiah, and Abigail Pickard Manning of Ipswich, int. July 26, 1823.

Nehemiah, of Brooklyn, N. Y., and Catherine A. Means, Nov. 25, 1842.*

Parker, Dr., and Elizabeth Jackman, both of Byfield Rowley, Aug. 2, 1773.

CLEFERD (see also Clifford), Richard, of Kingston, and Judeth Woodman, int. Dec. 17, 1741.

CLEFFORD (see also Clifford), Isack, and Elizabeth Pulcefer, Aug. 13, 1693. CT. R.

Peter, and Hannah Edwards of Salisbury, int. Mar. 23, 1805.

*Intention also recorded.

CLEMENS (see also Clement), Abraham, and Hannah Gove, May 10, 1683.

CLEMENT (see also Clemens, Clements, Clemment), Abiah, of Haverhill, and Daniel Little, int. Sept. 5, 1712.
Anna, of Beverly, and John Rea of Salem, Nov. 2, 1733. C. R. 7.
Dorothy, Mrs., and Archelaus Adams, Aug. 26, 1741.*
Elisabeth, and John Brown, Esq., Jan. 14, 1762.*
Hannah, and Daniel Balch, Aug. 19, 1756.*
Jonathan, and Mary Greenleaf, Nov. 30, 1721.*
Joseph, and Hannah Atkinson, Mar. 4, 1730-31.*
Joseph [jr. int.], of Newburyport, and Sarah Atkinson, Jan. 17, 1765.*
Nathaniel [resident in Newbury. int.], and Mary Adams, Mar. 27, 1751.*
Phebe, and Paul Pearson, int. Oct. 30, 1762.
Rachel, and Thomas Noyes, 3d, int. Jan. 29, 1757.
Rebecca S., of Newburyport, and Parsons Ordway, int. Sept. 16, 1843.
Sarah, Mrs., and Richard Hazzen of Haverhill, Oct. 22, 1719.*
Sarah, of Haverhill, and Daniel Pilsbury, jr., int. Oct. —, 1735.
Sarah, of Newburyport, and Moses Coffin, Feb. 7, 1768.*

CLEMENTS (see also Clement), Faune, and Mrs. Dorothy Freez, Mar. 7, 1718.*
Moses [jr. dup.], of Haverhill, and Sarah Bayley [at Haverhill. dup.], May 16, 1780. [May 17. dup.]*

CLEMMENT (see also Clement), Lydia, and Joseph Osgood of Salisbury, Dec. 15, 1774.*

CLERK (see also Clark), Aaron, Dea., of Wells, and Judith Coffin, Nov. 23, 1786.*
Abigail, and Samuel Brookins, Apr. 19, 1790.*
Eleanor [of Newburyport. int.], and Nathaniel Lunt, May 20, 1798. C. R. 1.*
John, and Ann Furness, both of Salem, May 29, 1734. C. R. 7.
Moses, and Polly Hale of Newburyport, int. Apr. 5, 1786.

.*Intention also recorded.

CLIFFORD (see also Cleferd, Clefford), Alice P., and William Falls of West Newbury, Oct. 7, 1832.*
David, and Sarah Poor, Nov. 4, 1808.*

CLIFT, Samuel, and Lydia Dogget, both of Marshfield, Oct. 10, 1734. C. R. 7.

CLOUGH, Caroline A., of Newburyport, and Joseph L. P. Colby, int. Nov. 29, 1845.
Ebenezar, of Rowley, and Elizabeth Thurla, int. June 18, 1777.
Ezra, and Bethiah Duty, both of Byfield-Rowley, Mar. 15, 1759.
Ezra, and Sarah Pearson, Dec. 1, 1762.*
Hannah, of Salisbury, and Hilton Woodman, int. Oct. 1, 1741.
Sara, and Daniel Merrill, May 14, 1667.
Thomas, of Amesbury, and Martha Timmins, Aug. 6, 1758.*

CLOUGHLIN, Peter, and Esther Wool, both of Rowley, Nov. 17, 1813. C. R. 5.

CLYDE, Charles, of Derry, N. H., and Abigail A. Winckley, June 16, 1842.*

COATS (see also Coots), David, Capt., of Newburyport, and Mehetable Thirston, June 24, 1765.*
Elisabeth, and Edward Edwards, int. Feb. 28, 1746-7.
Elisabeth, of Newburyport, and Thomas Greenleaf, int. May 23, 1789.
Jonathan, and Sarah Beckett [of Gloucester. int.], at Gloucester, June 18, 1752.*
Martha, and Mathew Pettingell, May 27, 1752.*
Mary, and Daniel Poor, Jan. 29, 1761.*

CODMAN, John, Rev., of Dorchester, and Mary Wheelwright, Jan. 19, 1813.*

COFFIN (see also Coffrin), Abel, and Anna Brown [Bruer. int.] of Danvers, at Danvers, Sept. 2, 1765.*
Abel, and Rebecca Pecker of Haverhill, int. Apr. 2, 1816.
Abigail, and Robert Morgan, resident of Newbury. July 13, 1727. C. R. 7.

*Intention also recorded.

COFFIN, Abigail, Mrs., and [Rev. int.] Aaron Whittemore of
Suncook, N. H., Feb. 2, 1743-4.*
Abigail, and Joseph Remick, Dec. 12, 1752.*
Abigail, and Richard Carr of Salisbury, May 17, 1778.*
Abigail, and Noyes Hopkinson, Aug. 13, 1792.*
Abigail, and Hackett Martin, both of Newburyport, Dec. 5,
1821.
Abigel, Mrs., of Nantucket, now resident in Newbury, and
Jedediah Fitch of Norwich, resident in Newbury, Sept.
13, 1701.*
Alice, and Joshua Colby, int. Sept. 23, 1835.
Amos, and Hannah Brown of Newburyport, int. Aug. 21, 1779.
Amos, jr., and Sally Cook of Newburyport, int. Jan. 1, 1803.
Amos, and Mary Newman of Newburyport, int. Aug. 29, 1846.
Ann, and Enoch Thurla, Mar. 9, 1797.*
Ann, and Thomas Lane, Nov. —, 1833. [int. Jan. 5, 1833.]*
Anna, and Thomas Dutton, Nov. 17, 1767.
Anna, and Richard Lovring, Feb. 24, 1784.*
Anne, and Robert Sergant of Amesbury, Jan. 22, 1740-41.*
Apphia, and Benjamin Jaques, May 20, 1725.*
Apphia, Mrs., and Capt. Ichabod Jones of Falmouth, May 8,
1746.*
Benjamin, and Miriam Woodman, Oct. 28, 1731.*
Benjamin, 3d, and Mary Eliot, Jan. 25, 1759.*
Benjamin, and Mary Maugridge of Portsmouth, N. H., int.
July 29, 1821.
Betsey, and William Merrill, Sept. 30, 1802.*
Charles, Dr., and Hephzibah Carnes of Boston, July 1, 1773.*
Charles, jr., and Susanna Woodbridge Ayer of New Milford,
Oct. 19, 1802.
Charles, and Lucretia James of Kensington, N. H., int. June
27, 1823.
Daniel, and Rebecca Bartlet, July 15, 1725.*
Daniel, and Lydia Moulton of Hampton, Jan. 11, 1726-7.
C. R. 7.
David, and Mary Pike, Aug. 23, 1759.*
David, jr., and Sarah Smith of Newburyport, int. July 28,
1813.
Deborah, and Joseph Knight, Oct. 31, 1677.
Dolly Farnham, and Rev. Eliphelet Gillet of Hallowell, int.
Jan. 16, 1801.
Dorcas, and Samuel Plumer of Newburyport, int. Sept. 1,
1781.

*Intention also recorded.

COFFIN, Dorothy [wid. C. R. 2.], and John Francis of Medford, Apr. 22, 1731.*

Ebenezer, and Mary Newhall of Newburyport, int. Sept. 25, 1793.

Edmund, Dr., and Shuah Bartlet, both of Kittery, at Kittery, Nov. 15, 1732.

Edmund, and Mary Moody of Newburyport, int. Sept. 15, 1792.

Edmund, and Lucy Kimbal, 2d w. [of Ipswich. int.], Apr. 25, 1809. C. R. 1.*

Elener, and Timothy Toppan, July 19, 1722.*

Eliphalet, of Exeter, and wid. Judeth Noyes, int. Feb. 3, 1710.

Eliphalet, and Lydia Emery, Jan. 17, 1760.*

Elisabeth, and Joseph Rosewell, Aug. 29, 1721.*

Elisabeth, and Isaac Johnson, jr., Jan. 3, 1760.*

Eliza P., and Daniel O. Sparhawk of Boston, int. Oct. 2, 1841.

Elizabeth, and Steven Greenleafe, Nov. 13, 1651.

Elizabeth, and Joseph Smith, June 29, 1749.

Elizabeth, and Charles Doyal, July 28, 1791. C. R. 2.*

Elizabeth L., and Moses Colman of Newburyport, Apr. 10, 1839.*

Emery, and Sarah Bartlett, both of Newburyport, Jan. 1, 1828.

Enoch, and Mrs. Mehitabel Moodey, Jan. 5, 1715-16.*

Eunice, and Joseph Pilsbury, jr., Jan. 26, 1766.*

Eunice, and Stephen Goodwin, int. Sept. 11, 1789.

Eunice, and Nathan Emery Coffin, May 5, 1803.*

Frances Maria, and William Hanscom, June 27, 1833.*

Hannah, and John Currier, jr., Dec. 31, 1795.*

Hannah [2d w. C. R. 1.], and Enoch Thurla, Nov. 30, 1802. [1803. C. R. 1.]*

Hannah C., and William Lunt, July 8, 1841.*

Hannah W., a. 23 y., d. Nathaniel and Hannah, and Charles Woodman of Dover, N. H., a. 23 y., merchant, b. Dover, N. H., s. Charles and Dorothy, of Dover, Sept. 9, 1845.*

Harriet, and John D. Cook of Newburyport, int. Jan. 1, 1825.

Hector, Capt., and Mary Caswell Cook of Newburyport, int. Dec. 25, 1807.

Hector, and Mary J. Sargent of Newburyport, int. Mar. 7, 1846.

Hezekiah, and Anna Hale, Jan. 16, 1800.*

Hezekiah, and Sally Currier of Amesbury, int. Jan. 16, 1811.

*Intention also recorded.

Coffin, Ichabod, and Judith Bartlet, Aug. 21, 1775.*
Jacob, and Sarah Greenleaf, Nov. 23, 1780.*
James, and Florence Hooke, Nov. 16, 1685.
Jane, and John Webster, Nov. 2, 1727. [Nov. 11. int.]*
Joanna, and Makepeace Horton, Mar. 3, 1724-5.*
Joanna, and Elias Davis of Newburyport, int. Oct. 14, 1831.
John, and Judeth Greenleaf, Apr. 22, 1713.*
John, jr., and Hannah Chaney, Apr. 28, 1726.*
John, of Newburyport, and Mary Palmer, Nov. 18, 1781.*
John, and Louis [Lois. int.] Sargent of Amesbury, at Ames-
    bury, Jan. 19, 1797.*
John, and Judith Moody of Salisbury, at Salisbury, July 14,
    1799.*
John, jr., and Elizabeth Brewster of Newburyport, int. Apr.
    19, 1823.
John, 3d, and Margaret Maria A[tkinson. int.] Towle, Dec.
    13, 1828.*
Joseph, and Margeret Morss, July 15, 1725.*
Joseph, jr., and Olive Fowler, Feb. 13, 1749-50.*
Joseph, 4th, and Mary Lunt, Jan. 30, 1752.*
Joseph, 4th, and Sarah Grant Joy, Feb. 9, 1758. c. r. 8.*
Joseph, 4th, and Elisabeth Jillings, Jan. 2, 1759.*
Joseph, jr., and Ruth Brown, Apr. 14, 1767.*
Joseph, and Judith Toppan, Dec. —, 1791.*
Joseph, and Margaret Sutherland of Brunswick, int. Aug. 20,
    1803.
Joseph, and Mary Cazwell Cook of Newburyport, int. Dec. 6,
    1806.
Joseph, widr., a. 59 y., ship carpenter, s. Amos and Hannah,
    and Theodate Lane of Newburyport, a. 38 y., b. Hampton,
    N. H., d. Jeremiah and Lucy, June 11, 1845.*
Joseph D., and Elizabeth Rogers of Newburyport, int. Feb. 4,
    1831.
Joshua, and Sarah Bartlet, Jan. 21, 1755.*
Joshua, and Clarissa Harlow Dutch, at Exeter, N. H., Dec. 2,
    1817.
Joshua, and Anna W. Chase of Philadelphia, Pa., at Philadel-
    phia, Apr. 28, 1835.
Judeth, and Parker Noyes, Dec. 11, 1707.*
Judeth, and Nathaniel Greenleaf, June 7, 1714.*
Judeth, and Samuel Bartlet [3d. int.], Jan. 2, 1716-17.*
Judith [Lydia. int.], and Richard Carr of Salisbury, Nov. 18,
    1715.*

*Intention also recorded.

COFFIN, Judith, and Dea. Aaron Clerk of Wells, Nov. 23, 1786.*
Judith, and Josiah Vose of Litchfield, May 23, 1790.*
Lemuel, and Ruth Brown, June 29, 1789.*
Louisa, and Thomas H. Gould, Nov. 30, 1837.*
Lucia T., and Edwin T. Chase, Esq., of Philadelphia, Pa., at Philadelphia, June 14, 1841.
Lydia, and Samuell Tod, Mar. 28, 1717.*
Lydia, and Oliver Hale, jr., Sept. 30, 1784.*
Margaret, and Paul Lunt of Newburyport, int. Jan. 13, 1775.
Margaret, and Thomas Emery, Nov. 27, 1806.*
Margaret E., and Ralph C. Huse of Newburyport, June 27, 1837.*
Martha A., and Washington McKenzie of Essex, int. July 20, 1844.
Mary, and Joseph Little, Oct. 31, 1677.
Mary, and Henry Jaques, Jan. 24, 1711-12.*
Mary, and Jonathan Ropes [jr. int.] of Salem, Dec. 10, 1761.*
Mary, and Amos Pearson of Newburyport, Feb. 5, 1778.
Mary, and Benjamin Burbank, Apr. 16, 1780.*
Mary, and Capt. Ebenezer Stocker of Newburyport, Dec. 8, 1782.*
Mary, and Edmund Knight, Nov. 9, 1786.*
Mary, and Enoch Toppan, Feb. 2, 1794.*
Mary, and Nathaniel Noyes, jr. of Newburyport, Nov. 12, 1815.*
Mary C. [Mrs. c. R. 10.], and Charles C. Doyle of Newburyport, Oct. 13, 1831.*
Mary Jane, and Charles Chase, int. June 27, 1823.
Mary Johnson, and Capt. Michajah Lunt, jr., Dec. 13, 1831.*
Mercy [Mary. int.], and Enoch Hunt, Jan. 5, 1735-6.*
Mercy, and John Danford, 3d, int. Jan. 21, 1763. ("The Banns Forbid by Mercy Coffin.")
Mirriam, and Abner Lunt, jr., Apr. 9, 1751.*
Moses, and Anne Dole, Nov. 28, 1732.*
Moses, and Mary Atkinson, Feb. 14, 1765.*
Moses, and Sarah Clement of Newburyport, Feb. 7, 1768.*
Moses, and Mary Jones of Southampton, int. Feb. 22, 1800.
Moses, and Harriet Little, Dec. 3, 1829.*
Nancy, of Newburyport, and John Little, int. Oct. 21, 1848.
Nathan Emery, and Eunice Coffin, May 5, 1803.*
Nathaniel, and Sarah Dole, Mar. 29, 1693.

*Intention also recorded.

COFFIN, Nathaniel, jr. [s. John. int.], and Patience Hale, Mar. 1, 1738-9.*

Nathaniel, and Susanna Hazeltine [of Chester. N. H. int.], May 2, 1809. c. r. 1.*

Nath[anie]l, and Mary Patten of Kensington, Nov. 24, 1814.*

Nathaniel, Capt., of Newburyport, and Hannah M. Woodman, Apr. 25, 1819.*

Newell S., and Nancy Warner of West Newbury, Sept. 3, 1822.*

Olive, and Joseph Rowell, Mar. 1, 1763.*

Peter [3d. int.], and Mary Currier of Amesbury, at Amesbury, Sept. 1, 1743.*

Phebe, and Moses Merrill, Apr. 7, 1757.*

Polly, and Daniel Smith, Nov. 23, 1807.*

Rachel, and Samuel Bartlet, Sept. 30, 1756.*

Rachel, of Newburyport, and Samuel Loud, int. Mar. 15, 1816.

Rebecca, and Will[ia]m Merrill, jr., Sept. 12, 1813.*

Richard, and Abigail Hale, Nov. 30, 1738.*

Richard, and Anna Pettengill, May 9, 1799.*

Richard, Capt., and Elizabeth Fletcher Webster of Haverhill, int. Feb. 1, 1810.

Ruth, and Anthony Somerby Stickney of Newburyport, Mar. 6, 1770.*

Ruth, and Philip D. Adams, Dec. 30, 1841.*

Sally, and Capt. James Lattimore of Newburyport, May 22, 1808.*

Sally, and John Litch, Mar. 31, 1814.*

Sally, Mrs., and Joshua Moody of Cornville, Me., Jan. 5, 1836.*

Samuel, and Anne Pettingell, May 27, 1752.*

Samuel, and Lydia Bartlett, June 17, 1777.*

Samuel [jr. int.], and Lydia Noyes, Apr. 25, 1803.*

Samuel, jr., and Rebecca B. Chase, Mar. 27, 1832.*

Samuel, of Georgetown, and Mary Ann Scribner, int. Sept. 28, 1844.

Sarah, and Joshua Bayley [jr. int.], Feb. 4, 1706.*

Sarah, and James Noyes, jr., int. May 13, 1713.

Sarah, and William Ripp, Jan. 1, 1729-30.*

Sarah, and Oliver Knight, Oct. 27, 1742.*

Sarah, Mrs., and Rev. Daniell Little of Wells, June 7, 1759. c. r. 9.*

*Intention also recorded.

COFFIN, Sarah, and Henry Peirce, Mar. 10, 1763.*
Sarah, and Moses Brown, jr., int. Nov. 12, 1763.
Sarah, and James Bradbury of Haverhill, Nov. 6, 1783.*
Sarah, and Caleb Knight of Newburyport, Feb. 10, 1785.*
Sarah, and Eliphalet Hills, jr., Dec. 14, 1809.*
Sarah, and Capt. Joseph Hoyt of Newburyport, int. Apr. 21, 1810.
Sarah, and Samuel Pickard of Rowley, May 13, 1823.*
Sarah, and Francis Lee, Apr. —, 1837.*
Statira R., and Enoch Richards of Charlestown, int. Aug. 6, 1845.
Stephen, jr., and Sarah Boardman, Aug. 16, 1722.*
Stephen, of Salisbury, and Sarah Knight, Jan. 30, 1752. c. r. 2.*
Stephen, and Susanna Brickett, May 23, 1776.*
Stephen, and Anna Morland, Aug. 26, 1801.*
Steven, and Sara Atkinson, Oct. 8, 1685.
Susan B., a. 29 y., d. Edmund and Lucy, and Washington Adams of Newburyport, a. 30 y., merchant, s. Moses and Marcy, May 10, 1846.*
Susanna, and James Boyd, Aug. 11, 1757.*
Susanna, and Theodore L. Grant of Newburyport, Feb. 3, 1814.*
Tristram, and Judith Somerby, Mar. 2, 1652.
Tristram [jr. int.], and Mrs. Martha Chaney, Nov. 17, 1715.*
Tristram, jr., and Dorothy Tufts, late of Medford, Mar. 22, 1721-2.*
Tristram, jr., and Anne Davis of Amesbury, int. Nov. 12, 1757.
Tristram, jr., and Sally Merrill, Jan. 3, 1792.*
William, and Susanna Wheeler, Dec. 14, 1749.*
William, and Eliza P. Thing, Nov. 2, 1822.*
William, and Mary Jane Ilsley, Jan. 29, 1833.*
William B., a. 22 y., shipwright, s. Joseph and Mary C., and Mary Chase, a. 19 y., d. Nathaniel and Sarah, Sept. 21, 1847.*

COFFRIN (see also Coffin), Anne, and William Nichols of Londonderry, Oct. 18, 1724.*
Jane, and William Rogers, July 20, 1725.*
Robert, and Mrs. Abigail Annis, Dec. 7, 1727.*

*Intention also recorded.

COGSALL (see also Cogswell), Sarah, Mrs., and William Noyes, Nov. 6, 1685.

COGSWELL (see also Cogsall), Abigail Redford, of Haverhill, and Abraham Chase, int. Aug. 23, 1794.
James, of Manchester, a. 27 y., blacksmith, b. Manchester, s. James and Mary, and Lydia G. Follansbee, a. 29 y., b. Georgetown, d. Moses and Ruth, Oct. 21, 1847.
Peter, of Newburyport, and Hannah Dumer, int. Aug. 19, 1786.

COKER, Abigail, and John Brocas of Boston, June 17, 1731.
Ann, and Joseph Parker, Oct. 31, 1734.*
Benjamin, and Martha Pearly, May 31, 1678.
Benjamin, jr., and Mrs. Anne Price, Nov. 24, 1692.
Benjamin [jr. int.], and Mary Weed, Dec. 7, 1706.*
Benjamin, and Elisabeth March, Jan. 29, 1732-3. c. r. 7.
Benjamin, and Sarah Pearson, int. Dec. 9, 1749. (Coker forbids this posting.)
Benjamin, and Sarah Pearson, int. Dec. 15, 1749. ("Benjm. Coker Designs to take Sarah Pearson Person without any Estate & will not oblidged himself to pay any of her late Husbands Debts namely Capt. Jeremiah Pearson late of Newbury Deceased.")
Catharine G., and David Ordway, both of West Newbury, Sept. 7, 1836.
Elisabeth, d. Harthorn and Terza, and Hezekiah Collings, s. Joseph, of Lynn, Dec. 19, 1734. c. r. 6.
Elizabeth, and John Mitchel, Mar. 11, 1724-5. c. r. 7.
Hanna, and Daniell Lunt, May 16, 1664.
Hannah, and Stephen Perley of Ipswich, Mar. 17, 1715.*
Hawthorn, and Tirza Bartlet, Dec. 17, 1708.*
John, and Susanna Adams, int. Dec. 14, 1805.
Joseph, and Sara Hathorne. Apr. 13, 1665.
Judith, and John Gerrish, Feb. 14, 1727-8.*
Lydia, d. Harthorn and Terza, and Amos Blake, s. Aaron and Martha, of Hampton, Jan. 26, 1742-3. c. r. 6.
Mary, and Joseph Mors, jr., Apr. 2, 1724.*
Mary, and Peter Doliver of Marblehead, int. Mar. 2, 1752.
Mary, and Sam[ue]ll Abbot, Feb. 14, 1757.*
Mary, and Artemas Thayer of Milford, Nov. 10, 1814.*
Miriam, and William Thurlow, Dec. 9, 1813.*

*Intention also recorded.

COKER, Sally Tappan, and Benjamin Lunt, jr., Mar. 31, 1813.*

Samuel, s. Harthorn and Terza, and Miriam Collins, d. Richard and Sarah, both deceased, 1: 11 m: 1752. c. r. 6.*

Sara, and James Smith, July 26, 1667.

Sarah, and Richard Long, Dec. 30, 1717.

Sarah, and Daniel Allin of Boston, Dec. 8, 1720.*

Sarah, and Isaac Ordway, Dec. 1, 1814.*

Thomas, and Sarah Greenleaf, May 3, 1781.*

William, and Crissia Hunt Noyes, Aug. 29, 1822.*

William, and Mary H. Adams of Newburyport, int. Mar. 19, 1836.

COLBURN, Nathaniel, of Leominster, and Abigail Chase, Dec. 1, 1803.*

COLBY (see also Colebe, Colebey, Coleby, Collbee), Abraham, of Rowley, and Sarah Buckman, Nov. 21, 1712.*

Ann E., and Ephraim W. Flanders, Feb. 4, 1844.*

Benj[ami]n, and Sally Pettengill, Apr. 3, 1805.*

Benja[min], jr., Capt. and Abigail Lunt, May 14, 1827.*

Benja[min], and Mary G. Lane, int. Mar. 22, 1828.

Betsy, and Andrew Lunt, June 2, 1795.*

Caroline C., and Abraham Goodwin, int. Oct. 29, 1842.

Chase, of Amesbury, and Esther Hardy, Mar. 13, 1777.*

Chase, and Martha Rogers, int. Oct. 15, 1791.

Dorothy, and Josiah Rogers, int. Apr. 7, 1798.

Elisabeth, and William Arnold, Apr. 27, 1750.*

Eliza, and Samuel Huse of Newburyport, int. May 23, 1830.

Emily, and Ariel Pearson, jr. of Newburyport, Oct. 19, 1839.*

Enoch, and Sally Dodge, Mar. 12, 1809.*

Enoch, and Margaret D. Burns of Newburyport, int. Nov. 1, 1834.

Felix D., and Lydia Ann Boaden of Newburyport, Nov. 6, 1834.*

Geo[rge] J. L., and S. Arabella Thompson of Francestown, N. H., int. Dec. 26, 1846.

Hannah, and Samuel Kendrick, both of Amesbury, Sept. 22, 1737. c. r. 7.

Hannah, and Ariel Pearson, Apr. 28, 1817.*

Hannah F., and John Lee of Salisbury, int. Nov. 7, 1829.

Harriet, and George Brown of Concord, int. Aug. 9, 1834.

John, and Eunice Emery of Hampstead, int. Mar. 17, 1777.

*Intention also recorded.

COLBY, John, jr., of Amesbury, and Mary Jackman, Dec. 29, 1818.*

John, jr., of Warner, N. H., and Mary M. Denney, Dec. 3, 1832.*

John W. S., a. 29 y., shipwright, b. Amesbury, s. John and Mary, and Mary Ann Tilton, a. 22 y., d. Samuel S. and Eliza J., June 17, 1849.*

Joseph L., jr., and Eliza H. Brown, May 23, 1824.*

Joseph L. P., and Caroline A. Clough of Newburyport, int. Nov. 29, 1845.

Joseph Lunt, and Salley Foot, July 2, 1796.*

Joseph Lunt, and Hannah Fowler of Salisbury, int. July 26, 1812.

Joshua, and Elisabeth Jenkins, June 8, 1787.*

Joshua, jr., and Sally Doyal of Newburyport, int. May 2, 1812.

Joshua, and Alice Coffin, int. Sept. 23, 1835.

Lydia, and Daniel Smith, July 27, 1825.*

Makepiece, and Sarah Pressey of Amesbury, int. Sept. 27, 1760.

Margaret, and William Bailey, Oct. 24, 1815.*

Mary, and Jotham Sawyer, resident in Newbury, int. Sept. 25, 1779.

Mary, a. 31 y., d. Joseph L. and Hannah, and Michael W. Bartlett, a. 29 y., school teacher, b. West Newbury, s. John E. and Nancy, of West Newbury, Aug. 20, 1846.*

Mary Conner, and John Gawn, int. July 28, 1804.

Mary E., and Enoch P. Lunt, int. [Mar. or Apr.] 17, 1847.

Patience, and Joseph Stanwood, Apr. 23, 1835.*

Salley, and John French of Atkinson, int. July 21, 1800.

Sarah, of Newburyport, and Thomas Kennison, int. Nov. 6, 1790.

Sarah, and Thomas Cook, jr. of Newburyport, int. Mar. 15, 1828.

Thomas, and Dorothy Williams, Aug. 4, 1784.*

Thomas, of Deer Island, and Elisabeth Thurla, int. Apr. 29, 1798.

Thomas C., and Abigail Kindrick, int. Mar. 27, 1807.

William, Capt., of Amesbury, and Mary Long, int. July 5, 1805.

William T., and Mary Jane Currier, Oct. 23, 1828. [Nov. 18. dup.]*

*Intention also recorded.

COLE, Augustus K., a. 20 y., victualer, s. N. W. and Sarah S., and Lydia E. Atkinson, a. 18 y., d. Jacob and Elizabeth, Aug. 5, 1849.*

Benjamin, and Jane Mitchell, June 18, 1752.*

Elizabeth G[age. c. r. 10.], and Samuel Cawley, Aug. 24, 1816.*

Jane, and Samuel Aubin, Jan. 17, 1732-3.*

Moses, jr., of Newburyport, and Louisa Currier, int. Mar. 8, 1833.

Robert, of Great Britain, and Abigail Tenney of Rowley, Aug. 31, 1715.

Robert, and Mrs. Susanna Atkinson, Nov. 11, 1742.*

Robert, of Newburyport, and Eunice Sweasy, int. Nov. 10, 1777.

Robert, and Sally Downs, Nov. 13, 1826.*

Sarah, and Henry Lunt, 3d [4th. dup.], Nov. 18, 1707.*

Sarah, and Hezekiah Coleby, Sept. 3, 1730.*

Sarah H., Mrs., and Henry Short, jr., May 9, 1844.*

COLEBE (see also Colby), Ruggles, of Amesbury, and Abigail Davis, Mar. 15, 1732-3.*

COLEBEY (see also Colby), Susanna, and Micah Hoit, both of Amesbury, Feb. 4, 1725-6. c. r. 7.

COLEBY (see also Colby), Elisabeth, of Amesbury, and Daniel Pillsbery, int. Dec. 20, 1752.

Hannah, of Amesbury, and Edmund Greenleaf, int. Oct. 21, 1769.

Hezekiah, and Sarah Cole, Sept. 3, 1730.*

Hezekiah, jr., and Mary Wait, Nov. 25, 1760.*

John, and Elisabeth Hogin, June 29, 1748.*

Joshua, and Sarah Peabody, int. Apr. 7, 1761.

Mary, and Ezra Howard, Oct. 30, 1752.*

Molly, and James Buswell, Aug. 6, 1761.*

Sam[ue]ll, and Dorothy Crocker, Feb. 22, 1753.*

Tabitha, and Jonathan Bernard, both of Amesbury, Oct. 6, 1726. c. r. 7.

Thomas, and Mary Wells, Nov. 5, 1731.*

COLEMAN (see also Colman), Ann [Mrs. int.], and Daniel Tenny of Bradford, May 15, 1733.*

*Intention also recorded.

COLEMAN, Benjamin, and Anne Brown, July 5, 1743.*
Dorcas, and John Tilseton, July 4, 1648.
Eunice, and Israel Turner, Feb. 3, 1814.*
Jane, and Samuel Hereman of Rowley, Oct. 16, 1729.*
John, and Ann Wicom, Apr. 26, 1732.*
Lydia, and Moses Richardson, Mar. 1, 1704.*
Mary, and Abraham Adams [4th. int.], Nov. 18, 1737.*
Molly [Polly. int.], and Joseph Searl of Rowley, June 7, 1781.*
Phebe, and Dudley Tyler of Rowley, int. Oct. 23, 1738.
Sarah, of Newington, and Enoch Toppan, int. Sept. 8, 1756.
Thomas, and Mary John[son. T. C.], July 11, 1651.
Thomas, and Phebe Pearson, int. Jan. 6, 1701-2.

COLINS (see also Collins), Mary, wid. Jonathan, of Hampton, d. John Green of Hampton, and Ben[jamin] Brown, s. John, 28: 10 m: 1727-8. C. R. 6.

COLL (see also Call), David, and Rebeckeh Edwards, May 14, 1752.*

COLLBEE (see also Colby), Dorothy, of Amesbury, and Samuel Watts of Haverhill, Nov. 13, 1727. C. R. 7.

COLLEYER, Samuel, and Sally Ordway of Newburyport, int. Mar. 26, 1825.

COLLINGS (see also Collins), Hezekiah, s. Joseph, of Lynn, and Elisabeth Coker, d. Harthorn and Terza, Dec. 19, 1734. C. R. 6.

COLLINS (see also Colins, Collings), Abigail, of Salisbury, and Richard French, int. Feb. 12, 1798.
Elizabeth, and Gilman P. Allen of Essex, Mar. 5, 1840.*
George, and Sarah E. Somerby of Newburyport, int. Oct. 21, 1848.
Hannah, and John Kimbal, July 17, 1796.*
Hannah H., and Edward S. Toppan of Boston, int. Mar. 3, 1845.
James, and Mary Beckett, both of Salem, Oct. 8, 1730. C. R. 7.
Martha, of Salisbury, and Nathan Presbury, at Salisbury, Dec. 13, 1727.

*Intention also recorded.

COLLINS, Mary, of Newburyport, and William Lydston, int.
June 11, 1812.
Mary, and Jacob G. Clarkson of Amesbury, int. Jan. 24, 1846.
Miriam, d. Richard and Sarah, both deceased, and Samuel
Coker, s. Harthorne and Terza, 1: 11 m: 1752. c. r. 6.*
Richard, and Rachel Dow, d. John, of Hampton, Mar. 1,
1738-9. c. r. 6.
Sarah, and Charles H. Ireland, Apr. 14, 1839.*
Susannah, and Jacob Gale, Oct. 20, 1735.*
William, resident in Newbury, and Betty Brown, Feb. 22,
1778.*
William, of Newburyport, and Sally Goodwin, Oct. 21, 1813.*
William, jr., and Harriet F. Bartlet of Newburyport, int. Feb.
25, 1837.

COLLIS (see also Corliss), Mary [Sarah. int.], and John
Ingersol, Mar. 19, 1761.*

COLLY (see also Calley), Elisbaeth, of Newburyport, and
Daniel Adams, Dec. 25, 1777.*

COLMAN (see also Coleman), Benjamin, Dea., and Sarah
Stickney of Newburyport, int. Oct. 6, 1778.
Benjamin, jr., and Mary Chute, June 29, 1780.*
Caleb, and Sally Burbank of Boscawen, int. Sept. 12, 1795.
Charles H., a. 29 y., school teacher, s. Daniel T. and Ann, and
Deborah L. Dinsmore of Boston, a. 27 y., b. Auburn, Oct.
20, 1846.*
Clarissa M., and Richard S. Hewlett of Winchester, Vir., int.
July 31, 1824.
Clarissa M., and Jacob Hearl of Shapleigh, Me., Sept. 28,
1829.*
Daniel, and Nancy Pike, Nov. 23, 1815.*
Daniel Thurston, and Nancy Harris, Feb. 3, 1818.*
Dorothy P., of Newburyport, and William Thurston of Ban-
gor, Me., ——, 1837.
Elizabeth L., and Joseph Moulton, July 12, 1838.*
Eunice, and Elisha Barnard. int. June 20, 1806.
Hannah, and Nathaniel Harriman of Rowley, at Rowley, May
21, 1742.*
Hannah T., and Marshall French of Reading, Apr. 24, 1814.*

· *Intention also recorded.

COLMAN, Jeremiah, of Newburyport, and Mary Chute of Rowley, June 8, 1808. C. R. 5.
John, and Lois Danforth, July 16, 1765.*
Judah, and Hephsibah Boynton, June 12, 1711.
Mary, and Stillman Mores, Aug. 11, 1829.
Moses, and Dorothy Pearson, Feb. 7. 1782.*
Moses, and Betty Emery, Dec. 5, 1787.*
Moses, of Newburyport, and Elizabeth L. Coffin, Apr. 10, 1839.*
Sarah, and Abner Spofford of Rowley, at Rowley, Dec. 23, 1734.*
Sarah E., a. 25 y., d. Daniel and Nancy, and Rev. Elbridge G. Little of Manayunk, Pa., a. 31 y., b. Hampstead, s. Joseph and Rebecca, July 12, 1848.*
William, and Susannah Thurston of Rowley, at Rowley, May 17, 1792.*
William [Capt. C. R. 5.], and Zervia Temple, Apr. 19, 1809.*
William, Capt., of Boscawen, and Mrs. Hannah Brown, June 12, 1816.*
William, a. 25 y., butcher, s. D. T., and Hannah B. Dinsmore of Auburn, N. H., a. 23 y., b. Auburn, N. H., Sept. 26, 1848.*

COLTER, Sarah [Colten. int.], of Ipswich, and Stephen Lavenuke, Sept. 22, 1741.*

COMERFORD, David A., of Newburyport, and Rachel Stanwood, int. Jan. 7, 1813.

CONANT, Mary W., of Rowley, and Timothy W. Emerson, int. May 9, 1834.

CONDRE (see also Condry), Timothy, and Elisabeth Becket of Gloucester, int. Aug. 28, 1756.

CONDRY (see also Condre), Ann, and Charles Knight, jr. of Newburyport, int. Nov. 9, 1833.
Dennis, of Newburyport, and Ann Lowell, Apr. 8, 1813.*
Elizabeth, and John Calley of Newburyport, Dec. 21, 1806.*
Rhoda, and Bartholomew Brown of Newburyport, int. Nov. 3, 1804.
William, of Newburyport, and Rhody Gerrish, May 28, 1786.*

*Intention also recorded.

CONE, Jonathan, of Campton, N. H., and Elizabeth Bartlet of Newburyport, Jan. 26, 1773.

CONGSTON, Elizabeth, and John How, baker, both of Boston, ——, 1729. c. r. 7.

CONNAWAY, Mary, of Ipswich, and Richard Flood, at Ipswich, Nov. 26, 1729.

CONNELLY (see also Connerly), Catharine, and Isaac Wharf, at Gloucester, Sept. 9, 1744.

CONNER (see also Connor), Edmund, and Dorcas Hunt, Jan. 12, 1792.*
Eliza, Mrs., and William C. Remick, July —, 1822.*
Gideon, and Mary Lunt, Aug. 23, 1787.*
Mary, and Samuel Chase, int. Aug. —, 1768.
Moses, and Abigail Lull, Dec. 14, 1721.
Ruth, and Samuel Beverly of St. Johns, N. F., Nov. 11, 1776.*
William, and Nancy Hervy of Newburyport, int. Sept. 17, 1791.

CONNERLY (see also Connelly), James, and Judith [L. c. r. 10.] Stickney, May —, 1826.*

CONNOR (see also Conner), Gideon, and Hannah Sanborn of East Kingston, N. H., int. Jan. 2, 1808.
Polly, and Enoch Lunt, jr., int. Dec. 22, 1785.
William, and Mary Hooper, Mar. 11, 1755. c. r. 8.*

CONSTANT, Victor, and Lois Smith, Dec. 2, 1821.*

COOCH (see also Couch), Joseph, and Mary Noyes, Oct. 23, 1740.*
Joseph, and Mrs. Alice Rowell, Apr. 25, 1744.*
Joseph, jr., and Judith Webster, Nov. 9, 1756. [Said Cooch takes said Judith naked, and is not obliged to pay any of her former husband's debts. int.]*
Joseph, and Mary Newman of Newburyport, int. Nov. 24, 1769.
William, jr., and Mrs. Lydia Mitchell, Nov. 11, 1741.*
William, and Mrs. Elisabeth Merrill, Mar. 23, 1742-3.*

*Intention also recorded.

COOK (see also Cooke), Abigail H., and Daniel H. Knight, both of Newburyport, July 25, 1839.

Caroline R., of Newburyport, and William Lecraw, jr., int. Oct. 11, 1845.

Elias, of Newburyport, and Sarah Dustin, July 13, 1777.*

Elizabeth, and Joseph Chandler of Atkinson, N. H., Jan. 7, 1768.

Hannah, of Newburyport, and Johnson Lunt, int. Feb. 23, 1771.

Hannah [Gage, resident in Kensington, N. H. int.], and Jeremiah Lunt, Mar. —, 1808. c. r. 1.*

James, Capt., and Betsy Blumpey, both of Newburyport, Oct. 14, 1838.

Joanna, Mrs., and William Wood [of Falmouth. int.], June 30, 1743.*

John, of Whitehaven, Eng., and Mary Gore, Nov. 13, 1757. c. r. 8.

John D., of Newburyport, and Harriet Coffin, int. Jan. 1, 1825.

Margaret, of Salem, and Isaac Marshal, int. June 5, 1801.

Maria, and Henry Hunt, Nov. 20, 1836.*

Mary, Mrs., and Ephraim Hunt, Nov. 22, 1739.*

Mary, of Newburyport, and Richard Adams, int. Apr. 3, 1818.

Mary Ann, of Newburyport, and Frederick W. Myrick of Nantucket, July 24, 1839.

Mary Caswell, and Capt. Hector Coffin, int. Dec. 25, 1807.

Mary Cazwell, of Newburyport, and Joseph Coffin, int. Dec. 6, 1806.

Mary Jane, and Joseph Lunt, 3d, Jan. 7, 1834.*

Moses, of Newburyport, and Mary Thurlo, Feb. 20, 1815.*

Moses, and Rebekah Stanwood, int. June 4, 1825.

Moses E., and Eunice M. Brookings, Aug. 11, 1844.*

Ruthy A., of Newburyport, and Edward Sealey, int. June 4, 1814.

Sally, of Newburyport, and Amos Coffin, jr., int. Jan. 1, 1803.

Samuel, and Mrs. Judith Bartlet, Feb. 18, 1745-6.*

Samuel, jr., of Newburyport, and Mary Safford, July 4, 1830.*

Sarah E., of Newburyport, and William H. Gray of Exeter, Dec. 27, 1839.

Thomas, of Newburyport, and Lucy Adams, Nov. 24, 1807.*

Thomas, jr., of Newburyport, and Sarah Colby, int. Mar. 15, 1828.

*Intention also recorded.

COOK, Zebedee, of Newburyport, and Sarah Knight, int. Nov. 15, 1783.

COOKE (see also Cook), Elisabeth, and Jacob Pilsbury, int. Jan. 15, 1736-7.

COOLIDGE Philip, and Sarah Brooks of Ipswich, Oct. 14, 1726.*

COOMBS (see also Coomes), Lydia, and William Knap, July 2, 1761.*
Martha, and Benjamin Knight, jr., Nov. 25, 1762.*
Haskel, ——, d. Neal, deceased, Aug. 17, 1810.
Mary, and Samuel Shackford, July 9, 1740.*
Philip, and Lydia Johnson, July 10, 1735.*
Samuel, and Bridgit Hannah Cotten, Nov. 26, 1747.*
Susanna, Mrs., and Eliazer Kezer, Jan. 17, 1743-4.*
William, and Jane Greenleaf, July 17, 1760.*

COOMES (see also Coombs), Elisabeth, and Jeremiah Pearson of Rowley, July 4, 1754.*
Hugh, and Susanna Hunt, int. Feb. 2, 1753.

COOPER (see also Coopper), Abigail, and Richard Carr Rogers, June 19, 1766.*
Benjamin, and Susanna Butler, Oct. 23, 1754.*
Betsey, and Moses Lovring of Salisbury, N. H., int. Feb. 15, 1805.
David, and Ruth Rogers, July 9, 1767.*
Elisabeth, and Richard Lowell of Rowley, Nov. 4, 1736.*
Ellis, and James Merrill, Nov. 11, 1768.*
Hannah, and Jonathan Hilliard of Hampton, Nov. 9, 1732.*
John, and Elisabeth Goodridge, Oct. 10, 1715.*
John [of Rowley. int.], and Miriam Thurston, May 25, 1773.*
Josiah, and Sophia Pattee of Amesbury, int. July 13, 1815.
Mary, and Cornelius Page of Haverhill, Dec. 9, 1729.*
Mary, of Rowley, and Jacob Pearson of Byfield Rowley, May 31, 1753.
Moses, and Abigail Lowell of Rowley, Feb. 24, 1736-7.*
Moses, and Hannah Rogers, int. July 21, 1759.
Moses [jr. int.], and Mary Kymbal, Apr. 13, 1762.*

. *Intention also recorded.

COOPER, Moses, jr., and Miriam Jones of Southampton, int. Aug. 4, 1764.

Rachel, and John [Jonathan. int.] George, Nov. 24, 1795. [Dec. c. R. 2.]*

Rebeckah, and Thomas Carter of Leominster, Aug. 12, 1800.*

Ruth, and Caleb Tilton of Andover, Aug. 24, 1801.*

Sarah, and Daniel Green, July 2, 1735. c. R. 7.*

Simeon, and Elizabeth Brown of Southampton, int. May 11, 1776.

Simeon, and Abigail True, int. Dec. 15, 1807.

Simeon, and Anna Merrill, May 11, 1831.*

Timothy, and Abigail Smith, Jan. 1, 1735-6.*

William, jr., and Judeth Carter of Kingstown, int. Jan. 19, 1748-9.

COOPPER (see also Cooper), John, and Sarah Salmon, Jan. 6, 1703.*

Sarah, and Edmund Moores, Jan. 2, 1676.

COOTS (see also Coats), John [Coats. int.], and Anne Titcombe, Dec. 8, 1725.*

COPPS (see also Cops), Simeon, and Molly Noyes, Dec. 24, 1794. c. R. 2.*

COPS (see also Copps), Josiah, of Haverhill, and Mary Swett, May 28, 1731.*

CORLEW, Joshua [John. int.], of Charlestown, and Hannah D. Loring, Feb. 24, 1841.*

CORLEY, Johana, and James Ordway, Oct. 4, 1687. CT. R.

CORLISS (see also Collis), Mary, of Windham, N. H., and Caleb Reed, int. Mar. 9, 1818.

CORNING, Joshua, widr., of Beverly, and Mary Green, wid., of Salem; May 30, 1733. c. R. 7.

Malachi, of Beverly, and Eunice Leach of Salem, July 21, 1726.

*Intention also recorded.

CORNISH, James, Capt., of Bristol, Eng., and Mrs. Mary
Woodbridge, Oct. 12, 1730. c. r. 7.
John, resident in Newbury, and Mary Chesemore, int. Aug. 11,
1716.

CORSER (see also Courser), Stephen, of Boscawen, N. H.,
and Rachel Noyes, Mar. 1, 1795.*

CORSON, Emily, of Exeter, N. H., and David Moody, ——,
1834. [Dec. 26, 1833. int.]*

COTTELL (see also Cottle), Ezra, and Mary Woodbridg,
July 6, 1695.

COTTEN, Bridgit Hannah, and Samuel Coombs, Nov. 26,
1747.*
Mary, Mrs., of Portsmouth, and Stephen Greenleaf, 3d, int.
May 7, 1715.

COTTLE (see also Cottell), Anne, and William Titcomb, May
15, 1683.
Edmund, and Anne Clark, Nov. 10, 1726.*
Johanah, and Daniel Perie, Feb. 9, 1687. ct. r.
Joseph, and Ann Webster of Salisbury, Sept. 18, 1735. c. r. 7.
Mercy, and Joseph Greenleaf, jr., Feb. 26, 1760.*
Thomas, and Mrs. Hannah Lowell of Amesbury, at Amesbury,
Jan. 6, 1725-6.

COUCH (see also Cooch), Joseph, and Mary Toppan, May
18, 1737.*
Joseph, of Boscawen, N. H., and Sarah Pilsbery, Feb. 10,
1785.*
Mary, and Jonathan Norton, Aug. 11, 1743.*
Mary, of Newburyport, and Moses Toppan, int. Feb. 9, 1793.
Mary Ann, of Newburyport, and Eleazer Johnson, jr., int. Oct.
12, 1822.
Sarah, and Richard Carr, Apr. 16, 1746.*
William, and Elisabeth Richardson, Jan. 1, 1718-19.*
William, and Elisabeth Matthews, Jan. 21, 1725-6.*

COUGHLIN, Michael, and Mary Watson, int. Nov. 11, 1820.

*Intention also recorded.

COURSER (see also Corser), Elesabeth, and John Bowle [jr. int.], Dec. 7, 1744.*
Hannah, and Joseph Atkinson of Exeter, N. H., Dec. 9, 1756.*
John, and Tabith Kenney, Mar. 8, 1716-17.*
John, jr., and Jane Nichols, Nov. 24, 1742.*
Margaret, and Ebenezer Flood, int. Jan. 7, 1737-8.

CRAM, Robert, of Exeter, and Prudence Jenkins, Dec. 7, 1758.*

CREASEY (see also Cresey), Elizabeth, of Rowley, and Amos Daniels, at Rowley, Feb. 9, 1797.
Michael, of Newburyport, and Hannah Currier, June 29, 1820.*

CREESSY (see also Cresey), Betsey, of Rowley, and Amos Dwinnel, int. Nov. 19, 1796.

CRESEY (see also Creasey, Creessy, Cresy), Abel, of New-
• buryport, and Betty Hidden, int. Oct. 5, 1765.
Ann [Keizer. int.], and John George, Feb. 15, 1761.*
Anne, and Samuel Hidden of Rowley, int. May 7, 1759.
Mary [wid. int.], and James Stickney, Dec. 26, 1772. [Said Stickney takes said Mary naked so that he will not have to pay any of her former husband's debts. int.]*
Phebe A., of Newburyport, and Benjamin Pettingell, 3d, int. Nov. 13, 1847.
Sam[ue]ll, jr., and Mary Sweet, Apr. 19, 1757.*

CRESY (see also Cresey), Mary, and Daniel Stickney, Apr. 1, 1777.*

CROAD, Sarah, and Benjamin Goodridg, Nov. 16, 1678.

CROCKER, Abigail M., of Salisbury, and Jefferson Currier, int. Sept. 27, 1845.
Dorothy, and Sam[ue]ll Coleby, Feb. 22, 1753.*
James, and Mrs. Dorothy Currier of Amesbury, at Amesbury, Nov. 18, 1725.
John S., and Mary Jane Evans of Newburyport, int. Mar. 14, 1849.

*Intention also recorded.

CROCKER, Lowell, widr., ship carpenter, s. Joseph Morse of
Salisbury, and Ruth Flanders, wid., Feb. 16, 1845.*
Sarah Ann, a. 18 y., d. Lowell, and Spofford McQuillen, a.
21 y., ship carpenter, s. Robert and Mehitable, Nov. 16,
1847.*

CROCKET (see also Crockett), Andrew, and Jane Emery of
Newburyport, June 15, 1812.*
Isaac, and Betsy Becket, Feb. 4, 1798.*

CROCKETT (see also Crocket), Charles C. [P. int.], of Con-
cord, N. H., and Hannah S. Chase, May 11, 1835.*
Elizabeth, and Philander Anderson, int. May 26, 1882.
Jane, and Luther Carkin of Newburyport, int. Apr. 19, 1828.

CROCKFORD, John, and Sarah Tucker, int. Mar. 19, 1752.
("I John Crockford do Purpose to take Mrs. Sarah
Tuckers Person naked and without any of her former
Husbands Estate so that I will not be oblidge to pay any
of her Husbands Debts namely Benjamin Tucker late of
Newbury.")

CROFOOT, Hosea T., of Newburyport, a. 28 y., bookbinder,
s. Ira and Betsy, and Ellen W. Clarke of Newburyport, a.
27 y., b. Newburyport, d. Samuel and Abby, of Newburyport, June 28, 1847.

CROMARTIE, William, of London, and Frances Allen of
Boston, Oct. 5, 1762. c. r. 8.

CROMBIE, Dorcas, of Rowley, and Benjamin Pillsbury, at
Rowley, Oct. 10, 1769.*
Mary, and John Hodgkins, jr. of Ipswich, at Ipswich, July
16, 1789.*

CROMLONE, Gyles, and Allice Wiseman, Sept. 10, 1648.

CROMWELL, John, and Joan Butler, Nov. 2, 1662.

CROOKER, Sarah, of Minot, Me., and John Atkinson, int.
Sept. 12, 1824.

*Intention also recorded.

CROON, Nicholas, resident in Newbury, and Martha Poor, int. Feb. 15, 1734-5.

CROSS, Daniel, and Abigail Bowley, int. July 20, 1804.
Harriet H., of Portland, and John Stickney, int. Dec. 10, 1824.
Jane B., a. 25 y., b. Newburyport, d. John and Martha, of Newburyport, and Johnson Robinson, jr., a. 25 y., mariner, s. Johnson and Esther, Nov. 5, 1849.*
Mary [ofIpswich. int.], and Robert Mitchell, Dec. 2, 1731.*
Mary, and John Nowell, Aug. 6, 1753. c. r. 9.*
Moses, and Ann Goss, July 17, 1753.*
Ralf, and Sarah Johnson, Oct. 31, 1728.*
Ralph, jr., and Miriam Atkinson, Sept. 21, 1757. [Sept. 24. c. r. 9.]*
Robert, of Amesbury, and Mary Cabot Tyng, int. Oct. 9, 1829.
Stephen, and Hannah Beck, Nov. 20, 1759. c. r. 9.*
Thomas, and Mary Dole, Dec. 2, 1762.*

CROWELL, Betsy, and Jedediah Saunders, Feb. 5, 1818.*

CROWNINSHIELD, William, and Sarah Plumer, Feb. 12, 1787.*

CUMINGS (see also Cummings), Witter, and Hannah Harrod, of Boston, int. Mar. 1, 1739-40.

CUMMINGS (see also Cumings, Cummins), Elizabeth M., of Newburyport, and Ebenezer S. Sweetser, int. Oct. 2, 1841.
Martha E., a. 17 y., b. Rowley, d. George and Eliza, of Rowley, and Ira Thompson of Rowley, a. 19 y., shoemaker, b. Rowley, s. Ira and Hannah, of Rowley, Nov. 8, 1846.

CUMMINS (see also Cummings), Charlottee, and Joseph Pearson, Feb. 15, 1820.*

CURIER (see also Currier), Hannah, and Tristam Brown, Oct. 28, 1799. c. r. 5.

*Intention also recorded.

CURRIER (see also Curier), Abigail, and Edmund Worth, Dec. 23, 1740.*

Abigail, of Haverhill, and Daniel Chase, jr., int. Feb. 16, 1793.

Abigail, of Newburyport, and Samuel Poor, int. Apr. 12, 1834.

Alfred, and Nancy B. Fowler, int. July 18, 1840.

Alice, and Amos Davis of Amesbury, Nov. 7, 1745.*

Amos, and Hannah Bodge [Badger. c. r. 2.], Dec. 22, 1793.*

Ann G., and Alfred Wood, both of Newburyport, July 31, 1839.

Apphia, of Salisbury, and Enoch Pilsbury, int. Aug. 20, 1756.

Bartlet J., and Susan L. Goodridge of West Newbury, int. Feb. 6, 1829.

Benj[ami]n, and Abigail Atkinson, Nov. 25, 1802.*

Benjamin, and Caroline J. Gallishan of Newburyport, int. Sept. 5, 1835.

Bernard, of Amesbury, and Mrs. Mary Emery, Oct. 23, 1739.*

Charles, of Newburyport, and Ann Hale, Nov. 29, 1827.*

Charles A., and Mary J. Mixer of Newton, int. Nov. 18, 1848.

Daniel Rogers, and Sarah Thurla, Oct. 14, 1802.*

Daniel Rogers, and Sally Merrill of Rowley, int. Dec. 31, 1808.

Diamond, and Elisabeth Woodman, Jan. 2, 1754.*

Dorothy, Mrs., of Amesbury, and James Crocker, at Amesbury, Nov. 18, 1725.

Dorothy, of Amesbury, and Joseph Hoyt, int. Oct. 29, 1762.

Dudley, of Salem, N. H., and Sarah Ordway, May 11, 1780.*

Edward, of Newburyport, and Lois Gerrish, int. Aug. 3, 1805.

Edwin, of Newburyport, and Ursula Fowler, Nov. 16, 1843.*

Elizabeth [of Haverhill. dup.], and John Worth, at Haverhill, Feb. 19, 1722-3.*

Elizabeth C., and Henry H. Hilliard of Boston, Sept. 10, 1837.*

Emeline, of Newburyport, and Michael Atkinson, jr., int. Oct. 3, 1835.

Esther, and Daniel Herrick of Hopkinton, Jan. 24, 1786.*

George, of Newburyport, and Almira Wells, Dec. 25, 1831.*

Grace, of Haverhill, and Nathan Kinerson, int. Jan. 7, 1804.

Hannah, and Michael Creasey of Newburyport, June 29, 1820.*

*Intention also recorded.

CURRIER, Hannah, and Harrisan [G. int.] Johnson of Newburyport, Dec. 21, 1843.*

Hannah S., of Salisbury, and William J. Currier, int. Jan. 10, 1846.

Harriet, and Thomas Merrill, jr., Feb. 6, 1833.*

Jefferson, and Abigail M. Crocker of Salisbury, int. Sept. 27, 1845.

Joanna Gerrish, and Joseph B. Tucker of Newmarket, N. H., Jan. 14, 1827.*

John, of Amesbury, and Mary Johnson, Jan. 23, 1728-9.*

John, and Mary Poor, Dec. 14, 1772.*

John, jr., and Hannah Coffin, Dec. 31, 1795.*

John, Dea., and Elisabeth Burditt of Malden, int. June 1, 1802.

John, jr., and Clarissa Carr, int. Nov. 19, 1830.

Jonathan, Capt., of South Hampton, N. H., and Judeth Wiliams, Apr. 19, 1744.*

Joseph, and Nancy Jackman, Mar. 9, 1809.*

Joseph H., of Newburyport, and Sarah Jane Hawes, int. Oct. 30, 1830.

Joseph H., of Newburyport, a. 23 y., mason, s. William and Abigail, of Newburyport, and Sarah Ann Gould of Newburyport, a. 24 y., b. Newburyport, d. Samuel and Ann, of Newburyport, May 12, 1847.

Joshua, and Mary Pingrey of Rowley, at Rowley, Aug. 15, 1776.*

Lavina, and William T. Merrill of Newburyport, int. Nov. 7, 1846.

Louisa, and Moses Cole, jr. of Newburyport, int. Mar. 8, 1833.

Lydia, and Edward Harris, July 8, 1762.*

Lydia A., of Amesbury, and Jeremiah D. Jewett, int. May 27, 1848.

Mary, of Amesbury, and Peter Coffin [3d. int.], at Amesbury, Sept. 1, 1743.*

Mary, and Samuel Beacham, June 5, 1754.*

Mary, of Newton, N. H., and John Bayley, jr., int. Sept. 8, 1787.

Mary, and David Wells, Apr. 12, 1792.*

Mary, and Samuel March of Salisbury, Aug. 23, 1793.*

Mary, and Joseph Bartlet, 3d, Jan. 4, 1797. c. R. 2.*

Mary Ann, and Joseph G. Flanders, Sept. 3, 1838.*

Mary C[offin. int.], and Charles Whitmore, Feb. 1, 1826.*

*Intention also recorded.

CURRIER, Mary H., of Newburyport, and Samuel Northend,. Nov. 11, 1841.
Mary Jane, and William T. Colby, Oct. 23, 1828. [Nov. 18. dup.]*
Mehitable, of Amesbury, and Joseph Gerrish [3d. int.], at Amesbury, Jan. 1, 1761.*
Molly, of Haverhill, and Abel Emerson, Nov. 18, 1777.*
Moses, and Azubah Hill of Rowley, Apr. 25, 1803.*
Moses A., and Dolly E. Blasdell of Salisbury, int. Oct. 19, 1844.
Moses C., and Eunice Atkinson, Sept. 15, 1835.*
Moses Coffin, and Prudence B. Rogers, Oct. 2, 1821.*
Nancy A., and Samuel Somerby, Jan. 22, 1843.*
Nancy D., and John Sawyer of West Newbury, Apr. 22, 1839.*
Nathaniel, and Phebe Adams, int. Apr. 18, 1795.
Nicolas, and Mary Plumer, Dec. 23, 1762.*
Nicolas, of Newburyport, and Sarah Plumer, int. Mar. 24, 1767.
Olive Ann, and George Worthen, int. Dec. 20, 1847.
Richard, and Elizabeth Knight, May 5, 1743.*
Richard [jr. int.], of Methuen, and Anna Knight, Dec. 18, 1777.*
Ruben, of Southampton, and Ruth Bartlet, int. Sept. 28, 1804.
Salley, and Thomas Brown, Nov. 11, 1797.*
Sally, and William Dickey, Sept. 5, 1799.*
Sally, of Amesbury, and Hezekiah Coffin, int. Jan. 16, 1811.
Samuel, of Haverhill, and Abigail Kelley, June 30, 1714.*
Samuel, and Margery Perkins, Dec. 8, 1757.*
Samuel, and Anna Bayley, int. Dec. 10, 1791.
Samuel C., and Sarah Ann Merrill, int. Oct. 1, 1837.
Sarah, and Enoch Flood, jr., int. Sept. 22, 1801.
Sarah, of Newburyport, and Benjamin Dutton, Nov. 15, 1801.*
Sarah C., a. 20 y., d. William, and David Brown, a. 23 y., ship carpenter, s. James and Lucy, Oct. 22, 1846.*
Sarah T., and Amos Bray of Gloucester, Nov. 27, 1826.*
Sawyer, and Elizabeth Merrill of Newburyport, int. Nov. 23, 1833.
Simon T., and Mary S. Hills of Rowley, Apr. 28, 1830.*
Solomon Haskell, and Sarah Davenport of Newburyport, int. Jan. 9, 1808.
Susan R., and David I. Goodridge of West Newbury, int. Aug. 30, 1837.

*Intention also recorded.

CURRIER, Susanna Haskell, of Newburyport, and Jeremiah Elliot, int. Oct. 14, 1813.

William [jr.c. R. 2.], of Amesbury, and Judeth Chase, Feb. 19, 1735-6.*

William, and Tabitha Pettingell, Sept. 29, 1748.*

W[illia]m, jr., and Elis[abeth] Todd, Mar. 4, 1760. C. R. 9.*

W[illia]m. 5th, of Newburyport, and Mary Gerrish, int. Oct. 2, 1802.

William, and Betsey Doyle, Aug. 19, 1812.*

William, jr., and Sarah N. Magoun of Pembroke, int. Nov. 9, 1831.

William E., and Fanny M. Pardee of Newburyport, int. Feb. 22, 1834.

William J., and Hannah S. Currier of Salisbury, int. Jan. 10, 1846.

CURSON, Elizabeth, of Roxbury, a. 25 y., d. Samuel and Margaret, and John A. Hoxie of Roxbury, a. 33 y., carpenter, s. John and Sally, of New York, Aug. 18, 1847.

Samuel, of Boston, and Margaret Searle, int. June 7, 1816.

CURTEEN, Anne [Nanne Curten. int.], and Peter Pilsbury, Oct. 17, 1751. C. R. 2.*

CURTICE (see also Curtis), Lydia, of Danvers, and Henry Dwinel, at Danvers, June 16, 1779.*

CURTIS (see also Curtice), Benjamin, and Rachel Hook of Salisbury, Dec. 8, 1762.*

Charity, and Joshua Dummer, int. May 16, 1840.

Reuben S., of Gloucester, and Elizabeth Somerby, Jan. 16, 1831.*

Sally, of Newburyport, and Stephen Pettingal, Aug. 2, 1815. C. R. 1. [int. June 15, 1816.]*

Sarah, and Thomas Upham, both of Marblehead, June 18, 1729. C. R. 7.

Timothy. of Newburyport, and Susanna Richards, Feb. 21, 1782.*

William, and Mary Lankister, Jan. 8, 1728-9.*

CUSHING, Jael, of Hingham, and John Lazell, Feb. 9, 1722-3. C. R. 7.

*Intention also recorded.

Cushing, Sarah, of Salisbury, and Col. Samuel Moody, int.
   May 13, 1779.
W[illia]m, of Newburyport, and Sarah M. Stone, int. Aug.
   21, 1847.

CUTLER, Ammi Ruhamah, Rev., and Mrs. Dorothy Bradbury,
   both of North Yarmouth, Aug. 14, 1734. c. r. 7.

CUTTER, Abigail, of Charlestown, and Silas Pillsbury, at
   Charlestown, May 27, 1797.*
Fanny H., of Newburyport, and Gorham Pilsbury, int. Apr. 7,
   1849.

CUTTING, Mary, and Samuel Moody, Nov. 30, 1657.

CYER, Mary Elizabeth, and Holbrook Burroughs, int. June
   2, 1838.

CYES, Elizabeth [Mary Elizabeth. int.], and James Manly
   Burroughs, July —, 1838.*

DALTON, Bethiah, of Andover, and Samuel Morss, at An-
   dover, Sept. 24, 1725.
Jeremiah, and Mary Noyes of New Marblehead, int. May 6,
   1761.
Jonathan, of Newburyport, and Sally Stickney, Sept. 30, 1793.*
Mary, and Leonard White of Haverhill, int. July 26, 1794.
Michael, and Mary Little, Feb. 5, 1733-4.*
Michal, and Mehitable Black of York, Nov. 23, 1730.*
Tristram, and Mrs. Ruth Hooper of Marblehead, at Marble-
   head [at Danvers. dup.], Oct. 4, 1758. [Oct. 24. dup.]*

DAM (see also Dame), Leader, and Melinda Goodridge, Sept.
   29, 1814.*
Mary, and Thomas Titcomb, Nov. ult., 1693.

DAME (see also Dam), Charles C., and Frances A. Little,
   Sept. 1, 1842.*
Luther, a. 22 y., school teacher, s. Joseph and Statira, of Kittery, and Sarah E. Tenney, a. 19 y., d. Richard and Hannah, Nov. 25, 1847.*
Olive, of Barrington, N. H., and John Chase, 3d., int. Mar. 8,
   1817.

*Intention also recorded

DANA, Daniel, Rev., D. D., of Newburyport, and Sarah Emery, Nov. 8, 1814.*

Lydia C., and Rev. Ed. Richard Tucker of Defiance, O., int. May 11, 1844.

Mary, and William Anderson, 3d of Londonderry, N. H., int. Sept. 25, 1830.

Sarah, and Isaac W. Wheelwright, int. Sept. 29, 1842.

Susan, and Rev. John M. C. Bartley of Hampstead, N. H., int. Jan. 12, 1837.

DANE, Edward [Dean. int.], and Abigail Hill, June 20, 1744.*

Henry, jr., of Andover, and Hannah Chase, int. Mar. 19, 1831.

James, of Andover, and Phebe [Rebeckah. c. R. 1.] Pilsbury, June 6, 1799.*

John, and Mary Moody, Oct. 29, 1761.*

John, of Andover, and Sally Moody, May 6, 1828.*

Philemon, and Hannah York of Ipswich, int. Mar. 20, 1741-2.

DANFORD (see also Danforth), Bethiah, and Joseph Flood, jr., July 1, 1756.*

Eliphalet, of Rowley, and Martha Burbank, Nov. 23, 1738.*

Francis, and Sarah Chase, Nov. 17, 1714.*

John, and Dorcas White, Nov. 24, 1714.*

John, and Elisabeth Fitts, Nov. 11 ,1735.*

John, 3d, and Mercy Coffin, int. Jan. 21, 1763. ("The Banns Forbid by Mercy Coffin.")

Jonathan, and Mary White, int. Jan. 21, 1703-4.

Jonathan [John, jr. int.], and Mercy Martin, Sept. 4, 1766.*

Joseph, and Bethyah Noyes, Dec. 13, 1717.

Oliver, and Anna Stickney, Oct. 14, 1756.*

Rebecka, and Francis Akers, Apr. 18, 1718.

Samuel, and Mehitable Brown, Jan. 13, 1736-7.*

Sarah, of Bradford, and David Pearson, jr., Nov. 6, 1750.*

DANFORTH (see also Danford, Danfourth), Anna, and Josiah Carr, Mar. 11, 1792.*

Daniel, and Eunice Poor, Oct. 1, 1798.*

Elizabeth, wid., of Andover, and Ebenezer Dow, at Andover, June 12, 1760.

Joseph, Lt., and Anna Quimbe, May 22, 1800.*

Joseph, and Jane Fairweather, ——, 1844. [Nov. 23. int.]*

*Intention also recorded.

DANFORTH, Joshua J., and Mary C. Boddily, Nov. 21, 1833.*
Joshua J., and Mary J. Knight, Dec. 1, 1836.*
Lois, and John Colman, July 16, 1765.*
Mary P., a. 26 y., d. Samuel and Edna, and Nathaniel Little,
    jr., a. 26 y., farmer, s. Tristram and Sarah, May 22, 1845.*
Myra, and Joseph Bailey, Nov. 23, 1826.*
Rebeckah, and John Buckley of Haverhill, Sept. 30, 1800.*
Rhoda [Rebecca. int.] B., and John Newman, Sept. —, 1833.*
Richard, and Mary White, int. June 30, 1702.
Ruth, and Abner Woodman, Apr. 11, 1769.*
Samuel, and Ednah Plumer, Nov. 10, 1803.*
Sarah, and Moses George of Peeling, N. H., Feb. 26, 1838.*
Simeon, and Judith Stickney, both of Rowley, July 9, 1801.
    C. R. 5.
William, and Hannah Rogers, Nov. 1, 1827.*

DANFOURTH (see also Danforth), Anna, and Joseph Downer,
    May 23, 1779.*

DANIEL (see also Daniels), Abigail, and Joshua Beck of
    Portsmouth, Apr. 20, 1716.*

DANIELS (see also Daniel), Amos, and Elizabeth Creasey
    of Rowley, at Rowley, Feb. 9, 1797.
George W., of Rowley, a. 29 y., shoemaker, b. Rowley, d.
    Philemon and Lucy, of Rowley, and Sarah J. Dwinnels of
    Rowley, a. 17 y., b. Rowley, d. Israel and Martha, of
    Rowley, July 2, 1846.
William, and Alice Wadleigh of Salisbury, at Salisbury, Dec.
    10, 1718.
William, and Relief Fellows of Rowley, Dec. 6, 1817.*

DARLING, John, of Kingston, and Hannah Mors, Oct. 18,
    1738.*

DARRAH, William, and Susan R. Noyes [int. Dec. 14.],
    1833.*

DAUKINS (see also Dawkins), Adeline, and Samuel D. Wood-
    man, int. Oct. 23, 1849.

*Intention also recorded.

DAVENPORT (see also Daverport), Dorcas, of Boston, and
Anthony Stickne, int. Nov. 26, 1746.
Sarah, of Newburyport, and Solomon Haskell Currier, int.
Jan. 9, 1808.

DAVERPORT (see also Davenport), William, and Mrs. Sarah
Gerrish, Apr. 3, 1740.*

DAVIDSON (see also Davinson, Davison), Isabella, and
Aaron Radcliffe, int. July 19, 1845.
Mary, of Newburyport, and Solomon Thurla, Apr. 14, 1787.*

DAVINSON (see also Davidson), Abigaill, and Zachariah
Fitch of Boston, Aug. 14, 1718.*
Johannah, Mrs., and John Lane, Nov. —, 1693.

DAVIS (see also Davise), Aaron, and Mary Knap, Nov. 10,
1761.*
Abigail, and Ruggles Colebe of Amesbury, Mar. 15, 1732-3.*
Abigail, and Stephen Wyat, Nov. 25, 1759.*
Abigail Haskel, of Newburyport, and David Pettengill, jr.,
int. Mar. 9, 1805.
Abraham, of Gloucester, and Mary Greenleaf, Jan. 10, 1732-
3.*
Amos, of Amesbury, and Alice Currier, Nov. 7, 1745.*
Ann, of Newburyport, and Benjamin Ordway, Dec. 27, 1829.*
Anne, of Amesbury, and Tristram Coffin, jr., int. Nov. 12,
1757.
Belinda Hills, and Ebenezer Bray Robbins, Mar. 28, 1831.*
Benj[amin], and Ruth Brown, Nov. 19, 1728. c. R. 7.
Benjamin [jr. int.], and Sarah Moody, Mar. 27, 1753.*
Benja[min], and Mary Sheppard, at Boston, Mar. 10, 1761.
Benjamin, and Martha E[veline. int.] Morse, Nov. 2, 1829.*
Betsey, and Samuel Morss, Nov. 20, 1811.*
Charles A., and Mary W. Hooker of Newburyport, int. Nov.
5, 1831.
Charles S., and Hannah M. Spooner of Newburyport, int.
Aug. 3, 1849.
Cornelius, and Elisabeth Hidden of Rowley, at Rowley, Aug.
29, 1696.*
Daniel, see Dow, Daniel.

*Intention also recorded.

DAVIS, Eben P., and Rhoda A. Thatcher of Plainfield, Ct., int. Aug. 31, 1844.

Ebenezer, of Gloucester, and Mary Pearson, Sept. 11, 1755.*

Ebenezer, and Lydia Ann Rappell, int. Mar. 10, 1838.

Elias, and Eliza[beth] Taylor, Aug. 8, 1820.*

Elias, of Newburyport, and Joanna Coffin, int. Oct. 14, 1831.

Elias Jackman, and Salley Walker of Newburyport, May 30, 1799.*

Eliphalet, of Exeter, N. H., and Mary Jackman, Sept. 10, 1775.*

Elisabeth, and Moses Emery, int. Oct. 15, 1743.

Elisabeth, and Daniel Cheney, Feb. 17, 1757. [1756. C. R. 2.]*

Elizabeth, and Robert Rogers [s. Thomas sr. int.], Aug. 8, 1709.*

Elizabeth, and Jonathan Norwood, both of Gloucester, Mar. 26, 1734. C. R. 7.

Elizabeth, of Newburyport, and Eliphalet Jaques, int. Aug. 30, 1810.

Elizabeth, and Patrick Burrill, Dec. 7, 1813.*

Elizabeth S., and John Goodwin, jr., May —, 1826.*

Enoch, and Mary Huse, May 8, 1740.*

Ephraim, and Elizabeth Kingsbury, June 9, 1687. CT. R.

Ephraim, and Lydia Emery, May 5, 1726.*

Eunice, and Nathan Flood, Jan. 10, 1770. (He took "the said Eunice naked & so would not be obliged to pay any of her former husband's debts.")*

Francis, of Amesbury, and Judith Foster, int. Aug. 31, 1780.

Hannah, and William Wilson, both of Haverhill, Feb. 26, 1735-6. C. R. 7.

Hannah, of Haverhill, and Aquila Chase, int. Mar. 12, 1736.

Hannah, and Jonathan Griffen, Nov. 12, 1761.*

Hannah, Mrs., and [Capt. C. R. 1.] Benjamin Perkins, Oct. 22, 1811.*

Hannah, and Samuel Kilborn, May 13, 1821.*

Hannah H., and Thomas Gould, Jan. 11, 1838.*

Hannah S., and Benjamin S. Rogers of Rowley, Jan. 12, 1835.*

Hiram D., of Boston, and Mary K. Smith, int. May 14, 1842.

James [jr., of Haverhill, and Sarah Wiggens, "late of Blue poynt." int.], Aug. [16. CT. R.], 1693. ["He renouncing any right, claime or interest in her former husband James Wiggens his estate." int.]*

*Intention also recorded.

DAVIS, James, and Rebecca Fitz, Jan. 6, 1813.*

James A., a. 22 y., painter, s. Alex. J. and Mary, and Mary
J. Chase, a 18 y., d. Josiah and Esther, Dec. 12, 1848.*

James W., of Newburyport, and Mary Jane Eastman, int. Apr.
1, 1837.

Jane N., and Daniel P. Noyes, int. Oct. 6, 1849.

Jemima, and William Rogers, int. July 15, 1809.

Jeremiah, and wid. Mary Joye of Amesbury, at Amesbury, Mar.
5, 1688-9.

Joanna, of Salisbury, and William Stickney, 3d, int. Nov. 12,
1757.

Johanna, of Haverhill, and Jacob Chase, Aug. 24, 1716.*

John, and Sara Carter, Apr. 8, 1681.

John, jr., of Amesbury, and Elizabeth Beetle, June 28, 1708.

John, and Hannah Heath of Haverhill, June 29, 1715.*

John, formerly of Virginia, resident in Newbury, and Abigail
Smith, int. July 3, 1778.

John, and Priscilla Bartlett, Apr. 18, 1784.*

John O., of Georgetown, and Charlotte Larkin, Nov. 20, 1843.

Joseph, and Bette Wells of Chester, int. Dec. 14, 1734.

Joseph, of Newburyport, and Hannah Akers, July 10, 1774.*

Judith [wid. int.], and Henry Bradley. Jan. 7, 1695-6.*

Lydia, wid., and Samuel Kenny, widr., Dec. 7, 1749. C. R. 7.*

Lydia, and Daniel Richardson, Nov. 21, 1751. C. R. 2.*

Lydia, of Sandown, N. H., and Timothy Noyes, int. Dec. 21,
1784.

Lydia E., a. 23 y., d. Oliver and Zilpah, and Ira S. Tilton, a.
26 y., clothier, s. Josiah and Rhoda, Oct. 12, 1845.*

Margaret, and Samuel Trott of Boston, May 25, 1760. C. R. 8.

Maria, of Newburyport, and George Goodwin, int. Jan. 9,
1836.

Maria, of Pembroke, N. H., and Oliver Hale, int. Sept. 24,
1836.

Martha, and William Rogers, int. Oct. 26, 1771. ("William
Rogers Takes her the Said Martha Davis Naked without
any of her former husbands Estate & so will not be
Obliged to pay any of her former husbands debts.")

Mary, and Stephen Roggers, Jan. 1, 1717. C. R. 7.

Mary, and Joseph Peasely, both of Haverhill, June 8, 1724.

Mary, and James Lecount of Rowley, at Rowley, Jan. 6, 1736.*

Mary, of Gloucester, and Nathaniel Bayley, int. June 20, 1747.

Mary, and Stephen Greenleaf, at Gloucester, Jan. 24, 1747-8.

*Intention also recorded.

DAVIS, Mary, and Jassiel Harraman of Plaistow, N. H., Mar. 19, 1752. C. R. 2.*

Mary, of Gloucester, and Jeremiah Wheelwright, int. Aug. 3, **1754.**

Mary, and Daniel Plumer of Gloucester [at Gloucester. dup.], May 19, 1763.*

Mary, and Amos Rogers [jr. int.], Dec. 28, 1769.*

Mary, and Samuel Rogers, June 3, 1784.*

Mary, and Jacob Webber of Hopkinton, N. H.; Jan. 8, 1816.*

Mary B., of Georgetown, a. 19 y., b. Georgetown, d. John, of Georgetown, and Green Wildes of Georgetown, a. 20 y., shoemaker, b. Georgetown, s. Ephraim and Huldah, of Georgetown, Oct. 10, 1846.

Mercy, and Daniel Lowell of Amesbury, Aug. 29, 1765.*

Moses, and Lydia Merrill, Nov. 17, 1759.*

Nathaniel, and Mary Lowel, Sept. 28, 1732.*

Nathaniel, jr., and Betty Flanders of Salisbury, int. May 8, 1766.

Obadiah S., and Juliann C. Hayes of Strafford, N. H.; int. Dec. 1, 1835.

Obadiah S., and Mrs. Mary J[ane. int.] Andrews, Aug. 28, 1843.*

Oliver, and Zilpah Pearson, Mar. 6, 1809.*

Patty, of Billerica, and Abraham Taylor, int. Mar. 15, 1799.

Rachel, and George Naish, Aug. 29, 1754. C. R. 8.

Rebecca B., and Moody Ordway, both of West Newbury, Sept. 30, 1836.

Rebeckah [d. Samuel, deceased. int.], and Abiel Kelly, Jan. 5, 1696.*

Richard, of Newburyport, and Hannah Flanders, Apr. 27, 1777*.

Richard, and Salley Rogers, July 17, 1800. C. R. 5.

Robert, and Dorothy Pearson, Nov. 3, 1776.*

Ruth, and Cutting Pettengell [jr. int.], Aug. 26, 1756.*

Ruth, and Nathan Chase, June 22, 1763.*

Sally. and James Leatherby of Newburyport, Dec. 29, 1796.*

Sally, and Moses Chase, Nov. 7, 1814.*,

Samuel, of Amesbury, and Mirriam Gardner, Jan. 23, 1749-50.*

Samuel, and Ruth Annis, Oct. 28, 1756.*

Samuel, of Newburyport, and Rebecca Adams, int. Oct. 14, 1797.

Sarah, and Joseph Moers, int. Aug. 12, 1734.

*Intention also recorded.

DAVIS, Sarah, of Newburyport, and Dudley Porter of Marble-head, Sept. 25, 1767.

Stephen, and Betty Sawyer, Jan. 25, 1786.*

Susan, of Gloucester, and Eliphalet Poor, int. Oct. 28, 1817.

Susanna, and Nathaniel Hooper of Wiscasset, int. Mar. 25, 1749.

Susanna, and Benjamin Ordway, Dec. 25, 1775.*

Susannah, and John Black, both of Haverhill, Jan. 1, 1729-30. c. R. 7.

Thomas, and [Mrs. c. R. 2.] Lydia Greenleaf, Dec. 28, 1778.*

William [of Haverhill. int.], and Mary Kelly, Dec. 31, 1700.*

William, jr., of Newburyport, and Ruth Hale, int. Aug. 17, 1793.

William, of Amesbury, and Nancy Jackman, int. June 11, 1831.

William A., of Newburyport, a. 23 y., sailmaker, b. Newbury-port, s. Benjamin and Elizabeth, of Newburyport, and Hannah A. Thurlow, a. 20 y.; d. John and Lois, Aug. 10, 1846.*

Zachary, and Judith Brown, Feb. 4, 1680-81.

DAVISE (see also Davis), Elisabeth, and Samuele Batchelder [of Hampton. int.], May 14, 1707.*

DAVISON (see also Davidson), Daniel, and Elisabeth Plomer, both of Ipswich, Nov. 4, 1726.

Joanna, Mrs., and Richard Kent, Jan. 6, 1674.

John, of Newburyport, and Eunice Sawyer Moulton, int. May 18, 1787.

John, and Joanna Dodge of Ipswich, at Ipswich, May 31, 1792.*

Mary, and Jacob Sheaf of Boston, Nov. 22, 1710.*

Moses, of Salem, and Martha Ann March of Newburyport, Nov. 29, 1832.

Sarah, and Stephen Dudley of Exeter, July —, 1708.*

DAWKINS (see also Daukins, Dockins), Hannah M., a. 18 y., b. England, d. William and Charlotte, and James Ogden of West Newbury, a. 23 y., farmer, b. Lincolnshire, Dec. 11, 1847.*

Jane, and Stephen Woodman, Aug. 8, 1843.*

*Intention also recorded.

DAY (see also Dayes), Abigail L. M., and Jeremiah Downs, Oct. 27, 1830.*

Abraham, jr. of Bradford, and Elisabeth Little, Jan. 12, 1764.*

Amos, of Newfield, and Hannah Robbins, Dec. 2, 1811.*

Bayley, of Bradford, and Hannah Carlton, May 5, 1787.*

Elizabeth, of Bradford, and Daniel eKnt, at Bradford, Apr. —, 1792.*

James, and Sarah Flood, Jan. 10, 1797.*

James, and Mary Louder, July 4, 1822.*

Jeremiah, and Betsey Hall Eldridge, May 7, 1822.*

Moses, of Bradford, and Patty Carlton, int. Oct. 18, 1785.

Nancy, of Gloucester, and James Bray, int. Oct. 5, 1816.

Susanna, and Jonathan Woodman, at Gloucester, June 22, 1777.

DAYES (see also Day), Abraham, of Bradford, and Mary Bailey, Jan. 25, 1737-8.*

DEALANE (see also Delany), Phillip, and Jane Atkinson, int. Oct. 26, 1695.

DEAN (see also Deane), Abigail, and Capt. Joseph Brown, Dec. 2, 1777.*

Betty, and Timothy Noyes, Jan. 10, 1770.*

Edward, of Ipswich, and Lydia Emery, May 31, 1716.*

Edward, and Abigail Hills, Mar. 18, 1756.*

John, of Salem, and Sarah Atkins, Sept. 1, 1763. c. r. 8.

John Gardner, and Mary Russel Peirce of Newburyport, int. Jan. 1, 1833.

Lucretia, of Exeter, and Amos Morse, int. Sept. 15, 1817.

Mary, of Ipswich, and Francis Follensby, int. Sept. 3, 1748.

Mary, and William Greenleaf, June 18, 1782.*

Mary Ann, and Moses Fowler, Oct. 23, 1835.*

Oliver, and Anna Pilsbery, int. July 9, 1796.

Samuel, and Margery Greenough, Feb. 19, 1761.*

Sarah, and [Capt. c. r. 2.] Moses Sargent Moody, Sept. 15, 1787.*

DEANE (see also Dean), Henry L., Rev., of Brookfield, and Catharine Tenney of Newburyport, Oct. 3, 1838.

Lydiah, and Thomas Bancraft of Reading, Oct. 31, 1717.

*Intention also recorded.

DEARBORN, George L., of Somersworth, N. H., a. 25 y., physician, b. Wakefield, s. Lewis, of Somersworth, and Susan A. Nason, a. 21 y., b. Ashland, d. Levi and Sarah, Nov. 29, 1849.*

Harrison W., and Lois Adams, Jan. 22, 1839.*

Nancy, of Deerfield, N. H., and Gideon R. Lucy, int. June 10, 1837.

Sally, of North Hampton, N. H., and Thomas M. Leavitte, int. Sept. 27, 1810.

DECKER, Margeret, and Joseph Pekkinton of Ipswich, Mar. 2, 1725-6.*

DEERING, Humphry [Sergt. int.], and Sarah Mar[ch], Dec. 25, 1705.*

DEFORD, Julia A. E., of Newburyport, a. 23 y., d. Samuel T. and Catharine, and Louis Worcester of Newburyport, a. 28 y., lawyer, b. Gloucester, s. David, Apr. 10, 1848.

DELAND, Abigail, of Salem, and Thaddeus Eaton, int. Oct. 17, 1813.

Lydia, and Josiah Ward, both of Salem, Nov. 6, 1781.

DELANE (see also Delany), Jane, and John Dole, Sept. 1, 1730.*

DELANO, Betsey, of Newburyport, and Jacob Whitmore, int. Apr. 25, 1824.

Otis, of Milford, a. 24 y., caulker, b. Medford, s. Charles and Bethiah, of Medford, and Sarah Merrill, a. 24 y., d. Thomas and Abigail, Oct. 8, 1846.

DELANY (see also Dealane, Delane), Dorothy, of Newbury, port, and William Dutton, int. Oct. 29, 1823.

DELAWN, Tabitha, and John Downin, Nov. 4, 1731. c. r. 7.

DELISLE, Eliza A., and Capt. Abner Lane, Apr. —, 1831.

DELPRATT, James, and Mary Bartlett, Apr. 9, 1778.*

*Intention also recorded.

DENISON, Elisabeth, and ——— Rayner, at Rowley, Nov. 12, 1662.

Mary, and William Bolton, Nov. 22, 1659.

Mary, Mrs., and Capt. Daniel Wise, both of Ipswich, Dec. 16, 1740. c. r. 7.

DENNEN, Elisabeth, of Gloucester, and Dan[ie]ll Bailey, May 23, 1750. c. r. 9.*

DENNET (see also Dennett), Charles, and Mary Downer, July 25, 1805.*

DENNETT (see also Dennet), Abigail, and Thomas Knox, July —, 1808.*

Mary, and James Riale [Ralle. int.], July 4, 1810.*

Thomas G., and Hannah Stevens of Andover, int. Mar. 9, 1821.

DENNEY (see also Denny), Mary M., and John Colby, jr. of Warner, N. H., Dec. 3, 1832.*

Nancy, of Warner, N. H., and John Woodwell, jr., Aug. 19, 1820.*

DENNIS, George W., and Mary Adams, int. Aug. 20, 1831.

John J., and Jane Wright, int. May 5, 1849.

Michael Doak, of Newburyport, and Sally Woodwell, int. June 21, 1799.

Polley, of Newburyport, and Moses Ordway, int. Aug. 25, 1804.

DENNY (see also Denney), Francis G., of Warner, N. H., and Joseph A. Atkinson, Nov. 24, 1825.*

DEUTY (see also Duty), Matthew, and Deborah Goodridge, Jan. 4, 1722-3.*

Samuel, jr., and Bethiah Pearson of Rowley, Nov. 14, 1749.*

DEXTER, John, and Deborah Ann Lunt, Nov. 12, 1837.*

DIAMOND, Abihail, wid., of Amesbury, and Richard Bartlett, widr., at Amesbury, Nov. 11, 1718.

*Intention also recorded.

DICASON (see also Dickinson), Mary [of Rowley. int.], and Daniell Pearson, Dec. 9, 1708.*

DICKERSON (see also Dickinson), Mary, of Rowley, and Samuel Plumer, int. Mar. 29, 1823.

.**DICKEY**, William, and Sally Currier, Sept. 5, 1799.*

DICKINSON (see also Dicason, Dickerson), Lucy, of Rowley, and Enoch Noyes, at Rowley, July 4, 1739.*
Sarah, of Byfield Rowley, and Parker Pillsbury, Mar. 24, 1774.*

DICKSON, John [Dreser. int.], of Rowley, and Hannah Boynton, Apr. 2, 1724.*

DINSMORE, Deborah L., of Boston, a. 27 y., b. Auburn, and Charles H. Colman, a. 29 y., school teacher, s. Daniel T. and Ann, Oct. 20, 1846.*
Hannah B., of Auburn, N. H., a. 23 y., b. Auburn, N. H., and William Colman, a. 25 y., butcher, s. D. T., Sept. 26, 1848.*
John, Esq., of Londonderry, and Mrs. Mary Rogers, ————, 1808 or 9. [Mar. 29, 1809. int.]*

DISCOW, Judith, Mrs., and Benjamin Pidgeon, July 12, 1742.*

DISNEY, Eunice Knight, and Jesse Thurlo, Nov. 27, 1813.*
George, and Polly Shaw, int. Sept. 25, 1789.
John, and Fanny Lunt, ————, 1830. [Jan. 2. int.]*
Mary, and Nathaniel Goodwin, jr., Apr. 8, 1817.*
Thomas, and Phebe Woodman, Jan. 20, 1825.*

DIVALL, Mary, and Stephen Lavenuck, Sept. 25, 1672.

DIVINE, John, and Sarah Jane Noyes, Aug. 22, 1831.
Michael, and Elsey Murray Moulton, Jan. 11, 1807.*

DOCKINS (see also Dawkins), William, of West Newbury, and Elizabeth Rogers, int. June 7, 1842.

*Intention also recorded.

DOD, Andrew, and Polly Thurla, Apr. 20, 1799.*

Philip, and Elizabeth Golding, both of Boston, July 6, 1726.
C. R. 7.

DODG (see also Dodge), William, of Newburyport, and
Abiah Lurvey, int. May 21, 1796.

DODGE (see also Dodg), Abraham, of Newburyport, and
Amelia Noyes, Sept. 16, 1783.*

Abraham, jr., and Dolly York, Apr. 9, 1809.*

Amelia, and Methuselah Bointon, Aug. 17, 1806.*

Bethiah, of Rowley, and John Noyes, at Rowley, Feb. 29,
1768.*

Daniel, and Martha Moody, both of Newburyport, Dec. 3,
1769.

Daniel, of Newburyport, and Lucy Adams, int. Oct. 15, 1814.

Elizabeth, and John Merrill, A. M., Sept. 22, 1814.*

Emily, and Francis H. Abbot, Dec. 18, 1820.*

Hannah, and William Smith, May 25, 1818.*

Joanna, of Ipswich, and John Davison, at Ipswich, May 31,
1792.*

John, of Newburyport, and Rebeckah Jaques, int. Sept. 22,
1804.

Lydia, of Newburyport, and James B. Christian of St. John's,
Apr. 5, 1833.

Martha, of Rowley, and Amos Rogers, jr., int. Jan. 18, 1805.

Mary, of Newburyport, and James S. Pettingell, int. May 31,
1834.

Mary G., and John E. Remick, both of Newburyport, Dec. 31,
1838.

Paul, and Jenny Pearson, June 28, 1799.*

Robert, and Elizabeth Wade of Ipswich, at Ipswich, Feb. 25,
1796.*

Ruth W[ade. int.], and John P[rentiss. int.] Adams of Dover, N. H., Mar. 29, 1824.*

Sally, and Enoch Colby, Mar. 12, 1809.*

Sarah L., of Newburyport, a. 21 y., b. Newburyport, d. Silas
and Marcia, and Paul Lunt, jr., a. 36 y., cordwainer, s.
Paul and Mary, Nov. 21, 1849.*

Thomas, of Beverly, and Abigail Stickney, July 25, 1781.*

William [P. int.], Esq., of Salem, and Sarah Dole, Apr. 9,
1807.*

Zecheriah, and Catharine Noyes, Dec. 15, 1804.*

*Intention also recorded.

DOE, Mary, of Romney, N. H., and Samuel Chase, jr., int. Sept. 2, 1810.

DOEL (see also Dole), Richard [Dole, jr. int.], and Sarah Ilsley, Apr. 3, 1706.*

DOGGET (see also Doggett), Lydia, and Samuel Clift, both of Marshfield, Oct. 10, 1734. C. R. 7.

DOGGETT (see also Dogget), John [Dagett, of Marshfield int.], and Rebecca Browne, June 22, 1697.*

DOLE (see also Doel), Abigail, and John Plumer, 3d, Apr. 4, 1751.*
Abner, and Mary Jewit, Nov. 1, 1694.
Abner, and [Mrs. int.] Sarah Belcher [of Boston. int.], at Boston, Jan. 5, 1698.*
Abner, jr., and Mary Kent, Sept. 3, 1730.*
Affia, and Josiah Bartlet, Aug. 18, 1767.*
Amos, of Rowley, and Abigail Stevens, int. Jan. 26, 1774.
Anna [Anne. int.], and William Ilsley, jr., Nov. 24, 1747.*
Anna, and David Stickny, Mar. 20, 1750.*
Anna L[ongfellow. int.], and Joseph Hale, jr., Oct. 30, 1800.*
Anne, and Moses Coffin, Nov. 28, 1732.*
Benjamin, and Sarah Clarke, Dec. 21, 1731.*
Betsy, and Benjamin Ilsley, Oct. 8, 1794.*
Daniel, and Sarah Pearson, Mar. 8, 1753.*
David [jr. int.], and Judith Pearson, Oct. 12, 1781.*
Ebenezer, of Hallowell, and Hannah Balch, Nov. 14, 1814.ᵏ
Edmund, Lt., of Rowley, and wid. Elizabeth Dole, at Rowley, Nov. 23, 1779.*
Edmund, of Bangor, and Judith Thurston, June 9, 1811.*
Elias P., of Salisbury, and Hannah G. Wadleigh, int. Jan. 7, 1832.
Elisabeth, and John Brown, jr., Jan. 20, 1712-13.*
Elisabeth, and Henry Dole, Oct. 4, 1742.*
Elisabeth, and Abner Greanleaf, jr., Jan. 12, 1762.*
Elisabeth, and Joseph Johnson, jr. of Newburyport, May 19, 1767.
Elisabeth, and Joseph Woodman of Newburyport, int. Sept. 1, 1781.

*Intention also recorded.

DOLE, Elizabeth [d. Richard, jr. int.], and Joshua Plumer, Nov. 6, 1699.*

Elizabeth, and David Bailey, Feb. 22, 1738-9.*

Elizabeth, and Joseph Wadleigh, jr. of Brentwood, Feb. 9, 1775.*

Elizabeth, wid., and Lt. Edmund Dole of Rowley, at Rowley, Nov. 23, 1779.*

Enoch, and Molly Plummer, Sept. 26, 1784.*

Enoch, jr., and Martha Noyes, May 31, 1808.*

Eunice, and John Thirston, June 25, 1765.*

Eunice, and Nicolas Lunt, Jan. 25, 1768.*

Eunice, and Benjamin Wheeler of Danvers, Mar. 3, 1818.*

Eunice S. [T. int.], and Caleb Woodbury, jr., Dec. 16, 1832.*

Fanney, of Rowley, and Jewett Ilsley, int. Aug. 5, 1786.

Friend, and Phebe Young of Wellfleet, int. Nov. 16, 1793.

Greenleaf, and Selina Titcomb of Newburyport, int. Apr. 11, 1818.

Hanah, Mrs., and Lt. Jonadab Waite, int. Dec. 13, 1699.

Hanah, Mrs., and Robert Greenough, jr. of Rowley, Jan. 20, 1704-5.

Hannah, and John Moodey, May 18, 1692. CT. R.

Hannah [sr. int.], and Edmund Goodridg, Nov. 16, 1701. [Oct. 3, 1702. int.]*

Hannah, and Luke Sweet of Newburyport, May 9, 1765.*

Hannah, and Stephen Poor, int. Nov. 16, 1771.

Hannah Plummer, and Jonas Bartlet, May 18, 1800.*

Henry, and Sarah Brocklebank, Nov. 3, 1686. CT. R.

Henry, and Mary Hale, Nov. 13, 1728.*

Henry, and Elisabeth Dole, Oct. 4, 1742.*

Henry, and Anne Poor, int. Aug. 20, 1772.

Henry, jr., of Limerick, and Sally Butler, Feb. 21, 1808.*

Henry Lunt, and Mary Ilsley, June 12, 1809.*

Isaiah, and Lydia Noyes, May 10, 1770.*

James, and Hannah Carleton of St. Johnsbury, Vt., int. June 2, 1815.

Jane, and Joseph Noyes, Aug. 17, 1711.*

Jane, and Matthew Perkins, Jan. 23, 1763.*

Jane, of Salisbury, and Samuel Moody, jr., int. Jan. 11, 1765.

Jeremiah, and Abigail Chase, Nov. 11, 1773.*

John, and Mrs. Mary Gerrish, Oct. 23, 1676.

John, and Hannah Tod of Rowley, int. Jan. 15, 1708.

John, and Jane Delane, Sept. 1, 1730.*

*Intention also recorded.

DOLE, John, jr., and Sarah Plumer, Mar. 6, 1745-6.*
John, 3d, and Abigail Lunt, June 27, 1765.*
John, and Mary Toppan of Newburyport, int. Jan. 3, 1807.
Jonathan, and Prudence Greenleaf, Apr. 28, 1725.*
Jonathan, jr., and Jane Noyes, Jan. 4, 1749-50.*
Joseph, and Lidya Noyes, Feb. 1, 1716-17.*
Judith, and John Rolfe [jr. int.], Oct. 7, 1715.*
Judith, and Nathaniel Mighill of Rowley, int. Aug. 28, 1776.
Judith, and John Emery Bartlet of Newburyport, int. May 8, 1807.
Judith, and George Adams, jr., Dec. 22, 1823.*
Judith C[lark. int.], and Moses Bartlet, June 13, 1822.*
Love, and Joshua Titcomb, Dec. 19, 1751.*
Lydia, and Enoch Thurlow, Jan. 26, 1815.*
Mary, and Joshua Boynton, int. Apr. 30, 1708.
Mary, and John Gerrish, Dec. 14, 1723.*
Mary, and Benjamin Lunt, 3d, Sept. 28, 1749.*
Mary, Mrs., and Capt. William Woodbridge, Dec. 14, 1749.*
Mary, and Jonathan Titcomb, May 9, 1751.*
Mary, and Samuel Plumer, 3d, Apr. 8, 1755.*
Mary, and Thomas Cross, Dec. 2, 1762.*
Mary, and Jacob Hale, Sept. 1, 1774.*
Mary, of Rowley, and Samuel Edgley, int. June 5, 1824.
Mary A. H., wid., a. 41 y., b. Sussex Vale, N. B., d. Samuel
    and Sally, of New Brunswick, and Dr. Charles Proctor,
    widr., of Rowley, a. 43 y., physician, b. Rowley, s. Benj-
    [amin] and Anna, of Rowley, Nov. 29, 1849.*
Moses, and Lydia Hobson [Hopson. int.] of Rowley, at Row-
    ley, Apr. 9, 1765.*
Moses, and Sally Thurla, June 27, 1799.*
Moses [3d. C. R. 1.], of Danvers, and Sally Boardman Tit-
    comb, Nov. 9, 1815. [Nov. 8. C. R. 1.]*
Nathan, and Phebe Harris of Rowley [of Ipswich. int.], at
    Rowley, June 6, 1754.*
Nathaniel, and Elisabeth Noyes, Nov. 26, 1730.*
Nathaniel, and Judith Noyes, Jan. 15, 1761.*
Nathaniel [of New Milford. int.], and Elisabeth Pearson,
    Nov. 5, 1799.*
Nath[anie]ll and Mary Somerby, Nov. 1, 1763. C. R. 9.*
Oliver, and Nabby Carlton, Nov. 24, 1790.*
Patience, and John Hale, jr., July 25, 1716.*
Phebe Thurlo, and Enoch Pearson, Sept. 13, 1821.*

*Intention also recorded.

DOLE, Phebe Y[oung. c. r. 10.], and Henry Stickman of New-
  buryport, Mar. 11, 1816.*
Polly, and Thomas Gage, Oct. 18, 1799. c. r. 5.
Priscilla, and Samuel C[olby. c. r. 5.] Shute, both of Rowley,
  Apr. 5, 1823.
Richard, and [Hannah. t. c.] Rofe, wid., —— 3, 1647.
Richard, and Sara Greenlefe, June 7, 1677.
Richard, sr., and Hannah Broklebank, Mar. 4, 1678.
Richard, jr., and Elizabeth Stickney of Rowley, int. June 2,
  1709.
Richard, jr., and Sarah Emmery, jr., May 21, 1719.*
Richard, jr., and Mrs. Susanna Noyes, Jan. 14, 1745-6.*
Richard, 3d, and Martha Merrill, Oct. 16, 1759.*
Ruth, and Thomas Plumer, Nov. 3, 1767.
Ruth, and Philip Butler of Newburyport, Sept. 18, 1782.*
Sally, of Rowley, and Thomas Somersby, jr. of Newburyport,
  June 4, 1803. c. r. 5.
Samuel, and Elisabeth Knight, Oct. 30, 1720.*
Samuel, jr., and Mary Gunneson, Apr. 7, 1752.*
Samuel, jr., and Hannah Little, Nov. 20, 1777.*
Sarah, and Nathaniel Coffin, Mar. 29, 1693.
S[arah, Mrs. int.], and William Johnson of Woburn, Jan. 1,
  1707.*
Sarah, and Tristram Little, Oct. 30, 1707.*
Sarah, and Jonathan Woodman, jr., Jan. 31, 1722-3.*
Sarah, and James Knight, May 22, 1740.*
Sarah, Mrs., and Daniel Perkins of Boxford, Nov. 27, 1740.*
Sarah, and Joseph Warner, Aug. 8, 1749.*
Sarah, of Rowley, and Lt. Jethro Pearson of Exeter, June 7,
  1753.
Sarah, of Salisbury, and John March, 3d, int. Oct. 23, 1756.
Sarah, and Joshua Moody [jr. int.], May 4, 1758.*
Sarah, and Enoch Plumer, Oct. 9, 1759.*
Sarah, and Jonathan Poor, Nov. 8, 1759.*
Sarah, and Henry Adams, jr., int. Nov. 7, 1767.
Sarah, and Amos Carlton, Oct. 3, 1780.*
Sarah, and William [P. int.] Dodge, Esq. of Salem, Apr. 9,
  1807.*
Sarah, and Joel R. Peabody of Topsfield, int. Nov. 18, 1841.
Seth J., of Rowley, and Mary Ann Poor, Nov. 22, 1825.*
Sewall, of Rowley, and Jane M. Knight [int. Nov. 10.],
  1832.*

*Intention also recorded

DOLE, Silas, and Judith Rolf, Sept. 25, 1777.*
Stephen, and Seusanah Noyes, Nov. 29, 1716.*
Stephen, and Susanna Adams, Mar. 15, 1768.*
Susan H., and Rev. John P. Cleaveland of Salem, Nov. 6, 1827.*
Tabitha [Mrs. int.], and John Noyes [3d. int.], Nov. 17, 1715.*
Thomas, of Lancaster, and Hannah Plumer, May 16, 1744.*
William, and Mary Brocklbanck, Oct. 13, 1684.
William, jr., and Rebeckah Person of Rowley, int. Jan. 9, 1713-14.
William, and Judeth Jaques, Apr. 3, 1755.*
William, and Edna Thurston, May 28, 1786.*
William, and Abigail Plumer, Dec. 4, 1842.*

DOLIBER (see also Doliver), Ruth, Mrs., of Marblehead, and Capt. Joseph Atkins, Nov. 18, 1734. c. r. 7.

DOLIVER (see also Doliber), Peter, of Marblehead, and Mary Coker, int. Mar. 2, 1752.

DONNALD, Joseph [Dwinnel, of Newfield. int.], and Rebekah Dresser, Apr. 2, 1795.*

DONNELL (see also Donnels), Abigail Ann, and Joseph Small, Dec. 18, 1832.*
Elizabeth, and Daniel Brown, Apr. 6, 1823.*
George, jr., and Phebe [T. int.] Wormsted, Nov. 7, 1833.*
Mary, and Rufus Barton [Baston. int.], Dec. 18, 1832.*
Zechariah, and Sarah Hardy, June 22, 1769.*

DONNELS (see also Donnell), George, and Betsey Pettengill, Apr. 3, 1805.*

DOOR, Bathsheba, and Enoch Evans, Sept. 24, 1817.*

DORMAN (see also Dorming), Jesse, of Newburyport, and Rebeckah Goodwin, Oct. 5, 1797.*

DORMING (see also Dorman), Joseph, and Mary Jillings, int. Dec. 2, 1761.

*Intention also recorded.

DOUGHERTY, Daniel, of Newburyport, and Sally Carlton, int. June 11, 1785.

DOVE, Will[ia]m, Capt., and Sarah Williams, both of Salem, June 1, 1730. C. R. 7.

DOW, Abby C., a. 20 y., d. Daniel and Joanna, and Robert Morss of Boston, a. 29 y., accountant, s. Robert and Mary, of Boston, Nov. 18, 1846.*
Benjamin P., and Margaret A. Campbell of Newburyport, int. Nov. 30, 1838.
Daniel [Davis. C. R. 10.], and Joanna Morse Pettingell, Aug. 13, 1810.*
Ebenezer, and wid. Elizabeth Danforth of Andover, at Andover, June 12, 1760.
Eliphaz, of Salisbury, and Elis[abeth] Flood, Sept. 2, 1729. C. R. 7.
Elisabeth, and Enoch Moody, Feb. 26, 1778.*
Elizabeth, and Benjamin Merrill, Feb. 4, 1739-40.*
Elizabeth, and Daniel Hale, 3d, July 17, 1776.*
Hepzebah, of Rowley, and John Frazer, at Rowley, June 6, 1754.*
John, and Elisabeth Moodey, Jan. 29, 1735-6.*
John, and Betsey Bickford, int. Mar. 7, 1835.
Judith, of Plaistow, and Sewell Short, int. Jan. 16, 1807.
Lydia, and John Poor, 4th, Feb. 16, 1769.*
Margaret, of Ipswich, and Henry Grinleaf, Aug. 24, 1727. C. R. 7.
Mary, and Edward Beacham, int. Nov. 15, 1755.
Mary, and Jacob Merrill, Feb. 8, 1778.*
Rachel. d. John, of Hampton, and Richard Collins, Mar. 1, 1738-9. C. R. 6.

DOWN (see also Downs), Joseph, and Elisabeth Silver, Apr. 7, 1763.*

DOWNER, Abigail, and Abner Rogers, Feb. 24, 1800.*
Amos, and Abigail Burrill of West Newbury, Sept. 11, 1828.*
Andrew, and Susanah Huntington, Dec. 20, 1699.*
Andrew, and Sarah Pike, July 15, 1756.*
Betsey, of West Newbury, and George Gould, Oct. 27, 1842.*
Daniel, and Judith Pilsbury, Dec. 11, 1796.*

*Intention also recorded.

DOWNER, Gideon, and Judith Merryl, Mar. 28, 1729. c. R. 7.
Hannah, and Robert Rogers, Jan. 8, 1784.*
John, and Hannah Pierson, Jan. 4, 1726-7.*
Joseph, and Mary Knight, July 9, 1660.
Joseph, and Abigail Merrill, Mar. 6, 1733-4.*
Joseph, and Anna Danfourth, May 23, 1779.*
Judith, and William Rogers [jr. int.], Aug. 29, 1749. c. R. 2.*
Martha, and Ezekiel Rogers, ———, 1810 or 11. [July 28, 1810. int.]*
Mary, and John Poor, Nov. 6, 1740.*
Mary, and Charles Dennet, July 25, 1805.*
Nancy, and W[illia]m Gould of West Newbury, int. Apr. 7, 1827.
Nancy M., of Newburyport, and Joseph Pickett, Nov. 28, 1838.*
Nanny, and Nathan Longfellow, Sept. 10, 1799.*
Paul P., and Hannah Moody, Mar. —, 1811.*
Samuel, and Sarah Moody, ———, 1808. [Apr. 16. int.]*
Sarah, and Joshua Ordway, Oct. 9, 1759.*
Sarah, and Isaiah Rogers, Jan. 15, 1783.*
Sarah, of Newburyport, and Edmund Nicols, int. Apr. 17, 1802.
Solomon, and Phebe Pearson of Haverhill, June 12, 1783.*
Stephen, and Susanna Chisemore, Dec. 9, 1773.*
Susanna, and Daniel Rogers, jr., Oct. 19, 1785.*

DOWNIN (see also Downing), John, and Tabitha Delawn, Nov. 4, 1731. c. R. 7.

DOWNING (see also Downin), David, and Susanna Beacham, Mar. 7, 1762.*
John, and Martha Smith, Mar. 10, 1755.*
John, and Sarah Hartshorn of Plaistow, N. H., int. Feb. 1, 1783.
Martha, and Richard Richards, Dec. 18, 1782.*
Sarah, and Benj[amin] Howard of Newburyport, Nov. 13, 1794.*
Susanna, Mrs., and Moses George, Oct. 27, 1752.

DOWNS (see also Down). Hannah Dole, and Ira Ricker of Newburyport, int. Sept. 20, 1821.
Jeremiah, and Abigail L. M. Day, Oct. 27, 1830.*

*Intention also recorded.

DOWNS, Massey, and Samuel Lunt, May 6, 1802.*
Prince Lumbard, and Sarah Morse, int. Sept. 8, 1798.
Salley Coffin, of Newburyport, and Jedediah Kilborn, int. Nov.
    17, 1804.
Sally, and Ebenezer Harris of Ipswich, int. May 17, 1823.
Sally, and Robert Cole, Nov. 13, 1826.*
Susan S., and John B. Chase, Oct. 16, 1824.*
Thomas, and Hannah Cavender, Sept. 5, 1800.*
Thomas, and Lydia Miller, int. Apr. 4, 1821.
William, and Elisabeth Hunt, int. Dec. 26, 1771.

DOWS (see also Dowse), Jonathan, of Charlestown, and Mary
    Blanchard of Littleton, Mar. 26, 1734. c. r. 7.

DOWSE (see also Dows), Samuel, and Alice Call, both of
    Charlestown, Oct. 2, 1733. c. r. 7.

DOYAL (see also Doyle), Charles, and Elizabeth Coffin, July
    28, 1791. c. r. 2.*
Sally, of Newburyport, and Joshua Colby, jr., int. May 2,
    1812.

DOYLE (see also Doyal), Ann, of Newburyport, and Daniel
    Wells, int. Aug. 6, 1825.
Ann, and Moses Plumer of Amesbury, int. Oct. 16, 1830.
Betsey, and William Currier, Aug. 19, 1812.*
Charles C., of Newburyport, and [Mrs. c. r. 10.] Mary C. Cof-
    fin, Oct. 13, 1831.*
Harriet, and Nathaniel Chase, Apr. 18, 1822.*
Martha Thurston, and John Woodwell Hunt, int. Mar. 22,
    1828.
Sally, and Amos Wood of Newburyport, int. Nov. 22, 1817.
Tamzon, of Newburyport, and Samuel W. Wells, int. Sept. 19,
    1835.

DRESOR (see also Dresser), Samuel, of Ipswich, and Sarah
    Moulton, int. Nov. 17, 1733.

DRESSER (see also Dresor, Dressor), Daniel, of Ipswich,
    and Esther Plumer, at Ipswich, May 24, 1792.*

DRESSER, Jane, and John Folansbe, June —, 1792.*
John, of Ipswich, and Abigail Poor, Oct. 27, 1757.*
Moses, resident in Newbury, and Sarah Murray, int. Mar. 1,
    1781.
Rebekah, and Joseph Donnald [Dwinnel, of Newfield. int.],
    Apr. 2, 1795.*
William O., and Mary W. Hale, May 12, 1837.*

DRESSOR (see also Dresser), Elisabeth, and James Ball, Feb.
    6, 1789.*
Mary, and Samuel Wallis, Aug. 23, 1789.*
Mercy, of Rowley, and Moses Longfellow, int. Mar. 16, 1804.
Polley, and Benjamin Nelson of Rowley, int. Feb. 20, 1802.

DREW, Lydia, of Peeling, N. H., and Amos Chase, jr., int.
    Oct. 19, 1816.

DROWNE, Samuel, of Newburyport, and Frances Loisa
    Brooks, ——, 1811. [Mar. 9. int.]*

DRURY, Lidia, of Framingham, and Joseph Pike, at Framing-
    ham, Dec. 5, 1722.

DUDDING, Thomas, and Grace Brickwood, both of Boston,
    ——, 1729. C. R. 7.

DUDLEY, Stephen, of Exeter, and Sarah Davison, July —,
    1708.*

DUGGIN (see also Duggins), John, and Elisabeth Ireland,
    Sept. 17, 1791. C. R. 1.*
Mary, and Josiah Pettengill, int. Dec. 18, 1801.

DUGGINS (see also Duggin), Elizabeth, and Benjamin Ran-
    dall Foss, Aug. 24, 1813.*
William, and Mary Symons, Oct. 2, 1783.*

DULIN, Mary, and Benjamin W. Robinson, int. Nov. 10, 1827.

DUMER (see also Dummer), Elisabeth, Mrs., and Moses Hale,
    int. Jan. 5, 1703-4.

*Intention also recorded.

Dumer, Elisabeth, Mrs., and Rev. Jedediah Jewett of Rowley, Nov. 11, 1730.*

Hannah, and Peter Cogswell of Newburyport, int. Aug. 19, 1786.

Jane, Mrs., and Henry Sewall, Mar. 25, 1646.

John, and Mrs. Sarah Peirce, int. Dec. 8, 1704.

Mehitable, Mrs., and Moses Hale, Nov. 8, 1744.*

Richard, and Mrs. Elizabeth Apleton, Nov. 2, 1673.

Sarah N., a. 29 y., b. Rowley, d. Samuel and Joanna, of Rowley, and Joshua N. Kent, a. 29 y., farmer, s. Jacob and Mary, Nov. 11, 1845.*

DUMMER (see also Dumer), Abigail, and William Dummer, May 28, 1811.*

Catharine [Mrs. dup.], and Enoch Bartlet of Haverhill [at Haverhill. dup.], Aug. 21, 1755.*

Catherine, and Oliver Canney, Aug. 14, 1826.*

Elisabeth, and Moses Little, 3d, Aug. 6, 1786.*

Elizabeth, Mrs., and Rev. Christopher Toppan, June 28, 1739.*

Jeremiah, of Hallowell, and Hitty Moody, May —, 1792.*

John, and Hannah Titcomb, Feb. 20, 1755.*

John, and Susannah Duty of Rowley, at Rowley, Aug. 27, 1789.*

Joseph G., and Mary P. Peabody of Boxford, int. Aug. 15, 1835.

Joshua, and Deborah Jewett of Rowley, int. May 6, 1820.

Joshua, and Charity Curtis, int. May 16, 1840.

Mary, and Nathaniel Pearly, Esq. of Hallowell, Feb. —, 1796.*

Richard, and Dorothy Light, Jan. 22, 1712-13.*

Richard, and Judith Greenleaf, June 6, 1754.*

Richard [jr. int.], and Hannah Northend of Rowley, at Rowley, June 21, 1785.*

Samuel, and Eunice Noyes, May 16, 1765.*

Samuel, jr., and Joanna Tenny, Oct. 26, 1816. [1815. c. R. 2.]*

Shubael, of Salem, and Deborah Moody, Mar. 1, 1808.*

William, and Dorothy Northend of Byfield Rowley, June 2, 1761.*

William, and Abigail Dummer, May 28, 1811.*

DUNLAP, David, and Fanny Bartlet of Newburyport, int. Jan. 17, 1824.

*Intention also recorded.

DUNN, John, of Rowley, a. 26 y., carpenter, b. Quebec, L. C.,
s. Herbert and Honored, of Quebec, and Susan A. Edgerly
of Rowley, a. 19 y., b. Rowley, d. Samuel and Mary, of
Rowley, Feb. 17, 1848.

DUNNING, James, and Abigail A. Scott, int. Aug. 7, 1830.
Robert, of Brunswick, and Mary Obrien, int. Dec. 11, 1802.

DURANT, Edward, and Anna Jackson, both of Newton, Sept.
15, 1735. C. R. 7.
John [resident in Newbury. int.], and Content Peasle, Nov. 17,
1763.*

DURGAN (see also Durgin), George, and Phebe E. Stanford,
Apr. 21, 1837.*

DURGIN (see also Durgan), Ann, and Samuel Goodwin, int.
July 3, 1829.
George, and Margaret Green, int. Sept. 16, 1845.
Nicolas, and Mary Foster, int. Nov. 11, 1803.
Rebecca [of Durham. int.], and Enos Bartlet, Feb. 16, 1815.*
Sarah, and Thomas Tewksbury, Oct. 10, 1814.*

DUSTAN (see also Duston), Lydia, and Nathaniel Low Chase,
Apr. 8, 1773.*
Moses, and Mercy Flanders, May 4, 1775.*

DUSTEN (see also Duston), Anna, and Martin Morland [of
Newburyport. int.], Nov. 25, 1790.*

DUSTIN (see also Duston), Hannah, and Abel Woodman,
June 17, 1779.*
Sarah, and Elias Cook of Newburyport, July 13, 1777.*

DUSTON (see also Dustan, Dusten, Dustin, Dutson), Jonathan, and Elisabeth Wats, both of Haverhill, May 18,
1715.
Mary, and Samuel Wats, jr., both of Haverhill, May 25, 1715.

DUTCH, Charlotte, of Exeter, and Moses Atkinson, 3d, int.
May 22, 1808.
Clarissa Harlow, and Joshua Coffin, at Exeter, N. H., Dec. 2,
1817.
Margaret, of Wells, and Enoch Ilsley, int. Jan. 5, 1811.

*Intention also recorded.

DUTSON (see also Duston), David [Duston. int.], and Elisabeth Morrill, Mar. 23, 1743-4.*

DUTTON, Abigail, and Paul G. Lunt, Feb. 11, 1841.*
Abigail Coffin, and Thomas Merrill, Jan. 8, 1809.*
Adeline, and Henry Mann, May 27, 1828.*
Almira, of Newburyport, and Matthias Jackman, Dec. 19, 1841.*
Benjamin, and Sarah Currier of Newburyport, Nov. 15, 1801.*
Benjamin, and Sarah Norton of Newburyport, Oct. 2, 1808.*
Benjamin, and Martha Ann Ash, both of Newburyport, Oct. 9, 1836.
Eliza P., of Boston, and Daniel T. Fisk, int. Oct. 13, 1849.
Elizabeth, of Newburyport, and George Ash, Oct. 11, 1835.*
Elizabeth M., and Thomas S. Ordway, both of West Newbury, Dec. 27, 1824.
Harriet, and Samuel Noyes of Haverhill, Dec. 3, 1835.*
Mary, and David Parsons, Nov. 22, 1812.*
Mary March, and Benjamin Hale Cheever of Newburyport, int. Apr. 9, 1825.
Sarah, and William Harris of Newburyport, int. Nov. 1, 1823.
Stephen Coffin, and Phebe Folansbe of Newburyport, int. Dec. 3, 1797.
Stephen T., of Jay, Me., and Sarah Stickney, Oct. 6, 1825.*
Thomas, and Anna Coffin, Nov. 17, 1767.
Thomas, jr., and Mary Moulton, Nov. 27, 1788.*
Thomas, and Elisabeth Ford, Nov. 14, 1793.*
William, and Dorothy Delany of Newburyport, int. Oct. 29, 1823.
William F., and Sally Rogers of Newburyport, int. June 17, 1821.

DUTY (see also Deuty), Andrew, and Mehitable Woodman, Apr. 20, 1726.*
Apphia, and Samuel Boynton, May 14, 1766.*
Bethiah, and Ezra Clough, both of Byfield Rowley, Mar. 15, 1759.
Elisabeth, of Byfield Rowley, and Francis Pingry of Rowley, Dec. 13, 1759.
Jane, and Richard Goodridge, int. June 15, 1761.
John, and Mary Pilsbury, Mar. 24, 1774.*
John [jr. int.], and Lydia Rogers, Nov. 18, 1802.*

*Intention also recorded.

DUTY, Joseph, and Sarah [Mary. int.] Pike, Nov. 19, 1754.*
Judith, and Samuel Gould, Dec. 14, 1826.*
Lydia, and Jesse Rogers, Nov. 24, 1807.*
Mary, and Daniel Rogers, Jan. 3, 1798.*
Mehetabel, and Onesiphorus Page of South Hampton, N. H.,
    Apr. 28, 1767.*
Mehetable, of Byfield Rowley, and John Hamilton, "a Foreigner," Dec. 25, 1778.
Sarah, and John Uran of Rumford, Nov. 24, 1746.*
Susannah, of Rowley, and John Dummer, at Rowley, Aug. 27,
    1789.*

DWIER, Thomas, of Newburyport, and Abigail Rappell, int.
    Nov. 4, 1834.

DWINEL (see also Dwinnell), Henry, and Lydia Curtice of
    Danvers, at Danvers, June 16, 1779.*

DWINELS (see also Dwinnell), Eunice, of Rowley, and Daniel Rogers, int. Oct. 15, 1836.

DWINNEL (see also Dwinnell), Amos, and Betsey Creessy of
    Rowley, int. Nov. 19, 1796.
Joseph, see Donnald, Joseph.

DWINNELL (see also Dwinel, Dwinels, Dwinnel, Dwinnells,
    Dwinnels), Mercy, and Joseph Pilsbury [jr. int.], June
    26, 1781.*

DWINNELLS (see also Dwinnell), Jacob, and Dolly Varney
    Rogers, int. Aug. 1, 1831.

DWINNELS (see also Dwinnell), Sarah J., of Rowley, a. 17
    y., b. Rowley, d. Israel and Martha, of Rowley, and
    George W. Daniels of Rowley, a. 29 y., shoemaker, b.
    Rowley, s. Philemon and Lucy, of Rowley, July 2, 1846.

EAGAN (see also Egan), Anna, and Isaiah Whitticer, int.
    Nov. 5, 1803.

*Intention also recorded.

EARL, Demaris, of Newport, R. I., and Daniel Smith of South Kingston, R. I., May 15, 1727. c. r. 7.

Mary A., of Newburyport, and William H. Hynes, int. Oct. 21, 1848.

EASMAN (see also Eastman), Anne, of Salisbury, and Solomon Pike, at Salisbury, Jan. 23, 1723-4.

Betsey, of Henniker, and John Hardy, int. Sept. 25, 1801.

Edmund, and Hannah Hills, Apr. 28, 1747.*

Enoch, and Betsey Tyler, int. Sept. 12, 1804.

EAST, Joseph, of Dracut, and Hepsibah Ames of Wilmington, Feb. 3, 1732-3. c. r. 7.

EASTERBROOK (see also Estabrook), Hannah, Mrs., and Joseph Burrill, Feb. 9, 1743-4.*

Robert D., Rev., of Malden, and Caroline Goodwin, Nov. 6, 1832.*

EASTERBROOKS (see also Estabrook), Sarah [of Haverhill. int.], and John Emerson, at Haverhill, Oct. 26, 1784.*

EASTMAN (see also Easman), Daniel, of Salisbury, and Mary Jackman, May 15, 1760.*

Enoch, and Judith Adams, Nov. 21, 1808.*

Jeremiah, of Salisbury, and Edner Poor of Haverhill, Sept. 10, 1772.

Jonathan, of Salisbury, and Elizabeth Chase, May 21, 1812.*

Lucinda, and Gideon Rogers, jr., Dec. 10, 1835.*

Mary Jane, and James W. Davis of Newburyport, int. Apr. 1, 1837.

Phillip, and Mary Morse, Aug. 22, 1678.

Thomas, and Hannah Annis, Nov. 2, 1732. c. r. 7.

EATON, Anne, of Salisbury, and Thomas Arnold, at Salisbury, Nov. 10, 1747.*

Daniel, and Nanne Pike, both of Salisbury, Nov. 24, 1730. c. r. 7.

David, and Ruth Little, Oct. 23, 1811.*

Elisabeth, and Simon Noyes, Dec. 10, 1754.*

*Intention also recorded.

EATON, Elisabeth, and Edward Ordway, jr., of Haverhill, at
Haverhill, [bef. 1780].
Elisabeth, of Newburyport, and William Chase, int. Feb. 10,
1798.
Eunice Wells, of Northampton, N. H., and Clark Foss, int.
Aug. 23, 1818.
Forrest, of Dover, N. H., and Harriet. P. Gordon, Sept. 23,
1828.*
Henry, of Seabrook, N. H., and Abigail [M. int.] Perry, Nov.
—, 1833.*
Jacob, and Sarah Plomer, May 13, 172[6].*
John, and Hannah Fowler, both of Salisbury, Jan. 13, 1734-5.
C. R. 7.
John, of Haverhill, and Judeth Hale [at Haverhill. dup.],
Oct. 21, 1741.*
John, of Salisbury, and Nancy Wyatt, int. Oct. 11, 1811.
Jonathan, and Susan Saunders, Apr. 3, 1815.*
Sally, of Salisbury, and Samuel S. Berdge, int. Oct. 20, 1811.
Thaddeus, and Abigail Deland of Salem, int. Oct. 17, 1813.
Thomas, of Salisbury, and Eunice Moulton, Oct. 5, 1749.*

EDES, Jonathan, of Boston, and Joannah Willit, int. Mar. 24,
1711-12.

EDGERLY (see also Edgley), Susan A., of Rowley, a. 19 y.,
b. Rowley, d. Samuel and Mary, of Rowley, and John
Dunn of Rowley, a. 26 y., carpenter, b. Quebec, L. C., s.
Hubert and Honored, of Quebec, Feb. 17, 1848.

EDGLEY (see also Edgerly), Samuel, and Mary Dole of
Rowley, int. June 5, 1824.

EDMONDS (see also Edmunds), Jane, and Michael Ludon of
Danvers, int. Aug. 12, 1797.

EDMUNDS (see also Edmonds), Samuel, and Hannah Thurlo, Mar. 11, 1811.*

EDWARDS, Abraham, and Elisabeth Emerson, June 4, 1723.*
Abraham, of Boston, and Lydia Pilsbury, int. Nov. 22, 1806.
Betsey, of Salisbury, and W[illia]m Merrill, 3d, int. Apr. 13,
1827.

.*Intention also recorded.

EDWARDS, Edward, and Elisabeth Coats, int. Feb. 28, 1746-7.
Elisabeth, and Nicholas Pettingell, June 25, 1752.*
Elizabeth, Mrs., and Daniel Merrill, June 18, 1831.*
Hannah, of Salisbury, and Peter Clefford, int. Mar. 23, 1805.
Hannah, and Rufus Pray, Dec. —, 1824.*
Joseph, and Sarah Newman, Nov. 12, 1753.*
Joseph, and Anna Pettingall, int. Mar. 15, 1785.
Joshua, and Elizabeth Pulsifer of Wenham, int. July 5, 1819.
Mary, and James Browne, jr., Apr. 28, 1694.
Mary, and James Browne, Apr. 8, 1695.
Mary Ann, of Newburyport, and Samuel Hoyt Pingry of Haverhill, Oct. 11, 1832.
Rebeckeh, and David Coll, May 14, 1752.*
Rice [of Wenham. int.], and Rebecca Ford, Mar. 22, 1710.*
Trifene, wid., and Josiah Goodrich, int. Feb. 22, 1777.

EGAN (see also Eagan), George, and Charlotte Rogers, May 18, 1817.*
James, and Anna Eliet, June 15, 1795.*

ELA (see also Ely), Sarah, of Newburyport, and Joseph Stanwood, ——, 1808. [June 17. int.]*

ELDER, William, of Falmouth, and Mary Akers, Nov. 21, 1751.*

ELDRIDGE, Betsey Hall. and Jeremiah Day, May 7, 1822.*
Emma, of Salisbury, and Joseph Hodgkins, int. Sept. 26, 1810.
Ezekiel, and Elisabeth Butler, Apr. 5, 1750. ("This man convicted of and branded in ye hand for Polygamy after this marriage." C. R. 3.)*

ELIET (see also Elliott), Anna, and James Egan, June 15, 1795.*

ELIOT (see also Elliott), Elisabeth, and Leonard Smith, Dec. 19, 1754. C. R. 8.
Eliz[abeth], of Newtown, and Joseph Bright of Watertown, June 5, 1730. C. R. 7.
John, of Boscawen, N. H., and Susanna Welch, Sept. 11, 1781.*

*Intention also recorded.

ELIOT, Jonathan, and Mehitabel Chute [of Rowley. int.], Oct. 2, 1800.*
Mary, and Francis Bartlet, both of Amesbury, Sept. 9, 1741. C. R. 7.
Mary, and Benjamin Coffin, 3d, Jan. 25, 1759.*
Moses, and Sarah Pearson of Rowley, int. Oct. 5, 1800.
Samuel, of Boston, and Catharine Atkins, int. Apr. 21, 1786.
Skipper, and Joanna Blake of Salisbury, int. May 23, 1752.

ELITROP, Mary, and Francis Plumer, int. Apr. 12, 1700.

ELLEN, Anna, and Jacob Adams, Apr. 7, 1677.

ELLERY, Abigail, Mrs., of Gloucester, and Joshua Tufts, int. Sept. 11, 1741.

ELLIOT (see also Elliott), David C., a. 22 y., b. Dorchester, N. H., s. Isaac and Dorothy, of Dorchester, and Hannah F. Chesley, a. 20 y., b. Gilmanton, d. Timothy and Betsy, of Gilmanton, Nov. 25, 1847.*
Elizabeth, of Haverhill, and Moses Moody, 3d, int. Feb. 12, 1780.
Jeremiah, and Susanna Haskell Currier of Newburyport, int. Oct. 14, 1813.
Jeremiah, and Hannah Pilsbury Questron, int. May 26, 1821.
Milton, and Rebecca R. Wells, int. Jan. 15, 1828.
Naomi [of Amesbury. int.], and John Calf, at Amesbury, Oct. 31, 1739.*

ELLIOTT (see also Eliet, Eliot, Elliot, Ellit, Ellite), Hannah, and Rufus D. Lothrop of Rowley, int. Jan. 27, 1842.
Henry M., of Salisbury, and Lydia George, int. Mar. 31, 1841.
John, of the Royal Scots, and Sarah Bayard, in New Hampshire, July 17, 1761. C. R. 8.

ELLIS, Abigail, and Samuel Ellis, widr., both of Medfield, May 17, 1726. C. R. 7.
Samuel, widr., and Abigail Ellis, both of Medfield, May 17, 1726. C. R. 7.

ELLISON, Francis, and Dorcas Moores of Newburyport, Sept. 19, 1810.*

*Intention also recorded.

ELLIT (see also Elliott), Sarah, and Daniel Lunt, int. May 22, 1714.

ELLITE (see also Elliott), Francis, and Sarah Hodgskins, Oct. 4, 1742.*

ELSWORTH, Hannah, of Rowley, and Zechariah Beal, jr., at Rowley, Apr. 10, 1766.*
Jonathan, and Eunice Tenney, both of Rowley, Feb. 20, 1753.
Samuel, and Judith Listy of Amesbury, int. Aug. 30, 1774.

ELWELL, Christian, of Gloucester, and William Sampson, int. July 18, 1702.
Cristian, alias Samson, and James Smith of Preston, Conn., Feb. 26, 1712-13.*
Hannah M., and John F. Jennin, both of Rowley, Apr. 27, 1818. C. R. 5.
Martha, and James Warden of Newburyport, int. Jan. 7, 1793.

ELY (see also Ela), Daniel, of Newburyport, and Sarah Brookins, Nov. 6, 1774.*

EMERSON (see also Emmerson, Emmison), Abel, and Molly Currier of Haverhill, Nov. 18, 1777.*
Anna, of Hampstead, and Jeremiah Chase, jr., int. May 22, 1789.
Anstis, of Ipswich, and William Badger, int. Oct. 3, 1751.
Bulkley, and Mary Moody, July 13, 1752.*
Elisabeth, and Abraham Edwards, June 4, 1723.*
Elizabeth, and James Fagin, Dec. 9, 1834.*
Hannah, and John Woollcutt, Jan. 4, 1684.
Hannah, and Samuel Lowell of Rowley, at Rowley, Sept. 17, 1735.*
James, jr., of Haverhill, and Sarah Emerson [int. Feb. 9, 1758.]*
Joanna, and Joseph Harrandin [Harradan. int.] of Gloucester, Jan. 6, 1731-2.*
John. [Lt. int.], and Hannah Poor, Nov. 2, 1710.*
John, and Sarah Easterbrooks, at Haverhill, Oct. 26, 1784.*
Jonathan, of Salem, N. H., and Rhoda Bayley, int. Dec. 13, 1780.
Joseph, and Ruth Brown, Jan. 6, 1735-6.*

*Intention also recorded.

EMERSON, Mary, and Hugh Mathews, Aug. 28, 1683.
Mary, and Robert Lander [Lowder. int.], Feb. 8, 1801. C. R.
5.*

Nancy, of Hopkinton, and John Pearson, int. Oct. 23, 1813.
Nehemiah, of Haverhill, and Abigail Knight, Feb. 6, 1794.*
Polly, of Hampstead, N. H., and Richard Jaques, int. May 15,
1792.

Richard, of Haverhill, and Mary Morss [at Haverhill. dup.],
Jan. 2, 1738-9.*

Samuel, and Mary Green of Boston, int. Jan. 30, 1753.
Sarah, and James Emerson, jr. of Haverhill [int. Feb. 9,
1758.]*

Thomas, and Anna Kimball, int. Nov. 21, 1785.
Timothy W., and Mary W. Conant of Rowley, int. May 9,
1834.

Watts, of Hampstead, and Molly Merrill, Apr. 2, 1794.*

EMERY (see also Emmery, Emory), Abigail, wid., and John
Stickne, jr., May 30, 1720.*

Abigail, and Gideon Bartlet, Dec. 16, 1725.*
Abigail, and Ebenezer Hacket, Mar. 24, 1752.*
Abigail, and Ephraim Boynton, Feb. 19, 1756.*
Abigail, and Jeremiah Jewett of Rowley, July 15, 1797.*
Amos, and Anna Moody of Newburyport, int. Jan. 9, 1784.
Ann, and Woodbridge Brown of Abington, Nov. —, 1736.*
Anna, and Abel Merrill, Jan. 4, 1776.*
Anne, and James Ardway, Nov. 25, 1648.
Anne, and Tristram Little, jr., Apr. 10, 1711.*
Anthony, and Hannah Plumer, int. Mar. 21, 1711.
Benjamin, and Sarah Samson, July 8, 1754.*
Benjamin, of Rumford, N. H. [Pennacook. C. R. 2.], and Sarah
Bayley, Mar. 12, 1761.*

Betty, Mrs., and Col. Daniel Spofford of Rowley, Apr. 12,
1780.*

Betty, and Moses Colman, Dec. 5, 1787.*
Bithia, and Henry Bodwell, May 4, 1681.
Charles, and Mary Elizabeth George of Newburyport, int. Jan.
5, 1828.

Daniel, and Sarah Brocklebank of Rowley, at Rowley, Feb. 28,
1757.*

Dan[ie]ll, and Hannah Tappin, Nov. 26, 171[8. int.]*
David, and Abigail Chase, Jan. 27, 1731-2.*

*Intention also recorded.

EMERY, David, and Mary Hale, Dec. 30, 1756.*

David, and Betty Little, Aug. 22, 1785.*

David [of Newburyport. int.], and Sarah Smith, Apr. 22, 1812.*

Ebenezer, and John Hoog, Apr. 21, 1669.

Elisabeth, and Caleb Moodey, jr., June 15, 1727.*

Elizabeth [d. Sergt. John. int.], and John Kelly [jr. int.], Nov. —, 1696.*

Elizabeth, of West Newbury, and Flavius Emery, Nov. 1, 1826.*

Enoch, and Sarah Sarjant of Haverhill, int. June 26, 1784.

Ephraim, Lt., and Polly Russell of Bradford, at Bradford, Sept. —, 1785.*

Eunice, of Hampstead, and John Colby, int. Mar. 17, 1777.

Flavius, and Elizabeth Emery of West Newbury, Nov. 1. 1826.*

Hanna, and Richard Bartlet, Nov. 18, 1673.

Hannah, and Samuel Chase, Dec. 8, 1713.*

Hannah, and Edward Holman, May 19, 1726.*

Hannah, and Jonathan Griffin, May 12, 1752.*

Hannah, and Daniel Hills, May 10, 1757.*

Hannah, and Paul Little of Falmouth, May 20, 1762.*

Hannah, and Samuel Moody [jr. c. ʀ. 2.], Apr. 25, 1790.*

Hannah, and Robert Howell, Oct. 6, 1814.*

Jacob, and Lydia Noyes, int. Nov. 5, 1804.

James, and Ruth Watson of Haverhill, Dec. 10, 1719.

Jane, of Newburyport, and Andrew Crocket, June 15, 1812.*

John, and Mary Webster [wid. John, of Ipswich. ᴛ. c.], Oct. [29. 1650. ᴛ. c.]

John, and Mary Sawyer, June 13, 1683.

John [sr. int.], and Abigel Bartlet, May 27, 1700.*

John, jr., and Hanah Mors, int. Feb. 2, 1704-5.

John [3d. int.], and Mrs. Mehitable Short, Dec. 30, 1714.*

John, and [Mrs. int.] Mary March, Jan. 2, 1723-4. [He takes her without any estate, refusing to pay any debts of her former husband, Capt. James March. int.]*

John, and Rebecca Walker of Bradford, int. July 21, 1733.

John, jr., and Ednah Noyes, Apr. 7, 1756.*

John, 3d, and Elisabeth Woodman, Oct. 1, 1767.*

John [jr. int.], and Betty Smith, Dec. 27, 1770.*

John, jr., and Susanna Bartlet, int. Oct. 19, 1781.

Jonathan, and Mary Woodman, Nov. 29, 1676.

*Intention also recorded.

EMERY, Jonathan, jr., and Ruth Richardson, int. Oct. 27, 1705.*

Joseph, and Elizabeth Merrill, Oct. 2, 1693. CT. R.

Joseph, of Andover, and Abigail Long, int. Aug. 17, 1738.

Joshua [s. John, jr. int.], and Sarah Smith, Mar. 27 or 28, 1728.*

Joshua, of Haverhill, and Sarah Short, at Haverhill [after 1729].

Joshua, of Haverhill, and Sarah Short, Aug. 29, 1754.*

Josiah, and Abigail Moodey, Nov. 25, 1714.*

Josiah, and Rebekah Woodman, Nov. 20, 1770.*

Judeth, and Daniel Hale of Rowley, Dec. 29, 1720.*

Judeth, and Samuel Smith, Dec. 2, 1742.*

Judeth, Mrs. [wid. C. R. 2.], and Stephen Huse, July 30, 1729.*

Judith, and Cutting Moulton, Nov. 25, 1784.*

Lydia, d. Sergt. John, deceased, and Joseph Browne, int. May 23, 1696.

Lydia, and Edward Dean of Ipswich, May 31, 1716.*

Lydia, and Ephraim Davis, May 5, 1726.*

Lydia, and Moses Emery, Mar. 14, 1737-8.*

Lydia, and Eliphalet Coffin, Jan. 17, 1760.*

Lydia, and Moses Short, July 24, 1781.*

Martha, and Nathaniel Bayley, Aug. 6, 1761.*

Mary, and Samuell Sawyer, Mar. 13, 1670-71.

Mary, and Jonathan Wiggens, Nov. 9, 1703.

Mary, and Ens. Thomas Noyes [jr. int.], Jan. 5, 1726-7.*

Mary, Mrs., and Bernard Currier of Amesbury, Oct. 23, 1739.*

Mary, and William Smith, May 20, 1747.*

Mary, and David Batcheldor of Hampton Falls, N. H., Jan. 1, 1771.*

Mary, and David Ordway, jr., Aug. 9, 1802.*

Mary, and John Remick, Oct. 2, 1806.*

Mehitable, and Ezekiel Little of Boston, May 24, 1801.*

Michael, and Sarah Sargent of Amesbury, int. Oct. 5, 1804.

Mirriam, and John Moody, Oct. 18, 1750.*

Molly, and John Chase, jr. [4th. int.], Oct. 2, 1781.*

Moody, and Abigail Priscot, Oct. 18, 1795.*

Moses, and Lydia Emery, Mar. 14, 1737-8.*

Moses, and Elisabeth Davis, int. Oct. 15, 1743.

Moses, and Hannah Jackman, May 29, 1745. C. R. 7.*

Moses, jr., and Ruth Bodwell, Dec. 15, 1768.*

Moses [jr. int.], and Sarah Hale, Sept. 27, 1770.*

*Intention also recorded.

EMERY, Moses, and Betsey Folansbe, Sept. 24, 1803.*
Moses, and Caroline Smith of Newburyport, int. Nov. 19, 1814.
Nathan, and Susanna Noyes, int. Aug. 5, 1777.
Nathaniel, Lt., and Sarah Short, Nov. 11, 1777.*
Nathaniel, Lt., and Abigail Longfellow, May 21, 1795.*
Nathaniel, and Mary Quimbe, Nov. 27, 1799.*
Nicholas, Capt., and Sarah Robinson, both of West Newbury,
    Feb. 5, 1822.
Polly, of Atkinson, N. H., and John Woodman, jr., int. Oct.
    25, 1785.
Ruth, and William Moulton, jr., Apr. 24, 1716.*
Ruth, and John White, 3d of Haverhill, May 7, 1772.*
Salley, and William Harris, Sept. 23, 1804.*
Sally, and Richard Rand, Nov. 2, 1807.*
Samuel, and Elizabeth Woodwell of Salem, at Salem, Apr. 16,
    1747.*
Samuel, and Ruth Annis, Nov. 25, 1760.*
Sarah, and Isaac Baily, June 13, 1683.
Sarah, Mrs., and Ambros Berry, June 3, 1728.*
Sarah, and David Chase, Nov. 24, 1729.*
Sarah, and Henry Adams, Nov. 20, 1746.*
Sarah, and John March, 3d, Mar. 5, 1761.*
Sarah, and Enoch Noyes, Oct. 30, 1765.
Sarah, and Ezekiel Merrill, June 1, 1773.*
Sarah, and John Bayley, Nov. 16, 1786.*
Sarah, and Nathaniel Noyes of Salisbury, N. H., ——, 1808
    or 9. [Nov. 25, 1808. int.]*
Sarah, and Rev. Daniel Dana, D. D. of Newburyport, Nov. 8,
    1814.*
Sarah Jane, a. 21 y., d. Thomas, and Lewis G. Farrington of
    West Newbury, a. 21 y., shoemaker, s. Ebenezer and Ruth,
    of West Newbury, May 1, 1845.
Stephen, and Ruth Jaques, Nov. 29, 1692.
Stephen, and Lydia Jackman, Feb. 25, 1714-15.*
Stephen, 3d, and Hannah Rolfe. May 5, 1732.*
Stephen, 4th, and Deliverance Stiles of Boxford, int. Sept. 1,
    1743.
Stephen, 3d, and Sarah Moody, Nov. 6, 1760.
Stephen, jr., and Sarah Bartlet, int. Apr. 22, 1780.
Stephen, 3d, and Hannah Little, May 4, 1783.*
Thomas, and Ruth March, Oct. 10, 1770.*
Thomas, and Elisabeth Hale, Dec. 4, 1796.*

*Intention also recorded.

EMERY, Thomas, and Margaret Coffin, Nov. 27, 1806.*
Thomas, jr., and Mary Hoyt of Amesbury, int. Mar. 19, 1818.
William, of Contoocook, N. H., and Mary Chase, int. Aug. 4,
1749.

EMMERSON (see also Emerson), Samuel, and Sarah Lowell
of Rowley, Nov. 16, 1729.*

EMMERY (see also Emery), Daniel [widr. c. r. 2.], and wid.
Judeth Knight, Nov. 29, 1723.*
Edward, and Sarah Sibley, Dec. 19, 1719.*
John, and Abigail Stiles of Boxford, at Boxford, Dec. 18,
1753.*
Sarah, jr., and Richard Dole, jr., May 21, 1719.*

EMMES, Elizabeth, and Phineas Glesen, both of Framingham,
Jan. 24, 1732-3. c. r. 7.

EMMISON (see also Emerson), Hannah, of Amesbury, and
Hugh Pike [jr. int.], at Amesbury, Nov. 24, 1715.*

EMMONS, Mercia, of Newburyport, and Tristram Rogers,
——, 1810 or 11. [Nov. 3, 1810. int.]*

EMORY (see also Emery), Elizabeth, Mrs., and Rev. Moses
Hale of Boxford, Dec. 28, 1775.*
Hittey, and Nathan Morss, Oct. 20, 1741.*

ENGLAND, Dan[ie]l B., a. 26 y., blacksmith, s. John and
Sarah, and Sarah Hale, a. 22 y., d. Oliver and Sarah,
July 5, 1846.*
Eliphalet, and Elisabeth Pearson, July 7, 1785.*
Elisabeth, and Ebenezer Brown, Sept. 18, 1785.*
Elizabeth [wid. int.], and Daniel Chase, May 7, 1777.*
Elizabeth, and Paul H. Grant, July 17, 1810.*
Francis, and Prudence Hills, May 10, 1757.*
Hannah, and John H[azen. int.] Perry, Oct. 15, 1806.*
John, and Sarah B. Jaques, Dec. 3, 1818.*
Lydia C., and William Francis Follansbee of Newburyport,
int. Apr. 13, 1833.
Pamela, and John Bailey. Mar. 4, 1837.*
Prudence, and Samuel Hills, July 24, 1766.*

*Intention also recorded.

ENGLAND, Samuel, of Newburyport, and Hannah Poor, Dec.
    10, 1795. [1794. c. r. 2.]*
Stephen, of Biddeford, and Sarah Willet, Sept. 9, 1731.*
Stephen, and Abigail Pilsbury, Dec. 18, 1755.*
Stephen, and Elizabeth Bayley, Sept. 21, 1775.*
William, and Hannah Morss, Jan. 15, 1812.*
William, and Rhoda Morse, Oct. 31, 1815.*

ERWIN, Miriam, and W[illia]m Lakin, both of Groton, July
    29, 1731. c. r. 7.

ESTABROOK (see also Easterbrook, Easterbrooks), Sophia
    W., of Haverhill, and Nathaniel Morss, int. May 29,
    1847.

EUSTIS, Elizabeth, of Newburyport, and Jonathan Poor, int.
    Sept. 13, 1823.

EVANS (see also Evens, Evins), Benjamin, of Salisbury, and
    Jane Herriman, Aug. 19, 1762.*
Benjamin [G. int.], of Newburyport, and Sarah J. Stickney,
    July 11, 1833.*
David, and Letty Stockman, int. Nov. 16, 1844.
Enoch, and Bathsheba Door, Sept. 24, 1817.*
Ezekiel, of Salisbury, and Mary B. Johnson, int. Oct. 17, 1846.
Jane, and John Tillotson, May 24, 1655.
Julia Ann, and George W. Miles, Sept. 27, 1832.*
Mary E., and Dennis Small of Newburyport, int. Apr. 21,
    1844.
Mary Jane, of Newburyport, and John S. Crocker, int. Mar.
    14, 1849.
Sarah, d. James, of Berwick, Me., and Jonathan Roggers, jr.,
    s. Jonathan and Hannah, Nov. 25, 1747. c. r. 6.
Sarah A., of Newburyport, d. William and Sophronia, of New-
    buryport, and Joseph R. Thurlow, a. 24 y., mariner, s.
    Joseph L. and Ruth, Nov. 26, 1846.*
Thomas, and Prudence Stickney, Jan. 10, 1782.*

EVENS (see also Evans), David, and Mary Gardner of New-
    buryport, int. Jan. 5, 1805.
Mary, and Jona[than] Samson, Sept. 4, 1749.*

*Intention also recorded.

EVINS (see also Evans), Ann, and Samuel Palmer of Rowley, int. July 3, 1738.
Hannah, and Seth Flood, Nov. 22, 1744.*
William, and Lydia Chase, Jan. 30, 1715-16.*

EWELL, Thomas, of Ramsgate, Kent, Eng., now of Marblehead, and Mary Bartlett of Marblehead, July 5, 1735. c. R. 7.

EWENS, Sally, and Samuel Thurlow, jr., Sept. 15, 1818.*

FAGIN, James, and Elizabeth Emerson, Dec. 9, 1834.*

FAHERTY, Mary, of Newburyport, and Patrick Faherty, int. Dec. 5, 1846.
Michael, and Elisabeth Henry of Newburyport, int. Aug. 12, 1848.
Patrick, and Mary Faherty of Newburyport, int. Dec. 5, 1846.

FAIRBANKS, George A., and Abby Langley, both of Lowell, Oct. 5, 1841.
Lucretia, of Canton, and Joseph Longfellow, int. Mar. 27, 1841.

FAIRFIELD, Benjamin, of Wenham, and Martha Hale, Sept. 3, 1754.*

FAIRWEATHER, Jane, and Joseph Danforth, ———, 1844. [Nov. 23. int.]*
Susan F., and Giles A. Noyes, int. Oct. 6, 1849.

FALLS, William, of West Newbury, and Alice P. Clifford, Oct. 7, 1832.*

FANNIN (see also Fanning), Dorcas, and Thomas Brown of Hampton, Dec. 13, 1710.*

FANNING (see also Fannin), William, and Elizabeth Allen, Mar. 24, 1667-8.

*Intention also recorded.

FARLEY, Benjamin, of Bedford, and Joanna Page of Billerica, Jan. 19, 1732-3. c. r. 7.
Hannah, of Ipswich, and Abil Huse, jr., int. Apr. 21, 1738.

FARMER, Anthony [Capt. int.], and Eunice Rogers, Feb. 20, 1746-7.*

FARNAM (see also Farnum), Daniel, resident in Newbury, and Mrs. Sybil Anger of Cambridge, int. June 21, 1740.

FARNEM (see also Farnum), Jonathan, and Elizabeth Barker, both of Andover, Oct. 16, 1708.

FARNSWORTH, Phineas, and Zeubah Burt, both of Groton, Feb. 12, 1729-30. c. r. 7.

FARNUM (see also Farnam, Farnem), Anson W., and Susan Lunt of Newburyport, int. Nov. 18, 1826.
Samuel [Varnum. c. r. 1.], and Sarah Jackman, Apr. 24, 1806.*
Stephen, and Susan Smith, Nov. 26, 1829.*

FARRINGTON, Abigail, and Jacob Merrill, May 4, 1835.
Ann, and Gorham Hills, ——, 1836.
Ebenezer, and Ruth Bartlet, int. Oct. 8, 1803.
Lewis G., of West Newbury, a. 21 y., shoemaker, s. Ebenezer and Ruth, of West Newbury, and Sarah Jane Emery, a. 21 y., d. Thomas, May 1, 1845.
William B., and Martha Stevens, both of West Newbury, Dec. 11, 1839.

FARWELL, John, and Jane Lakin, both of Groton, July 10, 1735. c. r. 7.

FASGETT, Robert, and Sarah How, both of Marlboro, Dec. 1, 1730. c. r. 7.

FAVOR (see also Favour), Elizabeth, and Samuel Nowell, July 16, 1747. c. r. 2.*
Richard, and Mrs. Jemimah Rich, Sept. 24, 1741.*

*Intention also recorded.

FAVOUR (see also Favor, Feavor), Dorothy, and William McCullock, int. Aug. 25, 1759.

FEAVOR (see also Favour), John, and Hannah Brickit, June 28, 1716.*
John, and Dorothy Weed, int. Oct. 5, 1745.
Sarah, and Benjamin Procter, Sept. 25, 1740.
Willouby, and Jane Richardson, Dec. 30, 1725.*

FEILD, Mary, and John Woodman, July 15, 1656.

FELCH (see also Feltch), Chelmsford, of Lowell, and Elizabeth M. Mace, Dec 26, 1841.*
Daniel, of Newburyport, and Susan Lurvey, int. Mar. 4, 1809.
Irena, of Newburyport, and Joel Adams, July —, 1832.*
Joseph H., and Mary Haskell, Apr. 16, 1834.*
Mary M., and William L. Shuff, ——, 1840. [Apr. 18. int.]*
Nicholas, of Newburyport, and Melinda Bartlet, int. Sept. 28, 1839.
William A., and Lucy M. Page of Newburyport, Dec. 19, 1844.*

FELKER, Solomon P., and Elizabeth C. Nute of Newbury-port, int. July 7, 1849.

FELLOWS, Benjamin, and Lydia Akers, May 4, 1758.*
Betty, of Hopkinton, N. H., and Daniel Hale, 3d, int. May 14, 1785.
Eunice, of Ipswich, and John Wood, int. May 13, 1758.
Relief, of Rowley, and William Daniels, Dec. 6, 1817.*

FELT, Elisabeth, of Rowley, and Benjamin Poor, July 9, 1717.

FELTCH (see also Felch), Clara M., a. 32 y., b. Kensington, d. Jacob and Hannah, and John B. Nelson of Newbury-port, a. 30 y., merchant tailor, b. Newburyport, s. Samuel and Sarah, of Newburyport, July 18, 1849.*
Emeline M., and Hiram Janvrin, Dec. 10, 1843.*

FELTON, Cornelius, and Anna Morse, June 1, 1806.*
Hugh [a seafaring man. int.], and Lydia Brookins, Nov. 27, 1781.*
Lydia, and Benjamin Pirkins of Newburyport, int. Sept. 5, 1789.

*Intention also recorded.

FERGUSON (see also Forguson), James, and Dorcas Noyes, May 19, 1825.*

FESSENDEN (see also Fissenden), Moses, see Tupenden, Moses.

FEVERYEAR, Mary, of Boston, and Charles Peirce, jr., int. Mar. 24, 1759.

FIELDING, John, and Anna Longfellow, Mar. 6, 1777.*

FILBROOK (see also Philbrook), Zachariah, of Hampton, and Mary Lowle, July 9, 1715.*

FILLMORE, John, and Elizabeth B. McQuillen, int. Dec. 7, 1849.

FISH, Eleazer, and Nancy Mace, Dec. 26, 1819.*
Nathan, and Patience Shaddock, both of Groton, Oct. 2, 1730. c. r. 7.

FISHER, Reubin, Capt., and Mary Little, Oct. 13, 1811.*
William, of Boston, and Mary Sprague, Dec. 2, 1760.*

FISK, Daniel T., and Eliza P. Dutton of Boston, int. Oct. 13, 1849.
David, and Lidia Morse, Feb. 20, 1794. c. r. 2.*
Elizabeth, and Job Watson of Newburyport, Jan. 22, 1812.*
Jonathan, and Mary Chase, Nov. 17, 1823.*
Marcy, and Charles Chaplin of Rowley, Apr. 10, 1832.*
Samuel, of Boxford, and Judith Noyes, Feb. 1, 1737-8.*
Samuel, and Rebeckah Flood, Feb. 12, 1791.*
Samuel, jr., and Lydia E. Blake of Hampton, N. H., Nov. 20, 1834.*
Sarah, and Charls Stewart, both of Rowley, Dec. 31, 1741.
William, Dea. [Dr. int.], of Rowley, and Mrs. Bethiah Goodrich, at Rowley, Dec. 19, 1753.*
William, and Mary A. Floyd, Oct. 25, 1841.*

FISSENDEN (see also Fessenden), Hannah, Mrs., and John Sewall, Oct. 27, 1674.

*Intention also recorded.

FITCH, Eleazer T., Rev., of New Haven, Conn., a. 56 y., Professor of Divinity, s. Nathaniel and Mary, of New Haven, and Mary C. Lunt of Newburyport, a. 45 y., b. Newburyport, d. Micajah and Sarah G., of Newburyport, Jan. 6, 1848.

Jedediah, of Norwich, resident in Newbury, and Mrs. Abigel Coffin of Nantucket, now resident in Newbury, Sept 13, 1701.*
Zachariah, of Boston, and Abigaill Davinson, Aug. 14, 1718.*

FITS (see also Fitz), Isaac, of Ipswich, and Mary Noyes, June 5, 1723.*

FITTS (see also Fitz), Eleanor, of Salisbury, and David T. Tucker, int. Nov. 14, 1845.
Elisabeth, and John Danford, Nov. 11, 1735.*
Elisabeth, of Ipswich, and Nehemiah Haskill, int. Nov. 6, 1762.
Emily, of Salisbury, a. 19 y., d. William and Priscilla of Salisbury, and Francis Ordway, a. 21 y., ship carpenter, s. Nathaniel and Polly, Oct. 29, 1845.*
Richard, and Sara Ordway, Oct. 8, 1654.
William, of South Hampton, and Elizabeth Abbot of Newburyport, Apr. 2, 1826. c. r. 10.

FITZ (see also Fits, Fitts), Rebecca, and James Davis, Jan. 6, 1813.*

FITZGERALD, Jane [Fitsgard. int.], "an Irish woman," and Joseph Scott of England [of White Haven, Great Britain. int.], Dec. 28, 1736. c. r. 7.*

FLANDERS, Andrew S., and Olive Kimball of Dover, N. H., int. Nov. 1, 1845.
Anna, of Amesbury, and Samuel Marsh, int. Feb. —, 1789.
Betty, of Salisbury, and Nathaniel Davis, jr., int. May 8, 1766.
Charles, and Eliza Somerby of Newburyport, int. Sept. 14, 1822.
Daniel, and Anna Merrill, Dec. 16, 1784.*
Daniel, jr., and Sarah Bailey of Newburyport, int. Dec. 3, 1807.

*Intention also recorded.

FLANDERS, Eliphalet, and Betsy Bailey, int. Apr. 13, 1807.
Elisabeth, of Salisbury, and Benjamin Greenfeild, int. Apr. 2,
    1737.
Elisabeth, and John Flood, jr., Sept. 22, 1765.*
Ephraim W., and Ann E. Colby, Feb. 4, 1844.*
Hannah, and Moses Flood, int. Jan. 3, 1772.
Hannah, and Richard Davis of Newburyport, Apr. 27, 1777.*
Harriet M., and Albert G. Maxwell, int. Dec. 7, 1833.
Jesse E., and Lydia B. Perkins, int. June 23, 1832.
Joanna, of Salisbury, and Nathan Bartlet, at Salisbury, Mar.
    5, 1740-41.*
John, and Hannah Bayley, Mar. 31, 1777.*
John, of Newburyport, and Esther Park, int. Mar. 13, 1830.
Joseph F., and Sarah W. Flanders, Feb. 17, 1825.*
Joseph G., and Mary Ann Currier, Sept. 3, 1838.*
Joseph G., and Jane Clarke, int. May 1, 1847.
Lydia, and Charles Brown of Newburyport, int. Oct. 22, 1823.
Lydia [A. int.], a. 18 y., d. John and Ruth, and James Ander-
    son, a. 22 y., caulker, s. Robert and Jane, June 2, 1849.*
Mary, and Silas Rogers [jr. int.], Mar. 6, 1785.*
Mercy, and Moses Dustan, May 4, 1775.*
Nathan A., ship carpenter, and Harriet M. Gurney of New-
    buryport, d. Nathaniel, of Newburyport, Nov. 2, 1844.*
Richard, and Mercy Whiten [Whitney. int.], Aug. 19, 1740.*
Ruth, wid., and Lowell Crocker, widr., ship carpenter, s. Joseph
    Morse of Salisbury, Feb. 16, 1845.*
Sarah E. J., of Newburyport, and Alexander Whittier, int.
    May 31, 1845.
Sarah W., and Joseph F. Flanders, Feb. 17, 1825.*
Tabitha, and Samuel Merrill, jr., Jan. 1, 1746-7.*

FLOID (see also Floyd), Catharine, and Jonathan Cheney, jr.
    of Rowley, int. July 4, 1834.

FLOOD (see also Floyd), Aaron, and Betsey George of New-
    buryport, Mar. 17, 1799.*
Abigail, and Joseph Rogers, int. Jan. 26, 1805.
Anna, and Moses Godfrey [of Kingston. int.], Sept. 15, 1765.*
Benjamin, and Mrs. Elizebeth Morey, Apr. 22, 1741.*
Daniel, and Sarah Laboree, Jan. 5, 1735-6.*
Ebenezer, and Margaret Courser, int. Jan. 7, 1737-8.
Ebenezer, and Nancy Cary, int. Oct. 13, 1803.

*Intention also recorded.

FLOOD, Elis[abeth], and Eliphaz Dow of Salisbury, Sept. 2, 1729. C. R. 7.

Elisabeth, of Hampton, N. H., and Joshua Vickery, int. Jan. 3, 1772.

Enoch, and Mary Goodridge, May 31, 1753.*

Enoch, and wid. Grace Mackenly, Jan. 24, 1771.*

Enoch, jr., and Sarah Currier, int. Sept. 22, 1801.

Esther, and Ebenezer Barton, May 5, 1710.*

George, and Mary Pin, June 8, 1767.

Gideon, and Hannah Rogers, Oct. 18, 1775.

Hannah, and Gideon Rogers, int. Sept. 2, 1775.

Hannah, and Abner Perkins, Jan. 3, 1776.*

Hannah, and Allen Morison, Nov. 13, 1795.*

James, and Elizabeth Shoars, both of Boston, Sept. 10, 1730. C. R. 7.

James, and Sarah Rogers, Jan. 16, 1770.*

John, and Jane Philips, Oct. 14, 1736.*

John, and Abigail Labore, int. Jan. 23, 1741-2.

John [resident in Newbury. int.], and Jane Hooper [July 21, int.], 1753. C. R. 9.*

John, jr., and Elisabeth Flanders, Sept. 22, 1765.*

Joseph, and Martha Acres, int. Jan. 5, 1704-5.

Joseph, jr., and Bethiah Danford, July 1, 1756.*

Joseph, and Abigail Rogers, Jan. 20, 1777.*

Joseph, and Martha Goodridge, Nov. 7, 1799.*

Levi, and Elisabeth Smith, Nov. 24, 1802.*

Lydia, and William Burrill, int. Oct. 28, 1786.

Mark, and Katharine Labore, Nov. 11, 1741.*

Martha, and Israel Gardner, June 3, 1755.*

Moses, and Mary Harris of Dover, Nov. 20, 1738.*

Moses, and Hannah Flanders, int. Jan. 3, 1772.

Moses, and Jane Russell, Mar. 1, 1800.*

Nathan, and Eunice Davis, Jan. 10, 1770. ("He took the said Eunice naked & so would not be obliged to pay any of her former husband's debts.")*

Patty, and Aquilla [Augustus. int.] Mayew [of Rye. int.], June 17, 1802.*

Peter, and Lucy Snow, Jan. 12. 1803. [May 21, 1803. int.]*

Rebeckah, and Samuel Fisk, Feb. 12, 1791.*

Richard, and Mary Connaway of Ipswich, at Ipswich, Nov. 26, 1729.

Ruth, and Ebenezer Sergeant, Jan. 1, 1769.*

*Intention also recorded.

FLOOD, Sarah, and Richard Urian of Contocook, Nov. 22, 1742.*

Sarah, and Ezekiel Rogers, Mar. —, 1780.*

Sarah, and James Day, Jan. 10, 1797.*

Sarah Evens, and William Burrill, Feb. 16, 1789.*

Seth, and Hannah Evins, Nov. 22, 1744.*

Stevens, and Annah Toby, July 21, 1772.*

FLORY (see also Flowry), Louisa Mary, of Newburyport, and Moody Lunt, Jan. 27, 1833.

FLOUD (see also Floyd), Phillip, and Sarah Poor, Mar. 1, 1721-22.*

FLOWRY (see also Flory), Lewis H., of Boston, and Fanny C. Goodwin, int. Apr. 26, 1845.

FLOYD (see also Floid, Flood, Floud, Flud), Aaron, and Hannah Stickney, Dec. 1, 1834.*

Abigail, and Samuel Holmes of Rowley, int. Sept. 9, 1831.

Amos, and Hannah Battis, July 5, 1809.*

Ann, and Silas D. Floyd, int. Oct. 9, 1847.

Benja[min] P., and Sarah P. Milton, Nov. 13, 1834.*

Ebenezer, jr., and Lois Pulsifer of Rowley, Jan. 7, 1833.*

Eliza W., and Asa Whitehouse, June —, 1840.*

Enoch, jr., and Sarah E. Hervey of Gloucester, int. Dec. 4, 1832.

Enos, and Polly Knight, Jan. 19, 1808.*

Eunice, and Robert Robinson of Boston, int. Aug. 8, 1846.

Hannah, and [Capt. int.] Mark Allen of Gloucester, Dec. 13, 1807.*

Hannah, Mrs., and Benjamin Jackman, Feb. 24, 1812.*

Hannah, and Caleb Woodwell, Dec. —, 1834.*

Harriet M., a. 23 y., d. John and Abigail, and Emanuel J. Bennett of New York, a. 23 y., cigar maker, b. New York City, s. John and Mary, of New York, Apr. 24, 1848.*

Huldah, and Gideon Rogers, jr., Aug. 2, 1815.*

Jane, and William Ilsley, Sept. 14, 1819.*

Joanna, and Benjamin Pettingell, jr., Sept. 11, 1824.*

John, and Elisabeth Harris of Newburyport, int. May 24, 1806.

John, jr., and Eliza B. Chace, int. Mar. 19. 1826.

John, jr., and Susan F. Towle of Newburyport, Jan. 7, 1829.*

Joseph, and Eunice Gould of West Newbury, int. May 19, 1849.

*Intention also recorded.

FLOYD, Lucy, and William Goodridge, Dec. 26, 1822.*
Lydia, and Giles Woodman, Jan. 25, 1827.*
Martha Ann, and Andrew M. Quimby of Rowley, Nov. 29, 1832.*
Mary A., and William Fisk, Oct. 25, 1841.*
Martha J., a. 16 y., d. Michael and Betsey, and Luther P. Gould, a. 23 y., shoemaker, s. John and Ruth, Aug. 3, 1845.*
Oliver, and Mrs. Jane White, May 27, 1810.*
Paul, and Sarah Willet of Newburyport, Sept. 11, 1811.*
Paul [jr. of Rowley. int.], shoemaker, s. Paul, and Adaline S. Plumer, a. 21 y., d. Silas, July 28, 1844.*
Paul, widr., a. 59 y., farmer, d. John and Polly [Elizabeth. dup.], and Sarah Norton, a. 48 y., d. Amos and Sarah, Jan. 21, 1845.*
Polly, and Robert Floyd, int. June 3, 1844.
Robert, and Sally Woodwell, Oct. 21, 1819.*
Robert, and Polly Floyd, int. June 3, 1844.
Sally, of Ipswich, and Reuben Jackman, int. Feb. 6, 1824.
Sarah, and Jonathan York, Nov. 15, 1807.*
Silas, and Ann Thurlo, Dec. 15, 1812.*
Silas D., and Ann Floyd, int. Oct. 9, 1847.

FLUD (see also Floyd), Anne, and Samuel Johnson of Andover, Nov. 23, 1727.*
John, and Lydia Kenna, Dec. 30, 1714.*

FOGG, Mary, and George Hardy, Nov. 24, 1686. CT. R.

FOLANSBE (see also Follansbee), Betsey, and Moses Emery, Sept. 24, 1803.*
James, Lt., and Sarah Plumer, Oct. —, 1789.*
John, and Jane Dresser, June —, 1792.*
Nehemiah, and Dorothy Hills. Dec. 16. 1784.*
Phebe, of Newburyport, and Stephen Coffin Dutton, int. Dec. 3, 1797.
Polly, and Daniel Pilsbury, int. Nov. 2, 1805.
Samuel, and Lydia Noyes, Nov. 26, 1800.*
Susanna, and David Bartlet [jr. C. R. 2.], Sept. 10, 1785.*

FOLANSBEE (see also Follansbee). Abial Pearson, of New Milford, and Lydia Pearson. int. Sept. 14, 1805.

*Intention also recorded.

FOLANSBEE, Jane, and Edward Woodman of Washington, int. June 8, 1804.
Lucy [H. int.], and Benjamin Brown, Oct. 25, 1806.*

FOLESOME (see also Folsom), Mary, of Exeter, and Daniel Morison, int. Mar. 27, 1707.

FOLINSBY (see also Follansbee), Thomas, jr., and Hannah March, Jan. 5, 1715-16.*

FOLLANSBE (see also Follansbee), Francis, and Hannah Cambel, Nov. 20, 1777.*
John, and Abigail Woodman, Dec. 9, 1779.*
Joshua, of Salisbury, and Mary Sawyer, Sept. 13, 1779.*
Moses, jr., of Weare, N. H., and Sarah Clark, Oct. 15, 1778.*

FOLLANSBEE (see also Folansbe, Folansbee, Folinsby, Follansbe, Follensbe, Follensby, Follingsby, Follinsbe, Follinsbee, Follinsbey, Follinsby), Clarissa, and David Buswell, Feb. 28, 1809.*
Hazen L., of Newburyport, a. 23 y., trader, b. Newburyport, s. Nathan and Catherine, and Rebecca B. Bartlett of Newburyport, a. 25 y., b. Newburyport, d. Samuel and Rebecca, of Newburyport, July 3, 1846.
John, and Judith Bailey, int. Nov. 11, 1809.
Lydia G., a. 29 y., b. Georgetown, d. Moses and Ruth, and James Cogswell of Manchester, a. 27 y., blacksmith, b. Manchester, s. James and Mary, Oct. 21, 1847.
Moses, and Priscilla Heath, June 14, 1756.
Nehemiah, and Priscilla Chase, June 2, 1808.*
Newman, and Mary Chase, Sept. 23, 1814.*
Polly, of Newburyport, and Henry Cromwell Jaques, int. May 9, 1807.
Sally, of Andover, and Moody Morse, Sept. 9, 1806.*
William, and Sarah Tukesbury, Aug. 17, 1806.*
William Francis, of Newburyport, and Lydia C. England, int. Apr. 13, 1833.

FOLLENSBE (see also Follansbee), Nabby, and Capt. John Carlton, Jan. 27, 1791. c. r. 2.
Sarah, and James Carr, Oct. 5, 1749.*

*Intention also recorded

FOLLENSBY (see also Follansbee), Francis, and Mary Dean of Ipswich, int. Sept. 3, 1748.
Hannah, and Eliphalet Rawlings of Bradford, Jan. 23, 1755.*
Moody, and Sarah Smith, Feb. 7, 1750.*
Sarah, and Ebenezer Knap, Aug. 9, 1750.*

FOLLET, Martha, and Capt. Othniel Homans, both of Boston, May 29, 1730. c. r. 7.

FOLLINGSBY (see also Follansbee), Thomas, and Mary Bancroft of Reading, at Reading, Feb. 18, 1734-5.*

FOLLINSBE (see also Follansbee), Ann, and Thomas Noyes, 3d, June 30, 1743.*
Hannah, and William Sawyer, jr., Apr. 2, 1735.*
Judeth, and Daniel Spaford of Rowley, Nov. 17, 1742.*
William, and Mehitable March, Oct. 2, 1733.*

FOLLINSBEE (see also Follansbee), Rachel, and Abial Goodridge, Apr. 23, 1776.*

FOLLINSBEY (see also Follansbee), John, and Susanna Moers, Nov. 20, 1760.*

FOLLINSBY (see also Follansbee), Abigail, and Richard Smith, Oct. 25, 1753.*
Anne, and Moses Chase, Nov. 10, 1684.
Francis, and Judeth Moodey, Dec. 15, 1719.*
Francis, and Mrs. Sarah Ripp, Oct. 27, 1741.*
Mary, and Robert Pike of Salisbury, Dec. 1, 1686. ct. r.
Mary, and Philip Chase, Apr. 17, 1712.*
Rebecca, and Thomas Chase, Nov. 22, 1677.
Thomas, sr., and Mrs. Jane Mosemore of Boston, int. Apr. 3, 1713.

FOLSOM (see also Folesome, Foulsom), David, of Newmarket, N. H., and Dorothy Johnson, int. Feb. 2, 1771.

FOOT, Dorothy, and Ebenezer Chase, May 18, 1741.*
Elisabeth, and Philip Read, Dec. 27, 1787.*
Elizabeth, and John Akerman, jr. of Newburyport, int. July 21, 1821.

FOOT, Enoch, of Newburyport, and Abigail Hale, Oct. 6, 1774.*

Mary, and Nathan Somerby of Newburyport, Aug. 1, 1775.*

Salley, and Joseph Lunt Colby, July 2, 1796.*

Thankful, of Newburyport, and Henry Pierce, int. Oct. 3, 1818.

William L., of Falmouth, and Judith Pearson, June 10, 1819.*

FOOTMAN, Mark W., of Somersworth, N. H., a. 28 y., manufacturer, s. Francis, of Durham, N. H., and Maria H. Nason, a. 27 y., d. Levi, Jan. 1, 1845.*

FORBES, Eli, Rev., of Gloucester, and Mrs. Sarah Parsons, Sept. 13, 1781.*

FORD, Christopher, resident in Newbury, and Elisabeth Robertson, July 2, 1780.*

Elisabeth, and Thomas Dutton, Nov. 14, 1793.*

Rebecca, and Rice Edwards [of Wenham. int.], Mar. 22, 1710.*

Sarah, of Newburyport, and Johnson Brookins, int. Nov. 24, 1770.

FOREMAN, Amos B., and Mary R. Porter of Newburyport, Mar. 4, 1833.

FORGUSON (see also Ferguson), Arthur, and Elisabeth Tilton, Feb. 2, 1762.*

FORSTER (see also Foster), Isaac, and Judith Hills, July 9, 1752.*

FOSDICK, Joanna, and Jonathan Blake, Jan. 16, 1727-8.*

Johannah, and Nathaniel Willit, Jan. 25, 1736-7. c. r. 7.*

Jonathan, and Mrs. Catharine Philips, both of Charlestown, May 9, 1729. c. r. 7.

Mary, of Charlestown, and [Capt. int.] George Borrow [Burroughs. int.], at Charlestown, Aug. 12, 1789.*

FOSS, Benjamin Randall, and Elizabeth Duggins, Aug. 24, 1813.*

Clark, and Eunice Wells Eaton of Northampton, N. H., int. Aug. 23, 1818.

*Intention also recorded.

Foss, Edwin, and Hannah Peirce, both of Rowley, Aug. 3, 1819. c. r. 5.

Geo[rge] E., of Ipswich, and Louisa Wood, Jan. 7, 1844.*

Hannah J., and Jacob Souter, int. Jan. 2, 1836.

John, and Esther Cheney, both of Rowley, Feb. 8, 1814. c. r. 5.

Lois, Mrs., and Obadiah Hills, both of Rowley, Nov. 31, 1814. c. r. 5.

Sarah, and Phillip Quimbe, Dec. 13, 1797.*

Titus, and Flora Fuller, int. Nov. 16, 1783.

FOSSAT, Thomas, and Ruth Jackson, July 3, 1791. c. r. 1.*

FOSTER (see also Forster), Abigail, and Peter Stanwood, int. Nov. 12, 1803.

Anna, of Ipswich, and Robert Mitchil, int. June 7, 1746.

Elisabeth, of Ipswich [of Chebacco. int.], and Nathan Page, at Chebacco parish, Ipswich, Apr. 19, 1758.*

Elisabeth, and Olliver Goodridge, int. June 14, 1788.

Elisabeth, of Boxford, and Moses Woodman, at Boxford, Nov. 29, 1798.*

Elizabeth, Mrs., of Charlestown, and Capt. Timothy McDaniel, of Co. Wicklow, Ireland, now of Boston, Aug. 11, 1732. c. r. 7.

Ephraim, of Andover, and Abigail Poor, Jan. 17, 1715-16.*

Hannah, and Ebenezer Virgin, both of Pennacook, Feb. 9, 1731-2. c. r. 7.

Isaac, and Lois Low, Apr. 24, 1755.*

Isaac, and Jane Longfellow of Rowley, int. Apr. 23, 1796.

Jesse, of Portsmouth, N. H., and Eliza Toppan, Oct. 1, 1818.*

John, of Charlestown, and Sarah Richardson, at Charlestown, May 31, 1692.

John, of Canterbury, and Sarah Kimbal, Aug. 25, 1800.*

Judith, and Francis Davis of Amesbury, int. Aug. 31, 1780.

Lois, of West Newbury, and Benjamin Pearson, int. Dec. 2, 1820.

Mary, of Rowley, and Joseph Plumer, at Rowley, Dec. 15, 1774.*

Mary, and William Plumer, Dec. 20, 1791. c. r. 2.*

Mary, and Nicolas Durgin, int. Nov. 11, 1803.

· *Intention also recorded.

FOSTER, Mary, of Boxford, and Charles Harrison Kimball, int. May 3, 1817.

Mehetable [of Ipswich. int.], and Noah J[ohnson. int.] Noyes [Sept. 26, int.], 1807. C. R. 1.*

Mercy, of Ipswich, and Isaac Plummer, int. Aug. 24, 1785.

Nathaniel, and Judeth Poor, Jan. 15, 1734-5.*

Nathaniel, jr., and Bridget Homan of Mountsweage, int. Mar. 4, 1758.

Nath[anie]ll, and Anna Mireck, Jan. 1, 1756.*

Rachel, and William Sargent, Mar. 24, 1780.*

FOULSOM (see also Folsom), Abraham, of Exeter, and Anne Chase, Oct. 27, 1703.*

Mary, and Georg March, June 12, 1672.

FOWLE, Stephen H., and Nancy Cheever of Newburyport, int. Jan. 24, 1829.

FOWLER, Abigail, and Capt. William Milberry of Newburyport, Oct. 14, 1792.*

Anna, and Reubin Greeley, int. Jan. 28, 1781.

Anne, and Samuel Jackman of Boscawen, N. H., int. Aug. 5, 1772.

Benjamin, of Ipswich, and Mary Thorla, May 26, 1731.*

Elisabeth, and Elexander Campbel, Sept. 21, 1786.*

Elizabeth, and Abraham Somerby, int. Nov. 1, 1835.

Hannah, and John Eaton, both of Salisbury, Jan. 13, 1734-5. C. R. 7.

Hannah, of Salisbury, and Joseph Lunt Colby, int. July 26, 1812.

Hannah, and Moses Stevens of Liberty, Me., July 17, 1836.*

Henrietta M., of Salisbury, and Benjamin Johnson, Mar. 10, 1844.*

Joseph, of Ipswich, and Sarah Bartlet, Dec. —, 1707.*

Lemuel, and Mary Boulter of Kensington, May 10, 1757.*

Martha, of Ipswich, and John Harris, int. Sept. 15, 1744.

Mary, of Ipswich, and Elezer Newhall, int. July 21, 1738.

Mary S., of Salisbury, and Adariel H. Hodgdon, int. July 6, 1833.

Molly, and Stanton Prentice of Newburyport. Sept. 24, 1784.*

Moses, and Mary Ann Dean, Oct. 23, 1835.*

Nancy B., and Alfred Currier, int. July 18, 1840.

*Intention also recorded.

Fowler, Olive, and Joseph Coffin, jr., Feb. 13, 1749-50.*
Samuel, and Mrs. Abigail Hogskins, July 1, 1742.*
Sarah, and John Hale, jr., May 1, 1750.*
Ursula, and Edwin Currier of Newburyport, Nov. 16, 1843.*

FOX, Charles J., of Newburyport, and Sybil Carkin, Dec. 3, 1835.*
Charles J., and Mary Sumner of Newburyport, int. Jan. 2, 1841.
Stephen R., of Newburyport, shoemaker, and Hester Scales of Concord, N. H., Dec. 25, 1844.
Stephen Russell, and Miriam Jackman, Feb. 17, 1811.*
William R., and Mary E. Carkin, both of Newburyport, June 20, 1833.

FRANCIS, Abigail, and David Mansfield, jr., July 10, 1817.*
John, of Medford, and [wid. c. r. 2.] Dorothy Coffin, Apr. 22, 1731.*
John, and Theodosia Lord, residents in Newbury, int. May 16, 1807.
John, and Theodosia Lord, Mar. 11, 1809.
Mary Ann, a. 29 y., d. John and Dorcas, and Castor Bean of Haverhill, a. 32 y., barber, s. James and Lydia, of Haverhill, May 18, 1845.
Thomas, and Rebekah Atkins, Nov. 3, 1776.*

FRANKLIN (see also Franklyn), Lydia, and James Scott, chandler, both of Boston, Sept. 8, 1730. c. r. 7.

FRANKLYN (see also Franklin), Mary, and Marmaduke Holmes, both of Boston, Apr. 23, 1731. c. r. 7.

FRAZER (see also Frieshur), Abigail, and Jacob Abbot, Jan. 7, 1716.
Anna, and David Ilsley of Newburyport, at Rowley, Apr. 4, 1789.*
Collin, and Anna Stuard, Nov. 10, 1685.
Elizabeth, and Joseph Somerby, jr. of Newburyport, June 10, 1779.*
Gershum, and Hannah Thirston, Jan. 9, 1718-9.*
Hannah, and Sam[ue]ll Goodridge, June 30, 1710.*

*Intention also recorded.

FRAZER, Hannah, and Samuel [Lemuel. int.] Spofford of Rowley, at Rowley, Apr. 9, 1785.*

John, and Elizabeth Little of Rowley, at Rowley, July 26,
1743.*

John, and Hepsebah Dow of Rowley, at Rowley, June 6,
1754.*

FREEMAN, Peter, and Charlotte Gardner, May 16, 1804.*

FREES (see also Freeze), George, and Mary Atkinson, Apr.
19, 1737.*

FREEZ (see also Freeze), Dorothy, Mrs., and Faune Clements, Mar. 7, 1718.*

FREEZE (see also Frees, Freez), Hannah, and Tho[ma]s
Haskins, Feb. 14, 1716-17. C. R. 7.

Jacob, and Elisabeth Adams, Dec. 17, 1761.*

James, and Mary Merrill [d. Daniel, deceased. int.], June 2,
1697.*

Mary, and Jonathan Moers of Newburyport, int. Oct. 18,
1766.

FRENCH, Betty, of Tewksbury, and James Merrill, int. Oct.
29, 1774.

Charles, of Boston, and Lucy Balch, Oct. —, 1821.*

Ether, and John Swett [father of Samuel. int.], Jan. 12,
1713-14.*

Hester [Esther. int.], and Daniel Pettingale, Mar. 26, 1708.*

Jane, and Jonathan Pettingell, int. Nov. 19, 1774.

Johanna, and Matthew Pettengall, int. Oct. 23, 1703.

John, and Sarah Noyes, Jan. 6, 1708.*

John, and Rebeccah Akers, Jan. 31, 1739-40.*

John, of Atkinson, and Salley Colby, int. July 21, 1800.

Julia, of Salisbury, and Micah Lewis, int. Oct. 2, 1839.

Lucy, and Benj[ami]n Woodwell, May 19, 1801.*

Lucy, Mrs., and Col. Ebenezer Hale, Sept. 28, 1835.*

Marshall, of Reading, and Hannah T. Colman, Apr. 24,
1814.*

Mary, of Salisbury, and James Jackman, 3d, at Salisbury, Dec.
8, 1721.

Mary, and Isaiah Ilsley, int. Nov. 28, 1783.

*Intention also recorded.

FRENCH, Nathaniel, and Jane Blane, Nov. 1, 1750.*
Phebe, and Daniel Somerby, jr. of Newburyport, int. Aug. 23, 1777.
Phillippa, and Josiah Pettingell, int. Oct. 22, 1774.
Phillippe [of Boston. int.], and Jonathan Call, at Boston, June 18, 1745.*
Reuben, and Tirzah Ring, Jan. 31, 1754. C. R. 8.
Richard, and Abigail Collins of Salisbury, int. Feb. 12, 1798.
Sarah [Mrs. dup.], and [Dea. dup.] Joseph Bradly of Haverhill, Sept. 20, 1748.*
Simon, of Salisbury, and Mrs. Abigail Noyes, May 8, 1707.*
William, and Olive Merrill of Londonderry, N. H., int. Apr. 2, 1808.

FRIEND, Henry, and Elisabeth Harris of Ipswich, int. Nov. 22, 1758.

FRIER (see also Fryer), Abigail, Mrs., of Berwick, and Dea. William Moodey, int. Dec. 11, 1714.

FRIESHUR (see also Frazer), John, and Susanna Wright [of Ipswich. int.], June 28, 1753.*

FRINK, Hannah, Mrs., and Daniel Weed, Feb. 15, 1742-3.*

FRISBIE, Levi, Rev., of Ipswich, and Mehitable Hale, June 1, 1780.*

FROST, Abigail, and Thomas Peirce, Feb. 8, 1732-3.*
Elisabeth, of Kittery, and Daniel Peirce, May 15, 1725.*
Elizabeth, and Moses May, both of Ipswich, July 3, 1734. C. R. 7.
Hannah, of Marblehead, and Charles Chase, int. Nov. 23, 1828.
Mehittable, Mrs. [d. Charles, of Kittery. int.], and Thomas Peirce, Jan. 5, 1697-8.*
Samuel, Capt., and Mary White, both of Boston, Aug. 22, 1727. C. R. 7.
Sarah M., of Newburyport, a. 21 y., b. Newburyport, d. Dependance and Jemima L., and William C. Merrill, widr., of Newburyport, a. 25 y., shipwright, b. Newburyport, s. Jacob and Dorothy S., June 21, 1847.

*Intention also recorded.

FROTHINGHAM, Dorothy, of Boston, and Capt. John
Quircke of Bristol, Eng., at Hampton, Feb. 3, 1724-5.
C. R. 7.

FRYE, Nathan, and Sarah Bridges, both of Andover, July 6,
1715.

FRYER (see also Frier), Nathaniel, and Mrs. Dorothy Woodbridg, Oct. 29, 1679.

FUDGE, James, and Mrs. Mary Allgreen, Nov. 9, 1816.*
Thomas, and Elizabeth Carey, int. Sept. 7, 1811.

FULLER, Edward, of Leominster, and Anna Thurston, Feb.
2, 1786.*
Flora, and Titus Foss, int. Nov. 16, 1783.
John P., and Sarah Jane Lunt, May 8, 1828.*
Sally O., of Danvers, and David R. Howard, int. Apr. 7, 1835.

FUMEY, John, of Ross, England, merchant, and Hannah Gibbons of Marblehead, Aug. 7, 1729. C. R. 7.

FURLONG, Lawrence, and Ruth Whitmore, Jan. 27, 1763.
C. R. 8.

FURNALD, Esther S., and Josiah Chase, jr., Feb. 5, 1817.*
William, of Kittery, and Mary Pearce of Boston, Aug. 22,
1734. C. R. 7.   . . . .

FURNESS, Ann, and John Clerk, both of Salem, May 29,
1734. C. R. 7.

FYFEILD, John, and Ann Lunt, Nov. 14, 1734 *

GAFFELL, Mary, and William Sutton, Oct. 27, 1679.

GAGE, Benjamin, and Lydia Mitchel, Dec. 31, 1764.*
Elisabeth, and Stephen Tilton, Jan. 20, 1761.*
Jonathan, and Martha Moodey, Apr. 27, 1730.*
Julia, of Bradford, and Uriah Bailey, int. Oct. 24, 1818.
Mary, of Bradford, and Benjamin Thirston, June 24, 1718.*

*Intention also recorded.

GAGE, Prudence, and Aaron Carlton, both of Bradford, Apr. 21, 1735. c. r. 7.
Sarah, and Samuel Barker, both of Andover, Oct. 16, 1708.
Sarah, and Richard Hale, jr., Nov. 30, 1749.*
Susanna, of Bradford, and Timothy Stevens, Oct. 11, 1743.*
Thomas, and Polly Dole, Oct. 18, 1799. c. r. 5.

GAINS, Judeth, of Ipswich, and Eliphalet Noyes, int. Oct. 3, 1746.
Mary, and Thomas Hibbut, at Gloucester, Sept. 25, 1764.

GALE (see also Gales), Daniel, of Salem, and Rebekah Swett, int. Dec. 9, 1700.
Henry, of Kingston, and Molly Atkinson, Aug. 10, 1795.*
Jacob, and Susannah Collins, Oct. 20, 1735.*
Lydia, of Salem, and Thomas Wells, at Salem, Oct. 12, 1704.*
Sarah, of Salem, and Daniel Grant, int. Apr. 14, 1738.

GALES (see also Gale), Bathsheba, and Joseph Clark, both of Hingham, July 20, 1731. c. r. 7.

GALLISHAN, Caroline J., of Newburyport, and Benjamin Currier, int. Sept. 5, 1835.
George K. W., of Andover, and Elizabeth E. Atkinson, Apr. 3, 1831.*

GALPIN (see also Galpine), Elizabeth, and George Tilley, sailor, both of Boston, June 17, 1727. c. r. 7.

GALPINE (see also Galpin), Katharine, and James Hodges, sailor, both of Boston, June 17, 1727. c. r. 7.

GARDINER (see also Gardner), Emerson, and Mary Brown, both of West Newbury, May 11, 1826.

GARDNER (see also Gardiner), Charlotte, and Peter Freeman, May 16, 1804.*
Henry, of Charlestown, and Sarah Noyes, Jan. 27, 1731-2.*
Israel, and Martha Flood, June 3, 1755.*
Joseph, of Charlestown, and Hannah Nelson, July 24, 1706.
Mary, of Newburyport, and David Evens. int. Jan. 5, 1805.
Mirriam, and Samuel Davis of Amesbury, Jan. 23, 1749-50.*

*Intention also recorded.

GARDNER, Norman, and Elisabeth Golding [Golden. int.], Nov. 5, 1761.*
Samuel, and Anne Myrick, Nov. 23, 1761.*

GAREN, Mary, of Newburyport, and Timothy Livingston, int. Aug. 22, 1805.

GARLAND, Elizabeth A., of Newburyport, and John A. Merrill, int. May 1, 1847.
Jacob, and Rebecca Sears, Jan. 17, 1681.
Sarah G., of Newburyport, and Benjamin H. Poor, int. Dec. 22, 1839.

GARNER, Susannah, wid., and Dea. John Worth, Oct. 25, 1742.*

GATCHELL (see also Getchell), Dorcas, of Salisbury, and Ebenezer Ayers, at Salisbury, Oct. 5, 1710.*

GAVET, Katherine, and Job Pilsbury, Apr. 5, 1677. [Apr. 8. CT. R.]

GAWN, John, and Mary Connor Colby, int. July 28, 1804.
John [Gavin. c. R. 10.], of Lowell, and Elvira Wade, Mar. 24, 1828.*

GAY, Lewis, and Mary March, both of Newburyport, Mar. 28, 1771.

GEE, Sarah, and Tho[ma]s Bennet, both of Boston, Oct. 12, 1734. c. R. 7.

GEORGE, Alice, of Haverhill, and Eliphalet Blaisdel, int. Oct. 23, 1812.
Amos P., and Alona C. Stanford, both of West Newbury, May 16, 1843.
Anne, of Haverhill, and James Pike, at Haverhill, Mar. 12, 1746-7.*
Betsey, of Newburyport, and Aaron Flood. Mar. 17, 1799.*
Betsey H., of Bradford, and Philip C. Stevens, int. Aug. 5, 1849.

*Intention also recorded.

GEORGE, Francis, and Mrs. Mary Hull, Nov. 14, 1745.*

Francis, and Mary Ambrose of Salisbury, int. Nov. 9, 1754.

George J., of Newburyport, and Jane S. Janvrin, int. Sept. 22, 1841.

Jacob Rice, and Polly Philips Chamberlin, both of Newburyport, June 15, 1808. C. R. 10.

James, and Tabitha Grenough, Dec. 24, 1793.*

Jemima, and Batt Moulton, both of Amesbury, May 29, 1730. C. R. 7.

John, and Ann Cresey [Keizer. int.], Feb. 15, 1761.*

John [Jonathan. int.], and Rachel Cooper, Nov. 24, 1795. [Dec. C. R. 2.]*

Lydia, and Henry M. Elliott of Salisbury, int. Mar. 31, 1841.

Maria, of Haverhill, and Nathaniel Morse, int. Sept. 11, 1842.

Maria L., of Newburyport, and Ebenezer Smith, Feb. 20, 1839.*

Martha, and James Hayes, Apr. 24, 1757.*

Mary Elizabeth, of Newburyport, and Charles Emery, int. Jan. 5, 1828.

Moses, and Mrs. Susanna Downing, Oct. 27, 1752.

Moses, of Peeling, N. H., and Sarah Danforth, Feb. 26, 1838.*

Nicolas, and Mary Jillings, int. May 18, 1755.

Phineas, and Susanna Thurlow, Mar. 19, 1823.*

Sarah, and Lazarus [M. int.] Goldsmith of Boston, ———, 1831. [June 11. int.]*

Sarah T., and Jeremiah S. Yale of Newburyport, int. Oct. 31, 1846.

William, and Susanna Pettengill, Dec. 22, 1803.*

W[illia]m H., and Harriet F. Johnson of Newburyport, June 27, 1832.

GERISH (see also Gerrish), Elisabeth, and Cutting Noyes, jr., Dec. 22, 1709.*

Jane, and Samuell Swett, Oct. 18, 1705.*

Keturah M., and Asa Merrill of Newburyport, int. July 20, 1833.

Sarah, and Isaac Pierson, Nov. 28, 1751. C. R. 2.*

GERNEY (see also Gurney), Elizabeth, of New York, a. 19 y., and Edward Tittle of Jamaica, a. 22 y., in New Hampshire, Sept. 21, 1727. C. R. 7.

*Intention also recorded.

GERRISH (see also Gerish), Abigail, Mrs., and William Stapleton [now resident in Newbury. int.], May 19, 1756.*
Ann M., and Philip H. Blumpey of Newburyport, int. Apr. 18, 1846.
Anna, and [Capt., 3. int.], Benjamin Junt. Junt 11, 1751.*
Anna, and Thomas Kelly, int. May 6, 1786.
Catherine, and Henry Adams, Mar. 2, 1768.*
Elisabeth, and Stephen March of Portsmouth, N. H., June 14, 1753.*
Elizabeth, and Lt. Steven Greenleaft, Oct. 23, 1676.
Eliza[beth], of Salem, and John Peirce, at Salem, June 4, 1730.
Elizabeth, and Samuel Moodey [3d. int.], Aug. 12, 1739.*
Elizabeth, and Capt. Benjamin Pierce of Newburyport, Dec. 27, 1792.*
Enoch, and Joanna Bennet of Newburyport, int. Oct. 15, 1780.
Enoch, and Keturah McHard Greenleaf of Newburyport, Apr. 30, 1811.*
Isabella H., and Daniel Silloway of Newburyport, int. Feb. 24, 1844.
Jane, and John Lunt, jr., Aug. 14, 1733.*
Jane, Mrs., and Rev. Phinehas Stevens of Contocook, Nov. 24, 1741.*
Jane, and Pearson Brown of Newburyport, int. Apr. 27, 1793.
Jane, and Foster Smith of Newburyport, Jan. 27, 1816.*
Johana, and Joshua Peirce, Jan. 20, 1704.*
John, and Mary Dole, Dec. 14, 1723.*
John, and Judith Coker, Feb. 14, 1727-8.*
Joseph, and Mrs. Mary Little, int. Feb. 26, 1703-4.
Joseph, and Mrs. Katharine Brown of Reading, at Reading, Feb. 16, 1731-2.
Joseph [3d. int.], and Mehitable Currier of Amesbury, at Amesbury, Jan. 1, 1761.*
Joseph, of Boscawen, N. H., and Mary Bartlet, int. Sept. 11, 1779.
Joseph, and Elizabeth Kent, int. Sept. 8, 1827.
Judith, and Daniel Thirston of Bradford, Sept. 10, 1761.*
Lois, and Edward Currier of Newburyport, int. Aug. 3, 1805.
Mary, Mrs., and John Dole, Oct. 23, 1676.
Mary, Mrs., and Capt. Anthony Gwyn of Bristol, Great Britain, Oct. 26, 1738.*

*Intention also recorded.

GERRISH, Mary, and Stephen Kent, Oct. 8, 1761.*

Mary, and William Currier, 5th of Newburyport, int. Oct. 2, 1802.

Mary Ann, and Jesse A. Thurlow, Sept. 12, 1836.*

Mary P., and Philip K. Hills of Newburyport, int. Aug. 15, 1846.

Mayo, and Betsy Rolf [Lunt. c. R. 2.], July 14, 1792.*

Mayo, and Hannah Thurlo, Oct. 9, 1814.*

Moses, and Mrs. Jane Sewall, Sept. 24, 1677.

Moses, and Mary Noyes, Nov. 12, 1714.*

Moses, and Elisabeth Peirce, Sept. 27, 1726.*

Moses, jr., and Mary Moodey, Apr. 18, 1728.*

Nathaniel, and Margaret Campbell of Newburyport, int. Jan. 1, 1803.

Paul, and Keturah Morse of Newburyport, int. Apr. 20, 1799.

Rebecca, and Robert Stanwood of Newburyport, June 28, 1810.*

Rebeckah, and Joshua March, jr., Jan. 1, 1752.*

Rhody, and William Condry of Newburyport, May 28, 1786.*

Sally, and Samuel Nason of Newburyport, Oct. 4, 1796.

Sally, of Salisbury, and Sam[ue]l Stocker, May 30, 1799.*

Samuel, and Ann Toppan, Oct. 30, 1735.*

Samuel, Maj., and Mrs. Sarah Johnson, May 19, 1761.*

Sarah, and Benjamen Woodbridge, Dec. 6, 1706.

Sarah, Mrs., and William Davenport, Apr. 3, 1740.*

Sarah, and Amos Stickney of Newburyport, int. Feb. 19, 1779.

Stephen [of Canterbury. int.], and Martha Chase, July 21, 1738.*

Stephen, of Contocook, and Joannah Hale, July 15, 1741.*

Stephen, and Ruth Page of Rowley, int. Nov. 21, 1772.

Thomasin, and Joseph Stevens, jr., Sept. 3, 1740.*

William, and Joanna Olliver, wid. John, Apr. 17, 16[45. T. C.].

William, and Elisabeth Mayo, Mar. 20, 1711-12.*

William, jr., and Mary Brown, Oct. 31, 1751.*

GETCHEL (see also Getchell), Judeth, and Benjamin Person, Nov. 2, 1717.

GETCHELL (see also Gatchell, Getchel), Hubbard, a. 26 y., carpenter, b. Sandford, Me., and Hannah R. Pilsbury, a. 25 y., d. Joshua and Sally, Nov. 27, 1848.*

*Intention also recorded.

GIBBINS (see also Gibbons), Susannah, wid., of Boston, and Matthew Johns, sailor, June 11, 1728. c. r. 7.

GIBBONS (see also Gibbins), Hannah, of Marblehead, and John Fumey of Ross, Eng., merchant, Aug. 7, 1729. c. r. 7.

GIBBS, Cutbury, and ———— Trotter, Dec. 9, 1652.

GIBSON, Abraham, and Mary W[h]eeler, both of Stow, Sept. 29, 1724. c. r. 7.
Edward, and Mrs. Mary Hoyte, Jan. 17, 1739-40.*
Mary, and Johnson Lunt, Dec. 8, 1756.*

GIDDING (see also Giddings), Martha, and David Scott, Dec. 28, 1750.*

GIDDINGS (see also Gidding, Giddins, Gidins), William, and Mary A. Jaques of West Newbury, int. Aug. 1, 1846.

GIDDINS (see also Giddings), Lydia, and David Whitmore, Dec. 5, 1758.*
Sarah, wid., of Chebacco, and John Bailey, int. Oct. 6, 1711.

GIDINS (see also Giddings), Jacob, and Lydia Bartlet, Dec. 6, 1737.*

GIFFORD, Nathaniel, and Mrs. Mary Button, both of Boston, Nov. 18, 1732. c. r. 7.

GILBERT, Abner, of Brookfield, and Hannah Jones of Southampton, Oct. 16, 1751. c. r. 7.
John C., of Newburyport, a. 31 y., mariner, s. William and Susannah, of Newburyport, and Abigail M. Weeks of Newburyport, a. 20 y., d. John and Hannah, of Newburyport, Sept. 6, 1846.
Jonathan, of Gloucester, and Abigail Rogers, Apr. 17, 1740.*

GILDEN, Daniel, and Sarah Putnam, both of Newburyport, Sept. 22, 1834.

*Intention also recorded.

GILE (see also Giles, Gyle), Hannah, of Plaistow, and John Serjant, int. Apr. 10, 1806.
John, of Andover, and Mary Ann Rogers, May 9, 1827.*

GILEMAN (see also Gilman), Maverick [of Exeter. int.], and Sarah Mayo, June 16, 1702.*

GILES (see also Gile), Elisabeth, Mrs., and Capt. William Allen of Salisbury, int. Sept. 21, 1745.
Hannah, and Jonathan Parsons, jr., Aug. 26, 1756.*

GILLET, Eliphelet, Rev., of Hallowell, and Dolly Farnham Coffin, int. Jan. 16, 1801.

GILLINGS (see also Jillings), Sarah, of Newburyport, and Samuel Lunt, int. Nov. 16, 1792.

GILMAN (see also Gileman), Lucas B., of Acton, and Lucy W. Rogers, int. Oct. 6, 1849.
Nicholas [of Exeter. int.], and Mrs. Sarah Clark, June 9, 1697.*

GILMORE, Georgiana R., and Sidney P. Smith, int. Dec. 15, 1847.

GIMSON (see also Jemson), Elisabeth, of Amesbury, and Benjamin Sawyer, at Amesbury, Feb. 3, 1714.

GINNINGS (see also Jennings), Mary, of Boston, and Samuel Long, int. July 25, 1745.

GIROTT, Elias, Capt., of Boston, and Mrs. Sarah Wade of Medford, June 3, 1730. c. r. 7.

GLADING, John, and Elizabeth Rogers, July 17, 1667.

GLASIER (see also Glazier), Beemsly, and Mrs. Ann Stevens, Apr. 17, 1739.*
Stephen, of Ipswich, and Sarah Pike. Jan. 3, 1727-8.*

*Intention also recorded.

GLAZIER (see also Glasier), Elizabeth, and Jedediah Kilburn, Dec. 12, 1793.*

Hannah, and Benjamin Moody, jr., Dec. 1, 1763. c. r. 9.*

GLEASON (see also Glesen), Jonathan, of Reading, and Lettice Peabody, int. Mar. 26, 1799.

GLESEN (see also Gleason), Phineas, and Elizabeth Emmes, both of Framingham, Jan. 24, 1732-3. c. r. 7.

Sarah, and Job Carly, both of Marlboro, Apr. 18, 1733. c. r. 7.

GLINES, John and Eunice Pickingpack, both of Newburyport, Dec. 2, 1819. c. r. 10.

Mary [Maria. int.] E., and Charles Wildes of Georgetown, Dec. 12, 1842.*

GLOVER, Daniel, of Marblehead, and Hannah Jillings, Dec. 1, 1757.*

Rachell, and Symon Thompson, Aug. 21, 1656.

Sara, and [Henry. t. c.] Shorte, Oct. 9, 1648.

Tabitha, of Salem, and Thomas Jillens, int. June 21, 1756.

GODDARD, Mary, and Richard Sanders Burk, both of Boston, Apr. 23, 1728. c. r. 7.

GODFREY (see also Godfree, Godfry), Jonathan, and Jane Apr. 22, 1730.*

Joseph, and Mary Sewall, Feb. 4, 1736-7.*

GODFREY (see also Godfree, Godfry), Jonathan, and Jane [Eunice. int.] Greenough [of Newburyport. int.], Feb. 25, 1767.*

Moses [of Kingston. int.], and Anna Flood, Sept. 15, 1765.*

GODFRY (see also Godfrey), Elizabeth, and Joseph Pilsbury, int. July 8, 1704.

Hannah, and Samuel Allen, Sept. 25, 1735.*

James, and Hanah Kimball, Feb. 10, 1700.*

Margret, and Joseph Richardson, July 12, 1681.

Mary, and John Ordway, Dec. 5, 1681.

Peter, and Mary Browne, May 13, 1656.

Peter, and Hannah Poer, jr., int. Sept. 10, 1703.

*Intention also recorded.

GODSTEAD, Anna, and William Reynolds [of Ireland. int.], resident in Newburyport, July 28, 1771.*

GOLD (see also Gould), ——, of the Isle of Shoals, and Ruth Richardson, int. Aug. 1, 1704.

GOLDEN (see also Goulding), Windsor, and Jane Sampson, Jan. 3, 1760.*

GOLDING (see also Goulding), Elisabeth [Golden. int.], and Norman Gardner, Nov. 5, 1761.*
Elizabeth, and Philip Dod, both of Boston, July 6, 1726. c. r. 7.

GOLDSMITH, Lazarus [M. int.], of Boston, and Sarah George, ——, 1831. [June 11. int.]*

GOOCH, James, jr., and Hester Plaisted, wid., both of Boston, Aug. 21, 1729. c. r. 7.
Mary, and George Gooden, both of Wells, June 9, 1729. c. r. 7.

GOODEN (see also Goodwin), George, and Mary Gooch, both of Wells, June 9, 1729. c. r. 7.

GOODHU (see also Goodhue), George, and Elisabeth Presbury, Jan. 30, 1734-5.*
George, and Elisabeth Sleeper, Apr. 7, 1747.*
Martha, of Ipswich, and Enoch Morss, int. Dec. 8, 1738.

GOODHUE (see also Goodhu), Anne, and George Patterson, Feb. 14, 1758.*
George, and Sarah Mors, Sept. 28, 1737.*
George, jr., of Newburyport, and Susanna [Joanna. c. r. 1.] Mitchel, Sept. 20, 1768.*
John, and Joanna Stickney, int. May 28, 1788.
Joseph, and Sarah Presbury, int. Mar. 6, 1741-2.
Joseph, and Johannah Mitchil, int. Mar. 1, 1745-6.
Joseph, and Ann Lees, Feb. 8, 1824.*
Sam[uel], and Mrs. Abig[ail] Bartlet, Nov. 6, 1717. c. r. 7.
Tamasin, and Benjamin Stanwood, ——, 1808. [May 7. int.]*

*Intention also recorded.

GOODIN (see also Goodwin), Elisabeth, and John Peas of
Salem, July 29, 1725.*
Sarah, and Samuel Woodberre, Feb. 16, 1738-9.*
Susanna, and Joseph Rusell of Boston, int. Nov. 3, 1739.

GOODING (see also Goodwin), Dorothy, and George Butler,
Nov. 4, 1712.*
Hanna, and Thomas Pettingill, Apr. 16, 1719.*
Martha, of Salisbury, and Soloman Hodgkins, int. Apr. 25,
1747.
Mary, and Isaac Knight, Feb. 20, 1714-15.*
Sarah, d. Richard and Mary, of Amesbury, and Joseph Howig,
s. John and Ebenezar, 5: 3 m: 1707. c. r. 6.

GOODRICH, Bethiah, Mrs., and Dea. William Fisk, of Row-
ley, at Rowley, Dec. 19, 1753.
Edward, and Lydia Staniford of Rowley, at Rowley, Dec. 4,
1788.
Hannah M., and Joseph Moody, int. Mar. 6, 1841.
Josiah, and wid. Trifene Edwards, int. Feb. 22, 1777.
Mary, wid., and Stephen Lunt, June 9, 1766.*
Nancy, of Newburyport, and Benja[min] Whitmore, int. Sept.
9, 1809.
Ruth, and John Savory, jr. of Bradford, int. July 4, 1810.

GOODRIDG (see also Goodridge), Abigel, and Samuel Saw-
yer, jr., Dec. 17, 1702.*
Benjamin, and Mary Jordan, Sept. 8, 1663.
Benjamin, and Sarah Croad, Nov. 16, 1678.
Daniel, and Mary Ordway, int. Nov. 16, 1698.
Edmund, and Hannah Dole [sr. int.], Nov. 16, 1701. [Oct. 3,
1702. int.]*
Hanah, and John Richards, Mar. 22. 1693-4.
Hannah, and Nathan[ie]ll Pettingall, sr., int. Oct. 16, 1703.
Jeremiah, jr., and Mary Roe [Poor. t. c.], ——, 1703.
Jeremy, and Mary Adams, Nov. 15, 1660.
Joseph, and Martha Moores, Aug. 28, 166[4?].
Mary, and Edward Woodman, Dec. 20, 1653.
Mary, and Arthur Thresher, Apr. 21, 1684.
Hannah, and Nathan[ie]ll Pettingall, sr., int. Oct. 16, 1703.
Phillip, and Mehittable Woodman, Apr. 16, 1700.*

*Intention also recorded.

GOODRIDGE (see also Goodridg), Abial, and Rachel Follinsbee, Apr. 23, 1776.*

Abigail, and James Bean, July 4, 1734.*

Abigail, of Boxford, and Benjamin Woodman, jr., int. Oct.
16, 1740.

Abigail, and Moses Boynton, May 13, 1742.*

Abigail, and Nathan Burbank, Oct. 18, 1742.*

Abigail, and William Bowley, Mar. 13, 1791. c. R. 2.*

Ann, and James Chase of Stratham, Aug. 10, 1736.*

Barnard, and Sarah Carr, Sept. 28, 1768.*

Benjamin, and Bethiah Woodberre, Nov. 7, 1738.*

Benjamin, and Sarah Smith, Sept. 3, 1747.*

Bethiah, and Dr. William Fisk of Rowley, int. Nov. 22, 1753.

Betsey, and Micaijah Poor, May 9, 1799.*

David L., of West Newbury, and Susan R. Currier, int. Aug.
30, 1837.

Deborah, and Matthew Deuty, Jan. 4, 1722-3.*

Edmund, and Lydia Stanwood, int. Oct. 11, 1788.

Elisabeth, and John Cooper, Oct. 10, 1715.*

Enoch, and Mary Greenleaf of Haverhill, at Haverhill, Jan.
17, 1749-50.*

Eunice, and Edmund Pilsbury, June 4, 1769.*

Ezekiel, and Rebecca Goodridge, Dec. 18, 1744.*

Ezekiel, and Molly Morss, Dec. 23, 1765.*

Hannah, and Jonathan Sibley, Nov. 27, 1730.*

Hannah, and William Turner, Mar. 30, 1732.*

Hannah, and Benjamin Pearson, jr., Nov. 11, 1778.*

Hannah, and Samuel Poor, jr., Sept. 20, 1796.*

Harriet, and William Ilsley, Nov. 28, 1813.*

Jeremiah, jr., and Abigail Lowell, Jan. 18, 1738-9.*

Jeremiah, and Susanna Lookin, Nov. 24, 1790.*

John [jr. int.], and Hannah Brown, Jan. 13, 1707.*

John [jr. int.], of Gloucester, and Elisabeth Woodman, Jan.
5, 1737-8.*

John, and Sarah Brown, Nov. 28, 1754.*

Joseph [jr. int.], and Bethia Thurlo, Oct. 11, 1722.*

Joseph, and Mary Bayley, Mar. 17, 1763.*

Joseph, Dr., and Mercy March, int. Dec. 19, 1778.

Joseph [3d. int.], and Susanna Plummer, Mar. 17, 1791. c. R.
2.*

Joseph, and [Mrs. c. R. 2.] Sarah Brown of Hamilton, Aug.
28, 1796.*

*Intention also recorded.

GOODRIDGE, Josiah, and Sarah Tenney of Rowley, Mar. 6, 1760.*

Martha, and Joseph Flood, Nov. 7, 1799.*

Mary, and Joseph Carlton of Bradford, Oct. 12, 1742.*

Mary, and Enoch Flood, May 31, 1753.*

Mehiteble, and Stephen Stickne, Jan. 17, 1732-3.*

Melinda, and Leader Dam, Sept. 29, 1814.*

Molly [Mary. int.], and James Trainer of Newburyport, July .24, 1791. c. R. 2.*

Oliver, and Ruth Woodman, Feb. 14, 1782.*

Olliver, and Elisabeth Foster, int. June 14, 1788.

Rebecca, and Ezekiel Goodridge, Dec. 18, 1744.*

Richard, and Jane Duty, int. June 15, 1761.

Sam[ue]ll, and Hannah Frazer, June 30, 1710.*

Sarah, and William Grant, Apr. 10, 1735.*

Susan L., of West Newbury, and Bartlet J. Currier, int. Feb. 6, 1829.

William, and Elisabeth Pilsbury, Feb. 5, 1734-5.*

William, and Lucy Floyd, Dec. 26, 1822.*

GOODWIN (see also Gooden, Goodin, Gooding), Aaron, of Essex, and Laura Moore of Ipswich, Nov. 27, 1839.

Abel, and Sarah Ann Goodwin, both of Newburyport, June —, 1840.

Abel L., and Sarah Jane Brown of Newburyport, int. Oct. 14, 1831.

Abraham, and Caroline C. Colby, int. Oct. 29, 1842.

Amos, and Esther Peirce of Newburyport, int. Oct. 18, 1766.

Amos, jr., and Ruth Thurlo, Dec. 24, 1807.*

Amos, 3d, and Sally Bartlet Stone, Dec. 16, 1820.*

[Mary. int.] Ann, and Simeon B. Noyes, Nov. 26, 1826.*

Ann, and Frederick Knight of Newburyport, Apr. 21, 1834.*

Ann E., and Daniel T. Morss of Newburyport, int. June 24, 1843.

Anna, and William C. Merrill, int. Nov. 3, 1845.

Belinda, of Amesbury, and John A. Little, int. Mar. 21, 1835.

Benj[ami]n, and Hannah Woodwell, Nov. 7, 1799.*

Benjamin, and Hannah Harriss of Newburyport, int. Apr. 24, 1802.

Benjamin, jr., and [Mrs. c. R. 10.]Hannah D. Kilborn, Dec. . 27, 1829.*

Betsy H[oyt. int.], and John L. Knight, Feb. 17, 1831.*

Goodwin, Caroline, and Rev. Robert D. Easterbrook of Malden, Nov. 6, 1832.*
Charity, of Newburyport, and David Mansfield, int. Sept. 4, 1818.
Charles, and Mary P. Brown, int. Oct. 27, 1829.
Daniel, and Elisabeth Bishop, int. Oct. 5, 1734.
Daniel, and Elisabeth Smith of Rowley, at Rowley, Apr. 10, 1746.*
Daniel, and Mercy Sawyer of Rowley, Dec. 14, 1756.*
Daniel, and Lucy Smith, Oct. 1, 1807.*
Daniel, and Abigail Shaw, Oct. 31, 1824.*
David, and Mehetable Jackson, int. Aug. 17, 1765.
Edward, and Susana Wheeler, June 5, 1668.
Elisabeth, and David Jewett of Rowley, int. Oct. 25, 1771.
Eliza Ann, of Newburyport, and Solomon Pilsbury, int. Apr. 6, 1837.
Elizabeth, and William Hale, Jan. 10, 1819.*
Elizebeth, and Abraham Grant, Dec. 28, 1726.*
Enoch, and Phebe Ann Chase, Dec. 9, 1841.*
Eunice, and Benjamin Woodwell Hale, Jan. 2, 1810.*
Ezra, of Amesbury, and Sally Moulton, at Amesbury, Nov. 30, 1797.*
Fanny C., and Lewis H. Flowry of Boston, int. Apr. 26, 1845.
George, and Maria Davis of Newburyport, int. Jan. 9, 1836.
Hannah, and Henry Somerby [jr. c. r. 1.], Mar. 22, 1798.*
Isaac, of Newburyport, and Dolly T. Robinson, Oct. 12, 1843.*
John, jr., and Elizabeth S. Davis, May —, 1826.*
Jonathan, of Amesbury, and Anne Satchel, Nov. 7, 1765.*
Jonathan, and Eliza Pearson of Newburyport, Oct. 4, 1829.*
Joseph, and Elisabeth Smith, int. May 28, 1803.
Joseph L., and Mary Peabody, int. Dec. 3, 1831.
Lydia, and Benjamin Bishop, Mar. 18, 1739-40.*
Major, and Sally Pettingell, Mar. 31, 1819.*
Martha, and Jonathan Hoag, Sept. 15, 1703.*
Martha, and David Poor, Sept. 5, 1729. c. r. 7.
Martha, and Stephen Hale, Mar. 1, 1755.*
Martha, and Charles W. Ayers of Portsmouth. N. H., int. Jan. 20, 1837.
Mary, and Daniel Knight, jr., Jan. 28, 1762.*
Mary, and Jonathan Peabody of Newburyport, Jan. 16, 1810.*
Mary, and John Poor, jr., Aug. 4, 1833.*

*Intention also recorded.

GOODWIN, Mary D., and Joseph Hall, jr., of Newburyport, int. May 11, 1844.

Moses, and Esther Adams, July 19, 1797.*

Nancy, and Nathaniel Tilton, jr., int. Nov. 27, 1830.

Nathaniel, and Catharine Lunt, int. Jan. 2, 1773.

Nathaniel, jr., and Mary Disney, Apr. 8, 1817.*

Nathaniel, and Sally Lunt, Feb. 5, 1822.*

Nathaniel, and Lois W. Brown of Newburyport, int. Oct. 22, 1843.

Rachel, and John Jemson of Salisbury, Mar. 14, 1738-9.*

Rebecca, and Benjamin Tilton, int. Oct. 27, 1827.

Rebeckah, and Jesse Dorman of Newburyport, Oct. 5, 1797.*

Richard, and Hannah Major [Mosier. CT. R.], Mar. 26, 1692.

Ruth, and Capt. Gideon Woodwell of Newburyport, July 31, 1781.*

Sally, and William Collins of Newburyport, Oct. 21, 1813.*

Sally L., wid., a. 43 y., d. Richard, of Bradford, and Thomas Grace, a. 33 y., shoemaker, Nov. 6, 1844.*

Samuel, and Abigail Beacham, int. Aug. 29, 1763.

Samuel, and Hannah Knight, Nov. 2, 1800.*

S[amuel. int.], and Ann Durgin [July 3. int.], 1829.*

Samuel, jr., a. 25 y., cooper, s. Samuel and Hannah, and Nancy K. Russell, a. 21 y., d. Samuel P. and Nancy K., Dec. 29, 1846.*

Samuel P., and Mary W. Sargent of Newburyport, int. July 12, 1844.

Sam[ue]ll, and Joanna Pettingell, Sept. 6, 1749.*

Sarah, Mrs., and Obadiah Richards, Dec. 22, 1727.*

Sarah, and Joseph Perkins, 3d, int. May 31, 1834.

Sarah Ann, and Abel Goodwin, both of Newburyport, June —, 1840.

Sarah L., a. 19 y., d. Nathaniel and Sarah, and Thurston S. Chase, a. 21 y., carriage builder, s. Josiah and Ester, Sept. 11, 1845.*

Stephen, and Eunice Coffin, int. Sept. 11, 1789.

Stephen, jr., and Elizabeth Thurlo of Boxford, int. Sept. 7, 1822.

Susanna, and Jacob Newman, Oct. 12, 1749.*

Thomas, and Lydia Smith of Newburyport, int. July 5, 1816.

William, and Alice Knight, Jan. 28, 1827.*

William, and Susan Baker of Salisbury, int. Dec. 11, 1828.

Willibee, of Amesbury, and Margaret Steward, int. Dec. 31, 1825.

*Intention also recorded.

GOOKIN, Hannah, and Capt. Partrick Tracy, July 25, 1749.*

GORDIN (see also Gordon), Timothy, and Lydia Whitmore, int. Dec. 29, 1781.

GORDON (see also Gordin, Gourdin, Gourding), Frances, of Exeter, and John Gordon, int. Feb. 18, 1814.
George, and Abigail Sawyer, Nov. 27, 1813.*
Harriet P., and Forrest Eaton of Dover, N. H., Sept. 23, 1828.*
John, and Frances Gordon of Exeter, int. Feb. 18, 1814.
Lydia, and William Wigglesworth, Feb. 2, 1836.*
Oliver S., of Boston, and Mrs. Eliza R. Atkinson of Newburyport, June 9, 1829.

GORE, Mary, and John Cook of Whitehaven, Nov. 13, 1757. c. r. 8.

GOSS, Ann, and Moses Cross, July 17, 1753.*

GOTT, Ann [of Gloucester. int.], and Benjamin Scott, at Gloucester, Jan. 13, 1736.*

GOUGH, John B., and Mary B. Cheney, Nov. —, 1838.*

GOULD (see also Gold), Abigail, of South Hampton, and Maj. Thomas Pike, int. May 20, 1756.
Abigail, and Francis Davis Rogers, Feb. 24, 1811.*
Ann, of West Newbury, and Joseph Rogers, Nov. 20, 1828.*
Elisabeth, of Dunstable, and Benjamin Moody, sr., int. Aug. 28, 1781.
Elisha P., and Mary Laskey, Dec. 27, 1825.*
Eunice, and James Rogers, Nov. 6, 1804. c. r. 5.*
Eunice, of West Newbury, and Joseph Floyd, int. May 19, 1849.
George, and Betsey Downer of West Newbury, Oct. 27, 1842.*
Harriet, and Paul Smith, Jan. 20, 1829.*
James, of West Newbury, and Mary Kent, June 15, 1829.*
John, and Ruth Stephens, Sept. 15, 1760.*
John, and Jane Bradbury of Kensington, N. H., int. Nov. 5, 1807.
John, and Ruth Rogers, Nov. 12, 1813.*

*Intention also recorded.

GOULD, Joseph, and Susanna Rogers, int. Apr. 21, 1787.
Joseph, and Mercy M. J. Cilley of Newburyport, int. June 17, 1848.
Luther P., a. 23 y., shoemaker, s. John and Ruth, and Martha J. Floyd, a. 16 y., d. Michael and Betsey, Aug. 3, 1845.*
Mary, and Richard Jackman, Nov. 25, 1780.*
Phebe, of West Newbury, and Francis R. Pilsbury, int. Nov. 16, 1827.
Priscilla, of Topsfield, and John Longfellow, at Topsfield, May 21, 1796.*
Rebecca, of West Newbury, and Joseph Steele, Aug. 9, 1843.*
Samuel, and Judith Duty, Dec. 14, 1826.*
Sarah, and Daniel Stickney, Mar. 11, 1755.*
Sarah, of Nottingham West, and Samuel Brown, int. Jan. 24, 1778.
Sarah Ann, of Newburyport, a. 24 y., b. Newburyport, d. Samuel and Ann, of Newburyport, and Joseph H. Currier, of Newburyport, a. 23 y., mason, s. William and Abigail, of Newburyport, May 12, 1847.
Silas, jr., and Bethany Parsons Tarr, Dec. 23, 1813.*
Thomas, and Hannah H. Davis, Jan. 11, 1838.*
Thomas H., and Louisa Coffin, Nov. 30, 1837.*
W[illia]m, of West Newbury, and Nancy Downer, int. Apr. 7, 1827.

GOULDING (see also Golden, Golding), Windsor, and Mary Benjy, Feb. 5, 1735-6.*
Winzer, and Elenor Pearson, July 18, 1732. C. R. 7.

GOURDIN (see also Gordon), John, of Exeter, and Hannah Willit, Dec. —, 1728.*

GOURDING (see also Gordon), Jonathan, of Exeter, and Sarah Sawyer, June 2, 1738.*

GOVE, Edward, of Seabrook, N. H., and Anna Brown, d. Stephen, late of Newbury, and Sarah, Nov. 1, 1775. C. R. 6.
Hannah, and Abraham Clemens, May 10, 1683.

GRACE, Benja[min], and Sarah Lunt, Jan. 22, 1822.*
Thomas, a. 33 y., shoemaker, and wid. Sally L. Goodwin, a. 43 y., d. Richard, of Bradford, Nov. 6, 1844.*

*Intention also recorded.

GRANGER, Lancelt, and Johane Adams, Jan. 4, 1653.

GRANT, Abraham, and Elizebeth Goodwin, Dec. 28, 1726.*
Daniel, and Sarah Gale of Salem, int. Apr. 14, 1738.
Daniel, and Elezabeth Hale of Exeter, int. Mar. 12, 1742-3.
Daniel, and Elizabeth Hall of Exeter, int. Mar. 12, 1742-3.
Francis, and Sollomon Keyes, Oct. 2, 1653.
Joshua, and Mercy Moulton, both of York, June 10, 1736.
    c. R. 7.
Paul H., and Elizabeth England, July 17, 1810.*
Sally, wid., a. 45 y., b. Atkinson, N. H., d. John and Martha
    Peaslee of Atkinson, N. H., and Joseph Worthen, widr.,
    a. 54 y., ship carpenter, b. Amesbury, s. George and Mary,
    of Amesbury, Sept. 7, 1848.*
Theodore L., of Newburyport, and Susanna Coffin, Feb. 3,
    1814.*
William, and Sarah Goodridge, Apr. 10, 1735.*

GRAVES, Hannah, of Salisbury, and Josiah Merrill, at Salis-
    bury, Oct. 30, 1746.*

GRAY, Abigail H., and Joseph Sewall of York, int. Sept. 27,
    1810.
Frederick, and Rebecca Badger, Mar. 17, 1814.*
James, Capt., of Epsom, N. H., and Susanna Parsons, Mar.
    20, 1777.*
Olive, of Biddeford, and Nathan Woodman, int. Nov. 2, 1749.
Rebecca, of Rowley, and William Moody, int. Sept. 22, 1835.
William H., of Exeter, and Sarah E. Cook of Newburyport,
    Dec. 27, 1839.

GREANLEAF (see also Greenleaf), Abner, jr., and Elisabeth
    Doel, Jan. 12, 1762.*
Ebenezer, and Hannah Titcomb, Dec. 21, 1760.*
Joshua, and Anna [Anne. int.] Kent, Dec. 1, 1763.*
Thomas, and Susanna Brown, Mar. 9, 1762.*

GREELEY (see also Greely), John B., of Newburyport, and
    Clarissa Jewett, int. July 27, 1823.
Margaret, Mrs., and Moses C. Pusey, both of Salisbury, June
    15, 1842.
Nathaniel, of Newburyport, and Ann Swett, Sept. 20, 1819.*
Reubin, and Anna Fowler, int. Jan. 28, 1781.
Sarah, Mrs., and John Bailey, Oct. —, 1833.

*Intention also recorded.

GREELY (see also Greeley, Griele), Benjamin, of Haverhill, and Hannah Poor, Mar. 18, 1745-6.*
Nathaniel, and Alice Hale of Newburyport, int. Oct. 16, 1847.

GREEN, Clarissa, wid., of Newburyport, a. 30 y., d. Jacob and Tabitha, and Thomas Caswell, widr., of Newburyport, a. 30 y., ropemaker, s. Samuel and Lydia, Feb. 24, 1846.
Daniel, and Sarah Cooper, July 2, 1735. c. R. 7.*
Eliphalet, and Mary Ann Merrill, Apr. 19, 1827.*
Emeline, and Thomas B. Patten, Nov. 7, 1833.*
John, and Sarah Stevens, int. July 5, 1735.
Margaret, and George Durgin, int. Sept. 16, 1845.
Mary, wid., of Salem, and Joshua Corning of Beverly, widr., May 30, 1733. c. R. 7.
Mary, of Boston, and Samuel Emerson, int. Jan. 30; 1753.
Mary Jane, and George P. Patten, July 29, 1834.*
Mary Jane, and Isaac Allen, int. Apr. 26, 1845.
Rebecka, and Thomas Banister, both of Bradford, Dec. 15, 1724. c. R. 7.
Sally, of Haverhill, and William Noyes, Sept. 17, 1800.*
Samuel H., and Elizabeth Cary, int. May 9, 1835.
Samuel W., widr., of Newburyport, a. 25 y., machinist, b. Newburyport, s. Ephraim and Sarah, of Newburyport, and Hannah M. Lander, a. 22 y., d. Henry and Lydia S., Apr. 23, 1848.*
Sarah, of Haverhill, and Ezekiel Bayley, at Haverhill, June 17, 1746.*
Silas, of Hampton Falls, N. H., and Sally Toppan, Mar. 20, 1808.*
Thomas, and Ann Cal[e]f, both of Boston, Jan. 11, 1725-6. c. R. 7.

GREENFEILD (see also Greenfield), Benjamin, and Elisabeth Flanders of Salisbury, int. Apr. 2, 1737.

GREENFIELD (see also Greenfeild), Tamzen, of Salisbury, and Benjamin Noyes, int. Aug. 29, 1761.

GREENLEAF (see also Greanleaf, Greenleafe, Greenleaft, Greenlef, Greenlefe, Greenlief, Grinleaf), Abigail, and William Ripp, Dec. 22, 1720.*
Abigail, and Jonathan Plumer, Nov. 27, 1760.*

*Intention also recorded.

GREENLEAF, Abigail A., a. 21 y., d. Peabody, and Moses Pettingell, jr., a. 17 y., seaman, s. Cutting, Nov. 20, 1844.*
Abner, and Mary Gutterson, May 19, 1757.*
Abner [jr. c. r. 2.], and Sarah Hale, Nov. 27, 1783.*
Ann, and Mathew Perkins, Dec. 22, 1748.*
Anna, and Joseph Spiller, Sept. 7, 1756.*
Benjamin, and Anne Woodbridge, Sept. 3, 1724.*
Benjamin, and Abigail Moodey, Aug. 26, 1726.*
Caleb, and Mrs. Mary Pearson, Nov. 23, 1742.*
Catherine, and Joseph Rawlings, jr., Jan. 12, 1798.*
Daniel D., a. 23 y., baker, s. Peabody and Dorothy, and Lucy
    G. Pettingell, a. 20 y., June 6, 1844.*
Daniell, and Sarah Moodey, Nov. 17, 1710.*
Deborah, and Moses Swett, Nov. 27, 1735.*
Edmund, and Abigell Somerby, July 2, 1691. [June. CT. R.]
Edmund, jr., and Lydia Brown, Mar. 12, 1718-19.*
Edmund [3d. int.], and Mary Hale, May 4, 1725.*
Edmund, jr., and Sarah Woodman, Apr. 18, 1754.*
Edmund, and Hannah Coleby of Amesbury, int. Oct. 21, 1769.
Edmund, of Canterbury, N. H., and Lydia Bartlet, ——, 1810
    or 11. [Jan. 26, 1811. int.]*
Edmund, of Newburyport, and Dorothy Lunt Jackman, int.
    Jan. 23, 1817.
Elisabeth, Mrs. [d. Capt. Stephen. int.], and Henry Clark,
    Nov. 7, 1695.*.
Elisabeth, and Thomas Oaks of Medford, Aug. 2, 1716.*
Elisabeth, and Ebenezer Choate of Ipswich, Sept. 3, 1730.*
Elisabeth, and Nathaniel Atkinson, jr., Nov. 30, 1738.*
Elizabeth, and Thomas Noyes, Sept. 24, 1677.
Elizabeth, and Ebenezer Noyes of Haverhill district, Jan. 7,
    1748. c. r. 2.*
Elizabeth, and Reuben Brown, June ——, 1810.*
Francis, and Anne Wycomb [Jan. 30. int.], 1748. c. r. 2.*
George, of Newburyport, and Elizabeth Cogswell Wheel-
    wright, Oct. 19, 1813.*
Hannah, Mrs., and Josiah Titcomb, jr., Dec. 10, 1745.*
Hannah, Mrs., and Capt. John Jones, resident in Newbury,
    int. Apr. 22, 1749.
Hannah, and William Woodman, May 13, 1766.*
Jacob, and Polley Stickney, int. Sept. 15, 1804.
Jane, Mrs., and Thomas Clark of Boston, Nov. 10, 1747.*
Jane, and William Coombs, July 17, 1760.*

*Intention also recorded.

GREENLEAF, John, and Mrs. Lyddia Peirce, May 13, 1716.
John, father of Parker, and Mrs. Lydia Peirce, int. June 2, 1716.
John, and Sarah Smith, Mar. 19, 1718-19.*
Jonathan, and Mary Presbe, int. Oct. 13, 1744.
Joseph, and Thomasin May [Mayo. int.], Nov. 18, 1707.*
Joseph, jr., and Mercy Cottle, Feb. 26, 1760.*
Joseph, and Elisabeth Hills of Newburyport, int. Oct. 24, 1801.
Joshua, and Judeth Moodey, Nov. 23, 1736.*
Joshua [jr. int.], and Sarah Pettingill, May 11, 1738.*
Joshua, jr., and Jane Ordway, Oct. 21, 1789.*
Judeth, and John Coffin, Apr. 22, 1713.*
Judeth, and John Knight [jr. int.], Jan. 9, 1720-21.*
Judith, and Richard Dummer, June 6, 1754.*
Judith [of Boston. int.], and Enoch Sawyer, at Boston, Oct. 17, 1793.*
Keturah McHard, of Newburyport, and Enoch Gerrish, Apr. 30, 1811.*
Lydia, and William Moulton, Sept. 16, 1742.*
Lydia [Mrs. c. r. 2.], and Thomas Davis, Dec. 28, 1778.*
Marjery, and Daniel Lunt [jr. int.], Sept. 25, 1746.*
Martha, and Ezra Moodey, Apr. 26, 1716.*
Martha, and Isaac Johnson, May 10, 1733.*
Martha, and Obadiah Horton, Aug. 14, 1755.*
Mary, d. Capt. Stephen, sr., deceased, and Joshua Moodey, int. May 1, 1696.
Mary, and Jonathan Clement, Nov. 30, 1721.*
Mary, and Rowland Bradbury, Nov. 15, 1723.*
Mary, and Nathan Noyes, Dec. 27, 1725.*
Mary, and Abraham Davis of Gloucester, Jan. 10, 1732-33.*
Mary, of Haverhill, and Enoch Goodridge, at Haverhill, Jan. 17, 1749-50.*
Mary, and Nathaniel Plumer, Oct. 5, 1750.*
Mary, and Nathan Peabody, June 2, 1754. c. r. 8.*
Mary, and Caleb Toppan, Apr. 14, 1762.*
Mary, and William Carr, int. Jan. 11, 1805.
Mary, of Newburyport, and Moses Pettingell, int. Mar. 9, 1811.
Mary, and Stephen Bailey, jr., ——, 1811. [July 30. int.]*
Mayo, and Sarah Merrill, Dec. 19, 1751.*
Nathaniel, and Judeth Coffin, June 7, 1714.*

*Intention also recorded.

GREENLEAF, Parker, and Mary Jaques, Nov. 24, 1715.*

Peabody, of Exeter, and Dorothy L. Jackman, int. Nov. 27, 1819.

Polly, Mrs., and Thomas Pettingell, July 29, 1822.*

Prudence, and Jonathan Dole, Apr. 28, 1725.*

Richard, and Mary Boucher [Mary Goucher of Boston. int.], at Boston, May 19, 1747.*

Richard, and Lois Rogers of Newburyport, int. Aug. 28, 1789.

Rookby, and John Clark of Kingston [Hampton. int.], Apr. 21, 1738.*

Ruth, and Mark Moors, jr., July 24, 1735.*

Sally, and Edward Phelan (Failing), Oct. 9, 1806.*

Samuel, and Mary Moodey, Oct. 3, 1721.*

Samuel, and Ann Bradbury, May 17, 1749.*

Samuel, jr., and Lois Rowell of Amesbury, int. Oct. 17, 1750.

Samuel, and Miriam Pilsbury, Sept. 12, 1792.*

Samuell, and Sara Kent, Mar. 1, 1685-6.

Sarah, Mrs., and Capt. Richard Kent, Jan. 30, 1709.*

Sarah, and Nathaniel Clark, Mar. 7, 1710.*

Sarah, and Tristram Knight, June 9, 1719.*

Sarah, Mrs., and Benjamin Bradstreet, Nov. 9, 1726.*

Sarah, and Moses Pearson of Rowley, Jan. 1, 1738-9.*

Sarah, and Joseph Whittier, jr. of Haverhill [at Haverhill. dup.], July 12, 1739.*

Sarah, Mrs., and Thomas Woodbridge, Nov. 21, 1749.*

Sarah, and Jacob Coffin, Nov. 23, 1780.*

Sarah, and Thomas Coker, May 3, 1781.*

Sarah, and Moses Lankister, int. June 28, 1805.

Sophia B., a. 21 y., d. Abner and Sophia B., and Andrew M. Paul of Newmarket, N. H., a. 24 y., iron moulder, b. Newmarket, N. H., s. Nathaniel and Mary, of Newmarket, Nov. 4, 1845.*

Stephen [jr. int.], and Mary Mackcres [Macrees. dup.], Oct. 7, 1712.*

Stephen, 3d, and Mrs. Mary Cotten of Portsmouth, int. May 7, 1715.

Stephen, and Mary Davis, at Gloucester, Jan. 24, 1747-8.

Susanna, and Timothy Greenleaf, May 26, 1743.*

Susanna, and Humphry Lane of Gloucester, int. Jan. 20, 1797.

Tamson, and Levi Shackford of Newburyport, Aug. 30, 1787.*

Thomas, and Elisabeth Hidden, Jan. 6, 1779.*

Thomas, and Elisabeth Coats of Newburyport, int. May 23, 1789.

*Intention also recorded.

GREENLEAF, Thomas, and Lydia Griffin of Gloucester, Nov. 9,
    1796.*
Timothy, and Susanna Greenleaf, May 26, 1743.*
Tristram, and Margaret Piper, Nov. 12, 1689.
Tristram, jr., and Dorothy Rolf, Nov. 5, 1728.*
William, and Mary Dean, June 18, 1782.*
Woodbridge, of Newburyport, and Mary Holman, July 25,
    1790.*

GREENLEAFE (see also Greenleaf), Elisabeth, and Edmund
    Titcomb, int. Nov. 18, 1704.
John, and Elizabeth Hills, Oct. 12, 1685.
Mary, and John Wells, Mar. 5, 1668.
Stephen, Capt., and Mrs. Hannah Jordan of Kittery, Me.,
    Sept. 17, 1713.
Steven, and Elizabeth Coffin, Nov. 13, 1651.
Steven, Ens., and Esther Swett, Mar. 31, 1679.

GREENLEAFT (see also Greenleaf), Steven, Lt., and Eliza-
    beth Gerrish, Oct. 23, 1676.

GREENLEF (see also Greenleaf), Mary, "Ms.," and Joseph
    Adams of Stratham, N. H., int. Nov. 29, 1746.
Sarah, and Peter Toppan [jr. int.], Apr. 28, 1696.*

GREENLEFE (see also Greenleaf), Sara, and Richard Dole,
    June 7, 1677.

GREENLIEF (see also Greenleaf), John [jr. int.], and Abi-
    gall Moodey of Salisbury, at Salisbury, May 7, 1713.*

GREENOUGH (see also Grenough), Elisabeth, and Capt.
    Henry Kingsbery, July 29, 1754.*
Epps, and Margaret Moor of Kittery, int. Dec. 11, 1730.
Hannah, and Richard Kelly, Oct. 18, 1725.*
Hannah, of Newburyport, and Samuel Poor, 3d, int. Dec. 19,
    1821.
James, of Bradford, and Mary Jaques, Dec. 13, 1759.*
James, and Tabitha Noyes, June 30, 1790.*
Jane [Eunice, of Newburyport. int.], and Jonathan Godfrey,
    Feb. 25, 1767.*
Joseph, of Boston, and Mrs. Betsey Heard of Newport, N. H.,
    Nov. —, 1839.

*Intention also recorded.

GREENOUGH, Judith, and Samuel Wyatt, July 27, 1756.*
Margery, and Samuel Dean, Feb. 19, 1761.*
Mary, and [Capt. int.] William Wyer [of Charlestown. int.],
Jan. 29, 1761.*
Moses, and Mary Lowell, int. Feb. 12, 1763.
Richard, and Hannah Sewall, July 20, 1738.*
Rob[er]t, jr., of Rowley, and Mrs. Hanah Dole, Jan. 20,
1704-5.
Robert, and Ednar Knight, Nov. 27, 1735.*
William, and Judeth Chase, int. Aug. 11, 1749.

GREENWOOD, Thomas S., of Ipswich, and Paulina A. Thurlow, May 18, 1829.*

GREGG, Samuel, of New Boston, and Lydia Bartlet, int. Feb.
24, 1804.
Sam[ue]ll, and Mary Moor, both of Londonderry, Sept. 22,
1731. C. R. 7.

GRENOLD, Peach, servant of Capt. Daniel Marquand, and
Timothy Moody, resident in Newbury, int. Dec. 24, 1749.

GRENOUGH (see also Greenough), Tabitha, and James
George, Dec. 24, 1793.*

GRIDLEY, Jeremy, and Mrs. Abigail Lewis, both of Boston,
May 22, 1734. C. R. 7.

GRIELE (see also Greely), Benjamin, of Haverhill, and Hannah Poor, at Haverhill [bef. 1715.].

GRIFFEN (see also Griffin), Ednah, and Nathan Merrill,
Dec. 25, 1760.*
Hannah, and William Rogers, Jan. 17, 1757.*
Jonathan, and Hannah Davis, Nov. 12, 1761.*

GRIFFIN (see also Griffen), Anna, of Sandown, N. H., and
Daniel Pressey, int. Feb. 23, 1816.
Catharine, and Amos Sargent, int. Feb. 28, 1841.
Daniel, and Beulah Bailey of Bradford, int. Jan. 31, 1735-6.
Eliphalet, and Jerusha Stickney, Nov. 6, 1755.*
George, of Bradford, and Judith Chase, Feb. 19, 1807.*

*Intention also recorded.

GRIFFIN, Jonathan, and Hannah Emery, May 12, 1752.*
Leonard, of Portland, and Ann Moulton, May 6, 1818.*
Lydia, and Lewis Page of Haverhill, Feb. 11, 1735-6.*
Lydia, of Gloucester, and Thomas Greenleaf, Nov. 9, 1796.*
Mark, of Gloucester, and Sally Ramsdal, int. Nov. 26, 1803.
Mark [jr. int.], and Mrs. Eliza Ann Young, Nov. —, 1833.*
Mark, jr., and Sarah D. Libby of Newburyport, int. Nov. 29, 1846.
Mary, and Daniel Sillaway, Sept. 7, 1687. CT. R.
Mary, and Edmund Mores [Morss. int. C. R. 2.], Jan. 16, 1728-9.*
Mary, of Charlestown, and Nehemiah Basset of Lynn, Feb. 3, 1731-2. C. R. 7.
Mary P., and Humphrey Lane, jr., Dec. 22, 1825.*
Ruben, and wid. Phillis Brown, int. June 14, 1783.
Sarah, and Phillip Hodgkins, Apr. 13, 1724.*
Shimuel, and Rebecca Annis, Nov. 6, 1716.*
Shimuel, and wid. Susanna Worth, Jan. 18, 1748-9. C. R. 2.*
William, and Molly Howard, Jan. 23, 1764.*
William R., and Harriet M. Pike of Newburyport, int. Oct. 28, 1843.

GRIFFIS, Robert, of Newburyport, and Nancy Bartlett, May 6, 1817.*

GRIFFITH, Joanna E., a. 22 y., d. Joseph and Elizabeth, and David Ross LeCraw of Newburyport, a. 23 y., mariner, b. Newburyport, s. William and Lydia, of Newburyport, May 10, 1847.
Joseph, and Elizabeth Thurlow, Dec. 16, 1821.*
Robert, jr., of Newburyport, and Charlottee Merrill, int. Feb. 7, 1840.

GRINLEAF (see also Greenleaf), Henry, and Margaret Dow of Ipswich, Aug. 24, 1727. C. R. 7.

GROE (see also Grow), William [Grow. int.], of York, and Joanna Poor, Feb. 9, 1715-16.*

GROVE, William, of Plymouth, Eng., and Mercy Hunt, Sept. 4, 1763. C. R. 8.

*Intention also recorded.

GROW (see also Groe), Mary S., of East Topham, Vt., and
J. William Merrill, int. Nov. 27, 1847.

GUNN, Lewis C., Esq., of Philadelphia, Pa., and Elizabeth
L. B. Stickney of Newburyport, Sept. 30, 1839.

GUNNESON (see also Gunnison), Mary, and Samuel Dole,
jr., Apr. 7, 1752.*

GUNNISON (see also Gunneson), Isaac, of Newburyport, and
Sarah A. Tilton, int. Jan. 11, 1832.
Jesse D., of Newburyport, and Mary S. Wormsted, int. June
5, 1841.
William, jr., of Newburyport, and Eliza Jane Lunt, int. Sept.
12, 1834.

GURNEY (see also Gerney), Caroline F., a. 19 y., d. Nathaniel and Harriet, and William Morton, a. 22 y., shipwright, s. James and Elizabeth, Nov. 24, 1847.*
Harriet M., of Newburyport, d. Nathaniel, of Newburyport,
and Nathan A. Flanders, ship carpenter, Nov. 2, 1844.*
John G., of Newburyport, and Mary Knowles, int. Feb. 16,
1839.

GUTRIDGE (see also Goodridge), Joseph, mariner, and Ann
Benington, both of Boston, Nov. 19, 1726. C. R. 7.
Boston, Nov. 19, 1726. C. R. 7.

GUTTERSON, Joseph, of Methuen, and Sarah Richardson,
Jan. 5, 1729-30.*
Mary, and Abner Greenleaf, May 19, 1757.*
Mary, and Joseph Lankister, int. Sept. 20, 1805.
[Abigail. int.], and Peter Rogers [May 6. int.], 1748. C. R. 2.*

GWYN, Anthony, Capt., of Bristol, Great Britain, and Mrs.
Mary Gerrish, Oct. 26, 1738.*

GYLE (see also Gile), Ezekiel, Maj., of Plaistow, N. H., and
Hannah Woodman, Feb. 14, 1819.*

HACKET (see also Hackett), Ebenezer, and Abigail Emery,
Mar. 24, 1752.*

*Intention also recorded.

HACKETT (see also Hacket, Hackit), Mehitabel, Mrs., and Capt. Thomas Carter, Oct. 9, 1809.*

HACKIT (see also Hackett), Mary, and Samuel Pilsbury, May 18, 1768.*

HADDOCK, Charles, of Haverhill, and Susanna Brickett, at Haverhill [bef. 1754].
Charles, of Haverhill, and Susanna Bricket, Oct. 22, 1767.*

HADLE (see also Hadley), Hanna, and Moses Ordway, int. Nov. 29, 1735.

HADLEY (see also Hadle, Hadly), Elizabeth, of Rowley, and Archelaus Lakeman, Jan. 11, 1775.*

HADLOCK, Abigail, and Edmund Lowel, Apr. 18, 1706.*
Abigail, and Stephen Ordway, jr., Mar. 28, 1750.*
Joseph, of Amesbury, and Prudence Thirlo, June 7, 1722.*

HADLY (see also Hadley), Joanna, of Amesbury, and James Blye, at Amesbury, Apr. 2, 1731.

HAGAT (see also Hagget), Isaac G., of Georgetown, a. 23 y., shoemaker, s. Stephen and Catharine, and Hannah M. Niles of Georgetown, d. W[illia]m and Hannah, Oct. 26, 1848.

HAGER, Eliza Ann, and John Q. Adams, int. Dec. 31, 1847.

HAGGET (see also Hagat), Eleanor, of Andover, and Jacob Bartlet, at Andover, Mar. 9, 1762.*

HAIL (see also Hale), Richard, and Mary Silver, Mar. 16, 1715.*

HAINES (see also Haynes), Matthias, of North Hampton, N. H., and Eunice Lunt, Nov. 30, 1828.*
Samuel W., of Newburyport, and Susan M. Rogers, Feb. 4, 1840.

*Intention also recorded.

HALE (see also Hail), Abigail, and Henry Poore, Sept. 12, 1679.

Abigail, and Richard Coffin, Nov. 30, 1738.*

Abigail, and Enoch Foot of Newburyport, Oct. 6, 1774.*

Abigail, and Joseph Stickney of Newburyport, Dec. 6, 1776.*

Abigail, and Moses Jaques, Aug. 15, 1782.*

Adeline, and James B. Knight, Sept. 27, 1836.*

Alice L., and Rev. John C. March, Apr. 23, 1832.*

Alice, of Newburyport, and Nathaniel Greely, int. Oct. 16, 1847.

Almira, and Stephen Kimball, jr., both of Newburyport, Oct. 18, 1838.

Amos, and Elisabeth Plumer, Oct. 17, 1786.*

Ann, and Richard Kent, jr., June 10, 1736.*

Ann, and Charles Currier of Newburyport, Nov. 29, 1827.*

Anna, and William Moodey [jr. int.], Dec. —, 1728.*

Anna, and Hezekiah Coffin, Jan. 16, 1800.*

Anne, and Daniel Knight, Dec. 11, 1733.*

Anne, and John Hidden, int. Nov. 21, 1767.

Aphia, and Samuel Robertson [Robinson. int.], May 30, 1732.*

Ap[phia. T. C. and CT. R.], and Benjamin Roafe, Nov. 3, 1659.

Benjamin, and Judith Swett, Dec. 18, 1729.*

Benjamin Woodwell, and Eunice Goodwin, Jan. 2, 1810.*

Bettee, and William Clark, Mar. 24, 1763.*

Betty, and Moses Bennet of Newburyport, Nov. 5, 1787.*

Charles H. [W. dup.], a. 26 y., carpenter, s. Ezra and Anna, and Sarah J. Adams of Derry, N. H., a. 23 y., b. Derry, d. Sewall and Sarah, May 5, 1846.*

Charles W., and Elizabeth A. Jackman, int. Jan. 9, 1847.

Daniel, of Rowley, and Judeth Emery, Dec. 29, 1720.*

Daniel, and Ednah Pickard of Rowley, at Rowley, June 16, 1749.*

Daniel, and Keziah Plumer, Jan. 9, 1755.*

Daniel, and Priscilla Brown of Haverhill, int. June 8, 1765.

Daniel, 3d, and Elizabeth Dow, July 17, 1776.*

Daniel, 3d, and Betty Fellows of Hopkinton, N. H., int. May 14, 1785.

Daniel [jr. int.], and Elisabeth Rawlings, Nov. 9, 1786.*

Daniel, and Betsy Chute of Rowley, Dec. 8, 1796.*

Daniel, Capt., and Mrs. Ruth Thurlo, May 1, 1811.*

. *Intention also recorded.

HALE, Daniel J., of Rowley, and Sarah Thurlow, int. Dec. 31, 1842.

Daniel K., and Elizabeth C. Pettengill, Apr. 29, 1838.*

David, jr., of Rindge, N. H., and Ann Plumer, Dec. 11, 1821. [Dec. 9, 1820. c. R. 1.]*

David, and Hannah Lunt, May 10, 1827.*

Dorothy, and Moses Woodman, Sept. 11, 1740.*

Ebenezer, and Sarah Wicomb of Bradford, int. Oct. 31, 1747.

Ebenezer, Col., and Mrs. Lucy French, Sept. 28, 1835.*

Ebenezer, Dr., and Sarah White Bannister of Newburyport, at Newburyport, June 13, 1844.*

Edmund, and Martha Sawyer, May 16, 1728.*

Edna, and George Little, Feb. 22, 1710.*

Edna, and Caleb Haskell, jr. of Newburyport, Apr. 10, 1781.*

Ednah, and Farnum How, May 8, 1791. c. R. 2.*

Ednar, and Abel Morss, jr., Nov. 11, 1736.*

Edward, of Newbury, Vt., and Mrs. Elizabeth L. Brown of Salisbury, Jan. 30, 1837.

Elezabeth, of Exeter, and Daniel Grant, int. Mar. 12, 1742-3.

Elisabeth [d. Richard. int.], and Edward Richardson, Dec. 11, 1696.*

Elisabeth, and George Thurla, May 25, 1726.*

Elisabeth, and Ebenezer Huse, Nov. 1, 1737.*

Elisabeth, and John Watkins, Oct. 28, 1746.*

Elisabeth, and John Ayre of Haverhill [at Haverhill. dup.], Jan. 27, 1746-7.*

Elisabeth, and Stephen Sweet, Mar. 30, 1758.*

Elisabeth, and Hugh Perterson, int. Feb. 27, 1790.

Elisabeth, and Thomas Emery, Dec. 4, 1796.*

Elizabeth, and George Toppan of Newburyport, Jan. 2, 1821.*

Enoch, and Mary Hills, Feb. 1, 1749-50.*

Enoch, and Mary Woodwell of Newburyport, int. Oct. 7, 1781.

Enoch, jr., and Eliza Lunt, Apr. 27, 1817. [May 27. c. R. 1.]*

Eunice, and Joseph Knight, int. Mar. 30, 1765.

Eunice, and John Waite of Ipswich, Oct. 21, 1773.*

Eunice W., of Newburyport, and Joseph B. Hervey, Nov. 4, 1832.

Ezekiel, and wid. Sarah Spofford [of Rowley. int.], at Rowley, Oct. 31, 1736.*

Ezekiel, and Mary Moodey, Sept. 6, 1743.*

Ezekiel, and Mary Sergeant of Amesbury, int. Apr. 13, 1750.

*Intention also recorded.

HALE, Ezekiel, and Hannah Balch of Bradford, int. Feb. 6, 1752.

Ezekiel, and Abigail Sargent of Methuen, at Methuen, Jan. 22, 1755. [Dec. 20, 1755. int.]*

Ezra, and Anna Knight, Oct. 30, 1764.

Ezra, and Nancy Adams, Jan. 1, 1800.*

Ezra, jr., and Almira Perkins, May 7, 1829.*

Ezra, jr., and Rebecca P. Adams of Derry, N. H., int. Apr. 14, 1839.

Hannah, and Thomas Wicum, Jan. 16, 1719.*

Hannah, and Ezra Pilsbury, Nov. 10, 1727.*

Hannah, and Joseph Atkinson, Jan. 23 1744-5.*

Hannah, and John Kelly, jr., July 3, 1749.*

Hannah, and Joseph Titcomb, 3d, Apr. 19, 1750.*

Hannah, and Joshua Pettengell, int. Aug. 25, 1770.

Hannah, and Abraham Plumer, both of Newburyport [Apr. 29. int.], 1809. C. R. 1.*

Henry. and Sarah Kelly [d. John. int.], Sept. 11, 1695.*

Henry, and Mary Bartlet, May 21, 1730.*

Hephsibah, and James Safford, Oct. 7, 1736.*

Isaac, and Ruth Jewett of Rowley, at Rowley, May 1, 1785.*

Jacob, and Mary March of Salisbury, at Salisbury, Jan. 11, 1738-9.*

Jacob [of Newburyport. int.], and Mercy [Eunice. int.] Brown, Nov. 16, 1769.*

Jacob, and Mary Dole, Sept. 1, 1774.*

Jacob, and wid. Mary Safford, int. June 6, 1783.

Jean, and William Cheever, Nov. 12, 1772.*

Joannah [sometime since of Beverly. int.], and Joseph [s. Capt. James. int.] Noyes, Feb. 15, 1710.*

Joannah, and Stephen Gerrish of Contocook, July 15, 1741.*

John, and Rebecca Lowle, Dec. 5, 1660.

John, and Sara Somerby, Dec. 8, 1663.

John, and Sarah Jacques, Oct. 10, 1683.

John, of Beverly, and Mrs. Sara Noyes [at Beverly. dup.], Mar. 31, 1684.

John, of Beverly, and Mrs. Elisabeth Clark [wid., sr. int.], Aug. 8, 1698.*

John, jr., and Patience Dole, July 25, 1716.*

John, and Mary Noyse, Sept. 14, 1732. C. R. 7.

John [jr. int.], and Mrs. Elenor Knight, Oct. 26, 1743.*

John, jr., and Sarah Fowler, May 1, 1750.*

*Intention also recorded.

HALE, John, and Mary Willet, Mar. 25, 1778.*
Joseph, and Mary Moodey, d. Sergt. Caleb, deceased, int. Dec.
   25, 1699.
Joseph, jr., and Mary Noyes, int. May 1, 1736.
Joseph, jr., and Mary Northend of Byfield Rowley, Nov. 19,
   1765.*
Joseph, jr., and Anna L[ongfellow. int.] Dole, Oct. 30, 1800.*
Joseph, of Salem, and Eunice Chute of Rowley, Sept. 18, 1806.
   C. R. 5.
Joseph Rawlings, and Lydia Rogers, June 15, 1818.*
Joshua, and Hannah Woodman, Oct. 13, 1726.*
Joshua, and Hannah Pemberton of Bradford, Jan. 13, 1761.*
Joshua, and Mehetabel Hale. Sept. 2, 1794.*
Judeth, and Tho[mas] Moodey, Nov. 24, 1692. CT. R.
Judeth, and John Eaton of Haverhill [at Haverhill. dup.],
   Oct. 21, 1741.*
Judith, and William Morss [jr. int.], June 17, 1729.*
Judith, and Oliver Hale, May 4, 1758.*
Judith, and John Bradstreet of Ipswich, Feb. 14, 1771.*
Judith, and John Waite of Ipswich, Dec. 29, 1785.*
Judith, and Joseph Tappan, 3d of Newburyport, May 19,
   1812.*
Lucy, and Stephen Kimball, jr. of Newburyport, June 11,
   1835.*
Lydia, and Josiah Bartlet, June 19, 1744.*
Lydia, and Moses Ayer, int. Oct. 2, 1804.
Martha, and Benjamin Fairfield of Wenham, Sept. 3, 1754.*
Martha, of Plaistow, and Edmund Pilsbery, at Haverhill,
   Oct. 22, 1761.*
Martha Greenleaf, and Nathaniel Cornelius Noonan, Sept. 14,
   1788.*
Mary, and Moses Little, sr., Jan. 5, 1714-15.*
Mary, and Edmund Greenleaf [3d. int.], May 4, 1725.*
Mary, and Henry Dole, Nov. 13, 1728.*
Mary, and Roger Merrill, Mar. 10, 1730-31.*
Mary, Mrs., and Rev. James Chandeler of Rowley [at Rowley.
   dup.], Dec. 14, 1736.*
Mary, and Joseph Hidden, Sept. 29, 1737.*
Mary, and David Emery, Dec. 30, 1756.*
Mary, and Enoch Little, Feb. 25, 1768.*
Mary, and Enoch Jaques, int. Jan. 8, 1772.
Mary [wid. int.], and Moses Chase, 3d, Mar. 9, 1784.*

*Intention also recorded.

HALE, Mary, and Rev. Elijah Parish, Nov. 7, 1796.*.
Mary, see Hall, Mary.
Mary Ann, and Aaron K. Hathaway of Woburn, Aug. 29, 1836.*
Mary W., and William O. Dresser, May 12, 1837.*
Matthew, and Mehetable Short of Amesbury, int. Feb. 3, 1760.
Mehetabel, and Joshua Hale, Sept. 2, 1794.*
Mehetable, and Daniel Clark, Jan. 28, 1752.*
Mehitable, and Abel Sawyer, sr., int. Feb. 4, 1779.
Mehitable, and Rev. Levi Frisbie of Ipswich, June 1, 1780.*
Mille, and Henry Noyes, Nov. 5, 1761.*
Moses, and Mrs. Elisabeth Dumer, int. Jan. 5, 1703-4.
Moses [Rev. int.], and Mrs. Mary Moody, Sept. 4, 1707.*
Moses [jr. int.], and Abigail Huse, Apr. 20, 1742.*
Moses, and Mrs. Mehitable Dumer, Nov. 8, 1744.*
Moses, and Mary More [Moore. int.] of Salem, at Salem, Nov. 21, 1763.*
Moses, jr., and Sarah Jewett of Bradford, int. Dec. 17, 1766.
Moses, Rev., of Boxford, and Mrs. Elizabeth Emory, Dec. 28, 1775.*
Moses, and Abigail Smith, June 15, 1786.*
Moses, 3d, and Anna Hills, Sept. 30, 1802.*
Moses, Capt., and Susan Toppan of Newburyport, int. Feb. 25, 1804.
Moses L[ittle. c. r. 10.], of Boston, and Mary L[ane. c. r. 10.] Miltimore, May 13, 1824.*
Nabby [Abigail. int.], and Thomas Merrill, July —, 1792.*
Nathan, and Elisabeth Kent, Aug. 27, 1713.*
Oliver, and Judith Hale, May 4, 1758.*
Oliver, jr., and Lydia Coffin, Sept. 30, 1784.*
Oliver, jr., and Sarah Toppan of Newburyport, July 4, 1821.*
Oliver, and Maria Davis of Pembroke, N. H., int. Sept. 24, 1836.
Patience, and Nathaniel Coffin, jr. [s. John. int.], Mar. 1, 1738-9.*
Phebe, and Samuel Newman of Newburyport, int. May 2, 1801.
Polly, and Timothy Shaw of Hampton Falls, N. H., int. Dec. 5, 1783.
Polly, of Newburyport, and Moses Clerk, int. Apr. 5, 1786.
Polly, and Samuel Knight of Rowley, at Rowley, June 10, 1791.

*Intention also recorded.

HALE, Priscilla, and Ebenezer Savery of Methuen, Dec. 11, 1790.*

Rebekah, and Jonathan Poer, int. Aug. 18, 1703.

Rebekah, and Moses Cheever, Jan. 15, 1770.*

Richard, jr., and Sarah Gage, Nov. 30, 1749.*

Ruth, and John Peirson of Rowley, Dec. 12, 1727.*

Ruth, and John Merrill [3d. int.], June 1, 1730.*

Ruth, and John Little, jr., Apr. 25, 1765.*

Ruth, and William Davis, jr. of Newburyport, int. Aug. 17, 1793.

Samuel, and Apphia Moodey, Aug. 26, 1714.*

Samuel, of Bradford, and Mrs. Sarah Hazzen, Dec. 30, 1723.*

Samuel, and Sarah Hasletine, both of Bradford, Dec. 13, 1725.

Samuel, jr., and Mrs. Elisabeth Pettingill, Apr. 18, 1745.*

Samuel, and Dorcas Lunt, Aug. 15, 1824.*

Samuell, and Sara Ilsly, July 21, 1673.

Sarah, and Stephen Chass, Dec. 17, 171[7. c. r. 2.]

Sarah [d. John. int.], and John Weed, jr., July 19, 1720.*

Sarah, and Joseph Person of Rowley, Jan. 1, 1722-3.*

Sarah, and Joshua Noyes, Apr. 7, 1730.*

Sarah, and Nathaniel Ordway, Apr. 13, 1736.*

Sarah, and Barnerd Brickit, Dec. 21, 1737.*

Sarah, and Capt. Jeremiah Pearle of Boxford, Nov. 10, 1741.*

Sarah, Mrs., and Humphery Atkinson, Aug. 25, 1743.*

Sarah, and Edmund Pilsbury of Haverhill, Nov. 22, 1759.*

Sarah, and Samuel Huse, int. Oct. 21, 1765.

Sarah, Mrs., and Rev. Nathaniel Noyes of South Hampton, N. H., Nov. 12, 1765.*

Sarah, and Edmund Knight, jr., Dec. 24, 1767.*

Sarah, and Moses Emery [jr. int.], Sept. 27, 1770.*

Sarah, of Bradford, and Moses Pilsbury, 3d, int. Nov. 2, 1771.

Sarah, of Hampstead, N. H., and Moses Atkinson, int. Aug. 4, 1781.

Sarah, and Abner Greenleaf [jr. c. r. 2.], Nov. 27, 1783.*

Sarah, and Paul Ilsley, int. Aug. 7, 1789.

Sarah, a. 22 y., d. Oliver and Sarah, and Dan[ie]l B. England, a. 26 y., blacksmith, s. John and Sarah, July 5, 1846.*

Simeon, and Eunice Noyes, June 18, 1771.*

Simeon, and Sarah Lunt, Dec. 15, 1774.*

Stephen, and Sarah Swet, Oct. 15, 1718.*

Stephen, and Martha Goodwin, Mar. 1, 1755.*

Stephen, and Elisabeth Tilton, int. Sept. 29, 1767.

*Intention also recorded.

HALE, Thomas, and Mary Hutchinson, May 26, 1657.

Thomas, and Sara Northend, May 16, 1682.

Thomas, jr., and Anna Short, int. Nov. 25, 1704.

Thomas, jr., and Abigail Pilsbury, Jan. 12, 1726-7.*

Thomas, 3d, and Mary Smith, Jan. 8, 1727-8.*

Thomas, and Alice Little, May 25, 1797.*

Thomas, Esq., and Mary Little, Sept. 17, 1822.*

Thomas, of New York, and Catharine C. Jordan of Savannah, Ga., Oct. 3, 1836.*

Thomasin, and Peter Morss, Mar. 30, 1726.*

William, of Rowley, and Martha Johnson, Nov. 6, 1753.*

William, and Ruth Peart of Manchester, int. Aug. 5, 1809.

William, and Elizabeth Goodwin, Jan. 10, 1819.*

William, jr., and Mary D. Plumer, int. Jan. 4, 1845.

William, and Mary Baston, int. Sept. 11, 1847.

HALL, Daniel, of Barrington, and Nancy H. Brown of Newburyport, Nov. 13, 1825.

Edmund, and Mrs. Elizabeth Calley, Feb. 21, 1813.*

Elisabeth, and Jacob Toppan, Sept. 27, 1748.*

Elizabeth, of Exeter, and Daniel Grant, int. Mar. 12, 1742-3.

Hannah, Mrs., and Edmund Bartlet, Oct. 3, 1745.*

Hannah, and Samuel Todd of Newburyport, int. May 10, 1822.

Isaac, and Elisabeth Johnson, Nov. 23, 1721.*

Joseph, jr., of Newburyport, and Mary D. Goodwin, int. May 11, 1844.

Lois S., of Georgetown, and James V. Rogers, int. May 11, 1840.

Martha, and John Toppan, Oct. 5, 1756.*

Mary [Hale. int.], and Joseph Chandler, Feb. 10, 1699-1700.*

Mary, of Hampton, and Daniel McKenny of Kittery, Dec. 18, 1732. c. R. 7.

Mary, and Lemuel Knight, int. May 21, 1791.

Peter, Capt., and Elizabeth Jackson, both of Portsmouth, May 10, 1732. c. R. 7.

Sarah, and Stephen Folsom, int. Mar. 23, 1805.

Sarah, of Canterbury, N. H., and Daniel Woodman, int. Nov. 8, 1828.

William, of North Kingston, R. I., and Mary Brown, wid. John, 18: 8 m: 1734. c. R. 6.

*Intention also recorded.

HALLODAY (see also Holliday), Sarah, of Ipswich, and
Thomas Stevens, int. Jan. 2, 1747-8.

HAMILTON, Hitty, of Rowley, and William Bailey, at Row-
ley, June 17, 1786.
John, "a foreigner", and Mehetable Duty of Byfield Rowley,
Dec. 25, 1778.

HANDSON (seee also Hanson), Martha, and Eliphalet Noyes,
int. Dec. 12, 1809.

HANIFORD, Lois, and Abner Moors Cheney, July 22, 1800.
c. r. 5.

HANSCOM, Frances, and Edwards Wines, int. June 12, 1840.
William, and Francis Maria Coffin, June 27, 1833.*

HANSON (see also Handson), Jeremiah, and Eliza B. Chase,
int. Apr. 14, 1824.
Lydia, and Thomas Ordway, Nov. 15,. 1807.*
Robard, s. Morill, of Dover, N. H., and Anna, and Miriam
Sargent, d. Ebenezer and Patience, Aug. 28, 1782. c. r. 6.

HARBUT (see also Harbutt), John, and Jane Peirce, May 9,
1753. c. r. 9.*

HARBUTT (see also Harbut), John, and Elisabeth Harridin
of Ipswich, int. Oct. 24, 1747.

HARDE (see also Hardy), Amos, of Bradford, and Mary
Chaney, Feb. 22, 1738-9.*
Beulah [Mrs. c. r. 2.], and Jonathan Philbrick, Aug. 6, 1756.*
Francis, of. Bradford, and Abigail Chaney, int. Nov. 16, 1738.
Francis, and Dorothy Wheeler of Hollis, N. H., int. Jan. 7,
1758.
Mary, and Joseph Lowle, int. Dec. 6, 1707.

HARDY (see also Harde), Charles, of Hampton Falls, N. H.,
and Hannah Ordway, Apr. 14, 1834.*
Deborah, of Bradford, and Joseph Bayley, int. Dec. 25, 1756.
Ephraim, of Bradford, and Susanna Cheney, Nov. 17, 1767.*

*Intention also recorded.

HARDY, Esther, and Chase Colby of Amesbury, Mar. 13, 1777.*
Francis, and Isabella Stanwood, Nov. 21, 1759. c. r. 9.*
Francis, of Newburyport, and Lucy M. Brown, int. Sept. 3,
    1831.
George, and Mary Fogg, Nov. 24, 1686. ct. r.
John, and Betsey Easman of Henniker, int. Sept. 25, 1801.
John [C. int.], Capt., of Newburyport, and Sarah Jane Brown,
    Dec. 19, 1828.*
Mary, wid., and Benjamin Poer, Apr. 13, 1696.*
Mary, of Bradford, and William Pilsbury, int. Oct. 2, 1762.
Moses, of Bradford, and Mary Boynton, Dec. 3, 1760.*
Nathaniel, and Eleanor Squire of Ashford, int. Feb. 15, 1777.
Sally, of Bradford, and Abner Bailey, 3d, int. Dec. 26, 1818.
Sarah, and Zechariah Donnell, June 22, 1769.*
Sarah J., wid., a. 35 y., d. Nicholas and Jane, and John Alter
    [Altex. int.] of Philadelphia, Pa., a. 38 y., merchant, b.
    Pennsylvania, s. Jacob and Elizabeth, May 3, 1846.*
Susanna [of Bradford. int.], and Benjamin Thurston [jr. Aug.
    31. int.], 1805. c. r. 1.*
William, of Newburyport, and Nancy Rier, Apr. 18, 1822.*

HARMON (see also Harmond), John, and Hannah J. Mil-
    ler, int. July 1, 1826.
John, and Eliza B. Chase, Aug. 30, 1826.*

HARMOND (see also Harmon), Eliza B., of Newburyport,
    and Henry Lunt, int. Nov. 10, 1837.

HARRAMAN (see also Harriman), Jassiel, of Plaistow, N.
    H., and Mary Davis, Mar. 19, 1752. c. r. 2.*

HARRANDIN (see also Harridin), Joseph [Haradan. int.],
    of Gloucester, and Joanna Emerson, Jan. 6, 1731-2.*

HARRIDIN (see also Harrandin), Elisabeth, of Ipswich, and
    John Harbutt, int. Oct. 24, 1747.

HARRIMAN (see also Harraman, Hereman, Herriman),
    Nathaniel, of Rowley, and Hannah Colman, at Rowley,
    May 21, 1742.*

*Intention also recorded.

HARRINGTON, Moses, of Cornish, N. H., and Abigail Chase, Oct. 22, 1795.*

HARRIS (see also Harrise, Harriss, Herris), Anne, and James Mulloone, Sept. 18, 1722.*

Benjamin, and Leucy Whitman of Stowe, int. Sept. 30, 1740.

Daniel, and Jerusha Howard, July 29, 1755.*

Ebenezer, of Ipswich, and Sally Downs, int. May 17, 1823.

Edward, and Lydia Currier, July 8, 1762.*·

Elisabeth, and John Badger [s. John. int.], Dec. 29, 1713.*

Elisabeth, of Ipswich, and Henry Friend, int. Nov. 22, 1758.

Elisabeth, of Newburyport, and John Floyd, int. May 24, 1806.

Elizabeth, and John Quill of Boston, Sept. 6, 1762. c. r. 8.

Giles, and Mary March, Nov. 26, 1747.*

John, and Martha Fowler of Ipswich, int. Sept. 15, 1744.

Josiah, of North Yarmouth, and Anna Knight, Oct. 2, 1793.*

Margeret, and John Wadley of Stratham, N. H., Aug. 8, 1744.*

Mary, of Dover, and Moses Flood, Nov. 20, 1738.*

Mary J., and Samuel S. Short, Sept. 24, 1841.*

Nancy, and Daniel Thurston Colman, Feb. 3, 1818.*

Phebe, of Rowley [Ipswich. int.], and Nathan Dole, at Rowley, June 6, 1754.*

Rachel, of Rowley, and John Webber, int. Jan. 6, 1759.

Ruth, and Abraham Bayley, July 29, 1762.*

Sally, and Benja[min] Perkins of Newburyport, June 1, 1823.*

Samuel, and Abigail Presbury, Feb. 1, 1738-9.*

Sarah, and John Kent, 4th, Oct. 1, 1747.*

Sarah, of Rowley, and Eliphalet Tenney, at Rowley, Oct. 13, 1755.*

Sarah, of Ipswich, and William Perkins, int. Oct. 3, 1818.

Susan S., and Thomas Caswell, Nov. 2, 1836.*

William, and Mary Lord of Exeter, N. H., int. Feb. 11, 1743-4.

William, and Salley Emery, Sept. 23, 1804.*

William, and Eliza Murray of Newburyport, int. Oct. 1, 1822.

William, of Newburyport, and Sarah Dutton, int. Nov. 1, 1823.

HARRISE (see also Harris), Jonathan [of Newburyport. c. r. 1.], and Anna Toppan, Apr. 10, 1788.*

*Intention also recorded.

HARRISS (see also Harris), Hannah, of Newburyport, and
Benjamin Goodwin, int. Apr. 24, 1802.
Samuel, jr., and Merinda Perkins, Nov. 16, 1831.*

HARROD, Hannah, of Boston, and Witter Cumings, int. Mar.
1, 1739-40.

HART (see also Hartt, Heart), Laurence, and Dorothy Jones,
Feb. 12, 1678.
Sarah, and Nathaniel Knap, Sept. 18, 1734. c. r. 7.*
Susan M., and Joseph Jackman, int. Aug. 7, 1846.
Thomas, of Portsmouth, N. H., and Anne Noyes, Nov. 14,
1762.*

HARTSHORN, Sarah, of Plaistow, N. H., and John Downing,
int. Feb. 1, 1783.

HARTT (see also Hart), Charles, and Rebeckah Kent, int.
May 26, 1705.

HARVEY, Abigail, Mrs., and Samuel Brown, Jan. 3, 1743-4.*

HASELTON (see also Hazeltine), Ruth, and William Ilsly,
Dec. 26, 1717.

HASKEL (see also Haskell), Nehemiah, Dea., of Newbury-
port, and Elisabeth Sawyer, int. Oct. 6, 1798.
Solomon, Dea., and Martha Smith, June 15, 1794.*
Tammey, and Joseph Bamford, June 9, 1796.*
William, and Elisabeth Nelson of Newburyport, int. Feb. 2,
1788.

HASKELL (see also Haskel, Haskill); Alexander, and Ra-
chael Stanwood, at Gloucester, Oct. 7, 1762.
Caleb, jr., of Newburyport, and Edna Hale, Apr. 10, 1781.*
Caroline, and George Lambert of Newburyport, int. June 4,
1836.
Eliza Ann, of Newburyport, and Will[ia]m R. Long, June 4,
1822.*
Jacob, of Newburyport, and Eunice Jaques, Dec. 23, 1819.*

*Intention also recorded.

HASKELL, Jacob, a. 26 y., school teacher, s. Jacob and Eunice, and Sarah E. Carr, a. 19 y., d. Dudly and Sarah Ann, Mar. 9, 1847.*

Joanna, of Newburyport, and Amos Pettingell, int. June 19, 1802.

John P. T., of Rochester, and Harriet M. Toppan of Newburyport, Nov. 16, 1832.

Mark, and Mary Ann Rundlett of North Hampton, N. H., int. Feb. 3, 1832.

Mary, of Newburyport, and Moses Pettingell, int. Nov. 28, 1823.

Mary, and Joseph H. Felch, Apr. 16, 1834.*

Mary N., and David T. Woodwell, Dec. 3, 1843.*

Nathan, of Newburyport, and Anna Lackey, int. May 12, 1804.

Rachel, and Joseph Mitchell, Feb. 7, 1786.*

Solomon, jr., and Harriet Orne of Newburyport, int. Jan. 5, 1830.

Stephen G., of Newburyport, and Mary G. Johnson, Dec. 1, 1836.*

HASKILL (see also Haskell), Nehemiah, and Elisabeth Fitts of Ipswich, int. Nov. 6, 1762.

HASKINS, Abigail, see Hodgkins, Abigail.

Tho[ma]s, and Hannah Freese, Feb. 14, 1716-17. c. R. 7.

HASLETINE (see also Hazeltine), Sarah, and Peter Merrill, Sept. 25, 1717.*

Sarah, and Samuel Hale, both of Bradford, Dec. 13, 1725.

HASTELETT, Sarah Ann, and Benjamin Goodwin Hunt, int. Oct. 6, 1827.

HASTINGS, Nathaniel, of Salem, N. H., and Lydia Bricket, Nov. 23, 1818.*

HASTY, Elizabeth P., of Newtown, N. H., and Abial Pearson, int. July 8, 1844.

HATCH, Luther, and Margaret L. Chase, int. May 31, 1845.

*Intention also recorded.

HATHAWAY, Aaron K., of Woburn, and Mary Ann Hale, Aug. 29, 1836.*

HATHORNE, Sara, and Joseph Coker, Apr. 13, 1665.

HATTLE, Margaret J., and George W. Rappel of Newburyport, int. Nov. 3, 1849.

HAWES, Richard, and Nancy Chase, May 12, 1818.*
Sarah Jane, and Joseph H. Currier of Newburyport, int. Oct. 30, 1830.

HAWKINS, Hannah, and Anthony Ilsley, Oct. 18, 1785.*
John, and Nancy C. Robinson, Aug. 23, 1824.*
Nancy C., and Caleb H. Howard, Nov. 29, 1826.*
William, resident in Newburyport, and Hannah Willet, int. July 1, 1780.

HAWLEY, W[illia]m, of Newburyport, and Lydia Hoyt, int. Nov. 18, 1848.

HAYES, Ebenezer G., of Newburyport, and Mary A. Merrill, int. July 4, 1847.
Elisabeth, and William Mireck, Oct. 15, 1730.*
Eloner, and Matthews Yong, Apr. 23, 1696.*
James, and Martha George, Apr. 24, 1757.*
Juliann C., of Strafford, N. H., and Obadiah S. Davis, int. Dec. 1, 1835.

HAYFORD, Barzilla, and Mary Howell, Apr. 21, 1812.*
Nathan, of Tamworth, N. H., and Judith Hunt, ——, 1808 or 9. [June 25, 1808. int.]*

HAYNES (see also Haines), Frederic, and Olive Merrill, Sept. 6, 1824.*
Jonathan, and Mary Moulton, Jan. 1, 1674.
Newell H., of Stoneham, a. 30 y., mechanic, b. Epsom, s. Caleb B. and Sarah, and Mary J. Merrill, a. 29 y., b. Deerfield, d. Joseph and Nancy, Nov. 29, 1849.*
Priscilla, of North Hampton, N. H., and Noah Little, int. Sept. 8, 1832.
Sara, and Joseph Hoton, Nov. 13, 1651.

*Intention also recorded.

HAZELTINE (see also Haselton, Hasletine, Hazelton), Anna,
and Amos Noyes, jr., Nov. 26, 1807. c. r. 1.
Deborah, of Haverhill, and John Merril, int. Aug. 7, 1708.
(Forbidden by Penuel Titcomb at the request of Sarah
Sawyer, singlewoman.)
Samuel [of Bradford. int.], and Ema Kent, June 10, 1701.*
Susanna [of Chester, N. H., int.], and Nathaniel Coffin, May
2, 1809. c. r. 1.*

HAZELTON (see also Hazeltine), Harriet E., of Salem, and
Enoch Plumer, jr., int. Apr. 12, 1845.
Nancy, of Newburyport, and Amos Noyes, jr., Nov. 26, 1807.*

HAZZEN, Hannah, of Boxford, and Joshua Morss, July 13,
1727.*
Richard, of Haverhill, and Mrs. Sarah Clement, Oct. 22,
1719.*
Sarah, Mrs., and Samuel Hale of Bradford, Dec. 30, 1723.*

HEAD, Joanna, and Joseph Pike [jr. int.], Dec. 28, 1710.*
Joseph, of Concord, and Sarah Bailey, Oct. 31, 1817.*

HEALY, Sarah, and Hugh March, sr., Dec. 3, 1685.

HEARD (see also Herd), Abigail, and William Brackenbury,
both of Ipswich, Sept. 3, 1707.
Betsey, Mrs., of Newport. N. H., and Joseph Greenough of
Boston, Nov. —, 1839.
Elisabeth, of Ipswich, and Anthony Somerby, int. Mar. 1,
1696-7.
Mary [Polly. int.], of Ipswich, and Edmund Boynton, at Ips-
wich, Mar. 22, 1792.*

HEARL, Jacob, of Shapleigh, Me., and Clarissa M. Colman,
Sept. 28, 1829.*

HEARN, Maurice, and Sally Mores Jewett, int. Nov. 1, 1812.

HEART (see also Hart), Ann, and John Lunt, Jan. 11, 1709.*

*Intention also recorded.

HEATH (see also Heth), Daniel S., and Abigail Locke of
Newburyport, int. Aug. 22, 1829.
Dudley, and Achsah Brown of Rowley, Mar. 28, 1811.*
Hannah, of Haverhill, and John Davis, June 29, 1715.*
Priscilla, and Moses Follansbee, June 14, 1756.
Richard, and Rebecca Newell, Oct. 15, 1812.*

HEBRON, Isabella, and Joseph Bartlet, Feb. 20, 1760.*

HEDMAN, Joseph, and Mary Smith, "Irish", both of Boston,
Nov. 5, 1728. C. R. 7.

HENDEN, Ann, and Henry Lynard, both of Boston, Dec. 2,
1741. C. R. 7.

HENDERSON, Charles, of Newburyport, a. 29 y., carpenter,
b. Newburyport, s. Samuel and Rhoda, of Newburyport,
and Olive Ann Battis, a. 25 y., d. Joseph and Olive, May
24, 1846.*
Lucy M., and Charles F. Wakefield, both of Lowell, Nov. 20,
1831.

HENDRICK, Hannah, wid., of Haverhill, and Henry Bradley,
at Haverhill, Apr. 17, 1729.

HENRY, Elisabeth, of Newburyport, and Michael Faherty,
int. Aug. 12, 1848.
Mary, and Jonathan Ingersol, Nov. 24, 1763.*
Molly, and John Low, int. Aug. 23, 1762.

HERBERT, see Harbut.

HERD (see also Heard), Hannah, of Ipswich, and John Butler, int. Aug. 27, 1748.

HEREMAN (see also Harriman), Samuel, of Rowley, and
Jane Coleman, Oct. 16, 1729.*

HERRICK, Daniel, of Hopkinton, and Esther Currier, Jan. 24,
1786.*
Joseph, of Salem Village, and Mrs. Mary March [wid. int.],
Jan. 29, 1706-7.*
Sarah, and Joseph Brown, both of Salem, Nov. 2, 1733. C. R. 7.

*Intention also recorded.

HERRIMAN (see also Harriman), Asa, and Joanna Beal, Mar. 5, 1761.*
Jane, and Timothy Toppan, Nov. 23, 1758.*
Jane, and Benjamin Evans of Salisbury, Aug. 19, 1762.*
Leonard, and Martha Plummer, both of Rowley, July 5, 1715.

HERRIS (see also Harris), Molly, and David Pilsbury, Mar. 24, 1801.*

HERVEY (see also Hervy), James M., of Boston, and Martha Ann Laskey, int. Feb. 13, 1836.
Joseph B., and Eunice W. Hale of Newburyport, Nov. 4, 1832.
Sarah E., of Gloucester, and Enoch Floyd, jr., int. Dec. 4, 1832.
Thomas, of Newburyport, and Rachel Quimby, Jan. 11, 1795.*

HERVY (see also Hervey), Nancy, of Newburyport, and William Connor, int. Sept. 17, 1791.

HETH (see also Heath), Jane, of Haverhill, and Joseph Kelley, Dec. 23, 1706.
Josiah, sr., of Haverhill, and wid. Martha Chase, int. May 9, 1713.

HEWES (see also Huse), Soloman, and Mrs. Martha Calef of Boston, int. June 19, 1700.

HEWLETT, Richard S., of Winchester, Vir., and Clarissa M. Colman, int. July 31, 1824.

HEWS (see also Huse), Clarissa, and Thomas Hunkins, Nov. 11, 1798.*
Mary, and Samuel Toppan [3d. int.], July 6, 1749.*

HIBBARD (see also Hibbut), Jeremiah, of Manchester, and Elizabeth Williams of Beverly, Jan. 17, 1733-4. C. R. 7.

HIBBUT (see also Hibbard), Thomas, and Mary Gains, at Gloucester, Sept. 25, 1764.

*Intention also recorded.

HICKEY, Elizabeth Swasey, of Newburyport, and Asa Chamberlin, int. Sept. 3, 1813.
Mary Jane, of Newburyport, and Silas Lunt, jr., int. Oct. 13, 1832.

HICKMAN, Eveline, and Charles Tyler, both of Newburyport, Nov. 28, 1837.
Gideon, and Mrs. Margaret Magowen, both of Newburyport, Nov. 17, 1836.
Mary E., of Newburyport, a. 24 y., b. Newburyport, d. Gideon and Mary, and Joseph Magowen of Newburyport, a. 32 y., mariner, b. Newburyport, s. Joseph and Margaret, of Newburyport, Sept. 6, 1846.

HIDDEN, Betty, and Abel Cresey of Newburyport, int. Oct. 5, 1765.
David, and Elizabeth Stickney of Newburyport, int. Dec. 12, 1781.
Elisabeth, of Rowley, and Cornelius Davis, at Rowley, Aug. 29, 1696.*
Elisabeth, and Thomas Greenleaf, Jan. 6, 1779.*
Elisabeth, and Jacob Adams, int. Oct. 3, 1789.
Hannah, and Samuel Stickney, ——, 1808 or 9. [Jan. 24, 1809. int.]*
Hannah J., Mrs., and Benj[ami]n G. Hunt, Jan. 21, 1838.*
Jacob, and Elisabeth Beal, Nov. 20, 1760.*
Jacob, and Jane Pettengill, Apr. 25, 1799.*
Jacob, and Betsey Jaques, int. Mar. 14, 1812.
Jacob, and Judith Clark, Sept. 10, 1812.*
Jacob, jr., and Hannah Johnson Thurlo, Dec. 16, 1821.*
James, of Rowley, and Jemima Moody, at Rowley, Sept. 26, 1748.*
John, and Elis[abeth] Beal, Nov. 20, 1760. c. r. 9.
John, and Anne Hale, int. Nov. 21, 1767.
John, and Mary Clanan of Newburyport, int. Nov. 29, 1793.
Joseph, and Mary Hale, Sept. 29, 1737.*
Joseph, jr., and Sarah Lunt, June 17, 1761.*
Lucy, and Dea. Silas Pearson, Jan. 2, 1802.*
Margeret, of Rowley, and Abraham Sawyer, Feb. 17, 1736-7.*
Mary, and Edmund Pettingall of Newburyport, int. Oct. 27, 1779.

. *Intention also recorded.

HIDDEN, Mary, and Benjamin Toppan, int. Jan. 17, 1784.

Molly, and Samuel Brown, at Gloucester, Dec. 7, 176-.

Robinson, of Gloucester, and [wid. int.] Katharine Beal, Nov. 21, 1775. [He takes said Katharine naked without any estate. int.]*

Ruth, and Edmund Morse of Newburyport, int. Nov. 22, 1783.

Samuel, of Rowley, and Anne Cresey, int. May 7, 1759.

Sarah, of Rowley, and Enoch Wells, int. Mar. 1, 1760.

Sarah, and John Cheever of Newburyport, int. Jan. 16, 1779.

Sarah, and John Smith, 4th [3d. int.], Jan. 31, 1788.*

Sarah T.[J. int.], and George W. Lunt of Newburyport, Jan. 8, 1825.*

Timothy, and Mehetabel Willet, May 26, 1776.*

HIGBE, Merrill, and Patty McCanty of Newburyport, int. Aug. 6, 1808.

HIGGENS, Salley, of Ipswich, and Nathaniel Plummer, int. Dec. 20, 1799.

HIGGINSON, Elizabeth, of Newburyport, and Nicholas Johnson, int. Nov. 11, 1831.

Sarah [of Boston. int.], and Dudley Atkins Tyng, Esq., at Boston, Oct. 18, 1792.*

Susan, of Newburyport, and James Frederick Otis of Portland, Me., int. Sept. 24, 1832.

HILDRITH, Azor B. F., of Chelsea, Vt., and Hannah L. Rier, Oct. 24, 1839.*

HILL (see also Hills), Azubah, of Rowley, and Moses Currier, Apr. 25, 1803.*

Betsey, and John Thurlow, both of Rowley, Mar. 28, 1811. C. R. 5.

Catharine, and William D. Jackman, May 28, 1837.*

Ednah, and Will[ia]m Hills, July 1, 1800.*

Eliphalet, and Abigail Webster, 2d w. [of Haverhill. int.], Nov. 31, 1816. C. R. 1.*

Elisabeth, of Westerly, R. I., and Capt. Edward Wyer of Charlestown, July 30, 1728. C. R. 7.

Hannah, and Joseph Pollard, both of Litchfield, Feb. 26, 1734-5. C. R. 7.

*Intention also recorded.

HILL, John, of Rowley, and Elizabeth Knapp of Salem, Jan. 28, 1816. c. r. 5.

Joseph, s. Samuel, of Kittery, Me., yeoman, and Miriam Sawyer, d. Stephen, yeoman, Oct. 24, 1744. c. r. 6.

Mary, of Billerica, and Nathaniel Patten of Windham, Conn., June 22, 1734. c. r. 7.

Robert, Quaker, and Elizabeth Stephens of Ipswich, Apr. 10, 1728. c. r. 7.

Sarah, and Jonathan Bullard, both of Sherborn, Dec. 8, 1733. c. r. 7.

Sarah, of Boston, and Lt. Enoch Huse, int. Oct. 26, 1782.

HILLIARD, Elizabeth C., a. 35 y., d. William and Betsy Currier, and Charles A. Olmstead, a. 28 y., shipwright, b. Perry, Me., s. Eliphalet, of Perry, Me., May 17, 1849.*

Henry H., of Boston, and Elizabeth C. Currier, Sept. 10, 1837.*

Jonathan, of Hampton, and Hannah Cooper, Nov. 9, 1732.*

HILLS (see also Hill), Abigail, and Isaac Bailey [jr. int.], Apr. 15, 1731.*

Abigail, and Edward Dane [Dean. int.], June 20, 1744.*

Abigail, and Edward Dean, Mar. 18, 1756 *

Abigail. and John Whittier [Whitcher. int.], June 12, 1800.*

Abigaill, and Joseph Brown, 3d, Dec. 26, 1723.*

Amos, and Nancy [Mary. int.] Chase, Apr. 25, 1793.*

Anna, and Moses Hale, 3d, Sept. 30, 1802.*

Benjamin, and Rebecca Ordway, Nov. 7, 1709.*

Benjamin, jr., and Anna Brickett, Sept. 27, 1774.*

Charles, of Rowley, and Mehitabel B. Chase, Dec. 3, 1818.*

Daniel, and Hannah Emery, May 10, 1757.*

Delia, and Capt. Nathan Perley, Apr. 28, 1813.*

Dorothy, and Nehemiah Folansbe, Dec. 16, 1784.*

Dorothy, of Rowley, and John Pearson, int. Sept. 14, 1805.

Edward [Edmund. int.]. and Prudence Ilsley, June 12, 1806.*

Eliphalet, and Sarah Whyman of Lancaster, at Lancaster, Sept. 18, 1783.*

Eliphalet, jr., and Sarah Coffin, Dec. 14. 1809.*

Elisabeth. of Newburyport, and Joseph Greenleaf, int. Oct. 24, 1801.

Elisha. of Portsmouth, N. H., and Jane Stevens, Oct. 31, 1765.*

*Intention also recorded.

HILLS, Elizabeth, and John Greenleafe, Oct. 12, 1685.
Emme, and Somers Clark, Nov. 26, 1735.*
Francis, and Hannah Tenney, Oct. 24, 1801. c. R. 5.
Gorham, and Ann Farrington, ———, 1836.
Hannah, and Abiell Long, Oct. 27, 1682.
Hannah, and Edmund Easman, Apr. 28, 1747.*
Hannah, and Nathaniel Bartlet, Jan. 12, 1773.*
Hannah, and Moses Wood of Bradford, Oct. 25, 1781.*
Henry, and Hannah Bodwell of Haverhill, at Haverhill, Sept.
    3, 1715.*
Henry, of Nottingham, and Dorcas Thirston, Nov. 11, 1736.*
Jacob, and Margaret Plats, Apr. 21, 1757.*
James, and Abigail Merrill, Dec. 26, 1723.*
John, and Mary Pilsbury, Mar. or Apr. —, 1728. [Mar. 30.
    int.]*
John, and Mary Snow of Haverhill, int. July 25, 1810.
John A., of Wells, Me., and Elizabeth L. Chase, Oct. 24,
    1839.*
Jonathan, and Abigail Bailey, int. Oct. 10, 1748. [Abigail
    Bayle forbids proceeding.]
Jonathan, and Hannah Merrill, Oct. 25, 1749.*
Joseph, and Anne Lunt, Mar. 8, 1664.
Joseph, and Priscila Chase, int. Feb. 26, 1703-4.
Joseph, Dr. [jr. int.], and Mrs. Hannah Britt, Sept. 10, 1730.*
Joshua, and Hannah Hunt, Dec. 27, 1739.*
Joshua, and Mary Noyes [Morse. int.], Nov. 13, 1766.*
Josiah, and Mary Bartlet, Sept. 30, 171[8. c. R. 2.]*
Josiah, and Elisabeth Stickny of Bradford, int. May 3, 1751.
Josiah, and Hannah Bayley, July 23, 1786.*
Judith, and Isaac Forster, July 9, 1752.*
Mary, and Jacob Adams, Aug. 31, 1742.*
Mary, and Enoch Hale, Feb. 1, 1749-50.*
Mary, and Charles Adams, Dec. 18, 1760.*
Mary S., of Rowley, and Simon T. Currier, Apr. 28, 1830.*
Moses, and Rebecca Hills, Jan. 28, 1734-5.*
Nathaniel, and Elisabeth Ordway, int. Mar. 16, 1771.
Nathaniel, and Caroline Parker, both of Newburyport, Mar.
    12, 1839.
Natt[haniel], and Ann Worm, int. Oct. 24, 1709.
Obadiah, and Sarah Merrill, Jan. 13, 1774.*
Obadiah, and Mrs. Lois Foss, both of Rowley, Nov. 31, 1814.
    c. R. 5.

*Intention also recorded.

HILLS, Philip K., of Newburyport, and Mary P. Gerrish, int. Aug. 15, 1846.
Polly, and Joseph Carlton, int. Feb. 6, 1806.
Prudence, and Francis England, May 10, 1757.*
Rebecca, and Moses Hills, Jan. 28, 1734-5.*
Rebekah, and Thomas Huse, Aug. 5, 1779.*
Rebekah, and Moses Jaques, July —, 1792.*
Ruth, and Nathaniel Mason of Boston, Sept. 1, 1743.*
Ruth, and John Chase, Feb. 16, 1762.*
Ruth, and Joseph Tenny, Dec. 17, 1771.*
Sally, and Ephraim Hutchins of Hampstead, N. H., int. Nov. 27, 1792.
Samuel, and Rebecca Thirston, Jan. 28, 1734-5.*
Samuel, and Prudence England, July 24, 1766.*
Samuel, and Prudence Bartlett, int. June 22, 1807.
Samuell, and Abigal Wheeler, May 20, 1679.
Sarah, and Samuel Woodman [jr. int.], May 7, 1761.*
Smith, and Mary Sawyer, Oct. [14. c. r. 2.], 1730.*
Smith, and Rachel Lowe, Jan. 30, 1744-5.*
Susanna, and Capt. John Ayer of Haverhill, Dec. 8, 1818.*
Thomas, and Betsey Chadwick of Bradford, at Bradford, Apr. —, 1783.*
William, and Amme Kelle, int. Jan. 31, 1712-13.
Will[ia]m, and Ednah Hill, July 1, 1800.*
William, jr., and Judith Chase, Jan. 21, 1802.*

HILTON, Hannah, and Jonathan Woodman, July 2, 1668.
Joseph [Ens. int.], of Exeter, and Rebecca Adams [jr. int.], Oct. 10, 1716.*
Joseph, and Margaret Pettengell, int. Dec. 25, 1762.
Mary, alias Downer, and Thomas Seers, Dec. 11, 1656.

HINCKLEY (see also Hinkley), Job, and Sarah Tufts, Dec. 9, 1723.*

HIND (see also Hynes), Ambrose, of Cambridge, and Anna Young of Medford, Apr. 22, 1734. c. r. 7.

HINKLEY (see also Hinckley), Gideon [of Brunswick. int.], and Mary Russell, Sept. 22, 1755.*
Salley, of Newburyport, and Daniel Lunt, int. May 29, 1803.

*Intention also recorded.

HOAG (see also Hoague, Hoog, Hoŵig), Benjamin, and Sarah Norris [of Exeter, N. H. int.], June 23, 1702.*
Jonathan, and Martha Goodwin, Sept. 15, 1703.*
Judith, and Thomas Nichols of Amesbury, 24: 3 m: 1720. c. r. 6. [int. 20: 2 m: 1721.]*
Martha, d. Jonathan, and Joseph Peasley, s. John, of Amesbury [of Haverhill. dup. c. r. 4.], Jan. 1, 1729. c. r. 6.

HOAGUE (see also Hoag), Abigail S., of Newburyport, and Edmund Smith, jr., int. Nov. 4, 1837.

HOBBS (see also Hobs), Polly, of Topsfield, and Samuel Safford, int. Jan. 10, 1807.
———, of Topsfield, and Mrs. Mehetible Searles of Rowley, June 21, 1804. c. r. 5.

HOBS (see also Hobbs), Hannah, of Rowley, and Joseph Titcomb, jr., int. Sept. 26, 1800.
Mary, and [John. c. c. and cr. r.] Kent, Feb. 24, 1664.

HOBSON (see also Hopson), Hannah, of Rowley, and John Batchelder, int. Mar. 21, 1809.
Humphery, of Rowley, and Priscilla Perkins, Mar. 5, 1745-6.*
Lydia, of Rowley, and Moses Dole, at Rowley, Apr. 9, 1765.*
Mary J., of Georgetown, a. 17 y., b. Rowley, d. Prescott and Dorothy, and Daniel Pearson of Georgetown, a. 18 y., shoemaker, b. West Newbury, s. William and Betsey, Mar. 11, 1848.
Nancy, and Henry Mason, June 5, 1832.*
Sarah, of Ipswich, and James Chase, int. May 7, 1819.
Tristram, of Ipswich, and Nancy Jackman, int. Apr. 27, 1820.
Tristram, of Rowley, and Mary E. Battis, int. Feb. 1, 1845.

HODGDON, Adariel H., and Mary S. Fowler of Salisbury, int. July 6, 1833.

HODGE (see also Hodges), Charles, and Elisabeth Titcomb, Sept. 9, 1742.*
Ellice, of Newburyport, and Jacob Chase, jr., int. Sept. 8, 1803.
Joanna, Mrs., of Salisbury, and Jonathan Beck, at Salisbury, Aug. 2, 1743.*

*Intention also recorded.

HODGEKIN, William, and Eliza[beth] Browne, Nov. 11, 1687. CT. R.

HODGES (see also Hodge), James, sailor, and Katharine Galpine, both of Boston, June 17, 1727. C. R. 7.
Sarah, of Rowley, and David S. Batchelder of Haverhill, June 2, 1808. C. R. 5.

HODGKINS (see also Hodgskins, Hogskins), Abigail [Haskins. int.], and George Bechem, Mar. 30, 1726.*
Hanah, and James Kent. [jr. int.], Dec. 23, 1707.*
John, jr., of Ipswich, and Mary Crombie, at Ipswich, July 16, 1789.*
Joseph, and Emma Eldridge of Salisbury, int. Sept. 26, 1810.
Joseph, and Mary Stark of Newburyport, Mar. 19, 1822.*
Joseph E., and Hannah L. H. Bayley of West Newbury, int. Nov. 6, 1835.
Patience, and Edward Wells, Dec. 1, 1743. C. R. 7.
Phillip, and Sarah Griffin, Apr. 13, 1724.*
Soloman, and Martha Gooding of Salisbury, int. Apr. 25, 1747.

HODGSKINS (see also Hodgkins), Anna, and Moses Peirce, jr., Dec. 26, 1762.*
Aquila, and Anna [Anne. int.] Moulton, May 29, 1761.*
Deborah, and Samuel Searls of Woodbery, Co. Devon, Great Britain, now resident in Newbury, int. Jan. 9, 1747.
Deborah, and Benjamin Pike, jr., Sept. 19, 1750.*
Francis, and Martha Pettengell, Nov. 16, 1760.*
Mary, and Jacob Pressy [jr. int.] of Amesbury, Feb. 22, 1758.*
Mehetable, Mrs., and Benajah Young, Dec. 11, 1744.*
Sarah, and Francis Ellite, Oct. 4, 1742.*

HOGAN (see also Hogin), Edward, and Anna Brown, int. Feb. 26, 1803.

HOGIN (see also Hogan), Elisabeth, and John Coleby, June 29, 1748.*

HOGSKINS (see also Hodgkins), Abigail, Mrs., and Samuel Fowler, July 1, 1742.*

*Intention also recorded.

HOIES, Catharine, wid., and Job Whipple, both of Ipswich, Mar. 2, 1731-2. C. R. 7.

HOIT (see also Hoyt), Micah, and Susanna Colebey, both of Amesbury, Feb. 4, 1725-6. C. R. 7.
Moses, and Mary Buzzell, Feb. 5, 1740-41.*
Nathan, and Mrs. Mary Pettingill, Apr. 28, 1742.*

HOITE (see also Hoyt), Hannah, and John Chase, jr., July 30, 1728.*

HOLBROOK, Joseph, of Newcastle, N. H., and Jane March, Nov. 29, 1770.*

HOLDGATE (see also Holgate), Elisabeth [of Haverhill. C. R. 2.], and John Morss, June 20, 1754.*

HOLEMAN (see also Holman), Elisabeth, and William Anderton, Oct. 28, 1725.*
John, of Sutton, and Hannah Cheney, Nov. 25, 1755.*
Joseph [Homan. C. R. 2.], and Bettee Richardson, June 7, 1764.*
Judith, and Benja[min] Cheney, Nov. 6, 1753.*
Mary, and John Bayley, jr. of Rowley, Nov. 4, 1756.*
Sarah, and Moses Lull of Rowley, July 8, 1755.*

HOLEMON (see also Holman), John, and Judeth Huse, May 23, 1728.*

HOLGATE (see also Holdgate), James, Dr., of Haverhill, and Mrs. Lydia Sawyer, Apr. 2, 1747. C. R. 7.

HOLLAND, Edward, and Mrs. Hannah Miller, Dec. 17, 1744.*
Hannah, of Exeter, N. H., and Juba Merrill, Aug. 3, 1777.*
John, and Rebeckah Ilsley, Aug. 28, 1792.*
Mary Wells, and John Stickney, jr., int. Dec. 27, 1782.
Nathaniel, and Sarah Wells, int. July 1, 1758.
Nathaniel, and Sarah Wells, Mar. 4, 1763.*

*Intention also recorded.

HOLLIDAY (see also Halloday), Francis, and Susanna Newman, July 31, 1754.*
John, and Mary Rogers, Dec. 19, 1751.*

HOLMAN (see also Holeman, Holemon, Holmon, Homan,
Homans), Edward, and Hannah Emery, May 19, 1726.*
Mary, and Woodbridge Greenleaf of Newburyport, July 25,
1790.*
Solomon, and Mary Brickit, May 23, 1722.*
Solomon, and Elisabeth Kelly, Apr. 18, 1738.*

HOLMES (see also Homes), Francis, and Mary Smith, Mar.
18, 1756.*
John, of Rowley, and Mary Carlton, Mar. 18, 1755.*
Marmaduke, and Mary Franklyn, both of Boston, Apr. 23,
1731. C. R. 7.
Mary, and Henry Poer, jr. of Rowley, int. Apr. 6, 1703.
Rebekah, and William Ridgill, both of Boston, Mar 16, 1726-
7. C. R. 7.
Samuel, of Rowley, and Abigail Floyd, int. Sept. 9, 1831.

HOLMON (see also Holman), Rachel, and Samuel Waters of
Sutton, Nov. 13, 1729.*
Sarah, and Abel Chase, Mar. 23, 1730-31.*

HOLT, Allis, and Joshua Mitchell, Mar. 10, 1756.*
John S., of Cambridge, a. 26 y., mason, s. Thomas, of Cam-
bridge, and Ann M. Ordway, a. 24 y., tailoress, d. John,
Sept. 1, 1844.*
Oliver, of Andover, and Mary Huse, abt. July 10, 1716.*

HOMAN (see also Holman), Bridget, of Mountsweage, and
Nathaniel Foster, jr., int. Mar. 4, 1758.
Joseph, 3d, of Marblehead, and Mary Chaney, Dec. 20, 1734.*
Thomas [Holeman. int.], of Sutton, and Deborah Huntinton,
at Amesbury, June 23, 1739.*

HOMANS (see also Holman), Abigail, and Nathan Alline,
Aug. 25, 1784.*
Nathaniel, and wid. Mary Stacey of Marblehead, Aug. 22,
1733. C. R. 7.
Othniel, Capt., and Martha Follet, both of Boston, May 29,
1730. C. R. 7.
Stephen, and Sarah Thurla, int. May 12, 1784.

*Intention also recorded.

HOMES (see also Holmes), Abigail, of Ipswich, and Nathaniel March, int. Nov. 11, 1747.

Elisabeth, and Henry Page, int. Aug. 4, 1804.

John, and Hannah Pearson, July 12, 1708.*

Hannah, and Stephen Knight, Oct. 16, 1729.*

Robert, and Esther Morse, Feb. 26, 1668.

HOOG (see also Hoag), John, and Ebenezer Emery, Apr. 21, 1669.

HOOK (see also Hooke), Elizabeth, and W[illia]m Hook, both of Salisbury, Sept. 6, 1734. c. R. 7.

Jacob, of Salisbury, and Mary March, Apr. 17, 1707.*

Jemima, and Jacob Blasdel, both of Amesbury, Oct. 19, 1727. c. R. 7.

Martha, and Richard Knight, May 10, 1786.*

Molly, of Salisbury, and Jacob Pettengell, int. Oct. 11, 1765.

Rachel, of Salisbury, and Benjamin Curtis, Dec. 8, 1762.*

Sally [of Salisbury. int.], and Rev. Abraham Moor, at Salisbury, May 10, 1796.*

W[illia]m, and Elizabeth Hook, both of Salisbury, Sept. 6, 1734. c. R. 7.

HOOKE (see also Hook), Florence, and James Coffin, Nov. 16, 1685.

Humphrey [of Salisbury. int.], and Mrs. Judith March, July 10, 1700.*

HOOKER, Mary W., of Newburyport, and Charles A. Davis, int. Nov. 5, 1831.

HOOPER, Jane, and John Flood [resident in Newbury, July 21. int.], 1753. c. R. 9.*

Mary, and William Connor, Mar. 11, 1755. c. R. 8.*

Nathaniel, of Wiscasset, and Susanna Davis, int. Mar. 25, 1749.

Phillis, and William Buck, int. Sept. 20, 1783.

Ruth, Mrs., of Marblehead, and Tristram Dalton, at Marblehead [Danvers. dup.], Oct. 4, 1758. [Oct. 24. dup.]*

Thomas Woodbridge, Capt., and Elisabeth Stickney Hunt, int. Mar. 21, 1801.

*Intention also recorded.

HOPKINS, Benjamin, Capt., of Wellfleet, and Esther Newman, Jan. 19, 1800.*
John, and Lucy Jewett of Rowley, at Rowley, July 7, 1763.

HOPKINSON, Charles, and Julia Ann Merrill [Morril. c. r.
10.], Sept. 23, 1824.*
John, and Elisabeth Noyes, Mar. 9, 1737-8.*
John, jr., of Bradford, and wid. Sarah Morss, June 18, 1742.*
John, of Bradford, and Lydia Noyes, Oct. 21, 1800.*
Jonathan, and Margaret Burbank, int. Mar. 4, 1737-8.
Maria, and Benjamin F. Young, Mar. 23, 1843.
Noyes, and Abigail Coffin, Aug. 13, 1792.*

HOPPIN, Opportunity, and Thomas Lunt, June 17, 1679.

HOPSON (see also Hobson), Samuel, of Rowley, and Bethia
. [Abiah. int.] Chase, Jan. 19, 1793.*
Sarah, of Rowley, and Paul Ilsley, May 28, 1761.*

HORN, Ephraim B., and Hannah Jaques, Sept. 21, 1815.*

HORTON, Daniel, and Elisabeth Chase, Nov. 15, 1759.*
Hannah, of Newburyport, and Chandler Burrough, int. Sept.
25, 1790.
Helen M., a. 16 y., d. James, of Newburyport, and Horace P.
Noyes, a. 25 y., farmer, s. Silas, June 23, 1844.*
James, of Newburyport, and Eunice L. Atkinson, Dec. 5,
1826.*
Joanna, and John Stickney, Sept. 9, 1756.*
John, and wid. Rebekah Andrews, both of Marblehead, Sept.
30, 1734. c. r. 7.
Makepeace, and Joanna Coffin, Mar. 3, 1724-5.*
Obadiah, and Martha Greenleaf, Aug. 14, 1755.*

HOTCHKISS, Caroline E., of Newburyport, and David Pettingell, 3d, int. May 11, 1839.
Levi J., of Newburyport, and Caroline Ireland, May 5, 1839.*

HOTON (see also Houghton), Joseph, and Sara Haynes,
Nov. 13, 1651.

*Intention also recorded.

HOUGHTON (see also Hoton), Mary, and Joshua Winnock, jeweller, both of Boston, Feb. 17, 1724-5. c. r. 7.

HOVEY (see also Hovy), Elisabeth, and Jonathan Thurston, Oct. 26, 1769.*
Hannah, and Enoch Little, June 5, 1759.*
John, and Betty Kimball of Bradford, int. Oct. 28, 1780.
Mary, of Boxford, and William Worcester, int. Sept. 29, 1733.
Mehitabel, and Stephen Jaques, Nov. 15, 1792.*
Samuel, and Mary Ilsley, Sept. 15, 1732.*
Sarah, of Rowley, and Bartholomew Pearson, Dec. 9, 1726.*
Sarah, and Wells Chase, Feb. 21, 1760.*

HOVY (see also Hovey), Luke, and Susannah Pilsbury, Oct. 25, 1698.
Sarah, and Nathan Pearson, July —, 1835.*

HOW (see also Howe), Charlotte, and William Mace, Dec. 17, 1839.*
Farnum, and Ednah Hale, May 8, 1791. c. r. 2.*
George, of Rowley, and Debby Chapman, June 9, 1798.*
John, baker, and Elizabeth Congston, both of Boston, ——, 1729. c. r. 7.
Sarah, and John Tharley, Mar. 2, 1684-5.
Sarah, and Robert Fasgett, both of Marlboro, Dec. 1, 1730. c. r. 7.
Sarah, and William Wigglesworth, Sept. 29, 1814.*

HOWARD, Abigail, and Moses Pilsbury, jr., Oct. 30, 1760.*
Abijah, of Thetford, Vt., and Hannah G. Lunt of Newburyport, ——, 1840.
Benjamin, and Millee Swett, Feb. 18, 1747-8.*
Benj[amin], of Newburyport, and Sarah Downing, Nov. 13, 1794.*
Benjamin, and Mrs. Lydia Caswell of Newburyport, July 27, 1816.*
Benjamin F., of Rowley, and Elizabeth F. Savory, int. Jan. 10, 1829.
Caleb H., and Nancy C. Hawkins, Nov. 29, 1826.*
Caroline, of Dracut, and Joseph B. Varnum, int. Oct. 17, 1846.
David R., and Sally O. Fuller of Danvers, int. Apr. 7, 1835.

*Intention also recorded.

HOWARD, Elsey Noyes, and Peter Lavelet of Newburyport, int.
Dec. 22, 1805.

Emily, and William Pemberton of Bradford, int. Nov. 22,
1820.

Esther M., and David Rogers, Feb. 3, 1814.*

Ezra, and Mary Coleby, Oct. 30, 1752.*

James, of Merrimac, a. 25 y., carpenter, s. Nathaniel and Jemima, and Mary R. Remick, a. 26 y., d. John and Mary,
Nov. 26, 1846.*

Jerusha, and Daniel Harris, July 29, 1755.*

John, and Lydia Richardson of Methuen, Nov. 13, 1776.*

John, of Deer Isle, and Mrs. Mary Chase Small, Dec. 15,
1811.*

Martha P., of Boston, and Charles D. Pettingell, int. Dec. 3,
1842.

Mary, and Zebulon Thayer, both of Braintree, July 30, 1729.
C. R. 7.

Mary D., and Moses P. Warren of Newburyport, int. May 25,
1822.

Molly, and William Griffin, Jan. 23, 1764.*

Nath[anie]l, of Newburyport, and Molly Noyes, May 12,
1784.*

Nath[anie]ll, and Mercy Safford of Ipswich, int. Jan. 15,
1756.

Roger S., and Martha Pike, int. Mar. 3, 1832.

Sarah, and Ezra P. Merrill of Newburyport, int. Aug. 6,
1820.

HOWE (see also How), Sally, and Eliphalet Williams of Salisbury, N. H., at Rowley, July 14, 1793.

HOWELL, Mary, and Barzilla Hayford, Apr. 21, 1812.*

Robert, and Fanny Chase. Nov. 30, 1809.*

Robert, and Hannah Emery, Oct. 6, 1814.*

HOWIG (see also Hoag), Joseph, s. John and Ebenezer, and
Sarah Gooding, d. Richard and Mary, of Amesbury, 5:
3 m: 1707. C. R. 6.

HOWLAND, Alice, and Hezekiah Keen, both of Pembrook,
Apr. 10, 1730. C. R. 7.

*Intention also recorded.

HOXIE, John A., of Roxbury, a. 33 y., carpenter, s. John and Sally, of New York, and Elizabeth Curson of Roxbury, a. 25 y., d. Samuel and Margaret, Aug. 18, 1847.

HOYES, see Hoies.

HOYT (see also Hoit, Hoite, Hoyte), Benjamin E., of Ipswich, and Elizabeth T. Moody, int. Aug. 27, 1836.

Charles F., of Salisbury, and Mary Jane Longfellow, int. May 18, 1838.

Ebenezer, and Sarah T. [Jane. c. R. 10.] Buswell, both of Newburyport, Aug. 14, 1824.

Elbridge G., and Mary Longfellow of Newburyport, int. Jan. 6, 1831.

Enos, and Mary Stevens, int. May 23, 1835.

Ephraim, and Abigail Beacham, June 25, 1761.*

Ezekiel, of Amesbury, and Rebecca Brown, Dec. 25, 1735.*

Hannah L., a. 23 y., d. Joseph and Martha, and Joseph Thurlow, jr., a. 34 y., seaman, s. Joseph and Sarah, Mar. 4, 1847.*

Hopee, of Amesbury, and Timothy Pike, resident in Newbury, at Amesbury, Aug. 4, 1726.

Jacob, and Mehetable Tompson, ——, 1788. [May 3. int.]*

Jane M., of Haverhill, and Joseph R. Chase, Oct. 20, 1832.

John C., of New York, and Mary H. Johnson, Sept. 15, 1832.*

Joseph, and Hannah Chace, Dec. 22, 1707.*

Joseph, and Ann Pettingill. May 6, 1731.*

Joseph, and Dorothy Currier of Amesbury, int. Oct. 29, 1762.

Joseph, Capt., of Newburyport, and Sarah Coffin, int. Apr. 21, 1810.

Joseph, and Martha Phipps, Mar. 27, 1816.*

Joseph, jr., a. 26 y., seaman, s. Joseph and Martha, and Lydia Mace of Newburyport, a. 25 y., b. Newburyport, d. Daniel and Lucy, of Newburyport, Nov. 4, 1845.*

Leonard, of Amesbury, and Caroline Whittier, Feb. 2. 1836.*

Lydia, and W[illia]m Hawley of Newburyport, int. Nov. 18, 1848.

Mary, and Christopher Bartlet, Dec. 17, 1663.

Mary, of Amesbury, and Thomas Emery, jr., int. Mar. 19, 1818.

Mary P., and Daniel P. Nelson of Rowley, ——, 1840. [Nov. 14. int.]*

Merriam, and William Short of Newburyport, Apr. 6, 1783.*

*Intention also recorded.

Hoyt, Moses, and Anne Nelson, Sept. 13, 1758. [Said Hoyt takes said Ann naked and so will not be obliged to pay any of her former husband's debts. int.]*

Moses, of Newburyport, and Mary Stickney, Mar. 6, 1766.*

Moses, and Judith Richards of Newburyport, int. Sept. 26, 1778.

Moses, and Hannah Merrill, Apr. 12, 1779.*

Susanna, of Amesbury, and Richard Kelle, at Amesbury, Sept. 28, 1721.

Thomas, of Manchester, and Abby H. Brown of Lowell, Dec. 19, 1839.

HOYTE (see also Hoyt), Mary, of Amesbury, and Moses Ingals of Andover, Feb. 21, 1712.

Mary, Mrs., and Edward Gibson, Jan. 17, 1739-40.*

HUBBARD, Ebenezer, Rev., and Charlotte Swasey of Ipswich, int. May 16, 1808.

Jane, and Tho[ma]s Champney, both of Cambridge, Sept. 18, 1730. c. R. 7.

John L., and Levina Poor, Oct. 25, 1835.*

HUDDLE, John, and Patience Evans Burrill, int. Dec. 6, 1823.

HUDSON, Deborah, and Joseph Bailey, Nov. 17, 1726.*

Deborah, Mrs., and Capt. Jeremiah Stevens of Salisbury, int. Mar. 1, 1737-8.

Hannah, Mrs., and William Samuel Ballard of Boston, Aug. 2, 1738. c. R. 7.

James, and Mary Rolfe, int. Sept. 29, 1744.

Judeth, and Jonathan Bootman [Bodman. c. R. 3.] of Gloucester, Dec. 27, 1733.*

Mary, Mrs., and Capt. Richard Brown, June 19, 1726. c. R. 7.

Mary, and William Richards, jr., Nov. 25, 1762.*

Rebeca, and Thomas Sweet, Jan. 3, 1760.*

Rebecca, Mrs., and Paul Shackford, Feb. 29, 1727-8.*

HUGGINS, Bridget, and John Webster, jr., Mar. 9, 1680-81.

Hannah, and Richard Woollery, Dec. 24, 1678.

* *Intention also recorded.

HUGHES (see also Huse), David A., and Elizabeth W. Hunt,
Oct. 4, 1817.*

Martha Ann, of Windham, N. H., and Nathaniel Pilsbury,
int. Nov. 16, 1839.

Mary Ann, of Ipswich, and Samuel Treadwell of Manchester,
May —, 1839.

HULGATE, James, Dr., of Haverhill, and Lydia Sawyer, int.
Mar. 19, 1746-7.

Priscilla, and David Bartlet, Jan. 31, 1754.*

HULL, Mary, Mrs., and Francis George, Nov. 14, 1745.*

HUMPHERYES, Benhemoth, resident in Newbury, and Mrs.
Mary Lord, int. Nov. 12, 1715.

HUNKINS, Jonathan, and Mary Noyes, Nov. 19, 1799.*

Robert [jr. dup.], of Haverhill, and Hannah Muzze [at Haverhill. dup.], Dec. 6, 1738.*

Thomas, and Clarissa Hews, Nov. 11, 1798.*

HUNT, Abigail, and Joseph Pirkins of Newburyport, int. Dec.
4, 1790.

Abigail, and Nathan Jelison, Mar. 28, 1835.*

Benj[ami]n G., and Mrs. Hannah J. Hidden, Jan. 21, 1838.*

Benjamin Goodwin, and Sarah Ann Hastelett, int. Oct. 6,
1827.

Caroline, and James Adams of Washington, D. C., May 26,
1828.*

Christian, and Eliphalet Noyes, July 20, 1760.*

Dorcas, and Edmund Connor, Jan. 12, 1792.*

Eleanor A., of Newburyport, and Jacob Chace, jr., int. Apr. 6,
1833.

Elias, of Newburyport, and Betty Lunt, Sept. 28, 1783.*

Elisabeth, of Amesbury, and John Kent [jr. int.], at Amesbury, Apr. 8, 1762.*

Elisabeth, and William Downs, int. Dec. 26, 1771.

Elisabeth, and Moses Quimbe, Apr. 25, 1790.*

Elizabeth C., and Charles Brown of Newburyport, int. Feb. 26,
1819.

Elizabeth Stickney, and Capt. Thomas Woodbridge Hooper,
int. Mar. 21, 1801.

*Intention also recorded.

Hunt, Elizabeth W., and David A. Hughes, Oct. 4, 1817.*

Enoch, and Mercy [Mary. int.] Coffin, Jan. 5, 1735-6.*

Enoch, and Mary Peirce, Mar. 15, 1736-7.*

Ephraim, of Bridgewater, and Katharine Acres, int. Oct. 8, 1698.

Ephraim, and Mrs. Mary Cook, Nov. 22, 1739.*

Gideon W[oodwell. int.], and Mary W[hite. int.] Brown, Feb. 5, 1834.*

Hannah, and Joshua Hills, Dec. 27, 1739.*

Hannah, and Andrew Leach of Manchester, Aug. 25, 1840.*

Henry, and Maria Cook, Nov. 20, 1836.*

Henry Swan, and Elizabeth Gardner Jackson of Newburyport, Mar. 20, 1809.*

Isaac J., and Mary Jane Platt of Newburyport, int. Sept. 12, 1829.

Isaiah, of Amesbury, and Ruth Lunt, Nov. 19, 1755. c. r. 9.

Isaiah, and Sarah Stickney, May 18, 1783.*

John Woodwell, and Martha Thurston Doyle, int. Mar. 22, 1828.

Josiah [Isaiah. int.], and Ruth Lunt, Nov. 19, 1755.*

Judeth, and Nathaniel Leach, Apr. 9, 1735.*

Judith, and Nathan Hayford of Tamworth, N. H., 1808 or 9. [June 25, 1808. int.]*

Lois, of Salisbury, and Joseph Jackman [jr. int.], July 31, 1806.*

Lydia, and Gideon W. Lattime, Nov. —, 1836.*

Margeret, and Ebenezer Barton, June 23, 1741.*

Mary, and John Salmon, both of Boston, May 29, 1735. c. r. 7.

Mary, of Newburyport, and Abraham Toppan, int. Jan. 9, 1773.

Mary, and Capt. William Noyes of Georgetown, Columbia, Mar. 17, 1812.*

Mercy, and William Grove of Plymouth, Eng., Sept. 4, 1763. c. r. 8.

Mercy B., and Benjamin Russell, Dec. —, 1835.*

Nathaniel, and Elisabeth Woodwell [Woodman. int.], Aug. 26, 1760.*

Nathaniel, jr., and Mary Pearson Clark of Newburyport, int. Mar. 3, 1821.

Samuel, and Joanna Bragdon of York, int. Nov. 26, 1808.

Sarah, and Daniel Swett of Newburyport, May 22, 1825.*

Susanna, and Hugh Coomes, int. Feb. 2, 1753.

Thomas, and Jane White, int. Aug. 24, 1809.

*Intention also recorded.

HUNTINGTON (see also Huntinton), Hanah, and William Chandler, jr., Nov. 29, 1692.

John L., and Elizabeth Ann Bayley, int. Oct. 5, 1849.

Sarah, d. John, deceased, and Abigail of Amesbury, and Micah Sawyer, s. Stephen and Sarah, deceased, Dec. 7, 1769. c. R. 6.

Susanah, and Andrew Downer, Dec. 20, 1699.*

HUNTINTON (see also Huntington), Deborah, and Thomas Homan [Holeman. int.] of Sutton, at Amesbury, June 23, 1739.*

HUSE (see also Hewes, Hews, Hughes), Abel, jr., and Elisabeth Little, Apr. 29, 1729.*

Abell, and Mary Sears, May 25, 1663.

Abigail, and Moses Hale [jr. int.], Apr. 20, 1742.*

Abil, jr., and Hannah Farley of Ipswich, int. Apr. 21, 1738.

Ann, and Samuel Stevens of Methuen, May 20, 1731. c. R. 7.

Ann P., and Charles E. Shuff of Newburyport, June 16, 1828.*

Caleb, of Belfast, and Sarah Smith, int. Oct. 26, 1805.

Dorothy, and Joseph Dole Plumer, Aug. 10, 1797. [Aug. 4, 1796. c. R. 1.]*

Ebenezer, and Elisabeth Hale, Nov. 1, 1737.*

Elizabeth, and Capt. Daniel Ladd, May 22, 1808.*

Elizabeth L., and John C. Randall, ——, 1842.

Enoch, Lt., and Sarah Hill of Boston, int. Oct. 26, 1782.

Hannah, Mrs., and Parker Mors, Mar. 14, 1736-7.*

Hannah, and Joseph Huse of Weare, N. H., Feb. 5, 1775.*

Hiram, and Hannah C. Arnold of Newburyport, int. July 11, 1841.

Israel, and Ruth Bodwell of Haverhill, Aug. —, 1716.*

Jacob P., and Harriet A. Knight of Salisbury, int. Mar. 10, 1849.

John, and Sarah Toppan, Oct. 25, 1716.*

John, and Dorothy Whittemore, May 19, 1768.*

John, and Elizabeth Tenney, Oct. 15, 1795.*

Joseph, and Molle Chase, Oct. —, 1737.*

Joseph, and Abigail Johnson, Dec. 2, 1762.*

Joseph, of Weare, N. H., and Hannah Huse, Feb. 5, 1775.*

Joseph, Capt., of Newburyport, and Sarah Moody, Mar. 5, 1776.*

*Intention also recorded.

HUSE, Joseph, and Elizabeth Lawrence of Newburyport, int
Apr. 6, 1816.
Judeth, and John Holemon, May 23. 1728.*
Keziah, and John Stevens of Amesbury, Sept. 13, 1733. C. R.
7.*
Martha, Mrs., and William Jenkins, Mar. 4, 1735-6. C. R. 7.
Mary, and Oliver Holt of Andover, abt. July 10, 1716.*
Mary, and Enoch Davis, May 8, 1740.*
Mary, and Daniel March, Apr. 6, 1742.*
Mary, of Newburyport, and Silas Moody, Esq., Sept. 5, 1841.*
Mary Jane, and John L. Lord, Dec. 2, 1835.*
Mollee, and Charles Pressey of Sandown, N. H., Apr. 5,
1764.*
Polly Chase, and William Burroughs of Newburyport, May
25, 1806.*
Ralph C., of Neyburyport, and Margaret E. Coffin, June 27,
1837.*
Ralph C., of Newburyport, and Sarah S. Barnard, int. Sept. 7,
1839.
Rebecca, and Dr. David Jewett. Mar. 30, 1809.*
Robert, of Hartland, Vt., and Mary [Lydia. int.] Jewet, Feb.
2, 1797.*
Ruth, and John Brown, Aug. 27, 1683.
Ruth, and Samuel Burnap of Reading, Dec. 1, 1726.*
Samuel, and Mary Mireck, July 14, 1726.*
Samuel, and Sarah Hale, int. Oct. 21, 1765.
Samuel, of Newburyport, and Eliza Colby, int. May 23, 1830.
Samuel, and Sarah Ann F. Smith of Newburyport, int. July
28, 1832.
Sarah, and Caleb Kimball, Apr. 17, 1735.*
Sarah, and William Bryant of Reading, Mar. 17, 1736-7.*
Sarah, and Nicholas Johnson, Mar. 22, 1736-7.*
Sarah, and Thomas Somerby of Newburyport, Sept. 6, 1786.*
Stephen, and Mrs. Judith Emery [wid. C. R. 2.], July 30,
1729.*
Theodore P., and Adar Norton of Newburyport, int. Aug. 16,
1840.
Thomas, and Sarah Moody, Jan. 2, 1777.*
Thomas, and Rebekah Hills, Aug. 5, 1779.*
Thomas [of Newburyport. int.], and Harriet L. Poor, May 5,
1836.*
William, and Anne Russell, int. July 22, 1699.
William, jr., and Mary Brown, Feb. 17, 1731-2.*

*Intention also recorded.

HUSSEY, Elizabeth A., of North Berwick, Me., and Samuel
     B. Bartlett, int. Jan. 6, 1849.

HUSTON, Deborah, and Dudly Rogers, Jan. 20, 1788.*

HUTCHINS, Elisabeth, of Bradford, and Jonathan Russel
     [both of Bradford. c. r. 7.], Sept. 19. 1722.
Ephraim, of Hampstead, N. H., and Sally Hills, int. Nov. 27,
     1792.
Hezekiah, and Hannah Noyes, July 5, 1750.*
Hezekiah [Lt. int.], and Mrs. Ann Sweet of Haverhill, at
     Haverhill, Jan. 29, 1761.*
Jonas, and Sarah Lee Johnson of Newburyport, int. Oct. 16,
     1841.
Joseph, of Newburyport, and Elizabeth Brown, June 8, 1812.*
Samuel, and Hanah Merrill, both of Haverhill, Jan. 4, 1715-
     16.

HUTCHINSON, John, of Andover, and Sarah Adams, Jan. 28,
     1714-15.*
Mary, and Thomas Hale, May 26, 1657.

HYDE, Mary L. W., of Cambridge, and Charles Wills, int.
     June 5, 1847.

HYNES (see also Hind), William H., and Mary A. Earl of
     Newburyport, int. Oct. 21, 1848.

ILSLEY (see also Ilsly), Abigail, of New Bradford, N. H.,
     and Friend Noyes, int. Mar. 17, 1792.
Abigail, and Moses Short, Oct. 25, 1826.*
Alice, and Asa Plummer, Sept. 26, 1784.*
Anna, and Daniel Sillaway, int. Apr. 6, 1808.
Anthony, and Hannah Hawkins, Oct. 18, 1785.*
Anthony, and Eliza Jane Bond, June 19, 1842.*
Anthony, and Mary N. Osgood of Newburyport, int. Dec. 7,
     1844.
Benjamin, and Betsy Dole, Oct. 8, 1794.*
Charlotte Ann, and James H. Small, int. May 25, 1847.
David, of Newburyport, and Anna Frazer [Frazier. int.], at
     Rowley, Apr. 4, 1789.*
Elisabeth, Mrs., and Capt. Thomas Noyes, July 24, 1740.*
Enoch, and Margaret Dutch of Wells, int. Jan. 5, 1811.

*Intention also recorded.

ILSLEY, Hannah, and Timothy Morse [Morss. int.], June 21, 1753. c. r. 9.*

Hannah, and Paul Adams, Apr. 30, 1785.*

Huldah S., a. 21 y., d. John and Huldah, and William Pickett, a. 33 y., ship builder, s. Joseph and Hannah, Oct. 15, 1846.*

Isaac, and Abigail Moodey, Mar. 16, 1720-21.*

Isaiah, and Mary French, int. Nov. 28, 1783.

Jane, and Benjamin Plumer, Nov. 3, 1748.*

Jewett, and Fanney Dole of Rowley, int. Aug. 5, 1786.

John, and Judith Webster, Sept. 24, 1767.*

John, and Elizabeth Rogers of Newburyport, int. Aug. 6, 1808.

John, and Huldah Dodge Stanwood of Newburyport, July 15, 1821.*

Jonathan, and Sarah Mors, Dec. 13, 1714.*

Jonathan, and Mary Adams, Nov. 24, 1778.*

Joseph, jr., and Hanah Pike, int. Oct. 25, 1701.

Joseph, and Pheby Jaques, Sept. 3, 1798.*

Lucy, and John J. Adams, Nov. 20, 1832.*

Mary, and Samuel Hovey, Sept. 15, 1732.*

Mary, and Richard Jaques of Gloucester, Jan. 13, 1785.*

Mary, and Henry Lunt Dole, June 12, 1809.*

Mary Jane, and William Coffin, Jan. 29, 1833.*

Moses, and Sarah Noyes, Mar. 21, 1764.

Parker, of Portland, and Phebe Ilsley, Oct. 25, 1792.*

Paul, and Sarah Hopson of Rowley, May 28, 1761.*

Paul, and Sarah Hale, int. Aug. 7, 1789.

Paul, jr., and Mary Moody, Oct. 18, 1821. [1820. c. r. 1.]*

Phebe, and Parker Ilsley of Portland, Oct. 25, 1792.*

Prudence, and Edward [Edmund. int.] Hills, June 12, 1806.*

Rebeckah, and John Holland, Aug. 28, 1792.*

Rowena, and Moses C. Knight of Newburyport, July 31, 1844.*

Ruth, and Enoch Rolfe, Jan. 4, 1753.*

Sarah, and Richard Doel [Dole, jr. int.], Apr. 3, 1706.*

Sarah, and Anthony Mors, Dec. 22, 1721.*

Sarah [Mrs. int.], and John Titcomb, Dec. 31, 1753.*

Sarah, and Sewell Adams of Londonderry, N. H., Dec. 7, 1820.*

Stephen, and Elisabeth Noyes, Oct. 27, 1757.*

Stephen [jr. c. r. 1.], and Ruth Short, Oct. 29, 1800.*

*Intention also recorded.

ILSLEY, Stephen, of Portland, and Ann Maria Woodwell, int. Apr. 14, 1822.

Stephen, and Susan H. Carr of Newburyport, Jan. 29, 1833.*

Thomas, and Hannah Jewett of Rowley, at Rowley, Dec. 24, 1760.*

Wade, and Clarissa Adams, Nov. 8, 1821.*

Wade, and Lydia Moser of Hampton, N. H., int. Mar. 31, 1827.

William, jr., and Anna [Anne. int.] Dole, Nov. 24, 1747.*

William, and Harriet Goodridge, Nov. 28, 1813.*

William, and Jane Floyd, Sept. 14, 1819.*

ILSLY (see also Ilsley), Elisha, and Hannah Poore, Mar. 14, 1667.

Joseph, and Sara Little, Mar. 3, 1681-2.

Joseph [3d. int.], and [Mrs. int.] Rebeckah Noyes, Nov. 28, 1717.*

Lydia, and John Person, Mar. 29, 1728.

Mary, and Samuel Moores, Sept. 12, 1656.

Sara, and Samuell Hale, July 21, 1673.

William, and Ruth Haselton, Dec. 26, 1717.

IMSON, Elizabeth, of Amesbury, and Benjamin Sawyer, int. Nov. 20, 1714.

INGALDS (see also Ingalls), Mary, and Will[ia]m Ravell, both of Marblehead, Nov. 8, 1726. c. r. 7.

INGALLS (see also Ingalds, Ingals), Hannah, and Moses Stickney [jr. int.], May 20, 1786.*

INGALS (see also Ingalls), Moses, of Andover, and Mary Hoyte of Amesbury, Feb. 21, 1712.

INGERSOL (see also Ingersoll), John, and Mary [Sarah. int.] Collis, Mar. 19, 1761.*

Jonathan, and Mary Henry, Nov. 24, 1763.*

INGERSOLL (see also Ingersol, Ingerson), David, of Gloucester, and Anna [Hannah. int.] Bradshaw, Apr. 12, 1756.*

David, of Gloucester, and Anna Kimbal, int. Aug. 22, 1801.

*Intention also recorded.

INGERSOLL, Elizabeth, of Salem, and William Burrows, late of
Jamaica, widr., Apr. 16, 1728. C. R. 7.
Zebulon, and Ruth Pike, Dec. 11, 1781.*

INGERSON (see also Ingersoll), Bathsua, and John Knight,
— [16-?].

IRELAND, Caroline, and Levi J. Hotchkiss of Newburyport,
May 5, 1839.*
Charles H., and Sarah Collins, Apr. 14, 1839.*
Elisabeth, and John Duggin, Sept. 17, 1791. C. R. 1.*
Geo[rge] C., and Mary L. Johnson of Newburyport, int. Nov.
25, 1848.
Jere R., of Newburyport, and Eliza B. Pickett, int. July 4,
1846.
Margaret, and Robert Jenkins, July 30, 1792.*
Mary, and Levi Carr, June 1, 1843.*
Nathaniel, and Mary Severance, Sept. 4, 1808.*

ISELIP (see also Islip), Abigail, and James Mackmilion, int.
Jan. 22, 1736-7.

ISLIP (see also Iselip), Thomas, and Abigail Waters, Feb. 23,
1719-20.*

JACKMAN, Abigail, and Humphry Bartlet, July 4, 1786.*
Abigail, a. 33 y., d. Joseph N. and Mary, and Asaph G. Spald-
ing of Milford, a. 29 y., printer, s. Asaph and Nancy,
Nov. 24, 1846.*
Abigail H., and John S. Mendum, Jan. 6, 1839.*
Amos, and Eliza Jane Bouer [Bowers. int.], Feb. 26, 1809.*
Amos, and Mary G [riffin. int.] Parsons, July 31, 1823.*
Antoinette, of Newburyport, and Charles N. Merrill, int. Dec.
8, 1840.
Apha, of Boscawen, and Ebben Woodman, int. Nov. 21, 1815.
Benjamin, and Dorothy Lunt, Aug. 9, 1744.*
Benjamin, of Rowley, and Elisabeth Noyes, Nov. 20, 1745.*
Benjamin, and Mrs. Hannah Floyd, Feb. 24, 1812.*
Benjamin, and Lydia Miller, int. Oct. 5, 1822.
Benjamin, and Elizabeth Perkins, int. Sept. 28, 1833.
David, and Abigail Moulton, July 17, 1760.*
David, jr., and Amelia Morse, int. Oct. 21, 1804.

*Intention also recorded.

JACKMAN, David, a. 39 y., farmer, s. David and Amelia, and
    Mary O. Morse, a. 33 y., d. Joseph, Feb. 20, 1845.*
David W., and Sally Jackman, Aug. 7, 1814.*
David W., and Sarah Somerby, Nov. 2, 1824.*
David W., and Lydia Morse, Apr. 7, 1829.*
Dorothy L., and Peabody Greenleaf of Exeter, int. Nov. 27,
    1819.
Dorothy Lunt, and Edmund Greenleaf of Newburyport, int.
    Jan. 23, 1817.
Eleanor P., a. 39 y., d. Matthias and Abigail, and William C.
    Merrill, a. 39 y., shipwright, s. William and Betsy, Jan.
    13, 1848.*
Elias, and Margaret Atkinson, Apr. 19, 1737.*
Elias, and Keziah Jackman, June 14, 1750. C. R. 7.
Elias, jr., and Dorotha Wise, Oct. 9, 1788.*
Elias, jr., and Irena Merrill of Salisbury, int. Oct. 27, 1837.
Eliza C., and John Warner [jr. C. R. 10.] of Londonderry,
    Sept. 5, 1822.*
Elizabeth, and Joseph Willit, May 15, 1706.
Elizabeth, and Dr. Parker Cleaveland, both of Byfield Row-
    ley, Aug. 2, 1773.
Elizabeth, and Daniel Bayley, jr. of Newburyport, int. Oct.
    10, 1777.
Elizabeth A., and Charles W. Hale, int. Jan. 9, 1847.
Emily, a. 20 y., d. Amos, and David Reed, a. 25 y., black-
    smith, s. David, Aug. 29, 1844.*
Enoch, and Molly Titcomb of Pelham, int. Apr. 2, 1803.
Esther, and Joseph Muzzy, Feb. 9, 1670.
George, and Hannah Bishop, at Rowley, Aug. 27, 1728.
George, and Mrs. Margaret Pervier, June 2, 1827.*
George W., and Lydia B. Longfellow, Feb. 25, 1825.*
George W., and Lydia C. Bartlett, July 16, 1834.*
Hannah, and Moses Retter, Mar. 25, 1741.*
Hannah, and David Adams, both of Rowley, Sept. 29, 1742.
Hannah, and Moses Emery, May 29, 1745. C. R. 7.*
Hannah, of Byfield Rowley, and Eliphaz Chapman, "a lay
    preacher" of Rowley, Aug. 18, 1772.
Harriet, and William Jackman, Dec. 30, 1834.*
Harriet, Mrs., and Samuel Lunt, jr., Oct. —, 1837.*
Harriet W., of Newburyport, and Hiram Roberts of Newton,
    July 3, 1833.
Harriet W., and Eben B. Whitmore, int. Oct. 24, 1846.

*Intention also recorded.

JACKMAN, Henry M., and Phebe S. Varnum, Oct. 22, 1840.*
Humphrey M., and Sarah Robinson, Oct. 31, 1836.*
James, 3d, and Mary French of Salisbury, at Salisbury, Dec.
   8, 1721.
James, and Martha Snell, Sept. 4, 1738.*
Jane, and Richard Knight of Haverhill, May 11, 1749.*
Jane, and John Stickney [4th. c. R. 2.] of Newburyport, Oct.
   9, 1788.*
Jeremiah N., and Sarah E. Lunt, Oct. 25, 1840.*
Joanna, and John Short, May 27, 1708.*
Joanna, and Joseph Bartlett, Nov. 3, 1825.*
John, and Hannah Smith, Nov. 28, 1717.
John, and Jenny Wise, Apr. 22, 1781.*
John, jr., and Mary Wheeler of Newburyport, int. Jan. 4,
   1817.
John L., and Nancy B. Ramsell of Salisbury, int. Mar. 26,
   1849.
Joseph, and Hannah Plomer, Aug. 3, 1720.*
Joseph, and Edith Tirrell of Kensington, Aug. 12, 1754.*
Joseph [jr. int.], and Lois Hunt of Salisbury, July 31, 1806.*
Joseph, and Mary Merrill, June 28, 1810.*
Joseph, and Elizabeth Stevens of Newburyport, int. Feb. 1,
   1812.
Joseph, and Susan M. Hart, int. Aug. 7, 1846.
Keziah, and Elias Jackman, June 14, 1750. c. R. 7.
Lydia, and Stephen Emery, Feb. 25, 1714-15.*
Lydia, and Benjamin Tenney, both of Byfield Rowley, Mar.
   18, 1783.
Lydia, and Henry Merrill, 3d, int. June 16, 1803.
Mary, and Joseph Morss [3d. int.], July 17, 1738.*
Mary, of Rowley, and George Thorla, jr., Mar. 23, 1758.*
Mary, and Daniel Eastman of Salisbury, May 15, 1760.*
Mary, and Eliphalet Davis of Exeter, N. H., Sept. 10, 1775.*
Mary, of Byfield Rowley, and John Barker of Bradford, Mar.
   27, 1781.
Mary, and Peter Ordway, July 24, 1783.*
Mary, and John Colby, jr. of Amesbury, Dec. 29, 1818.*
Mary Elizabeth, and Joseph Greenleaf Perkins, Dec. 27,
   1823.*
Mary W., of Newburyport, a. 16 y., d. John and Mary, of
   Newburyport, and Abram Somerby, a. 22 y., shoemaker, s.
   Samuel and Mary Ann, Jan. 8, 1845.*

*Intention also recorded.

JACKMAN, Matthias, and Almira Dutton of Newburyport, Dec. 19, 1841.*

Matthias A., and Nabby Warthen, Mar. 25, 1793.*

Mercy, and Jonathan Martin, May 25, 1756.*

Miriam, and Stephen Russell Fox, Feb. 17, 1811.*

Moses, and Elisabeth Short, int. Jan. 21, 1769.

Moses B., and Harriet Carr, Apr. 22, 1821.*

Moses B., a. 27 y., ropemaker, s. Richard and Elizabeth, and Mary E. Smith, a. 23 y., d. Samuel and Elizabeth, Nov. 25, 1847.*

Nancy, and Joseph Currier, Mar. 9, 1809.*

Nancy, and Tristram Hobson of Ipswich, int. Apr. 27, 1820.

Nancy, and William Davis of Amesbury, int. June 11, 1831.

Nicholas, and Mary Mors, May 29, 1718.

Nicholas, and Abigail Pettingill, July 2, 1724.*

Olive Pierce, and Joseph Boughdon Battis, Dec. 29, 1811.*

Polly, and Joshua Towle, int. Sept. 7, 1808.

Polly [Dolly. C. R. 10.], and Joseph Wadleigh, May 18, 1809.*

Rachel, and Elias Whiten, Dec. 27, 1711.*

Reuben, and Sally Floyd of Ipswich, int. Feb. 6, 1824.

Richard, and Elizabeth Plumer, June 26, 1682.

Richard, jr., and Elizabeth Major, int. Apr. 6, 1703.

Richard, and Mary Gould, Nov. 25, 1780.*

Richard, jr., and Abigail Akers, int. July 9, 1785.

Richard, and Abigail Blasdel of Amesbury, int. July 22, 1803.

Richard, and Martha Bointon, int. Sept. 5, 1840.

Ruth, of Byfield Rowley, and Elias Cheney, Mar. 9, 1768.

Sally, of Rowley, and Isaac Pearson, Sept. 15, 1794.*

Sally, and David W. Jackman, Aug. 7, 1814.*

Samuel, and Meriam Plomer, May 23, 1717.*

Samuel, of Boscawen, N. H., and Anne Fowler, int. Aug. 5, 1772.

Sam[ue]ll, and Mary Aires, Dec. 14, 1737. C. R. 7.

Sara, and Joseph Palmer, Mar. 1, 1664.

Sarah, and Enoch Adams, July 28, 1747.*

Sarah, and Samuel Farnum [Varnum. C. R. 1.], Apr. 24, 1806.*

Sarah A., a. 20 y., d. Joseph N. and Mary, and Charles C. Morse of Bradford, a. 21 y., shoemaker, b. Bradford, s. Benjamin and Abigail, of Bradford, June 3, 1846.*

Sarah E. [of Newburyport. int.], a. 22 y., d. Moses B. and Harriet, and Giles A. Adams, a. 26 y., carpenter, s. Richard, jr. and Abigail, Jan. 13, 1848.*

*Intention also recorded.

JACKMAN, Sarah M., and Thomas Robinson, Apr. 12, 1815.*
Simeon, and Sarah Morss, int. Sept. 29, 1770.
Stephen, and Mary Moers, Mar. 30, 1763.*
Stephen, and Nancy Merrill, June 22, 1828.*
Stephen, jr., and Elizabeth G. Burrill of Newburyport, Oct. 27, 1828.*
Timothy, and Hannah Chute of Rowley, Apr. 9, 1723.*
Timothy, jr., and Mary Thirston, both of Rowley, Apr. 2, 1751.
Timothy, 3d, of Byfield Rowley, and Molly Burbank of Bradford, Oct. 19, 1768.
William, and Mary Pierce, July 29, 1786.*
W[illia]m, jr., and Nancy Ball, int. June 26, 1815.
William, and Mrs. Nancy Ball, Nov. 18, 1816.
William, and Harriet Jackman, Dec. 30, 1834.*
William D., and Catharine Hill, May 28, 1837.*
William T., and Sarah M. C. Varnum, Dec. 17, 1835.*

,JACKSON, Abigail, and Enoch Parker, both of Newtown, July 14, 1736. c. r. 7.
Anna, and Edward Durant, both of Newton, Sept. 15, 1735. c. r. 7.
Daniel, and Lucy Burnam, int. Nov. 13, 1754.
Elizabeth, and Adam Pickett, both of Marblehead, Oct. 6, 1730. c. r. 7.
Elizabeth, and Capt. Peter Hall, both of Portsmouth, May 10, 1732. c. r. 7.
Elizabeth Gardner, of Newburyport, and Henry Swan Hunt, Mar. 20, 1809.*
John, and Polly Knight, Nov. 5, 1789.*
Mary, of Kittery, and Edmund Moodey, int. Mar. 17, 1732.
Mehetable, and David Goodwin, int. Aug. 17, 1765.
Ruth, and Thomas Fossat, July 3, 1791. c. r. 1.*
Sally, and Joseph Broughton, int. Oct. 26, 1808.
Sarah, of Bradford, and Ezra Rolfe, int. Oct. 27, 1705.
Sarah, Mrs., of Marblehead, and Capt. Daniel Brown of Exeter, Nov. 12, 1730. c. r. 7.

JACOBS, Abigail B., and Jona[than] M. Tucker, Sept. 11, 1843.
Joseph, of Ipswich, and Mary Bartlet, Apr. 29, 1723. c. r. 7.

· *Intention also recorded.

JACOBS, Sarah, Mrs., of Ipswich, and Ens. Moses Chase, int. May 10, 1713.

JACQUES (see also Jaques), Sarah, and John Hale, Oct. 10, 1683.

JAMES, Dudley, of Exeter, and Sarah Knight, Feb. 24, 1763.*
Lucretia, of Kensington, N. H., and Charles Coffin, int. June 27, 1823.

JANVRIN, Betsey, and John Scribner, Dec. 17, 1828.*
George, and Mary Chase, Nov. 21, 1839.*
Hiram, and Emeline M. Feltch, Dec. 10, 1843.*
Jane S., and George J. George of Newburyport, int. Sept. 22, 1841.
Joanna, and Lorenzo D. Ross, Mar. 17, 1833.*
John, and Elizabeth Chase, Oct. 24, 1842.*
Joseph, and Joanna Thurlo, Jan. 8, 1809.*
Joseph, jr., and Elizabeth Ladd of Newburyport, int. Dec. 7, 1833.
Mary E., a. 19 y., d. Joseph and Joanna, and Robert J. Torry, a. 21 y., stone cutter, s. Joseph and Ruth, Apr. 8, 1849.*
Ruth Ann, a. 17 y., d. Joseph and Joanna, and George A. Randall, a. 21 y., farmer, s. Eliphalet and Mary, Nov. 14, 1849.*

JAQUES (see also Jacques), Ann, and Robert Adams, jr., Oct. 29, 1725.*
Benjamin, and Apphia Coffin, May 20, 1725.*
Benjamin, and Mary Noyes, Dec. 5, 1727.*
Benjamin, and Mary Adams of Rowley, at Rowley, Mar. 25, 1760.*
Benjamin [jr. int.], and Judith Noyes, Mar. 4, 1762.*
Betsey, and Jacob Hidden, int. Mar. 14, 1812.
Charles, and Marcy Thurlo, Feb. 5, 1821.*
Daniell, and Mary Williams, Mar. 20, 1692-3.
David, and Dolley Richards of Newburyport, int. Nov. 24, 1804.
Deborah, and Cutting Lunt, Dec. 10, 1735.*
Deborah, and Capt. Israel Adams, Nov. 11, 1779.*
Deborah, and True Brown, jr. of Deerfield, N. H., Feb. 5, 1824.*

*Intention also recorded.

JAQUES, Eleanor, and James Noyes, May 7, 1747.*
Eleanor, and Benjamin Short, Dec. 16, 1813.*
Eliphalet, and Elizabeth Davis of Newburyport, int. Aug. 30,
  1810.
Eliphalet, and Lydia Adams, Jan. 3, 1737-8.*
Elisabeth, and Enoch Knight, Nov. 11, 1736.*
Elisabeth, and Moses Moodey, June 12, 1744.*
Elisabeth, and Amos Knight of Newburyport, Jan. 12, 1797.*
Ellanor, and Benjamin Short, Dec. —, 1808? c. r. 1.
Enoch, and Mary Hale, int. Jan. 8, 1772.
Enoch, and Joanna Plumer, Feb. 9, 1797.*
Enoch, jr., and Sally Williams Tilton of Newburyport, May
  26, 1811.*
Eunice, and Samuel Pearson, int. Dec. 5, 1767.
Eunice, and Jacob Haskell of Newburyport, Dec. 23, 1819.*
Florence, and James Safford, Apr. 5, 1763.*
Hanna, and Ephraim Plumer, Jan. 15, 1679.
Hannah, and Ephraim B. Horn, Sept. 21, 1815.*
Henry, and Anne Knight, Oct. 8, 1648.
Henry, and Mrs. Rebecca Pikering of Portsmouth, int. Apr.
  10, 1706.
Henry, and Mary Coffin, Jan. 24, 1711-12.*
Henry Cromwell, and Polly Follansbee of Newburyport, int.
  May 9, 1807.
John, and Sarah Jaques, June 12, 1746.*
Joseph, and Martha Brown, Mar. 4, 1756.*
Judeth, and William Dole, Apr. 3, 1755.*
Judith, and Abraham Mace [jr. int.] of Newburyport, Apr.
  26, 1795.*
Love, and Robert Adams, 3d, Sept. 7, 1738.*
Lydia, and Capt. Kindal Pearson of Wilmington, Jan. 30,
  1737-8.*
Lydia, and Tristram Lunt, Feb. 20, 1799.*
Martha, and Enoch Thurston of Newburyport, May 28, 1794.*
Mary, and Richard Brown, May 7, 1674. [1675. CT. R.]
Mary, and Parker Greenleaf, Nov. 24, 1715.*
Mary, and Samuel Peirce, Oct. 19, 1738.*
Mary, and James Greenough of Bradford, Dec. 13, 1759.*
Mary, of Gloucester, and Simon Thorla, int. Mar. 15, 1770.
Mary, and John Knight, Jan. 12, 1809.*
Mary, and Stephen Adams, jr., Jan. 27, 1814.*
Mary A., of West Newbury, and William Giddings, int. Aug.
  1, 1846.

*Intention also recorded.

JAQUES, Mehetabel, and Richard Smith, Oct. 11, 1779.*
Moses, and Sarah Woodman, Nov. 4, 1778.*
Moses, and Abigail Hale, Aug. 15, 1782.*
Moses, and Rebekah Hills, July —, 1792.*
Moses, jr., and Hannah Chase, int. Oct. 27, 1804.
Parker, jr., and Sarah Adams, Dec. 1, 1767.*
Pheby, and Joseph Ilsley, Sept. 3, 1798.*
Prudence, and Edmund Knight, June 11, 1751.*
Rebeckah, and John Dodge of Newburyport, int. Sept. 22, 1804.
Rhoda, and John Loud Tilton, Jan. 25, 1814.*
Richard, and Ruth Plumer, Jan. 18, 1681.
Richard, and Elisabeth Knight, Feb. 25, 1713-14.*
Richard, jr., and Mrs. Judith Noyes, Feb. 19, 1722-3.*
Richard, of Gloucester, and Mary Ilsley, Jan. 13, 1785.*
Richard, and Polly Emerson of Hampstead, N. H., int. May 15, 1792.
Richard, Lt., and Eunise Thurston, Nov. 28, 1799.*
Richard T., and Caroline Noyes, Aug. 20, 1837.*
Ruth, and Stephen Emery, Nov. 29, 1692.
Ruth, and James Short, Apr. 19, 1737.*
Sally, of Bradford, and Samuel Jewett, int. Mar. 5, 1814.
Samuel, and Mary Noyes, May 8, 1750.*
Samuel [jr. int.], and Eunice Chase, Aug. 12, 1779.*
Samuell, and Lydiah Pike, Dec. 12, 1717.
Sarah, Mrs., and Moses Little, jr., Feb. 12, 1716-17.*
Sarah, and John Jaques, June 12, 1746.*
Sarah, and Somersby Chase, Apr. 16, 1777.*
Sarah, and Dudley Rogers, jr. of Newburyport, int. Aug. 25, 1798.
Sarah, and Daniel G. Tilton of Newburyport, Nov. 4, 1811.*
Sarah B., and John England, Dec. 3, 1818.*
Sophia, and John Ladd, Aug. 25, 1814.*
Stephen, jr., and Mrs. Thankfull Taylor of Yarmouth, int. Feb. 21, 1712-13.
Stephen, and Mary Bartlett, July 6, 1783.*
Stephen, and Mehitabel Hovey, Nov. 15, 1792.*
Steven, and Debora Plumer, May 13, 1684.
Susanah, and Moses Noyes [jr. int.], May 21, 1738.*
Susannah Newman, and Benjamin Rolf of Portland, int. Apr. 30, 1803.
Theophilus, and Sarah Wood of Newburyport, int. Mar. 14, 1795.

*Intention also recorded.

JAQUES, William, and Lydia Bartlet of Newburyport, int. Mar. 11, 1815.
William, and Elizabeth Savory, May 3, 1825.*

JARVOTT, Rachel, of Boston, and Capt. Abraham Winter of Topsham, Devonshire, Eng., June 23, 1724. c. r. 7.

JEBSON (see also Jepson), Sarah, of Cambridge, and Samuel . Rolf, int. Jan. 10, 1698-9.

JEFFERS (see also Jeffry), James, and Judith Carr, Nov. 15, 1803.*

JEFFRY (see also Jeffers), Georg, and Elizabeth Walker, Dec. 7, 1665.

JELISON, Nathan, and Abigail Hunt, Mar. 28, 1835.*

JEMSON (see also Gimson), John, of Salisbury, and Rachel Goodwin, Mar. 14, 1738-9.*

JENKINS, Elisabeth, and Joshua Colby, June 8, 1787.*
Hannah, and Caleb Reed, int. July 13, 1822.
Lemuel, of Kittery, and Martha Smith, May 2, 1737. c. r. 7.
Mary, wid., and John Mudd, widr., shipwright, both of Boston, Feb. 15, 1727-8. c. r. 7.
Prudence, and Robert Cram of Exeter, Dec. 7, 1758.*
Robert, and Margaret Ireland, July 30, 1792.*
Robert, and Betsy Pritchard, Dec. 30, 1823.*
Sarah, and John Tarbox, Sept. 16, 1760. c. r. 8.
Sarah, and John Nason [resident in Newbury. int.], Nov. 20, 1763.*
William, and Mrs. Martha Huse, Mar. 4, 1735-6. c. r. 7.

JENNESS, Sarah Ann, of Haverhill, and John Atkinson, int. Jan. 8, 1831.

JENNIN (see also Jennings), John F., and Hannah M. Elwell, both of Rowley, Apr. 27, 1818. c. r. 5.

JENNINGS (see also Ginnings, Jennin), Mary Jane, and Thomas H[all. int.] Adams, Dec. 2, 1838.*

*Intention also recorded.

JEPSON (see also Jebson), John, of Boston, and Aphia Rolfe
[d. Benjamin. int.], Apr. 1, 1696.*

JEWEL (see also Jewell), Benj[ami]n, and Salley Row, Aug.
30, 1796.*

JEWELL (see also Jewel, Jewill), Abigail, and Micah Clark,
Apr. 15, 1779.*

JEWET (see also Jewett), Dummer, and Mary Staniford of
Ipswich, int. Oct. 12, 1754.
Ezekel, of Boxford, and Martha Thirston, Jan. 9, 1718-19.*
Hannah, and Joseph Plumer, jr., Jan. 20, 1684.
Jonathan, of Rowley, and Mrs. Rebeca Poor, Dec. 27, 1742.*
Mary [Lydia. int.], and Robert Huse of Hartland, Vt., Feb.
2, 1797.*
Mehitable, and Samuel Wiatt, Jan. 13, 1737-8.*
Samuel, and Lydia Walingford, both of Rowley, Apr. 26,
1743.
Sarah, of Rowley, and Moses Thorla, Aug. 5, 1756.*

JEWETT (see also Jewet, Jewit), Abigail, of Rowley, and
James Calef, Jan. 2, 1734-5.*
Anna, of Byfield Rowley, and John Morse of Chester, N. H.,
Oct. 15, 1778.
Bette, and Oliver Tenney of Rowley, Apr. 30, 1752.
Clarissa, and John B. Greeley of Newburyport, int. July 27,
1823.
David, of Rowley, and Elisabeth Goodwin, int. Oct. 25, 1771.
David, and Abigail Knight of Atkinson, N. H., int. Feb. 13,
1807.
David, Dr., and Rebecca Huse, Mar. 30, 1809.*
Deborah, of Rowley, and Joshua Dummer, int. May 6, 1820.
Eben[eze]r, and Elizabeth Ann Knight, both of Newburyport,
Jan. 20, 1828.
Hannah, of Rowley, and Thomas Ilsley, at Rowley, Dec. 24,
1760.*
Jacob, jr., of Rowley, and Elizabeth Northend of Byfield
Rowley, Nov. 19, 1771.
Jamima, of Rowley, and Josiah Smith, jr., Aug. 23, 1750.*
Jedediah, Rev., of Rowley, and Mrs. Elisabeth Dumer, Nov.
11, 1730.*

*Intention also recorded.

JEWETT, Jeremiah, of Rowley, and Abigail Emery, July 15, 1797.*

Jeremiah, Capt., of Rowley, and Eleanor Adams, Apr. 21, 1832.*

Jeremiah D., and Mary Smith, May 19, 1831.*

Jeremiah D., and Lydia A. Currier of Amesbury, int. May 27, 1848.

John [W. int.], of Rowley, and Susanna Cheney, Dec. 2, 1824.*

Lucy, of Rowley, and John Hopkins [Ropkins. int.], at Rowley, July 7, 1763.*

Mary Ann, and Frederick Lambert of Rowley, May 24, 1827.*

Maximillian, of Byfield Rowley, and Molly Pearson, Oct.5, 1780.*

Mehitabel Jane, and William Smith, Nov. 12, 1837.*

Moses, of Hopkintou, N. H., and Mary Sawyer of Byfield Rowley, Oct. 29, 1776.

Philomela, and Moses Johnson, both of Rowley, Sept. 29, 1810. C. R. 5.

Ruth, of Rowley, and Isaac Hale, at Rowley, May 1, 1785.*

Sally Mores, and Maurice Hearn, int. Nov. 1, 1812.

Samuel, and Sally Jaques of Bradford, int. Mar. 5, 1814.

Sarah, of Bradford, and Moses Hale, jr., int. Dec. 17, 1766.

Sarah, of Rowley, and Amos Poor, jr., int. Mar. 10, 1769.

Sarah, of Rowley, and Simeon Plumer, at Rowley, Jan. 18, 1770.*

William, jr., and Elizabeth Bowers of Newburyport, int. July 2, 1819.

William, and Betsey Lancaster of Rumney, N. H., int. Dec. 16, 1820.

JEWILL (see also Jewell), Thomas, and Ruth Badger, Feb. 17, 1701.*

JEWIT (see also Jewett), Eunice, of Rowley, and Joshua Noyes, int. Apr. 5, 1797.

Mary, and Abner Dole, Nov. 1, 1694.

Pheby, of Rowley, and Moses Adams [jr. int.], May 16, 1793.*

JILLENS (see also Jillings), Thomas, and Tabitha Glover of Salem, int. June 21, 1756.

*Intention also recorded.

JILLINGS (see also Gillings, Jillens), Elisabeth, and Joseph Coffin, 4th, Jan. 2, 1759.*
Hannah, and Daniel Glover of Marblehead, Dec. 1, 1757.*
Isaac, and Mary Pilcifer, Nov. 12, 1755.*
Mary, and Nicolas George, int. May 18, 1755.
Mary, and Joseph Dorming, int. Dec. 2, 1761.
Thomas, and Hannah Mireck, Nov. 18, 1725.*

JOHN (see also Johns), Charles, and Susan W. Smith, June 14, 1836.*

JOHNS (see also John), Matthew, sailor, and wid. Susannah Gibbins of Boston, June 11, 1728. c. R. 7.

JOHNSON (see also Johnston), Abigail, Mrs.; and Joseph Sweasy, Dec. 6, 1742.*
Abigail, and Joseph Huse, Dec. 2, 1762.*
Alfred, jr., of Belfast, Me., and Nancy Atkinson, Oct. 25, 1817.*
Almira, and William E. Knight, int. Dec. 3, 1840.
Anna, of Haverhill, and Joseph Poer, jr., int. Mar. 15, 1697-8.
Anna, and Dr. John Tenny of Bradford, May 4, 1775.*
Augusta, and Thomas A. Smith of Newburyport, Oct. 25, 1832.*
Benjamin, and Henrietta M. Fowler of Salisbury, Mar. 10, 1844.*
Betty, and Edward Sargent of Newcastle, N. H., Feb. 7, 1760.*
Brackett, and Mary Johnson, both of Greenland, N. H., Feb. 13, 1732-3. c. R. 7.
Bradstreet, and Susannah Brown, June 19, 1760.*
Daniel, of Newburyport, and Hannah Woodman, Oct. 5, 1764.*
Daniel, of Haverhill, and Mary Ann Smith, June ——, 1842.*
Dorothy, and David Folsom of Newmarket, N. H., int. Feb. 2, 1771.
Eleazer, and Sarah Bayley, Sept. 28, 1762.*
Eleazer, and Elizabeth Clarkson, Mar. 8, 1809.*
Eleazer, jr., and Mary Ann Couch of Newburyport, int. Oct. 12, 1822.
Eliazer, and Mrs. Elizabeth Toppan, Aug. 18, 1741.*
Elisabeth, and Isaac Hall, Nov. 23, 1721.*

*Intention also recorded.

JOHNSON, Elisabeth Le Breton, of Newburyport, and Charles Wills, int. Dec. 15, 1849.

Elizabeth C., of Newburyport, and Isaac Pearson, int. Jan. 15, 1820.

Elizebeth, and Joshua Bailey [3d. int.], Apr. 25, 1715.*

Hannah, and Simeon Chase, Sept. 9, 1772.*

Hannah, and Capt. William H. Pettingell of Newburyport, Oct. —, 1837.*

Harriet F., of Newburyport, and W[illia]m H. George, June 27, 1832.

Harrison [G. int.], of Newburyport, and Hannah Currier, Dec. 21, 1843.*

Henry, of Newburyport, and Susan Carey, int. Nov. 13, 1812.

Henry, of Newburyport, and Elizabeth Le Breton, int. Mar. 15, 1823.

Isaac, and Martha Greenleaf, May 10, 1733.*

Isaac, jr., and Elisabeth Coffin, Jan. 3, 1760.*

Isaac [5th. int.], of Newburyport, and Ann Toppan, Oct. 14, 1813.*

James, of Newburyport, and Charlottee Adams, int. Jan. 16, 1808.

Jane, and William Akerman, both of Newburyport, ——, 1832.

Jeremiah, and Hannah Newman of Newburyport, int. Sept. 8, 1821.

Joseph, jr., of Newburyport, and Elisabeth Dole, May 19, 1767.

Joseph T., and Hannah P. Toppan of Newburyport, int. Oct. 10, 1829.

Lucy Ann, and John S. Kimball of Newburyport, int. Aug. 23, 1834.

Lydia, and Philip Coombs, July 10, 1735.*

Lydia, and Capt. Samuel Knapp of Newburyport, June —, 1839.*

Martha, and William Hale of Rowley, Nov. 6, 1753.*

Martha. of Salem, and John Bayley, int. Dec. 11, 1802.

Mary, and Thomas Coleman, July 11, 1651.

Mary, and Francis Browne, Nov. 21, 1653.

Mary, and John Currier of Amesbury, Jan. 23, 1728-9.*

Mary, and Brackett Johnson, both of Greenland, N. H., Feb. 13, 1732-3. c. r. 7.

Mary, and David Moody, Oct. 13, 1757.*

*Intention also recorded.

JOHNSON, Mary, and Joseph Little, Nov. 11, 1766.*

Mary, of Rowley, and John Burbank, int. Apr. 4, 1777.

Mary, and Dudly Russel, May 9, 1802.*

Mary, and Ezra Lunt, July 7, 1808.*

Mary B., and Joshua Turner, both of Newburyport, Aug. 21, 1839.

Mary B., and Ezekiel Evans of Salisbury, int. Oct. 17, 1846.

Mary G., and Stephen G. Haskell of Newburyport, Dec. 1, 1836.*

Mary H., and John C. Hoyt of New York, Sept. 15, 1832.*

Mary L., of Newburyport, and Geo[rge] C. Ireland, int. Nov. 25, 1848.

Moses, and Anna Moody, Apr. 20, 1758.*

Moses, and Philomela Jewett, both of Rowley, Sept. 29, 1810. c. R. 5.

Nancy J., of Frankfort, Me., and William Lane, int. Nov. 26, 1842.

Nicholas, and Sarah Huse, Mar. 22, 1736-7.*

Nicholas, and Elizabeth Higginson of Newburyport, int. Nov. 11, 1831.

Nicholas, of Newburyport, a. 21 y., merchant, b. Newburyport, s. Henry and Mary A., of Newburyport, and Caroline Pettingell, a. 19 y., d. Moses and Mary, June 12, 1849.*

Obadiah, s. Edmon[d], of Hampton, and Judith Brown, d. John, deceased, 28 : 11 m : 1729-30. c. R. 6.

Obadiah, s. Edmund and Abigail, both deceased, of Kensington, N. H., and Ruth Rogers, d. Robert and Elizabeth, Nov. 5, 1761. c. R. 6.

Obadiah, s. Obadiah and Judith, deceased, of Kensington, N. H., and Content Rogers, d. Josiah and Patience, late of Newbury, Oct. 5, 1763. c. R. 6.

Paul, of Rowley, and Hannah Thorla, Dec. 9, 1779.*

Pharaoh, s. Nehemiah, of Lynn, and Lydia, former w., and Hannah Sawyer, d. Humphrey and Hannah, Jan. 23, 1782. c. R. 6.

Samuel, of Andover, and Anne Flud, Nov. 23, 1727.*

Samuel, of Rowley, and Susanna Searl of Byfield, Oct. 20, 1774.

Sarah, and Ralf Cross, Oct. 31, 1728.*

Sarah, and John Noyes, 3d, Nov. 18, 1729.*

Sarah, and David Chase, jr.. Mar. 20, 1755.*

Sarah, Mrs., and Maj. Samuel Gerrish, May 19, 1761.*

*Intention also recorded.

JOHNSON, Sarah Lee, of Newburyport, and Jonas Hutchins, int. Oct. 16, 1841.

Susannah, of Rowley, and Nathan Woodbury, at Rowley, Dec. 16, 1746.

Thomas, and Joanna Pilsbury, Dec. 7, 1726.*

William, and Martha Peirce, d. Col. Daniel, Nov. 9, 1702.*

William, of Woburn, and [Mrs. Sarah. int.] Dole, Jan. 1, 1707.*

William, Rev. [jr. int.], and Mrs. Betty Bradstreet, Aug. 30, 1731.*

William, Capt., and Mrs. Abigail Stickne, Feb. 14, 1733 or 34.*

Will[ia]m, Rev., and Mrs. Sarah Sergeant of Amesbury, int. Oct. 26, 1757.

William, jr., and Lydia Chase, Mar. 31, 1761.*

JOHNSTON (see also Johnson), James, of Newburyport, and Martha March, July 5, 1772.*

Sarah, of Amesbury, and Roger Merrill, int. Sept. 9, 1774.

Thomas, and Elisabeth Lowell, Feb. 12, 1765.*

JOHONNOT, Andrew, and Susannah Oliver, both of Boston, May 21, 1730. c. R. 7.

JONES, Abiah, and Nathaniel Lurvey, Nov. 2, 1785.*

Anne, and Capt. Paul White, Mar. 14, 1664.

Dorothy, and Laurence Hart, Feb. 12, 1678.

Evan, of Salisbury, and Elisabeth Ordway, Mar. 20, 1721-2.*

Evan, and Lydia Ordway, May 13, 1726.*

Hannah, of Southampton, and Abner Gilbert of Brookfield, Oct. 16, 1751. c. R. 7.

Hannah, and Enoch Titcomb, jr., Nov. 6, 1763. c. R. 9.*

Ichabod, Capt., of Falmouth, and Mrs. Apphia Coffin, May 8, 1746.*

John, of Rochester, Co. Kent, Eng., and Martha Mitchel, Mar. 25, 1744. c. R. 7.

John, Capt., resident in Newbury, and Mrs. Hannah Greenleaf, int. Apr. 22, 1749.

Mary, Mrs., and Thomas Woodbridg, June [12. c. c.; 4. CT. R.], 1672.

Mary, of South Hampton, N. H., and Joseph Lowell, int. Jan. 11, 1744-5.

*Intention also recorded.

JONES, Mary, and Jona[than] Bartlet, Oct. 12, 1749.*
Mary, of South Hampton, and Moses Coffin, int. Feb. 22, 1800.
Miriam, of South Hampton, and Moses Cooper, jr., int. Aug. 4, 1764.
Nathaniel, and Katharine Wigglesworth, both of Ipswich, Nov. 24, 1762.
Oliver O., and Hannah H. Pettingell, Nov. 23, 1836.
Samuell, of Exeter, and Mary Lunt, Dec. 26, 1728.*
Sarah, wid., and Joseph Kendall, widr., tanner, both of Boston, Oct. 27, 1725. c. r. 7.
Sarah, and Richard Mayler, resident in Newbury, int. Dec. 7, 1753.

JORDAN (see also Jordon), Hannah, Mrs., of Kittery, Me., and Capt. Stephen Greenleafe, int. Sept. 17, 1713.
Mary, and Benjamin Goodridg, Sept. 8, 1663.

JORDON (see also Jordan), Caroline C., and Thomas Hale of New York, int. Sept. 10, 1836.
Catharine C., of Savannah, Ga., and Thomas Hale of New York, Oct. 3, 1836.
Hannah, and Joseph Calef of Boston, Nov. 9, 1718.*

JOSEPH, Abigail, and Samuel Cheney, both of Byfield Rowley, Dec. 9, 1783.

JOY (see also Joye), Benjamin, of Salisbury, and Sarah Sawyer, Feb. 10, 1735-6.*
Sarah Grant, and Joseph Coffin, 4th, Feb. 9, 1758. c. r. 8.*

JOYE (see also Joy), Mary, wid., of Amesbury, and Jeremiah Davis, at Amesbury, Mar. 5, 1688-9.

KEEN, Hezekiah, and Alice Howland, both of Pembroke, Apr. 10, 1730. c. r. 7.
John, jr., and Mary Bisbee, both of Pembroke, Oct. 28, 1727. c. r. 7.

KEILY, Elmira, of Pittston, Me., and Levi D. Burrill, int. Sept. 3, 1848.

*Intention also recorded.

KEITH, Jane, and David Thayer, both of Mendon, Dec. 31, 1729. c. r. 7.

KEIZER (see also Kezęr), Eunice, and Richard Kent, jr., Feb. 19, 1787.*
Miriam, and Jonathan Martin, Dec. 14, 1790.*
Sarah, and Josiah Brown, Nov. 28, 1762.*

KELLE (see also Kelley), Amme, and William Hills, int. Jan. 31, 1712-13.
Esther, and Christopher Bartlet, Mar. 8, 1724-5.*
Richard, and Susanna Hoyt of Amesbury, at Amesbury, Sept. 28, 1721.

KELLEY (see also Kelle, Kelly), Abigail, and Samuel Currier of Haverhill, June 30, 1714.*
Elizabeth, of Salem, N. H., and Eliphalet Poor, int. Dec. 23, 1780.
Hannah, and Hugh Pike [jr. int.], June 30, 1714.*
Hannah, and Stephen Bailey, May 13, 1729.*
Joseph, and Jane Heth of Haverhill, Dec. 23, 1706.
Lydia, and William Carr, int. Dec. 30, 1809.
Mary, and Samuel Sawyer, July 9, 1728.*
Nath[anie]l, and Betsey Brown, Nov. 30, 1797.*
Prudence, and Benjamin Brown, Feb. 2, 1776.*
Ruth, and Parker Chase, Dec. 28, 1774.*
Samuel, of Haverhill and Abigail Plommer, Jan. 12, 1721-2.*
Sarah Barnard, and Gideon Baker, int. Aug. 23, 1809.
Susanna, and Moses Chase, 3d, June 17, 1760.*

KELLY (see also Kelley), Abiel, and Rebeckah Davis [d. Samuel, deceased. int.], Jan. 5, 1696.*
Anna Gerrish, and Jeremiah Woodman of Newburyport, Oct. 18, .1806.*
Benjamin, of Amesbury, and Rebecca Bartlet, Oct. 7, 1736.*
Daniel, and Mercy Smith, Oct. 30, 1734.*
Ebenezer, and Elisabeth Cheeny, Apr. 29, 1790.*
Elisabeth, and Solomon Holman, Apr. 18, 1738.*
Elizabeth, and Edmund Worth, Nov. 25, 171[8. int.].*
Emma [of Boston. int.], and Sylvanus Plummer, at Boston, Nov. 5, 1700.*

*Intention also recorded.

KELLY, Jane, of Haverhill, and James Brown [jr. int.], at
   Haverhill, Apr. 13, 1737.*
John, and Sara Knight, May 20, 1663.
John [jr. int.], and Elizabeth Emery [d. Sergt. John. int.],
   Nov. —, 1696.*
John, sr., and Lydia Ames of Bradford, Mar. 15, 1715-16.*
John, jr., and Hannah Somes, Dec. 31, 1723.*
John, jr., and Hannah Hale, July 3, 1749.*
John, and Mercy Pilsbury, Aug. 26, 1792.*
Jonathan, and Hester Morss [d. Dea. Benjamin. int.], July 6,
   1702.*
Judith, and Joseph Moodey, Nov. 27, 1722.*
Mary, and John Belcong[er], Apr. 12, 1666.
Mary, and William Davis [of Haverhill. int.], Dec. 31, 1700.*
Moses, and Lydia Sawyer, Nov. 10, 1757.*
Prudence, and John Knight [3d. int.], Oct. 18, 1749.*
Rebecca, and James Brown, jr., Jan. 2, 1701.
Rebecca, and Daniel Peasley of Haverhill, July 21, 1724.*
Richard, and Hannah Greenough, Oct. 18, 1725.*
Richard, jr., and Hannah Bartlet, Dec. 16, 1725.*
Richard, of Amesbury, and Judith Worth, May 17, 1781.*
Ruth, and Abel Merrill [jr. int.], Dec. 12, 1721.*
Sarah [d. John. int.], and Henry Hale, Sept. 11, 1695.*
Sarah [jr. int.], and Josiah Pilsbury, May 12, 1720.*
Thomas, and Anna Gerrish, int. May 6, 1786.
Timothy, and Joanna Newcomb, Dec. 28, 1783.*
Timothy, and Jane Burbank, May 19, 1808.*

KENDALL, George, of Georgetown, a. 28 y., shoecutter, b.
   Georgetown, s. George and Martha Bachiler, and Mary E.
   Kimball, a. 25 y., d. Charles H. and Mary, June 17,
   1847.*
Joseph, widr., tanner, and wid. Sarah Jones, both of Boston,
   Oct. 27, 1725. c. r. 7.

KENDRICK (see also Kenricke, Kindrick, Kinreck, Kinrick),
   Samuel, and Hannah Colby, both of Amesbury, Sept. 22,
   1737. c. r. 7.

KENISTON (see also Kennison, Kenniston, Kinerson, Kinison, Kinniston), Elizabeth S. [L. int.], and John F. Lee,
   Nov. 30, 1843.*

        *Intention also recorded.

KENISTON, Hannah G., d. Moses and Dolly, of Amesbury, and
Paul Adams, s. Richard, deceased, and Hannah, 28: 4 m:
1803. C. R. 6.
James R., and Sarah Ann Pearson of Salem, int. Dec. 23, 1847.
Jonathan, and Mary Ann Somerby, June 13, 1841.*

KENNA (see also Kenney), Lydia, and John Flud, Dec. 30,
1714.*

KENNE (see also Kenney), Samuel, and Mary Moores, Feb.
29, 1711-12.*
Samuel, and Mary Mulincum of Bradford, int. Oct. 29, 1743.
Thomas, and Phebe Thirston, Nov. 11, 1729.*

KENNEY (see also Canney, Kenna, Kenne, Kennie, Kenny),
Person, and Elizabeth Brown, both of Rowley, Jan. 12,
1814. C. R. 5.
Tabith, and John Courser, Mar. 8, 1716-17.*
Tabitha, and Samuel Akers, int. Jan. 21, 1715-16.

KENNIE (see also Kenney), David, Capt., and Mrs. Katharine
Steward, both of Boston, July 21, 1733. C. R. 7.

KENNING, Henry, of Salem Village, and Mrs. Magdaleane
Wiggins, int. May 14, 1698.

KENNISON (see also Keniston), Thomas, and Sarah Colby
of Newburyport, int. Nov. 6, 1790.

KENNISTON (see also Keniston), Abner, and Betsy Lowell
of Amesbury, int. Oct. 14, 1810.

KENNY (see also Kenney), Mary, and William Pilsbury, Dec.
13, 1677.
Mary, and Benajah Young, Apr. 6, 1747.*
Samuel, widr., and Lydia Davis, wid., Dec. 7, 1749. C. R. 7.*

KENRICKE (see also Kendrick), John, and Lydia Cheny,
Nov. 12, 1657.

KENT, Abigail, and Tho[ma]s Pool, both of Boston, Mar. 16,
1735-6. C. R. 7.

*Intention also recorded.

KENT, Abigail, and Benjamin Pettingell [of Falmouth. int.],
   Oct. 23, 1750.*
Abigail, and Thomas Little of Atkinson, N? H., int. Oct. 3,
   1772.
Abigail, and Ezekiel Bartlet, Mar. 6, 1788.*
Ann, and Enoch Moody [jr. int.], Apr. 14, 1798.*
Anna [Anne. int.], and Joshua Greanleaf, Dec. 1, 1763.*
Caroline, and John Kent, jr., Mar. 20, 1833.*
Clement, and Sarah Peterson, Dec. 5, 1750.*
Daniel, and Elizabeth Day of Bradford, at Bradford, Apr. —,
   1792.*
David, and Mary Rogers, May 22, 1843.*
Elisabeth, and Nathan Hale, Aug. 27, 1713.*
Elisabeth, and Samuel Burtt of Boston, Dec. 7, 1749.*
Elizabeth, and Nathan Sargent of Haverhill, Oct. 12, 1819.*
Elizabeth, and Joseph Gerrish, int. Sept. 8, 1827.
Elizabeth, and Jesse Adams, int. Nov. 16, 1835.
Elizabeth A., of Newburyport, and Abraham S. Lunt, int. Aug.
   12, 1835.
Elizabeth A., a. 19 y., d. James and Rhoda, and Mial M.
   Rogers, a. 21 y., shoemaker, s. Moody and Ann, Oct. 14,
   1845.*
Ema, and Samuel Hazeltine [of Bradford. int.], June 10,
   1701.*
Emma, and Spindelo Morrison, Apr. 3, 1740.*
Emme, and Thomas Chase, 3d, Nov. 24, 1726.*
Hannah, and Nathan Merrill, Sept. 6, 1699.*
Hannah, and [Capt. int.] Tho[ma]s Lord of Exeter, Aug. 8,
   1753. C. R. 9.*
Hannah G., and Moses Kent, jr., Dec. 17, 1822.*
Hannah O., and Isaac Adams, int. Oct. 12, 1839.
Jacob, of Plaistow, N. H., and Abigail Bayley, Dec. 26, 1752.*
Jacob, of Amesbury, and Mary Noyes, Mar. 14, 1812.*
James [jr. int.], and Hanah Hodgkins, Dec. 23, 1707.*
James, and wid. Elizabeth Woodbridge, Mar. 15, 1711.*
James, and Rhoda Rogers, Apr. 10, 1813.*
James G., and Sarah Jane Stickney, June 4, 1837.*
Jane, and Thomas S. Poor of Newburyport, Sept. 23, 1841.*
[John. C. C. and CT. R.], and Mary Hobs, Feb. 24, 1664.
John, jr., and Sara Woodman, Mar. 13, 1665.
John [4th. int.], and Sarah Little, Jan. 14, 1702.*
John, jr., and Abigail Merrill, Jan. 10, 1722-3.*

*Intention also recorded.

KENT, John, jr., and Sarah Mors [wid. c. R. 2.], June 20, 1737.*

John, 4th, and Sarah Harris, Oct. 1, 1747.*

John, and Elisabeth Hunt of Amesbury, at Amesbury, Apr. 8, 1762.*

John, of Danvers, and Hannah Toppan, May 14, 1822.*

John, and Elizabeth Northend, Sept. 14, 1823.*

John, jr., and Caroline Kent, Mar. 20, 1833.*

John N., and Harriet Moulton, Oct. 20, 1835.*

Joseph, and Jane Moody, Aug. 23, 1768.*

Joseph, and Jane Willcomb of Newburyport, int. Sept. 23, 1785.

Joseph, and Lois Little, June 25, 1815.*

Joshua N., a. 29 y., farmer, s. Jacob and Mary, and Sarah N. Dumer, a. 29 y., b. Rowley, d. Samuel and Joanna, of Rowley, Nov. 11, 1845.*

Judith, and Thomas Merrill, Mar. 16, 1704.*

Judith, and Paul Woodman, Sept. 7, 1814.*

Martha J., and John D. Rogers, Nov. 29, 1826.*

Mary, d. John, mariner, and Stephen Swett of Hampton, N. H., int. Dec. 27, 1695.

Mary, and Abner Dole, jr., Sept. 3, 1730.*

Mary, Mrs., and Capt. William Starke [Starkey. int.] of London, Great Britain, May 29, 1744.*

Mary, and Samuel Pilsbury, jr., Sept. 12, 1763.*

Mary, and James Gould of West Newbury, June 15, 1829.*

Mary Ann, of Newburyport, and John Pearson, jr., int. May 11, 1822.

Moses, of Newburyport, and Sarah Adams, Feb. 18, 1795.*

Moses, and Marcey Toppan, Mar. 3, 1799. c. R. 1.*

Moses, jr., and Hannah G. Kent, Dec. 17, 1822.*

Paul, and Alice Thurla, June 29, 1799.*

Rebecca, and Henry Kingsbury, Mar. 14, 1716-17.*

Rebeckah, and Charles Hartt, int. May 26, 1705.

Richard, and Mrs. Joanna Davison, Jan. 6, 1674.

Richard, Capt., and Mrs. Sarah Greenleaf, Jan. 30, 1709.*

Richard, Esq., and Mrs. Hannah Carter of Charlestown, at Charlestown, Sept. 8, 1724.

Richard [jr. int.], and Hannah Marriner, Nov. 7, 1734.*

Richard, jr., and Ann Hale, June 10, 1736.*

Richard, 3d, and Hannah Tilton, Sept. 26, 1759.*

Richard, jr., and Eunice Keizer, Feb. 19, 1787.*

*Intention also recorded.

KENT, Sara, and Samuell Greenleaf, Mar. 1, 1685-6.

Sarah, d. Sergt. John, and Jacob Toppan, int. May 15, 1696.

Sarah [wid. int.], and Bartholomew Thing of Exeter, N. H., Apr. 2, 1712.*

Sarah, and John Waite, Jan. 7, 1724-5.*

Sarah, and Beamsly Wells, Apr. 30, 1752.*

Sarah, Mrs., and Dudley Atkins, May 7, 1752.*

Stephen, and Mary Gerrish, Oct. 8, 1761.*

Stephen, jr., and Sarah Noyes, Mar. 17, 1808.*

Stephen, jr., and Susan Varina, Mar. 6, 1834.*

KETTELL, James, of Boston, and Harriet Stickney, Sept. 9, 1826.*

KEYES (see also Kyes), Ebenezer S., and Rebecca Plumer, Nov. 23, 1830.*

Eleazer F., and Mary L. Plumer, Mar. —, 1834.*

Mary, wid., a. 40 y., d. John, and Benj[amin] Spiller, widr., of Wenham, a. 64 y., shoemaker, b. Wenham, s. Samuel and Annis, of Wenham, Dec. 28, 1848.*

Sollomon, and Francis Grant, Oct. 2, 1653.

KEZER (see also Keizer), Eliazer, and Mrs. Susanna Coombs, Jan. 17, 1743-4.*

KIAH, Benjamin, and Nabby Atkison, Nov. 25, 1802. c. R. 1.

KILBORN (see also Kilbourn, Kilburn), Eliphalet, and Mary Thorla, Dec. 23, 1779.*

Elisabeth, of Newburyport, and Charles Bartlett, int. Sept. 13, 1845.

Eliza Ann, of Newburyport, and Joseph Russell, jr., Nov. 25, 1823.*

Elizabeth C., and Jeremiah Spiller, Dec. 19, 1825.*

Hannah D. [Mrs. c. R. 10.], and Benjamin Goodwin, jr., Dec. 27, 1829.*

Hannah D., of Newburyport, and W[illia]m H. Pierce, int. Oct. 24, 1846.

Hannah P., of Newburyport, and Nicholas R. Brown, int. May 6, 1843.

James, and Elizabeth Thurston, Nov. 26, 1807.*

*Intention also recorded.

KILBORN, Jedediah, and Salley Coffin Downs of Newbury-
port, int. Nov. 17, 1804.
John C., and Hannah Ross, Sept. 25, 1825.*
Mary P., and George S. Shute of Newburyport, int. Nov. 18,
1837.
Nathan, and Sarah Plumer, June 12, 1777.*
Nathan, and Susan Cilley of Newburyport, Jan. 9, 1837.*
Samuel, and Hannah Davis, May 13, 1821.*
Sarah Jane, and Joseph Cheney, Oct. 10, 1838.*
Thomas, of Rowley, and Anne Plummer, Oct. 17, 1780.*
Thomas, and Hannah Pike, Dec. 28, 1819.*

KILBOURN (see also Killborn), Jedediah, and Mary Knight
Pettingell, Dec. 12, 1814.*

KILBURN (see also Kilborn), Jedediah, and Elizabeth Glazier, Dec. 12, 1793.*

KIMBAL (see also Kimball), Abigail, of Rowley, and Daniel
Morrison, int. Nov. 8, 1712.
Anna, and David Ingersoll of Gloucester, int. Aug. 22, 1801.
Anna, of Newburyport, and Samuel Willie, int. Nov. 10, 1804.
Caleb, jr., and Hannah Noyes, Nov. 25, 1766.*
Caleb, jr., and Ednah Woodman, Nov. 27, 1800.*
Daniel, of Boxford, and Sarah Pearson, int. Oct. 11, 1789.
John, and Hannah Collins, July 17, 1796.*
Joseph, and Rachel Chase of Haverhill, int. Dec. 26, 1800.
Judith, and Asa Sergeant, July 24, 1766.*
Lucy, 2nd w. [of Ipswich. int.], and Edmund Coffin, Apr. 25,
1809. c. r. 1.*
Polly, and Moses Brown, Nov. 20, 1794.*
Royal, of Portland, and Nancy Toppan, Dec. 5, 1824. c. r.
10.*
Sarah, of Exeter, and William Moody, jr., Oct. 18, 1787.*
Sarah, and John Foster of Canterbury, Aug. 25, 1800.*
Thomas, and Anny Carr, Oct. 23, 1794.*
True, Rev., and Jane Short, May 7, 1784.*

KIMBALL (see also Cimbal, Kimbal, Kimble, Kymbal), Almira, of Boxford, and William Moody, jr., int. Oct. 13,
1825.
Anna, and Thomas Emerson, int. Nov. 21, 1785.

*Intention also recorded.

KIMBALL, Benja[min], and Eliza Bean of Kingston, N. H.,
   Aug. 16, 1827.*

Betsy, and Thomas Lankaster, June 12, 1806.*

Betty, of Bradford, and John Hovey, int. Oct. 28, 1780.

Caleb, and Sarah Huse, Apr. 17, 1735.*

Charles Harrison, and Mary Foster of Boxford, int. May 3,
   1817.

Elis[abeth], and Ebenezer Carlton, both of Bradford, Aug.
   18, 1729. C. R. 7.

Eliza, of Kingston, N. H., and Solomon Pilsbury, int. Mar.
   14, 1840.

Elizabeth, and Thomas Bayley, int. Oct. 8, 1774.

Hanah, and James Godfry, Feb. 10, 1700.*

Hannah, and Nathan Rogers, Apr. 2, 1772.*

Hannah, and Joseph Woodman [jr. int.] of Sanbornton, May
   16, 1805.*

Hannah, and Lewis Rogers, June 22, 1829.*

John, and Susanna Knight, Oct. 10, 1782.*

John G., and Phebe Rogers [2d. C. R. 10.], Nov. 20, 1828.*

John S., of Newburyport, and Lucy Ann Johnson, int. Aug.
   23, 1834.

Leanord W., and Phebe Pilsbury, both of Boston, July 16,
   1829.

Loraney, and Paul Rogers of Newburyport, int. Sept. 2, 1826.

Lucretia H., of Ipswich, and William W. Perkins, int. Oct. 22,
   1836.

Mary Ann, and George Blood, both of Worcester, May —,
   1839.

Mary C. [Ann. int.], a. 14 y., d. Benjamin, and Edward Rogers, jr., a. 21 y., shoemaker, s. Edward and Mary, July 31,
   1844.*

Mary E., a. 25 y., d. Charles H. and Mary, and George Kendall of Georgetown, a. 28 y., shoecutter, b. Georgetown, s.
   George and Martha Bachiler, June 17, 1847.*

Mehittable, and Joseph Thirston, int. Nov. 21, 1695.

Nathaniel, jr., of Ipswich, and Sarah Stickney of Byfield Rowley, May 15, 1783.

Olive, of Dover, N. H., and Andrew S. Flanders, int. Nov. 1,
   1845.

Stephen, jr., of Newburyport, and Lucy Hale, June 11, 1835.*

Stephen, jr., and Almira Hale, both of Newburyport, Oct. 18,
   1838.

*Intention also recorded.

KIMBLE (see also Kimball), Benj[amin], and Lorana Rogers, Oct. 30, 1803. c. r. 5.*
Martha, and Daniel Chase, Aug. 25, 1683.

KINDRICK (see also Kendrick), Abigail, and Thomas C. Colby, int. Mar. 27, 1807.
Edmund Bayley, and Abigail Pilsbery, May 27, 1787.*
Judith [Mrs. int.], and Dea. Abner Bayley, Apr. 7, 1785.*
Mary, and Abner Bayley, jr., Sept. 26, 1788.*
Samuel, and Tabitha Tenny, int. May 7, 1791.

KINERSON (see also Keniston), Nathan, and Grace Currier of Haverhill, int. Jan. 7, 1804.

KING, Deborah, of Boston, and John Calef, int. May 23, 1702.
John, and Mary Brown of Salisbury, at Salisbury, Nov. 23, 1725.

KINGSBERY (see also Kingsbury), Benjamin, and Eunice Rowell of Amesbury, int. Apr. 14, 1753.
Henry, Capt., and Elisabeth Greenough, July 29, 1754.*

KINGSBURY (see also Kingsbery, Kinsbury), Elizabeth, and Ephraim Davis, June 9, 1687. ct. r.
Elizabeth, and Samuel Titcomb, Sept. 2, 1740.*
Hannah, and Ambros Berrye, Jan. 10, 1716-17.
Hannah, and Timothy Pike, jr., Mar. 24, 1757.*
Henry, and Rebecca Kent, Mar. 14, 1716-17.*
John, of York, and Mary Stickney, Dec. 29, 1715.*
John, and Mrs. Patience Toppan, June 5, 1739.*
Mary, and Samuel Barnard of Amesbury, Mar. 1, 1759.*

KINISON (see also Keniston), Timothy, and Abigail Longfellow, Nov. 7, 1821.*

KINNISTON (see also Keniston), Martha, and Charles Thompson, Feb. 13, 1796.*

KINRECK (see also Kendrick), James, and Judith Bayley, int. Dec. 17, 1763.

*Intention also recorded.

KINRICK (see also Kendrick), Catherine, and Samuel Ordway
    of Haverhill, Apr. 19, 1813.*
Dudley, and Mary Williams, Apr. 21, 1763.*

KINSBURY (see also Kingsbury), Susan, and Joseph Pik, Jan.
    29, 1661.

KNAP (see also Knapp), Anna, and Benjamin Choat, Aug.
    10, 1754.*
Ebenezer, and Sarah Follensby, Aug. 9, 1750.*
Ebenezer, jr., and Anne Pilsbury, Nov. 17, 1757.*
Hannah, and Joseph Noyes, jr., Jan. 14, 1761.*
John, and Mary Wiatt, Dec. 10, 1731.*
John, of Newburyport, and Anne Adams. Apr. 28, 1767.
Mary, and Aaron Davis, Nov. 10, 1761.*
Nathaniel, and Sarah Hart, Sept. 18, 1734. c. r. 7.*
Nathaniel, jr., and Mary Mireck, June 14, 1757.*
Nathaniell, and Elisabeth Moody, Sept. 18, 1754.*
Nath[anie]ll, and Elisabeth Morgaridge, Jan. 19, 1763.*
Samuel, and Mary Robinson, Jan. 17, 1738-9.*
Sarah, and Jonathan Whitmore, Jan. 29, 1760. c. r. 9.*
Susan M., and Nathaniel K. Merrill, July 21, 1825.*
William, and Lydia Coombs, July 2, 1761.*

KNAPP (see also Knap, Knaps), Elizabeth, of Salem, and
    John Hill of Rowley, Jan. 28, 1816. c. r. 5.
Joseph J., of Newburyport, and Mary Pierce, July 24, 1828.*
Robert H., of Newburyport, and Emily Brookings, int. Mar.
    11, 1831.
Samuel, Capt., of Newburyport, and Lydia Johnson, June —,
    1839.*
Sarah Ann, of Conway, N. H., and Jesse Adams, int. Sept. 22,
    1849.

KNAPS (see also Knapp), Ebenezer, and Mrs. Sarah Butler,
    Nov. 15, 1743.*

KNIGHT, Abigail, and Jonathan Person, Jan. 24, 1722-3.*
Abigail, and Abel Merrill of Falmouth, Nov. 22, 1759.*
Abigail, and Nehemiah Emerson of Haverhill, Feb. 6, 1794.*
Abigail, of Atkinson, N. H., and David Jewett, int. Feb. 13,
    1807.

*Intention also recorded.

KNIGHT, Adams, and Alice Little, Nov. 6, 1798.*
Adams, jr., and Mary Little, Dec. —, 1833.*
Alice, and William Goodwin, Jan. 28, 1827.*
Amos and Elis[abeth] Pettingell, Oct. 6, 1763. c. r. 9.
Amos, of Newburyport, and Elisabeth Jaques, Jan. 12, 1797.*
Ann, and Richard Trusdel of Newburyport, int. Sept. 19, 1818.
Ann, and Joseph Lunt, Dec. 1, 1831.*
Anna, and Ezra Hale, Oct. 30, 1764.
Anna, and Moses Tenny, Nov. 18, 1776.*
Anna, and Richard Currier [jr. int.] of Methuen, Dec. 18, 1777.*
Anna, and Josiah Harris of North Yarmouth, Oct. 2, 1793.*
Anne, and Henry Jaques, Oct. 8, 1648.
Anne, and John Merill [jr. int.], May 15, 1725.*
Benjamin, jr., and Jane Toppan, Jan. 6, 1719-20.*
Benjamin, jr., and Martha Coombs, Nov. 25, 1762.*
Benjamin, and Hannah Beal of Newmarket, int. Dec. 13, 1791.
Bezaleel, and Jemima Bishop, Sept. 16, 1754.*
Caleb, of Newburyport, and Sarah Coffin, Feb. 10, 1785.*
Charles, and Abigail Leigh, Sept. 1, 1808. c. r. 1.
Charles, jr., of Newburyport, and Ann Condry, int. Nov. 9, 1833.
Daniel, and Anne Hale, Dec. 11, 1733.*
Daniel, jr., and Mary Goodwin, Jan. 28, 1762.*
Daniel H., and Abigail H. Cook, both of Newburyport, July 25, 1839.
David, and Mary Weed, Oct. 18, 1759. c. r 9.*
David, and Dolly Noyes, May 18, 1793.*
Deborah, and Nathaniell Atkinson, Jan. 22, 1707.*
Edmund, and Jane Little, May 25, 1741.*
Edmund, and Prudence Jaques, June 11, 1751.*
Edmund, jr., and Sarah Hale, Dec. 24, 1767.*
Edmund, and Mary Coffin, Nov. 9, 1786.*
Ednar, and Robert Greenough, Nov. 27, 1735.*
Edward, Capt., of Dusley, Gloucestershire, England, and Elizabeth Brightwell of Suffolk, Eng., Aug. 13, 1731. c. r. 7.
Elenor, Mrs., and John Hale, Oct. 26, 1743.*
Eliphalet, and Elisabeth Ordway, June 6, 1745.*
Elisabeth, and Richard Jaques, Feb. 25, 1713-14.*
Elisabeth, and Samuel Dole, Oct. 30, 1720.*
Elisabeth, and Edward Sweasi, Dec. 24, 1741.*
Elisabeth, and Friend Noyes, Oct. 17, 1785.*

*Intention also recorded.

KNIGHT, Elisabeth, and Oliver Martin, Mar. 28, 1786.*
Elisabeth, and Enoch Lunt, jr:, int. Feb. 17, 1792.
Eliza Ann, and Benjamin Lunt Atkinson, July 26, 1821.*
Elizabeth, and Anthony Morse, May 8, 1660.
Elizabeth, and Cutting Noyes, Feb. 25, 1673.
Elizabeth, and Samuel Plumer, July 22, 1711.*
Elizabeth, and Richard Currier, May 5, 1743.*
Elizabeth, and Pike Noyes, Feb. 18, 1819.*
Elizabeth Ann, and Eben[eze]r Jewett, both of Newburyport,
    Jan. 20, 1828.
Elizabeth [P. int.], and Amos Little, June 17, 1832.*
Enoch, and Elisabeth Jaques, Nov. 11, 1736.*
Enoch, and Lucy Woodman, Nov. —, 1797. C. R..1.
Eunice, Mrs., and Ichabod Woodman, Dec. 20, 1739.*
Foster, of Salem, widr., a. 35 y., tanner, b. Salem, s. Enoch and
    Lucy, and Mary C. Knight of Newburyport, a. 32 y., b.
    Newburyport, d. Hale and Nancy, Nov. 25, 1847.
Frederic, and Sarah C. Knight, Nov. 2, 1834.*
Frederick, of Newburyport, and Ann Goodwin, Apr. 21,
    1834.*
George, and Judith Moody, Feb. 3, 1725-6.*
George [jr. int.], of Falmouth, and Priscilla Merrill, Nov. 16,
    1769.*
George W., and Caroline Lunt, Dec. 22, 1837.*
Hale, and Anna Brooks, Jan. 1, 1797. C. R. 1.
Hannah, and James Noyes, Mar. 31, 1684.
Hannah, and John Beard of Wilmington, Apr. 10, 1744.*
Hannah, and Samuel Goodwin, Nov. 2, 1800.*
Hannah, of Newburyport, and Greenleaf Mores, int. Dec. 11,
    1802.
Hannah, and John Poor, jr., Oct. 30, 1817.*
Hannah, of Newburyport, and David Stickney, int. Apr. 22,
    1826.
Harriet A., of Salisbury, and Jacob P. Huse, int. Mar. 10,
    1849.
Henry, and Priscilla Merrill, Dec. 5, 1722.*
Hephzibah, and David Noyes, Nov. 9, 1756.*
Isaac, and Mary Gooding, Feb. 20, 1714-15.*
Isaac [jr. int.], and Hannah Toppan, June 15, 1736.*
Jacob, and Deborah Noice, Oct. 17, 1734. C. R. 7.
James, and Mary Plumer, July 13, 1708.*
James, and Sarah Dole, May 22, 1740.*

*Intention also recorded.

KNIGHT, James, jr., and Eunice Noyes, Feb. 8, 1785.*
James, jr., and Harriet N. Lunt, int. Aug. 26, 1843.
James B., and Adeline Hale, Sept. 27, 1836.*
Jane, and Benjamin Thurston, Jan. 20, 1785.*
Jane Little, and Stephen Noyes [jr. int.], ——, 1804. C. R. 1.
    [Apr. 3. int.]*
Jane M., and Sewall Dole of Rowley [Nov. 10. int.] 1832.*
Jane M., and Daniel McDonald of Boston, int. Dec. 6, 1845.
Jemima, and William Chapman, Dec. 11, 1799. C. R. 1.
John, and Bathsua Ingerson, —— [16—?].
John, and Rebecca Noyes, Jan. 1, 1671.
John [jr. int.], and Judeth Greenleaf, Jan. 9, 1720-21.*
John [3d. int.], and Prudence Kelly, Oct. 18, 1749.*
John, of Plaistow, N. H., and Sarah Merrill, Nov. 7, 1751.*
John, and Mehetabel Adams, July 21, 1763. C. R. 9.*
John, and [Mrs. C. R. 2.] Martha Burroughs [Burrill. C. R. 2.],
    June 28, 1792. ("The s'd John Knight declared before
    several witnesses that he took s'd Martha Burroughs
    naked, i. e. without any of her own earnings or without
    anything that was her former husbands." C. R. 2.)*
John, and Mary Jaques, Jan. 12, 1809.*
John, 3d, and Lydia N. Webster, July 27, 1834.*
John L., and Betsy H[oyt. int.] Goodwin, Feb. 17, 1831.*
John L., and Martha Ayers, int. Oct. 2, 1847.
Jonathan, and Eunice Presbury, Dec. 1, 1747.*
Jonathan, of Newburyport, and Anna Somerby, Dec. 19,
    1805.*
Jonathan, and Roxanna Brown of Newburyport, int. Feb. 6,
    1830.
Joseph, and Deborah Coffin, Oct. 31, 1677.
Joseph, jr., and Rebecca Noy[es], Apr. 29, 1708.*
Joseph, and Ann Moodey, Jan. 21, 1747-8.*
Joseph, and Sarah Plumer, Dec. 6, 1753.*
Joseph, and Eunice Hale, int. Mar. 30, 1765.
Joseph, and Anne Rogers, Jan. 24, 1769.*
Joseph, and Sarah Brown, May 31, 1809.*
Judeth, wid., and Daniel Emmery [widr. C. R. 2.], Nov. 29,
    1723.*
Judith, and Daniel Noyes, Dec. 29, 1702.*
Katharine, and Nathan Poor, Apr. 5, 1764.*
Lemuel, and Mary Hall, int. May 21, 1791.
Lydia, and Oliver Clark, Jan. 12, 1742-3.*

*Intention also recorded.

KNIGHT, Mary, and Joseph Downer, July 9, 1660.
Mary, and Timothy Noyes, Jan. 13, 1680.
Mary, and Stephen Thirston, Oct. 14, 1706.
Mary, and John Pettingill, Feb. 16, 1720-21.*
Mary, Mrs., and Samuel Pettingill [jr. int.], Aug. 1, 1745.*
Mary, and Bezalleel Woodbury, int. Dec. 18, 1788.
Mary, and John Swanskins, Aug. 24, 1795.*
Mary, and Eliphalet Randall, ——, 1836. [Jan. 23. int.]*
Mary, C., of Newburyport, a. 32 y., b. Newburyport, d. Hale
    and Nancy, and Foster Knight of Salem, widr., a. 35 y.,
    tanner, b. Salem, s. Enoch and Lucy, Nov. 25, 1847.
Mary J., and Joshua J. Danforth, Dec. 1, 1836.*
Moses, and Hannah Akers, Nov. 29, 1737.*
Moses, a. 55 y., farmer, s. James and Eunice, and Lydia
    Stickney, a. 45 y., d. Amos and Hannah, Dec. 28, 1848.*
Moses C., and Eliza Bartlet of Newburyport, Apr. 28, 1831.*
Moses C., of Newburyport, and Rowena Ilsley, July 31,
    1844.*
Nancy, and Samuel P[erkins. c. r. 10.] Russell, Nov. 19,
    1818.*
Nathaniel, and Sarah Somerby, Oct. 15, 1719.*
Nathaniel, of Plaistow, N. H., and Abigail Merrill, Sept. 25,
    1750.*
Oliver, and Sarah Coffin, Oct. 27, 1742.*
Parker, and Molly Stockles of Newburyport, int. Nov. 26,
    1791.
Patience, and Daniel Pettengell, June 23, 1757.*
Paul, and Nabby Beal, int. Nov. 5, 1791.
Polly, and John Jackson, Nov. 5, 1789.*
Polly, and Enos Floyd, Jan. 19, 1808.*
Prudence, and Benajah Titcomb [jr. int.], June 24, 1740.*
Rebecca, and Abiel Somerby, Nov. 13, 1661.
Rebecca, and Abraham Wheelwright, Sept. 25, 1780.*
Rebekah, d. John, and Robert Adams, int. July 13, 1695.
Rebekah, and Moses Rogers, Aug. 14, 1783.*
Rebekah, and Jacob Newman of Newburyport, Sept. 27,
    1819.*
Richard [jr. int.], and Hebsibah Person, Apr. 14, 1715.*
Richard, of Haverhill, and Jane Jackman, May 11, 1749.*
Richard, and Martha Hook, May 10, 1786.*
Richard, a. 21 y., farmer, s. Enoch and Mary T., and Caroline
    L. Tenney, a. 20 y., d. Daniel S. and Caroline, May 20,
    1847.*

*Intention also recorded.

KNIGHT, Samuel, of Rowley, and Polly Hale, at Rowley, June 10, 1791.

Sara, and John Bartlet, Mar. 6, 1659-60.

Sara, and John Kelly, May 20, 1663.

Sarah, and Thomas Noyes, Nov. 16, 1686. CT. R.

Sarah, and Samuel Moodey, Apr. 16, 1700.*

Sarah, and Matthew Adams, Apr. 4, 1707.*

Sarah, and William Chevers, Mar. 31, 1741.*

Sarah, and Ebenezer Sweasy, Nov. 23, 1749.*

Sarah, and Stephen Coffin of Salisbury, Jan. 30, 1752. C. R. 2.*

Sarah, and Dudley James of Exeter, Feb. 24, 1763.*

Sarah, and Daniel Lunt [jr. int.], Nov. 16, 1769.*

Sarah, and Zebedee Cook of Newburyport, int. Nov. 15, 1783.

Sarah, and Humphrey Morse, Feb. 11, 1808.*

Sarah, and John Noyes, jr., Feb. 24, 1812.*

Sarah, and James Short, jr., Sept. 28, 1819.*

Sarah C., and Frederic Knight, Nov. 2, 1834.*

Silas, and Ruth Short, July 26, 1810.*

Stephen, and Hannah Homes, Oct. 16, 1729.*

Stephen, and Susanna Noys, Nov. 16, 1752.*

Stephen, and Elisabeth Plumer, Sept. 23, 1760.*

Stephen, of Newburyport, and Mary Muzzey, int. Aug. 4, 1770.

Susan P., and Hugh McDonald of Boston, int. May 25, 1844.

Susanna, and John Kimball, Oct. 10, 1782.*

Thomas, and Anna Chase, int. Nov. 8, 1786.

Thomas, and Sally Bointon of Bradford, Mar. 27, 1791.*

Thomas, jr., and Sally Lunt, Nov. 3, 1824.*

Tristram, and Sarah Greenleaf, June 9, 1719.*

William, and Mary Lumbert, Dec. 28, 1813.*

William E., and Almira Johnson, int. Dec. 3, 1840.

KNOLTON (see also Knowlton), Ebenezer, and Sarah Lowle [d. Sergt. Benjamin. int.], Feb. 14, 1698.*

KNOULTON (see also Knowlton), Joanna, and John Smith, of Limerick, Ireland, int.], Oct. 30. 1751.*

KNOWLES, Louisa, of Newburyport, and Nathan Adams, Apr. 6, 1826.*

Mary, and John G. Gurney of Newburyport, int. Feb. 16, 1839.

*Intention also recorded.

KNOWLTON (see also Knolton, Knoulton), Anna, of New-
buryport, and Lt. Amos Atkinson, int. June 12, 1784.
Elisabeth, and Thomas Warren of Exeter, Eng., July 27,
1756.*
George, and Joanna Woodman, Sept. 21, 1732.*
Patty [Mrs. c. r. 2.], and Seth Plummer [of Hampstead. c. r.
2.], Sept. 2, 1796.*
Rebecca, and Newton Cannon, Dec. 3, 1761.*

KNOX, Thomas, and Abigail Dennett, July —, 1808.*

KYES (see also Keyes), Edward, of Ashford, and Sarah Whitmore, Feb. 15, 1801.*

KYMBAL (see also Kimball), Lucy, and Thomas Rogers, Jan.
4, 1764.*
Mary, and Moses Cooper [jr. int.], Apr. 13, 1762.*
Rebecca, and Jabes Ayers, Dec. 8, 1718.*

LABORE (see also Laboree), Abigail, and John Flood, int.
Jan. 23, 1741-2.
Katharine, and Mark Flood, Nov. 11, 1741.*

LABOREE (see also Labore), Sarah, and Daniel Flood, Jan.
5, 1735-6.*

LACKEY, Anna, and Nathan Haskell of Newburyport, int.
May 12, 1804.

LACOUNT (see also Lecount), Mary, of Newburyport, and
William York, int. May 8, 1808.

LADD, Daniel, Capt., and Elizabeth Huse, May 22, 1808.*
Dudley, of Meredith, N. H., and Abigail Plumer, June 26,
1811.*
Elizabeth, of Newburyport, and Joseph Janvrin, jr., int. Dec.
7, 1833.
John, and Sophia Jaques, Aug. 25, 1814.*
Josiah, of Exeter, and Sarah Mors, Jan. 3, 1737-8.*
Mary, and Caleb Richardson, July 31, 1682.
Salley, of Haverhill, and William Poor, int. Mar. 14, 1807.
William H., of Newburyport, and Sarah Lane, Mar. 22, 1841.*

*Intention also recorded.

LADD, William H., widr., of Newburyport, a. 38 y., mariner, b. Newburyport, s. Daniel and Elizabeth, and Harriet G. Brown, wid., a. 37 y., d. Joseph L., and Sarah Colby, Feb. 13, 1848.*

LAKE, Joshua, of Haverhill, and Henrietta Moulton, int. June 25, 1830.

LAKEMAN, Archelaus, and Elizabeth Hadley of Rowley, Jan. 11, 1775.*
Daniel, and Sarah J[ane. c. r. 10.] Atkinson, Apr. 3, 1831. c. r. 10.*
Hannah, and Joseph Chase, 3d, May 29, 1773.*
Margaret, and Josiah Magowin, Apr. 6, 1813.*
Mary, and Samuel Lurvey, Dec. 9, 1817.*
Susannah, and Benjamin Poor [jr. int.], at Rowley, Sept. 10, 1785.*

LAKIN, Jane, and John Farwell, both of Groton, July 10, 1735. c. r. 7.
W[illia]m, and Miriam Erwin, both of Groton, July 29, 1731. c. r. 7.

LAMB, Levi, and Lucy Pearson, Sept. 22, 1836.*

LAMBERT (see also Lambord, Lumbart, Lumbert), Frederick, of Rowley, and Mary Ann Jewett, May 24, 1827.*
George, of Newburyport, and Caroline Haskell, int. June 4, 1836.
Robert, mariner, of England, and Eliz[abe]th Yeale, wid., of Boston, May 21, 1728. c. r. 7.
William H., of Newburyport, and Statira M. Noyes, int. May 4, 1847.

LAMBORD (see also Lambert), Louisa F., of Ludlow, and Joseph P. Noyes, int. June 4, 1842.

LAMPHREY (see also Lamprey), Elizabeth, of Hampton, N. H., and John James Noyes, June 3, 1838.*

*Intention also recorded.

LAMPREY (see also Lamphrey), Lucy, of Kensington, N. H., and Moses Styles of Barnstead, N. H., June 28, 1821.
Sally, of Kensington, N. H., and John Boardman Lord, int. Oct. 5, 1811.

LAMSON, Caleb, and Abigail Chase, July 15, 1802.*
Charles, and Margaret Lucy Lovett, Apr. 24, 1834.*
Judith, and James Tayler of Andover, int. Mar. 19, 1819.

LANCASTER (see also Lanchester, Lankaster, Lankister), Betsey, of Rumney, N. H., and William Jewett, int. Dec. 16, 1820.
Elizabeth, and Joseph Rawlings, Oct. —, 1751. c. r. 2.*
Hannah, and Luke Larcumbe, Nov. 6, 1786.*
Henrietta M., and Leonard W. Pearson, Oct. —, 1840.*
Mary, and Samuel Butterfield, Nov. 23, 1785.*
Samuel, of Haverhill, and Lois Pike, Sept. 5, 1764.*

LANCEY, Joel, of Lee, N. H., and Ruth Weymouth, Dec. 2, 1838.*

LANCHESTER (see also Lancaster), Mary, d. Joseph, of Amesbury, and Timothy Mirrick, int. May 9, 1696.

LANDER, Augusta C., a. 20 y., d. Henry and Lydia, and John J. Noyes, a. 23 y., farmer, s. John and Sarah, Apr. 13, 1847.*
Hannah M., a. 22 y., d. Henry and Lydia S., and Samuel W. Green, widr., of Newburyport, a. 25 y., machinist, b. Newburyport, s. Ephraim and Sarah, of Newburyport, Apr. 23, 1848.*
Henry, of Newburyport, and Lydia S. Adams, June 18, 1820.*
Henry A., a. 27 y., shoemaker, s. Henry and Lydia, and Ann P. Clark of Newburyport, a. 24 y., b. Newburyport, d. Amos and Rebecca, June 4, 1848.*
Robert [Lowder. int.], and Mary Emerson, Feb. 8, 1801. c. r. 5.*

LANDRIGAN (see also Lanegin), Alice, and Alexander Barret, June 3, 1756. c. r. 8.

*Intention also recorded.

LANE, Abner, Capt., and Eliza A. Delisle, Apr. —, 1831.

Humphrey, jr., and Mary P. Griffin, Dec. 22, 1825.*

Humphry, of Gloucester, and Susanna Greenleaf, int. Jan. 20, 1797.

John, and Mrs. Johannah Davinson, Nov. —, 1693.

Joseph, Capt., and Abigail Smith, Aug. 31, 1796.*

Lydia D., and Samuel Lunt, jr., Nov. 27, 1834.*

Mary G., and Benja[min] Colby, int. Mar. 22, 1828.

Polly B. [Mary Baker. int.], of Rowley, and Samuel Pearson, at Rowley, Nov. 23, 1796.*

Reuben, and Nancy Parsons, May 4, 1813.*

Robert L., and Elizabeth P. Watson, both of Newburyport, ——, 1841.

Robert Sampson, and Caroline Lunt, Oct. 7, 1830.*

Samuel [jr. int.], of Gloucester, and Mercy Newhall, Jan. 28, 1762.*

Sarah, and William H. Ladd of Newburyport, Mar. 22, 1841.*

Susanna, of Gloucester, and James Thurlo, Nov. 22, 1818.*

Theodate, of Newburyport, a. 38 y., b. Hampton, N. H., d. Jeremiah and Lucy, and Joseph Coffin, widr., a. 59 y., ship carpenter, s. Amos and Hannah, June 11, 1845.*

Thomas, and Ann Coffin, Nov. —, 1833.*

William, and Lucretia Prescott of Hampton Falls, N. H., int. Nov. 6, 1830.

William, and Sophia C. Pressey of Newburyport, int. Nov. 1, 1838.

William, and Nancy J. Johnson of Frankfort, Me., int. Nov. 26, 1842.

Wingate, and Mary Merrill, May 2, 1839.*

LANEGIN (see also Landrigan), Eleanor Welch, and Joseph Laughton, Feb. 14, 1810.*

LANFORD, Harriet N., and Paul Adams, both of Newburyport, Nov. 27, 1838.

LANGLEY, Abby, and George A. Fairbanks, both of Lowell, Oct. 5, 1841.

Wiliam C., and Lydia Maria Thomas, int. Nov. 6, 1830.

LANKASTER (see also Lancaster), Thomas, and Betsy Kimball, June 12, 1806.*

*Intention also recorded.

LANKISTER (see also Lancaster), Joseph, and Mary Gutterson, int. Sept. 20, 1805.
Mary, and William Curtis, Jan. 8, 1728-9.*
Moses, and Sarah Greenleaf, int. June 28, 1805.

LAPHAM, Barker, of Bradford, and Ruth Chisimore, at Bradford, Feb. 10, 1795.*

LARCUMBE, Luke, and Hannah Lancaster, Nov. 6, 1786.*

LARKIN, Alice, and Joshua Noyes of Georgetown, int. May 3, 1843.
Caroline, and Orlando W. Morriil of Rowley, int. Oct. 22, 1831.
Charlotte, and John O. Davis of Georgetown, Nov. 20, 1843.
Joseph, and Almira C. White, Apr. 18, 1836.*
Mary Ann, and John Marshall, July 3, 1822.*
Mary Ann, d. Thomas and Hannah, and Joseph Yeaton, a. 35 y., farmer, s. Samuel and Sally, Apr. 17, 1845.*
Samuel, and Lorana Rogers, Dec. 25, 1823.*
Thomas, and Hannah Pearson of Rowley, int. Dec. 10, 1821.

LAROY, Sara [Lary. CT. R.], and Mathew Moore, Mar. 27, 1662.

LASKEY, Elizabeth, and Silas Wheeler, int. Aug. 29, 1846.
Martha Ann, and James M. Hervey of Boston, int. Feb. 13, 1836.
Mary, and Elisha P. Gould, Dec. 27, 1825.*
Thomas F., and Abigail Arbuckle of Beverly, int. Dec. 27, 1834.

LATTIME (see also Lattimore), Gideon W., and Lydia Hunt, Nov. —, 1836.*
James S., and Mary S. Smith of Lynn, int. Sept. 17, 1834.
Nicholas, and Mary Wheeler of Lynn, int. May 25, 1833.
Nicolas, of Newburyport, and Polly Woodwel, int. July 13, 1805.

LATTIMORE (see also Lattime), James, Capt., of Newburyport, and Sally Coffin, May 22, 1808.*

*Intention also recorded.

LAUGHTON, Joseph, and Eleanor Welch Lanegin, Feb. 14, 1810.*

LAVALETTE (see also Lavelet), Charles, and Eunice Cheever, both of Newburyport, Aug. 1, 1839.

LAVELET (see also Lavalette), Peter, of Newburyport, and Elsey Noyes Howard, int. Dec. 22, 1805.

LAVENUCK (see also Lavenuke), Steven, and Mary Divall, Sept. 25, 1672.

LAVENUKE (see also Lavenuck), Stephen, and Sarah Colter [Colten. int.] of Ipswich, Sept. 22, 1741.*

LAWRENCE, Elizabeth, of Newburyport, and Joseph Huse, int. Apr. 6, 1816.

LAWSON, David, resident in Newbury, and Martha Chase, Aug. 3, 1716.*
John, of Great Britain, and Abigail Waters, int. Sept. 29, 1710.

LAYTON (see also Leighton), Abigail, of Byfield Rowley, and John Uran, June 12, 1760.*

LAZELL, John, and Jael Cushing of Hingham, Feb. 9, 1722-3. c. r. 7.

LEACH, Andrew, of Manchester, and Hannah Hunt, Aug. 25, 1840.*
Eunice, of Salem, and Malachi Corning of Beverly, July 21, 1726.
Mary, and Thomas Adams, June 5, 1805.*
Nathaniel, and Judeth Hunt, Apr. 9, 1735.*

LEADIARY, Rachel, of Marblehead, and John Bailey, Nov. 14, 1721.

LEATHERBY, James, of Newburyport, and Sally Davis, Dec. 29, 1796.*
Sally, and James Murphy of Newburyport, July 31, 1806.*

*Intention also recorded.

LEAVITTE (see also Levit), Thomas M., and Sally Dearborn of North Hampton, N. H., Sept. 27, 1810.

LEAVOR, Lydia, of Rowley, and Daniel Thirston, int. Oct. 29, 1715.

LeBRETON, Elizabeth, and Henry Johnson of Newburyport, int. Mar. 15, 1823.
Peter, jr., and Sarah Ellen Chase of Newburyport, int. Oct. 3, 1823.

LECOUNT (see also Lacount), James, of Rowley, and Mary Davis, at Rowley, Jan. 6, 1736.*
Samuel, of Newburyport, and Elisabeth Cassadey, int. July 2, 1772.

LeCRAW, David Ross, of Newburyport, a. 23 y., mariner, b. Newburyport, s. William and Lydia, of Newburyport, and Joanna E. Griffith, a. 22 y., d. Joseph and Elizabeth, May 10, 1847.
William, jr., and Caroline R. Cooke of Newburyport, int. Oct. 11, 1845.

LEDAIN (see also Ludon), George, and Mary Adams of Boston, ——, 1729. c. r. 7.

LEE (see also Lees, Leigh), Francis, and Sarah Coffin, Apr. ——, 1837.*
John, of Salisbury, and Hannah F. Colby, int. Nov. 7, 1829.
John F., and Elizabeth S. [L. int.] Keniston. Nov. 30, 1843.*
Sarah, and Elijah P. White of Georgetown, int. Nov. 2, 1844.

LEEMAN (see also Leman), John, and Elisabeth Pilsbury, Jan. 28, 1747-8.*

LEES (see also Lee), Ann, and Joseph Goodhue, Feb. 8, 1824.*
Joseph, and Rebecca Taylor, July 4, 1824.*

LEFAVOUR, see Favour.

LEGROW, see Grow.

*Intention also recorded.

LEIBBY (see also Libby), Eliza Ann, and John E. Banks of Portsmouth, N. H., int. Oct. 13, 1849.

LEIGH (see also Lee), Abigail, and Charles Knight, Sept. 1, 1808. C. R. 1.
Benja[min], jr., of Newburyport, and Sally Jackson Pearson, May 12, 1813.*
Hall J., and Abigail Little, June 2, 1844.*
Hannah, and Michael Little, Jan. 12, 1809.*
Mary L., and Richard P. Plumer, int. Apr. 6, 1833.

LEIGHTON (see also Layton), John, of Newburyport, and Elizabeth Stickney, int. Sept. 30, 1812.
Jonathan, of Rowley, and Mrs. Mary Boynton, Apr. 25, 1739.*
Mary E., of Newburyport, and Nathaniel G. Pierce, int. Mar. 31, 1849.

LEMAN (see also Leeman), Henry, and Jane Perkins, Nov. 30, 1837.*

LENEX, James, and Mary Turner, Jan. 24, 1758. C. R. 8.

LEONARD (see also Lynard), Asa, of Somersworth, N. H., and Mary Ann Woodman, July 6, 1828.*
Salley, of Newburyport, and Capt. Orlando Bagley Merrill, int. Sept. 25, 1802.

LERVEY (see also Lurvey), Patience, and William Reed, int. Oct. 7, 1781.

LEVISTON, John, and Hannah Thompson, int. Nov. 27, 1832.

LEVIT (see also Leavitte), Ephraim, of Stratham, and Judeth Morss, int. Sept. 6, 1738.

LEWIS, Abigail, Mrs., and Jeremy Gridley, both of Boston, May 22, 1734. C. R. 7.
Ann, and Robert Morse, Oct. 30, 1654. CT. R.
Frederick [of Deerfield, N. H. int.], and Sarah Bartlet, Sept. 22, 1777.*
John, b. Carmanshire, Wales, and Susanna Pilsbury, May 4, 1749. C. R. 7.

*Intention also recorded.

Lewis, Jonas, and Rebeckah Chase, int. Oct. 5, 1805.
Mary Ann, and John C. Ramsdell, int. Aug. 19, 1843.
Micah, and Julia French of Salisbury, int. Oct. 2, 1839.
Paul, of Hingham, and Hannah Vincent of Weymouth, ——,
    1729. c. r. 7.
Susanna, Mrs., and John Wyat, jr., Feb. 20, 1745-6.*

LIBBY (see also Leibby), Sarah D., of Newburyport, and
    Mark Griffin, jr., int. Nov. 29, 1846.

LIGHT, Dorothy, and Richard Dummer, Jan. 22, 1712-13.*

LIGHTFOOT, Anne, and Daniell Thurston, Aug. 29, 1648.

LISTY, Judith, of Amesbury, and Samuel Elsworth, int. Aug.
    30, 1774.

LITCH, John, and Sally Coffin, Mar. 31, 1814.*

LITTLE, Abigail, and Richard Adams, jr., Apr. 30, 1821.*
Abigail, and Hall J. Leigh, June 2, 1844.*
Abner, a. 20 y., cordwainer, and Abigail Atkinson, a. 18 y.,
    Apr. 30, 1771.
Alice, and Thomas Hale, May 25, 1797.*
Alice, and Adams Knight, Nov. 6, 1798.*
Amos, and Hannah Moody, Nov. 8, 1785.*
Amos, and Elizabeth [P. int.] Knight, June 17, 1832.*
Ann, Mrs., and Stephen Sewall, Dec. 27, 1739.*
Ann, and [Capt. c. r. 1.] Moody Adams Thurlo, Mar. 28,
    1815. [Apr. 4. c. r. 1.]*
Anna, and William Atkinson, Apr. 10, 1804.*
Anna Mary, and Adams Moore of Littleton, N. H., int. May
    9, 1829.
Betty, and James Saunders of Salem, N. H., Dec. 15, 1774.*
Betty, and David Emery, Aug. 22, 1785.*
Betty, and Stephen Bartlet of Newburyport, June 9, 1796.*
Caroline, and Daniel S. Tenney, Dec. 19, 1826.*
Daniel, and Abiah Clement of Haverhill, int. Sept. 5, 1712.
Dan[ie]ll, Rev., of Wells [York Co. int.], and Mrs. Sarah
    Coffin, June 7, 1759. c. r. 9.*
David, and Abigail Noyes, Mar. 24, 1785.*
Ebenez[er], and Elisabeth Browne, Apr. 5, 1737.*

*Intention also recorded.

LITTLE, Ebenezer, and Eliza Adams, Dec. 30, 1822.*
Edmund, and Judeth Adams, Mar. 18, 1735-6.*
Edmund, jr., and Judith Bartlet, Aug. 2, 1789.*
Edmund, Capt., and Elisabeth Smith, Nov. 2, 1789.*
Ednah, and Stephen Toppan, Jan. 1, 1786.*
Elbridge G., Rev., of Manayunk, Pa., a. 31 y., b. Hampstead,
    s. Joseph and Rebecca, and Sarah E. Colman, a. 25 y., d.
    Daniel and Nancy, July 12, 1848.*
Elisabeth, and Abel Huse, jr., Apr. 29, 1729.*
Elisabeth, and Humphery Noyes, Nov. 22, 1743.*
Elisabeth, and Abraham Day, jr. of Bradford, Jan. 12, 1764.*
Eliza, and John Woodman, May 29, 1825.*
Elizabeth, and Anthony Mors, Jan. 21, 1717-18.
Elizabeth, of Rowley, and John Frazer, at Rowley, July 26,
    1743.*
Elizabeth, and John Carr of Salisbury, Nov. 24, 1774.*
Elizabeth, and Richard Stickney, Oct. 2, 1795.*
Elizabeth, and Samuel Brookings, jr., Mar. 11, 1823. [Mar. 12.
    C. R. 1.]*
Elizabeth, and Jacob Atkinson, Oct. 5, 1825.*
Elizabeth, wid., a. 31 y., d. James and Lucy Knight, and John
    M. Little, a. 31 y., farmer, s. Michael and Hannah, Nov.
    27, 1845.*
Enoch, and Elizabeth Worth, May 19, 1707.*
Enoch, and Sarah Pettengell, Feb. 19, 1755.*
Enoch, and Hannah Hovey, June 5, 1759.*
Enoch, and Mary Hale, Feb. 25, 1768.*
Enoch, jr., and Mary Bricket, Sept. 15, 1796.*
Eunice, and Robert Adams, jr., July 12, 1774.*
Ezekiel, of Boston, and Mehitable Emery, May 24, 1801.*
Forbes, and Sarah Baker, both of Marshfield, Nov. 30, 1733.
    C. R. 7.
Frances A., and Charles C. Dame, Sept. 1, 1842.*
Georg, and Elionar Barnard, July 19, 1681.
George, and Edna Hale, Feb. 22, 1710.*
George, of Hampstead, and Elisabeth Poor of Rowley, May
    29, 1754.
George, and Maria J. Brockway of Newburyport, Nov. 17,
    1839.*
Hannah, and Joseph Low, Jan. 15, 1746-7.*
Hannah, and Samuel Dole, jr., Nov. 20, 1777.*
Hannah, and Dr. Moses Sawyer, July 25, 1781.*

*Intention also recorded.

LITTLE, Hannah, and Stephen Emery, 3d, May 4, 1783.*

Hannah, d. Joseph and Hannah, and James Stickney, Mar. 18, 1802.*

Hannah, and Robert Adams, June 12, 1808.*

Harriet, and Moses Coffin, Dec. 3, 1829.*

Henry, and Lydia Little, Dec. 7, 1738.*

Henry, and Phebe Little [2d w. c. r. 1.], Oct. [20. c. r. 1.], 1816.*

Jacob, and Hannah Sawyer, int. Apr. 29, 1786.

Jane, and Edmund Knight, May 25, 1741.*

Jane, and Capt. Nicholas Brown, jr. of Newburyport, Feb. 27, 1808.*

Jane Noyes, a. 30 y., d. Henry and Phebe, and Richard Tenney, widr., a. 45 y., victualler, b. Rowley, s. David and Judith, Oct. 20, 1847.*

John [jr. int.], and Temperance Ripp, May 14, 1745.*

John, jr., and Ruth Hale, Apr. 25, 1765.*

John, and Hannah Noyes, Oct. 27, 1767.*

John, of Plymouth, and Salley Little, Nov. 18, 1801.*

John, jr., and Mary Tuksbury, ——, 1809. [Apr. 24, 1810. int.]*

John, jr., and Abigail Tewksbury, Mar. 25, 1817.*

John, and Ellen D. Morrill of Newburyport, int. Jan. 21, 1843.

John, and Nancy Coffin of Newburyport, int. Oct. 21, 1848.

John A., and Belinda Goodwin of Amesbury, int. Mar. 21, 1835.

John M., a. 31 y., farmer, s. Michael and Hannah, and Elizabeth Little, wid., a. 31 y., d. James and Lucy Knight, Nov. 27, 1845.*

Joseph, and Mary Coffin, Oct. 31, 1677.

Joseph, jr., and Bettee Merrill, Apr. 28, 1763.*

Joseph, and Mary Johnson, Nov. 11, 1766.*

Joseph, and Elizabeth Moody, Oct. 18, 1821. [1820. c. r. 1.]*

Joshua, and Eunice Atkinson, Jan. 5. 1775.*

Joshua [jr. int.], and Ann Toppan of Newburyport, Nov. 19, 1821.*

Joshua Bailey, of Danvers, and Lydia Little, May 28, 1827.*

Josiah, and Sarah Toppan, Mar. 23, 1770.*

Josiah, of Newbury, Vt., and Sophronia Balch. Jan. 24, 1814.*

Judith [d. Lt. Joseph. int.], and Cutting Moodey, Mar. 25, 1696.*

*Intention also recorded.

LITTLE, Judith, and Abraham Adams, jr., July 12, 1774.*
Judith, and Thomas Norwood of Newburyport, Jan. 7, 1783.*
Judith, and Amos Chase [jr. C. R. 2.], Sept. 24, 1794.*
Judith, and Asa Tarbell Newhall of Lynn, int. Sept. 12, 1807.
Lois, and Joseph Kent, June 25, 1815.*
Lucretia, of Newburyport, and Silas Little, int. Apr. 15, 1786.
Lydia, wid. Moses, and John Pike, Mar. 18, 1694-5.
Lydia, and Henry Little, Dec. 7, 1738.*
Lydia, and John Atkinson, Oct. 4, 1770.*
Lydia, and Joshua Bailey Little of Danvers, May 28, 1827.*
Maria, and Adams Moor, M. D. of Littleton, N. H., Aug. 14,
    1843.*
Mary, Mrs., and Joseph Gerrish, int. Feb. 26, 1703-4.
Mary, and Michael Dalton, Feb. 5, 1733-4.*
Mary, and John Berry, Jan. 22, 1740-41.*
Mary, and Jonathan Wiggin of Stratham, Oct. 1, 1761.
Mary, and John Moody, Mar. 9, 1762.*
Mary, and John Merrill, int. Jan. 25, 1771.
Mary, and Matthias Plant Sawyer, Dec. 13, 1775.*
Mary, and Silas Pearson, jr., Nov. 29, 1792.*
Mary, and William White Little of Danvers, Sept. 15, 1805.*
Mary, and Thomas Roberson, Apr. 17, 1806.*
Mary, and Capt. Reubin Fisher, Oct. 13, 1811.*
Mary, and Thomas Hale, Esq., Sept. 17, 1822.*
Mary, and Adams Knight, jr., Dec. —, 1833.*
Micajah, and Hannah Leigh [bet. Jan. 12 and Apr.], 1809.
    C. R. 1.
Michael, Esq., of Poland, and Salley Stover, Oct. 19, 1800.*
Michael, and Hannah Leigh, Jan. 12, 1809.*
Moses, sr., and Mary Hale, Jan. 5, 1714-15.*
Moses, jr., and Mrs. Sarah Jaques, Feb. 12, 1716-17.*
Moses, jr., and Abigail Bayley, June 5, 1743.*
Moses, 3d, and Mary Milk of Falmouth, in Casco Bay, Aug.
    15, 1757.*
Moses, 3d, and Elisabeth Dummer, Aug. 6, 1786.*
Moses, jr., and Anna Chase, Nov. 15, 1800.*
Moses P., and Jane W. Russell, Apr. 19, 1832.*
Nabby, of Amesbury, and Moses Chase, jr., July 10, 1800.*
Nancy, and Asa Adams, Nov. 20, 1826.*
Nanne [Anna. int.]. and John Peabody, Mar. 30, 1791.*
Nathan, and Hannah Mighill of Rowley, at Rowley, Nov. 12,
    1741.*

*Intention also recorded.

LITTLE, Nathaniel, Lt., and Mary Toppan, Apr. 7, 1782.*
Nathaniel, Lt., and Joanna Muzzey Plumer, Jan. 1, 1795.*
Nathaniel, and Edna Lunt, July 4, 1843.*
Nathaniel, jr., a. 26 y., farmer, s. Tristram and Sarah, and
    Mary P. Danforth, a. 26 y., d. Samuel and Edna, May
    22, 1845.*
Noah, and Jane Lunt, Nov. 15, 1801.*
Noah, and Priscilla Haynes of North Hampton, N. H., int.
    Sept. 8, 1832.
Noah, and Olive Littlefield, Dec. 27, 1838.*
Patience, and Ebenezer March, jr., Apr. 29, 1817.*
Paul, of Falmouth, and Hannah Emery, May 20, 1762.*
Paul, and Mehitabel Lunt, Sept. 12, 1805.*
Paul, and Sally R. Little [2d w. c. R. 1.], Sept. 15, 1818.*
Phebe [2d w. c. R. 1.], and Henry Little, Oct. [20. c. R. 1.],
    1816.*
Prudence, and James Smith [jr. int.], May 17, 1787.*
Richard, and Jane Noyes, Sept. 19, 1754.*
Ruth, and David Eaton, Oct. 23, 1811.*
Salla, and Simeon Adams, Apr. 13, 1790.*
Salley, and John Little of Plymouth, Nov. 18, 1801.*
Sally R. [2d w. c. R. 1.], and Paul Little, Sept. 15, 1818.*
Samuel, and Dorothy Noyes, Feb. 18, 1735-6.*
Samuel, of Haverhill, and Hannah Sewall, int. Dec. 4, 1736.
Samuel M., a. 25 y., farmer, s. Joseph and Elizabeth, and Mary
    Putnam Rolf, a. 27 y., d. Moses and Mary [Sarah. dup.]
    P., July 1, 1847.*
Sara, and Joseph Ilsly, Mar. 3, 1681-2.
Sarah, and John Kent [4th. int.], Jan. 14, 1702.*
Sarah, and Thomas Pike, Jan. 3, 1709.*
Sarah, and James Noyes, jr., May 30, 1729.*
Sarah, and Parker Titcomb, Oct. 11, 1737.*
Sarah, and William Pottle of Stratham, May 4, 1758.*
Sarah, and Samuel Thurlo, May 31, 1770.*
Sarah, and Tristram Little, Dec. 5, 1815.*
Sarah, and James Smith, jr., Dec. 22, 1817.*
Silas, and Lucretia Little of Newburyport, int. Apr. 15, 1786.
Stephen, and Judith Bayley, June 5, 1743.*
Stephen, and Anna Atkinson, June 2, 1795.*
Stephen, jr., and Mrs. Rebeckah Caldwall of Ipswich, at Ips-
    wich, Apr. 3, 1797.*
Stephen Moody, and Elisabeth Bricket, Oct. 9, 1794.*

*Intention also recorded.

LITTLE, Stephen William, and Hannah Morgan Russel [of
  Ipswich. int.], May 16, 1820. c. R. 1.*
Susannah, and Robert Adams, Oct 10, 1799.*
Temperance, and Enoch Merrill, May 31, 1778.*
Thomas, of Atkinson, N. H., and Abigail Kent, int. Oct. 3,
  1772.
Tristram, and Sarah Dole, Oct. 30, 1707.*
Tristram, jr., and Anne Emery, Apr. 10, 1711.*
Tristram, and Sarah Little, Dec. 5, 1815.*
William, and Salley Bayley of Bradford, int. Feb. 11, 1797.
Will[ia]m White, of Danvers, and Mary Little, Sept. 15,
  1805.*

LITTLEFIELD, Benj[ami]n B., and Almira T. Bailey of Ha-
  verhill, Oct. 7, 1838.*
Isaiah G., of Newburyport, a. 25 y., farmer, s. William and
  Betsey, and Mary E. Chase of Newburyport, a. 20 y.,
  Jan. 27, 1846.
Meribah, Mrs., of Kittery, and Nathaniel Bartlet, int. Sept.
  22, 1705.
Olive, and Noah Little, Dec. 27, 1838.*
Samuel, of Charlestown, and Lydia Ann Winder, Mar. 1,
  1842.*

LIVINGSTON, Timothy, and Mary Garen of Newburyport,
  int. Aug. 22, 1805.

LLOYD (see also Loyd), Amos P., of Newburyport, a. 26 y.,
  shoemaker, b. Henniker, N. H., s. John and Mary, and
  Mary C. Mace, a. 22 y., d. W[illia]m and Catherine, June
  17, 1849.*

LOCK (see also Locke), Joseph, and Salley Stanwood, int.
  Jan. 16, 1804.

LOCKE (see also Lock), Abigail, of Newburyport, and Daniel
  S. Heath, int. Aug. 22, 1829.

LONG (see also Longe), Abiell, and Hannah Hills, Oct. 27,
  1682.
Abigail. and Joseph Emery of Andover. int. Aug. 17, 1738.
Eliner, and Ebenezer Watson, Aug. 21, 1732.*

*Intention also recorded.

LONG, Enoch, and Abigail Bayley, Dec. 2, 1755.*
Eunice, of Newburyport, and Samuel Poor, jr., int. June 10, 1791.
Hanah, and Thomas Rogers, Aug. 18, 1702.*
Hannah, Mrs., and Moses Sawyer, Jan. 7, 1752. c. R. 7.
John, and Sarah Rawlings, Oct. 27, 1727.*
Mary, and Jonathan ———, Oct. 24, 1676.
Mary, and Benjamin Pettingill [jr. int.], June 15, 1736.*
Mary, and Capt. William Colby of Amesbury, int. July 5, 1805.
Rebecca, and Nicholas Rawlins, Oct. 31, 1679.
Rebecca, and Samuel Poor, jr., Dec. 19, 1733.*
Richard, and Sarah Coker, Dec. 30, 1717.
Robert, and Alice Short, ——— [164—?].
Robert, and Eliner Annis, May 19, 1724.*
Samuel, and Susanna Bacon, Nov. 20, 1733.*
Samuel, and Mary Ginnings of Boston, int. July 25, 1745.
Sarah, and William Russel [resident of Newbury. int.], Nov. 28, 1715.*
Sarah, and Enoch Merril, May 17, 1750. c. R. 7.
Sarah, of Chester, N. H., and Joseph Sawyer, jr., int. Apr. 27, 1793.
Shubiel, and Hanah Merrill [d. Abraham. int.], Aug. 26, 1695.*
Will[ia]m R., and Eliza Ann Haskell of Newburyport, June 4, 1822.*

LONGE (see also Long), Benj[amin], and Sarah Sawyer, ———, 1716. c. R. 7.

LONGFELLOW, Abigail, and Lt. Nathaniel Emery, May 21, 1795.*
Abigail, and Timothy Kenison, Nov. 7, 1821.*
Ann, and Henry Short, May 11, 1692.
Ann, and John Poor, Dec. 26, 1734.*
Anna, and Jóhn Fielding, Mar. 6, 1777.*
Anne, Mrs., and Abraham Adams, jr., int. Nov. 13, 1703.
David, and Susanna Adams, June 29, 1809.*
Edward, and Johannah Short, Oct. 6, 1743.*
Elisabeth, and Benjamin Woodman, Mar. 1, 1710-11.*
Jane, of Rowley, and Isaac Foster, int. Apr. 23, 1796.

*Intention also recorded.

LONGFELLOW, John, and Priscilla Gould of Topsfield, at Topsfield, May 21, 1796.*
John, and Lydia Brown, both of Rowley, Sept.ʼ4, 1803. c. r. 5.
Joseph, and Lucretia Fairbanks of Canton, int. Mar. 27, 1841.
Judith, and Sewel Moody, June 6, 1799.*
Judith, and Giles Rogers, int. Jan. 30, 1841.
Lydia B., and George W. Jackman, Feb. 25, 1825.*
Mary, of Newburyport, and Elbridge G. Hoyt, int. Jan. 6, 1831.
Mary Ann, and Stephen Adams, jr., Jan. 16, 1822.*
Mary E., of Newburyport, a. 20 y., b. Newburyport, d. John and Mary, of Newburyport, and Amos Lunt, a. 24 y., seaman, s. William and Hannah, Nov. 20, 1845.*
Mary Jane, and Charles F. Hoyt of Salisbury, int. May 18, 1838.
Moses, and Mercy Dressor of Rowley, int. Mar. 16, 1804.
Nathan, and Nanny Downer, Sept. 10, 1799.*
Nathan, and Eunice Adams, Feb. 24, 1814.*
Rebecca, and Ebenezer Damon Batchelder of Reading, Jan. 23, 1823.*
Samuel, and Rebecca Chase, Nov. 30, 1768.*
Samuel, and Martha Chaplin of Rowley, int. Jan. 1, 1780. (1790?)
Samuel, and Caroline Smith, ——, 1834. [Feb. 22. int.]*
Sarah, and Jonathan Pearson of Rowley, at Rowley, Apr. 16, 1740.*
Stephen, and Abigail Tompson, Mar. 25, 1714.*
William, and Mrs. Anne Sewall, Nov. 10, 1678. [1676.ct. r.]
William, and Hephsibah Plumer of Rowley, Jan. 24, 1739-40.*

LONGHORNE, Constance, and Jonathan Moores, abt. May 10, 1670.

LONGLAND, John, mariner, and Elisabeth Bramble, wid., both of Boston, Mar. 6, 1732-3. c. r. 7.

LOOK, Mary, and Stephen Bailey, int. Jan. 24, 1735-6.
Thomas, of Rowley, and Martha Mooers, Feb. 13, 1716-17.

LOOKIN, Susanna, and Jeremiah Goodridge, Nov. 24, 1790.*

*Intention also recorded.

LORD, Benjamin, of Newburyport, and Margaret Plummer, Apr. 22, 1806. c. r. 1.*

John Boardman, and Sally Lamprey of Kensington, N. H., int. Oct. 5, 1811.

John L., and Mary Jane Huse, Dec. 2, 1835.*

Mary, and William Chandler, Feb. 26, 1666.

Mary, Mrs., and Benhemoth Humpheryes, resident in Newbury, int. Nov. 12, 1715.

Mary, of Exeter, N. H., and William Harris, int. Feb. 11, 1743-4.

Mary, of Ipswich, and Daniel Adams, at Ipswich, Jan. 14, 1787.*

Samuel D., and Ann C. Lunt, June 28, 1826.*

Theodosia, and John Francis [residents in Newbury. int.], Mar. 11, 1809.*

Tho[ma]s [Capt. int.], of Exeter, and Hannah Kent, Aug. 8, 1753. c. r. 9.*

Thomas, of Newburyport, and Sally Newman, May 3, 1801.*

Thomas P., of Amesbury, a. 23 y., harness maker, s. Benjamin and Margaret, and Eliza A. Clarkson, a. 21 y., d. Jacob and Eliza Ann, Nov. 27, 1845.*

LORING, Hannah D., and Joshua [John. int.] Corlew of Charlestown, Feb. 24, 1841.*

John, and Meriam Ramsdell, Feb. 26, 1786.*

John T., of Newburyport, and Mary Rolf, int. July 18, 1840.

Laura H., and Thomas B. Patten, July 4, 1841.*

Mary, and Elisha Wheeler, both of Sudbury, Nov. 30, 1731. c. r. 7.

LOTHROP, John, of Rhode Island, goldsmith, and Ann Badge of Charlestown, Aug. 20, 1730. c. r. 7.

Rufus D., of Rowley, and Hannah Elliott, int. Jan. 27, 1842.

LOUD, Samuel, and Rachel Coffin of Newburyport, int. Mar. 15, 1816.

LOUDER (see also Lowder), Mary, and James Day, July 4, 1822.*

LOUGHRAN, Catherine, of Newburyport, and Michael O'Connell, Sept. 17, 1843.

*Intention also recorded.

LOVEJOY, Abiel T., and Thuda [Thudalinda. int.] L. Noyes, Mar. 10, 1814.*

LOVEL, Michael, and Mary Mors[e], both of Medfield, May 25, 1726. c. R. 7.

LOVERIT (see also Lovett), Abigail, and Edward Trask, Apr. 9, 1735. c. R. 7.

LOVET (see also Lovett), Thomas, of Hampton, N. H., and . Elizabeth Atkinson, int. Jan. 4, 1703-4.

LOVETT (see also Loverit, Lovet), Margaret Lucy, and Charles Lamson, Apr. 24, 1834.*
Priscilla [of Newburyport. int.], and William Stickney, 3d, July or Aug. 25, 1819. c. R. 1.*

LOVEWELL, Jonathan, and Bridget Behony, both of Dunstable, Oct. 16, 1734. c. R. 7.

LOVRING, Joseph, of Exeter, N. H., and Eunice Smith, Feb. 13, 1798.*
Moses, of Salisbury, N. H., and Betsey Cooper, int. Feb. 15, 1805.
Richard, and Anna Coffin, Feb. 24, 1784.*

LOW (see also Lowe), Asa, and Sally Brown of Rowley, Jan. 1, 1793.*
Elisabeth, and Thomas Williams, Apr. 29, 1762.*
John, and Molly Henry, int. Aug. 23, 1762.
Joseph, and Hannah Little, Jan. 15, 1746-7.*
Joseph, and Mary Porter of Wenham, at Wenham, Jan. 1, 1756.*
Lois, and Isaac Foster, Apr. 24, 1755.*
Mary, and Richard Martin, Feb. 1, 1781.*
Moses A., of Gloucester, a. 43 y., mariner, b. Gloucester, s. David and Elizabeth, and Anna M. Sargent, a. 32 y., d. Winthrop and Emily, Nov. 22, 1848.*
Nathaniel, and Hannah Ring of Gloucester, int. Nov. 22, 1760.
Sarah, and Ephraim Bayley, Dec. 6, 1781.*

*Intention also recorded.

LOWDEN, John, and Emma Morrison, Jan. 1, 1750.*

LOWDER (see also Louder), Elizabeth, and Richard Trusdel, jr., both of Newburyport, Sept. 10, 1823.

LOWE (see also Low), Abigail, and Ezra Chase, Oct. 13,
1743.*
Eunice, and Jacob Lufkin of Ipswich, May 13, 1762.*
Rachel, and Smith Hills, Jan. 30, 1744-5.*

LOWEL (see also Lowell), Edmund, and Abigail Hadlock,
Apr. 18, 1706.*
George, and Elisabeth Morss, June 28, 1732.*
John, and Hannah Rogers, Aug. 14, 1797.*
Jonathan, of Amesbury, and Hannah Ayer, Nov. 14, 1734.
C. R. 7.*
Margaret, and John Merrill, Apr. —, 1729.*
Mary, and Nathaniel Davis, Sept. 28, 1732.*

LOWELL (see also Lowel, Lowle), Abigail, of Rowley, and
Moses Cooper, Feb. 24, 1736-7.*
Abigail, and Jeremiah Goodridge, jr., Jan. 18, 1738-9.*
Abner, and Betsy Toppan of Newburyport, int. Dec. 31, 1824.
Ann, and Dennis Condry of Newburyport, Apr. 8, 1813.*
Anne [of Amesbury. int.], and William Bailey, at Amesbury,
Nov. 25, 1742.*
Betsy, of Amesbury, and Abner Kenniston, int. Oct. 14, 1810.
Daniel, of Amesbury, and Mercy Davis, Aug 29, 1765.*
Ebenezer, and Elisabeth Titcomb, Sept. 6, 1757.*
Elisabeth, and Joseph Parker, Aug. 9, 1762. [He "takes the
said Elisabeth naked, without any of her former husband's
estate." int.]*
Elisabeth, and Thomas Johnston, Feb. 12, 1765.*
Hannah, Mrs., of Amesbury, and Thomas Cottle, at Amesbury,
Jan. 6, 1725-6.
Hannah. of Salisbury, and Israel Bartlet, int. May 11, 1805.
John, Rev., and Mrs. Elisabeth Whiple of Hampton, N. H.,
int. Sept. 26, 1757.
Joseph, and Mary Jones of South Hampton, N. H., int. Jan.
11, 1744-5.
Joseph, and Eunice Toppan of Newburyport, int. Feb. 7,
1824.

*Intention also recorded.

LOWELL, Mary [Mercy. int.], and Francis Brown, May 5,
1741.*
Mary, and Moses Greenough, int. Feb. 12, 1763.
Priscilla, and Henry Merrill, May 5, 1748.*
Rachel, of Amesbury, and Abraham Merrill, int. Sept. 17,
1748.
Richard, of Rowley, and Elisabeth Cooper, Nov. 4, 1736.
Richard, and Mary Atkin, Jan. 16, 1752.*
Samuel, of Rowley, and Hannah Emerson, at Rowley, Sept. 17,
1735.*
Samuel, and Ann Titcomb, Aug. 27, 1752.*
Samuel, jr., and Lois Pike, int. Apr. 10, 1762.
Sarah, of Rowley, and Samuel Emmerson, Nov. 16, 1729.*

LOWLE (see also Lowell), Benjamin, and Ruth Woodman,
Oct. 17, 1666.
Elizabeth [d. John. dup.], and Phillip Nelson [at Rowley.
dup.], Jan. 1, 1666. [Nov. 1. dup.]
Elizabeth [d. Sergt. Benjamin. int.], and Francis Willet [jr.
int.], Jan. 29, 1695-6.*
Gideon, and Mary Swett, July 7, 1692. CT. R.
Joseph, and Mary Harde, int. Dec. 6, 1707.
Mary [d. Sergt. Benjamin. int.], and Thomas Williams, Jan.
15, 1695-6.*
Mary, and Zachariah Fillbrook of Hampton, July 9, 1715.*
Percival, and Mary Chandler, Sept. 7, 1664.
Rebecca, and John Hale, Dec. 5, 1660.
Richard, and Sarah Browne, Apr. 8, 1695.
Sarah [d. Sergt. Benjamin. int.], and Ebenezer Knolton, Feb.
14, 1698.*

LOWRY, Margaret, and Peter Pelham, both of Boston, Feb.
19, 1734-5. C. R. 7.

LOYD (see also Lloyd), Charles, of Newburyport, and Sally
Newman, Jan. 7, 1802.*

LUCY, Gideon R., and Mary Adams, May 5, 1831.*
Gideon R., and Nancy Dearborn of Deerfield, N. H., int. June
10, 1837.

LUDON (see also Ledain), Michael, of Danvers, and Jane
Edmonds, int. Aug. 12, 1797.

*Intention also recorded.

LUFKIN, Eunice, and Jonathan Carlton, Sept. 25, 1786.*
Jacob, of Ipswich, and Eunice Lowe, May 13, 1762.*
Rachel, of Ipswich, and John Smith, at Chebacco parish, Ipswich, June 18, 1747.*

LUL (see also Lull), Sarah, and Stephen Bridges of Newburyport, Feb. 2, 1786.*

LULL (see also Lul), Abigail, and Moses Conner, Dec. 14, 1721.
Elisabeth, of Rowley, and Richard Tyler of Boxford, Feb. 14, 1725-6.
Hannah, of Byfield Rowley, and Joseph Carr of Chester, Oct. 25, 1764.
John, of Byfield, and Susannah Ayer of Haverhill, at Haverhill, Feb. 8, 1727-8.
Lydia, and William Caldwell, both of Ipswich, Nov. 29, 1729. C. R. 7.
Mercy, of Byfield Rowley, and Parker Moores, May 20, 1762.
Moses, and Judith Stuart, both of Rowley, Apr. 11, 1754.
Moses, of Rowley, and Sarah Holeman, July 8, 1755.*
Samuel, of Byfield, and Hannah Ayer of Haverhill, at Haverhill, July 28, 1729.
Sarah, of Byfield Rowley, and Samuel Buck of Sutton, Nov. 23, 1775.
Thomas, of Rowley, and Hannah Poor, Dec. 5, 1716.*

LUMBART (see also Lambert), Davis, and Abigail Rolf, Dec. 24, 1789.*

LUMBERT (see also Lambert), Mary, and William Knight, Dec. 28, 1813.*

LUNT, Abigail, and Henry Lunt, Jan. 31, 1764. [He takes said Abigail naked and so will not pay any of Her former Husband's debts. int.]*
Abigail, and John Dole, 3d, June 27, 1765.*
Abigail, and Capt. Benja[min] Colby, jr., May 14, 1827.*
Abner, and Hannah Stickne, May 6, 1726.*
Abner, jr., and Mirriam Coffin, Apr. 9, 1751.*
Abraham, and Miriam Moulton, both of York, July 11, 1733. C. R. 7.

*Intention also recorded.

LUNT, Abraham S., and Elizabeth A. Kent of Newburyport,
int. Aug. 12, 1835.

Amos, a. 24 y., seaman, s. William and Hannah, and Mary E.
Longfellow of Newburyport, a. 20 y., b. Newburyport, d.
John and Mary, of Newburyport, Nov. 20, 1845.*

Andrew, and Betsy Colby, June 2, 1795.*

Ann, and Samuel Pettingale, Apr. 29, 1707.*

Ann, and Steven Moodey, both of Newbury, May 9, 1734.
C. R. 7.

Ann, and Samuel Plummer, Nov. 7, 1734.*

Ann, and John Fyfeild, Nov. 14, 1734.*

Ann C., and Samuel D. Lord, June 28, 1826.*

Anna, and Daniel Sylloway of Newburyport, Nov. 14, 1788.

Anne, and Joseph Hills, Mar. 8, 1664.

Bartholomew, and Susanna Young, int. Feb. 16, 1758. ("said
Lunt takes the said Susanna Young Naked & so will not
be obliged to pay any of her former husband's Debts.")

Bartholomew R[ussell. c. R. 1.], and Jane Chapman, Jan. 25,
1823.*

Benjamin, and Hannah Noyes, Jan. 16, 1712-13.*

Benjamin [jr. int.], and Mary Muzze, Dec. 15, 1725.*

Benjamin, 3d, and Jemima Worcester, July 15, 1748.*

Benj[a]m[in], 3d, and Mary Dole, Sept. 28, 1749.*

Benjamin [Capt., 3d. int.], and Anna Gerrish, June 11, 1751.*

Benjamin, jr., of Newburyport, and Judith Smith, int. Dec. 20,
1795.

Benjamin, jr., and Mary Pearson, Dec. 1, 1807.*

Benjamin, jr., of Newburyport, and Rooxbe Moody Lunt, int.
Feb. 11, 1809.

Benjamin, jr., and Sally Tappan Coker, Mar. 31, 1813.*

Betsy Rolf, and Mayo Gerrish, July 14, 1792.*

Betty, and Elias Hunt of Newburyport, Sept. 28, 1783.*

Betty, and Samuel Wheeler of Rowley, int. Jan. 19, 1788.

Caroline, and Robert Sampson Lane, Oct. 7, 1830.*

Caroline, and George W. Knight, Dec. 22, 1837.*

Catharine, and Nathaniel Goodwin, int. Jan. 2, 1773.

Charles [jr. int.], and Sarah Blake of Newburyport, Aug. 7,
1838.*

Cutting, and Deborah Jaques, Dec. 10, 1735.*

Cutting, and Alice Osborn of Newburyport, int. Oct. 4, 1806.

Daniel, and Mary Moody, June 24, 1679.

Daniel, and Sarah Ellit, int. May 22, 1714.

*Intention also recorded.

LUNT, Daniel, and Mary Pettingill, Jan. 21, 1719-20.*
Daniel [jr. int.], and Marjery Greenleaf, Sept. 25, 1746.*
Daniel [jr. int.], and Sarah Knight, Nov. 16, 1769.*
Daniel, and Salley Hinkley of Newburyport, int. May 29,
     1803.
Daniel, a. 23 y., cordwainer, s. Daniel A. and Elizabeth, and
     Julia A. Bartlet of Brentwood, N. H., a. 21 y., b. Brent-
     wood, d. Aaron and Matilda, of Brentwood, Nov. 27,
     1849.*
Daniel A., Capt., and Elizabeth D. Woodman, Feb. 13, 1825.*
Daniell, and Hanna Coker, May 16, 1664.
Deborah Ann, and John Dexter, Nov. 12, 1837.*
Dorcas, and Samuel Hale, Aug. 15, 1824.*
Dorothy, and Benjamin Jackman, Aug. 9, 1744.*
Dorothy, and Jonathan Moers, Jan. 22, 1771.*
Edna, and Nathaniel Little, July 4, 1843.*
Elisabeth, and John Webster, int. May 30, 1734.
Eliza, and Enoch Hale, jr., Apr. 27, 1817. [May 27. c. r. 1.]*
Eliza [Elizabeth. int.], and Thomas Pettingell, jr., Mar. 31,
     1820.*
Eliza Jane, and William Gunnison, jr. of Newburyport, int.
     Sept. 12, 1834.
Elizabeth, and Israell Webster, Nov. 9, 1669.
Elizabeth, and John Webster, June 17, 1734. c. r. 7.
Elizabeth, and Ehud Bartlet of Amesbury, Nov. 14, 1734.
     c. r. 7.
Elizabeth, and Samuel Wheeler, jr. of Rowley, at Rowley,
     Feb. 7, 1788.
Elkanah, and Ann Thorla, Mar. 24, 1728-9.*
Elkanah, jr., and Elisabeth Palmer, Apr. 5, 1759.*
Enoch, and Jane Rolfe, Dec. 23, 1762.*
Enoch, jr., and Polly Connor, int. Dec. 22, 1785.
Enoch, Capt., and Jane Brookins, int. Oct. 10, 1789.
Enoch, jr., and Elisabeth Knight, int. Feb. 17, 1792.
Enoch, jr., and Lydia Jaques Pearson, Aug. 13, 1794.*
Enoch P., and Mary E. Colby, int. [Mar. or Apr.] 17, 1847.
Ephraim, and Jane Noyes, Apr. 10, 1744.*
Eunice, and Nath[anie]ll Perkins, Dec. 21, 1757.*
Eunice, and Matthias Haines of North Hampton, N. H., Nov.
     30, 1828.*
Ezra, and Mary Johnson, July 7, 1808.*
Ezra, jr., and Joanna Pettingell, both of Newburyport, Apr.
     13, 1837.

*Intention also recorded.

LUNT, Fanny, and John Disney, ——, 1830. [Jan. 2. int.]*

George, Capt., and Caroline B. Chase, both of Newburyport, July 10, 1833.

George W., of Newburyport, and Sarah T. [J. int.] Hidden, Jan. 8. 1825.*

Hannah, and Benjamin Perkins, Jan. 8, 1746-7.*

Hannah, and James Short, jr., Nov. 24, 1766.*

Hannah, and Moses Stephens, Feb. 13, 1806.*

Hannah, and Joseph Weeks of Bartlett, N. H., Mar. 4, 1811.*

Hannah, and David Hale, May 10, 1827.*

Hannah G., of Newburyport, and Abijah Howard of Thetford, Vt., ——, 1840.

Harriet, and Thomas [Samuel. c. r. 10.] Small of Newburyport, Dec. 17, 1818.*

Harriet, and Charles P. Questrom of Newburyport, Nov. 27, 1838.*

Harriet N., and James Knight, jr., int. Aug. 26, 1843.

Henry [3d. int.], and Sarah Bricket, Jan. 1, 1701.*

Henry, 3d [4th. dup.], and Sarah Cole, Nov. 18, 1707.*

Henry, 4th, and Sarah Anderton, Mar. 24, 1724.*

Henry, and Elisabeth Stickne of Rowley. Mar. 28, 1724.*

Henry, jr., and Abigail Morrill of Salisbury, int. Apr. 25, 1741.

Henry, and Abigail Lunt, Jan. 31, 1764. [He "takes said Abigail naked and so will not pay any of Her former Husband's debts." int.]*

Henry, and Eliza B. Harmond of Newburyport, int. Nov. 10, 1837.

Jacob K., and Harriet Safford, June 2, 1835.*

Jacob W., of Newburyport, a. 21 y., livery stable keeper, s. Micajah and Sarah B., of Newburyport, and Frances E. Wood, a. 19 y., d. Hiram and Prudence, Jan. 30, 1849.*

James, jr., and Hannah Noyes of Tamworth, int. May 28, 1743.

Jane, Mrs., sr., and Joseph Mayo, int. Oct. 29, 1712.

Jane, and Isaac Morse, Mar. 22, 1738-9. c. r. 7.

Jane, Mrs., and Abner Perkins [of York. int.]. Oct. 3, 1745.*

Jane, and Henry Pierce, jr. of Newburyport, Oct. 9, 1787.*

Jane, and Noah Little, Nov 15, 1801.*

Jeremiah, and Hannah [Gage. int.] Cook [resident in Kensington, N. H. int.], Mar. —, 1808. c. r. 1.*

Jeremiah, Capt., and Lois Pearson Blanchard, Oct. 22, 1812.*

*Intention also recorded.

LUNT, Jeremiah, of Newburyport, and Mary Jane Lunt, int.
July 28, 1834.
Joanna, and Richard Pettengell, Nov. 27, 1755.*
Joanna, and Moses Chase, 3d, Apr. 21, 1783.*
Joanna, and Thomas Smith, int. Apr. 24, 1784.
Joanna, and Michael Atkinson, Apr. 17, 1794.*
John, and Mary Skerry, Nov. 19, 1668.
John, and Ann Heart, Jan. 11, 1709.*
John, jr., and Jane Gerrish, Aug. 14, 1733.*
John, of Rowley, and Ann Richardson, Mar. 18, 1734-5.*
John, mariner, of Poolton, parish of Wallasy, Cheshire, Eng.,
     and Mrs. Hannah Moodey, Aug. 17, 1747. C. R. 7.
John, and Sarah Becket, Sept. 20, 1769.*
Johnson, and Mary Gibson, Dec. 8, 1756.*
Johnson, and Hannah Cook of Newburyport, int. Feb. 23,
     1771.
Joseph, and Martha Noyes, Dec. 29, 1702.*
Joseph, and Joannah Adams, Dec. 4, 1708.
Joseph, and Mrs. Sarah Osgood of Andover, at Andover, Nov.
     24, 1738.*
Joseph [4th. int.], and Sarah Stickney, May 28, 1750. C. R. 7.*
Joseph, 3d [4th. int.], and Mercy Beal, Oct. 31, 1751.*
Joseph, and Sarah Knight Lunt of Newburyport, int. Apr. 22,
     1827.
Joseph, and Ann Knight, Dec. 1, 1831.*
Joseph, 3d, and Mary Jane Cook, Jan. 7, 1834.*
Joseph J., and Louisa E. Pressey of Newburyport, July 3,
     1836.*
Joshua, and Love Bartlet, Mar. 4, 1756. C. R. 8.
Josiah, and Abigail Allen, Nov. 21, 1751.*
Judith, and Parker Clark, jr., int. July 8, 1769.
Judith, and Richard Short, Apr. 25, 1776.*
Judith, and William Sargent, Dec. 13, 1813.*
Lydia, and Joseph Stanwood, int. Nov. —, 1765.
Lydia, and Nathaniel Plumer, jr. int. Nov. 11, 1786.
Lydia, and Gideon Woodwell Stickney of Newburyport, Oct.
     25, 1798.*
Lydia, and Joseph Hobson Morrill of Boscawen, int. Nov. 19,
     1804.
Marcia, and Charles Bailey, Apr. 4, 1822.*
Marcy, Mrs., and Moses Adams, jr., Dec. 26, 1811.*
Margaret, and John Adams [jr. C. R. 1.], June 22, 1800.*

*Intention also recorded.

Lunt, Martha, and Joshua Morse, int. Apr. 11, 1805.

Mary, and Nathaniel Badger, Mar. 27, 1693.

Mary [d. Ens. Henry. int.], and Joshua Winget of Hampton, Nov. 19, 1702.*

Mary, and Samuell Jones of Exeter, Dec. 26, 1728.*

Mary, and Josiah Noyes, Mar. 2, 1737-8.*

Mary, Mrs., and Samuel Brookins, June 16, 1741.*

Mary, and Joseph Coffin, 4th, Jan. 30, 1752.*

Mary, and Moses Toppan, Dec. 26, 1754.*

Mary, and Crispus Richards [resident in Newbury. int.], Jan. 28, 1783.*

Mary, and Gideon Connor, Aug. 23, 1787.*

Mary, Mrs., and Capt. John Woodwell, jr., Dec. 26, 1815.*

Mary, and Abraham Stickney, Jan. 5, 1817.*

Mary, and Stephen Caldwell of Newburyport, int. Jan. 21, 1819.

Mary Ann, and Hanson Ordway of West Newbury, Jan. 14, 1830.*

Mary C., of Newburyport, a. 45 y., b. Newburyport, d. Micajah and Sarah G., of Newburyport, and Rev. Eleazer T. Fitch of New Haven, Conn, a. 56 y., Professor of Divinity, s. Nathaniel and Mary, of New Haven, Jan. 6, 1848.

Mary Jane, and Jeremiah Lunt of Newburyport, int. July 28, 1834.

Mary M., and Joseph S. Bradbury of New York, May 27, 1838.*

Mary Muzzy, and Benjamin Small, Mar. 8, 1812.*

Mary S., and Philip [M. int.] Bollman of Newburyport, Aug. 2, 1827.*

Matthew, and Jane Moody, int. Feb. 6, 1741-2.

Matthew, and wid. Hannah Tenny, Apr. 18, 1771.*

Mehitabel, and Paul Little, Sept. 12, 1805.*

Mercy, and John Thurla, int. Nov. 2, 1790.

Micajah, jr., Capt., and Hannah G[iles. int.] Mulliken of Newburyport, May 29, 1826.*

Micajah, and Sarah B. Swett, int. July 7, 1827.

Michajah, jr., Capt., and Mary Johnson Coffin, Dec. 13, 1831.*

Moody, and Louisa Mary Flory of Newburyport, Jan. 27, 1833.

Moses, and Sarah Wise, June 9, 1771.*

Myra E., a. 20 y., d. Daniel A. and Elizabeth, and Justin Noyes, a. 28 y., farmer, s. John and Sarah, Nov. 27, 1849.*

*Intention also recorded.

LUNT, Nathan, and Patience Bryant of Newburyport, int. Oct. 14, 1784.

Nathaniel, and Eunice Noyes, Jan. 14, 1741-2.*

Nathaniel, and Eleanor Clerk [of Newburyport. int.], May 20, 1798. c. R. 1.*

Nicolas, and Eunice Dole, Jan. 25, 1768.*

Paul, of Newburyport, and Margaret Coffin, int. Jan. 13, 1775.

Paul, and Hannah Adams, Feb. 5, 1789.*

Paul, jr., and Mary Somerby, June 21, 1800.*

Paul, jr., a. 36 y., cordwainer, s. Paul and Mary, and Sarah L. Dodge of Newburyport, a. 21 y., b. Newburyport, d. Silas and Marcia, Nov. 21, 1849.*

Paul G., and Abigail Dutton, Feb. 11, 1841.*

Polly, and Jonathan Poor of Newburyport, int. Dec. 11, 1802.

Rachel, and Jonathan Barker of Greenland, Sept. 26, 1734. c. R. 7.*

Richard [jr. int.], and Sarah Bright [of Newburyport, July 16. int.], 1796.*

Rooxbe Moody, and Benjamin Lunt, jr. of Newburyport, int. Feb. 11, 1809.

Ruth, and Josiah [Isaiah. int.] Hunt [of Amesbury. c. R. 9.], Nov. 19, 1755.*

Sally, and Dunham Watson, Aug. 29, 1814.*

Sally, and Nathaniel Goodwin, Feb. 5, 1822.*

Sally, and Thomas Knight, jr., Nov. 3, 1824.*

Sally S[omerby. c. R. 10.], and Amos Poor, jr. of West Newbury, Apr. 21, 1831.*

Samuel, and Sarah Gillings of Newburyport, int. Nov. 16, 1792.

Sam[ue]l [jr. c. R. 1.], and Hannah Sweat, Jan. 18, 1797.*

Samuel, and Massey Downs, May 6, 1802.*

Samuel, jr., and Abigail L. Morrison of Sanbornton, N. H., int. Jan. 18, 1828.

Samuel, jr., and Lydia D. Lane, Nov. 27, 1834.*

Samuel, jr., and Mrs. Harriet Jackman, Oct. —, 1837.*

Sarah, d. Daniel, and Nicholas Noyes, jr., int. July 17, 1695.

Sarah, Mrs., and Andrew Stickne of Rowley, Dec. 12, 1727.*

Sarah, and Stephen Pettingill, Oct. 28, 1731.*

Sarah, and Isaac Spooner, Sept. 26, 1754.*

Sarah, and Joseph Hidden, jr., June 17, 1761.*

Sarah, and Simeon Hale, Dec. 15, 1774.*

Sarah, and Robert Michel of Newburyport, int. Sept. 13, 1794.

*Intention also recorded.

LUNT, Sarah, and Simon Adams, Oct. 17, 1799.*
Sarah, and Benja[min] Grace, Jan. 22, 1822.*
Sarah E., and Jeremiah N. Jackman, Oct. 25, 1840.*
Sarah Jane, and John P. Fuller, May 8, 1828.*
Sarah Knight, of Newburyport, and Joseph Lunt, int. Apr. 22, 1827.
Sarah L., and Henry Titcomb, jr. of Newburyport, int. Mar. 11, 1826.
Silas, jr., and Mary Jane Hickey of Newburyport, int. Oct. 13, 1832.
Skiper, and Elisabeth Browne, July 18, 1704.*
Stephen, and wid. Mary Goodrich, June 9, 1766.*
Susan, of Newburyport, and Anson W. Farnum, int. Nov. 18, 1826.
Susan M., of Newburyport, and David P[erkins. int.] Page Dec. 16, 1832.*
Susanna, and Walter Maddin, Aug. 12, 1763. C. R. 8.*
Tabitha, and Caleb Moodey [jr. int.], Jan. 1, 1722-3.*
Thomas, and Opportunity Hoppin, June 17, 1679.
Thomas, and Sarah Whitcher, Oct. 2, 1783.*
Tristram, and Lydia Jaques, Feb. 20, 1799.*
Tristram, and Clarissa A. Stevens of Newburyport, int. Oct. 16, 1841.
William, and Sarah Clark, Dec. 29, 1747.*
Will[ia]m [jr. int.], and Mary Stanwood, July 18, 1804.*
William, and Hannah Wyatt, Feb. 25, 1813.*
William, and Angelina Poor, Nov. —, 1833.
William, and Hannah C. Coffin, July 8, 1841.*
William. jr., and Ann Young of Newburyport, int. Aug. 29, 1846.
William, jr., and Mrs. Mary Blake of Newburyport, int. Nov. 10, 1849.
William I., of Newburyport, a. 25 y., pilot, s. Jeremiah and Lois P., of Newburyport, and Lydia S. Nutting of Newburyport, a. 18 y., d. Gay and China, of Newburyport, Oct. 8, 1846.

LURVEY (see also Lervey), Abiah, and William Dodg of Newburyport. int. May 21, 1796.
Jabez, of Newburyport, and Harriet Pearson, int. Nov. 4, 1815.

*Intention also recorded.

LURVEY, Jacob [of Newburyport. int.], and Hannah Boynton, Feb. 26, 1782.*
Letty, and William Stockman of Newburyport, Aug. 12, 1824.*
Lydia, and Bagley Weed of Newburyport, Dec. 24, 1815.*
Lydia, and Abner Pearson, July 30, 1825.*
Nathaniel, and Abiah Jones, Nov. 2, 1785.*
Richard, and Sally Elliott Mores, int. May 18, 1822.
Richard, and Sarah Jane Tobey, int. Feb. 20, 1848.
Samuel, and Mary Lakeman, Dec. 9, 1817.*
Susan, and Daniel Felch of Newburyport, int. Mar. 4, 1809.
Susan, and John Smith, 6th, June 8, 1809.*

LYDSTON, William, and Mary Collins of Newburyport, int. June 11, 1812.

LYLE, John, late of Belfast, Ireland, now of Boston, merchant, and Mrs. Hannah Newton of Boston, June 29, 1731. C. R. 7.

LYNARD (see also Leonard), Henry, and Ann Henden, both of Boston, Dec. 2, 1741. C. R. 7.

McARTHUR, Robert, mariner, and Elizabeth Mansfield, both of Boston, Nov. 16, 1726. C. R. 7.

McCANTY, Patty, of Newburyport, and Merrill Higbe, int. Aug. 6, 1808.

McCARTHY, Will[ia]m, of Kingsale, Ireland, mariner, and Margaret Pulsafer of Boston, June 25, 1729. C. R. 7.

McCAULA, Ann, and Owen Sullivan, int. July 14, 1849.

MACCLARN, Joseph, and Sarah Perkins, int. June 4, 1796.

MACCLURE (see also Mackclure), Ann, and [John. int.] Mireck, Sept. 2, 1725.*
Samuel, and Mary Badger, Dec. 27, 1733.*

McCULLOCK, William, and Dorothy Favour, int. Aug. 25, 1759.

*Intention also recorded.

McDANIEL, Timothy, Capt., of Co. Wicklow, Ireland, now of Boston, and Mrs. Elizabeth Foster of Charlestown, Aug. 11, 1732. C. R. 7.

McDONALD, Daniel, of Boston, and Jane M. Knight, int. Dec. 6, 1845.
Hugh, of Boston, and Susan P. Knight, int. May 25, 1844.

MACE, Abraham, and Abigail Barnard [of Amesbury. int.], Mar. 21, 1733-34.*
Abraham [jr. int.], of Newburyport, and Judith Jaques, Apr. 26, 1795.*
Daniel, and Priscilla Annis, July 1, 1735.*
Elizabeth, Mrs., and Asa Merrill, Oct. 24, 1811.*
Elizabeth M., and Chelmsford Felch of Lowell, Dec. 26, 1841.*
Elizabeth M., of Newburyport, a. 34 y., b. Newburyport, d. John and Martha, and Josiah P. Noyes, widr., a. 48 y., baker, b. Newburyport, s. Timothy and Elizabeth, of Newburyport, June 12, 1848.*
John, and Martha Norton of Newburyport, Oct. 29, 1812.*
Joseph, and Polly Marsh, int. Sept. 2, 1809.
Joseph, and Hannah Perkins of Newburyport, int. May 22, 1819.
Joshua, and Mrs. Amelia Boynton, Mar. 22, 1824.*
Judith, and Jonathan Peabody, int. May 5, 1821.
Judith, see Morse, Judith.
Lavina, and George W. Bray, Nov. 21, 1842.*
Lydia, of Newburyport, a. 25 y., b. Newburyport, d. Daniel and Lucy of Newburyport, and Joseph Hoyt, jr., a. 26 y., seaman, s. Joseph and Martha, Nov. 4, 1845.*
Mary, and Dea. Abial Somerby, Sept. 30, 1730.*
Mary, and Thomas Obrian, Sept. 7. 1755.*
Mary C., a. 22 y., d. W[illia]m and Catherine, and Amos P. Lloyd of Newburyport, a. 26 y., shoemaker, b. Henniker, N. H., s. John and Mary, June 17, 1849.*
Nabby, and William Ramsdel, int. Sept. 11, 1790.
Nancy, and Eleazer Fish, Dec. 26. 1819.*
Ruben, and Mary Chase, Sept. 20, 1739. C. R. 7.*
William, and Charlotte How, Dec. 17, 1839.*

McGRAY, James, and Elisabeth Babbidge, Nov. 28, 1753. C. R. 8.

*Intention also recorded.

McINTIRE, Eunice, of Portsmouth, and Samuel Brookins, Apr. 4, 1799.*

MACKANETENE, Matthew [of Haverhill. int.], and Grace Mitchill [wid. int.], Feb. 10, 1700.*

MACKCLURE (see also Macclure), Jane, and Joseph Spinne, Oct. 12, 1725.*

MACKCRES, Mary [Macrees. dup.], and Stephen Greenleaf [jr. int.], Oct. 7, 1712.*

McKEEL, Tho[ma]s, and Experience Marsh, both of Glo[u]cester, Apr. 30, 1735. c. R. 7.

MACKENLY, Grace, wid., and Enoch Flood, Jan. 24, 1771.*

McKENNY, Daniel, of Kittery, and Mary Hall of Hampton, Dec. 18, 1732. c. R. 7.

McKENZIE, Washington, of Essex, and Martha A. Coffin, int. July 20, 1844.

MACKHARD, William, and Mrs. Margeret Allin, Dec. 15, 1743.*

McKINSTRY, William, and Lydia Tenney, int. June 11, 1811.

MACKMILION, James, and Abigail Iselip, int. Jan. 22, 1736-7.
James, and Mrs. Judith Blake, Dec. 30, 1745.*

McLENNEN, Elisabeth, and William Smith, int. June 17, 1797.

McNEEL, James, and Rose Taylor of Londonderry, int. Mar. 29, 1811.

McQUILLEN (see also McQuillin), Elizabeth B., and John Fillmore, int. Dec. 7, 1849.

*Intention also recorded.

McQuillen, John P., a. 26 y., shipwright, s. David P. and Sophia, and Susan F. Merrill, a. 26 y., d. Jonathan and Sally, Oct. 5, 1845.
Naomia P., and Cha[rle]s D. Chipman, int. Apr. 5, 1848.
Spofford, a. 21 y., ship carpenter, s. Robert and Mehitable, and Sarah Ann Crocker, a. 18 y., d. Lowell, Nov. 16, 1847.*

McQUILLIN (see also McQuillen), John H. P., and Clarinda Caveley, int. Sept. 18, 1847.
Mary G., and Benjamin S. Pike, int. Apr. 26, 1839.
Robert R., and Elizabeth Seward of Newburyport, int. Oct. 10, 1846.

MACREES, Mary, and Stephen Greenleaf, Oct. 7, 1712.

MADDIN, Walter, and Susanna Lunt, Aug. 12, 1763. C. R. 8.*

MADDIX, Mary S., of Gloucester, and Abraham Stickney, int. Dec. 10, 1825.

MAGER (see also Major), Georg, and Susanna ——, Aug. 21, 1672.

MAGONIAR, Jasper, and —— Slowman, wid., int. ——, 1702.

MAGOUN (see also Magowen, Magowin), Mercy D., Mrs., and Luther Briggs, both of Pembroke, Aug. 3, 1834.
Sarah N., of Pembroke, and William Currier, jr., int. Nov. 9, 1831.

MAGOWEN (see also Magoun), Joseph, of Newburyport, a. 32 y., mariner, b. Newburyport, s. Joseph and Margaret, of Newburyport, and Mary E. Hickman of Newburyport, a. 24 y., b. Newburyport, d. Gideon and Mary, Sept. 6, 1846.
Margaret, Mrs., and Gideon Hickman, both of Newburyport, Nov. 17, 1836.

MAGOWIN (see also Magoun), Joseph, and Jane Peterson, both of Newburyport, Nov. 28, 1837.
Josiah, and Margaret Lakeman, Apr. 6, 1813.*

*Intention also recorded.

MAJOR (see also Mager), Elizabeth, and Richard Jackman, jr., int. Apr. 6, 1703.
Hannah, and Richard Goodwin, Mar. 26, 1692.

MAKEUM, Will[ia]m, merchant, and Lydia Pitts, both of Boston, July 1, 1725. c. r. 7.

MALBONE, Godfrey, of Newport, R. I., and Mrs. Katharine Brindley of Roxbury, Aug. 9, 1748. c. r. 7.

MALLARD, Priscilla, and Thomas Robbins, "late of Woller Hampton", Staffordshire, Eng., Dec. 1, 1703.*

MANLEY, Elizabeth, and Moses Blaisdell, int. Jan. 26, 1821.

MANN, Hewy, and Adeline Dutton, May 27, 1828.*
Jonathan, M. D., of Franklin, and Marietta Rollins, int. Sept. 14, 1844.

MANNING, Abigail Pickard, of Ipswich, and Nehemiah Cleaveland, int. July 26, 1823.
George W., of Ipswich, and Elizabeth Brookings, Dec. 26, 1833.*

MANSFIELD, David, jr., and Abigail Francis, July 10, 1817.*
David, and Charity Goodwin of Newburyport, int. Sept. 4, 1818.
Elizabeth, and Robert McArthur, mariner, both of Boston, Nov. 16, 1726. c. r. 7.
Salley, and Joseph Shephard of Newburyport, int. Aug. 24, 1805.

MANSON, Joseph [Munson. int.], of Scarboro, and Sarah Morse, June 27, 1749.*

MARCH, Abigail, and Joseph March, Jan. 5, 1715-16.*
Abigail, and Humphery Richards, Mar. 13, 1734-5.*
Anna, and Henry Brookins, Mar. 19, 1772.*
Anna, and Joseph Newell, June 10, 1790.*
Daniel, and Mary Huse, Apr. 6, 1742.*
Dorothy, and Robert Bayley of Newburyport, July 5, 1772.*

*Intention also recorded.

MARCH, Ebenezer, jr., and Patience Little, Apr. 29, 1817.*
Elisabeth, and Benjamin Coker, Jan. 29, 1732-3. C. R. 7.
Elisabeth, and William Blunt of Portsmouth, N. H., int. Sept. 9, 1769.
Elisabeth, and Mark Mores, Dec. 29, 1778.*
Elizabeth, and Samuel Mors, Feb. 23, 1712-13.*
Elizabeth, and William Rich of Lynn, Jan. 7, 1718-19.*
Elizabeth, of Newburyport, and Richard Ordway, int. Apr. 29, 1820.
Enoch, and Keturah True, int. Jan. 9, 1741-2.
Eunice, and Seth Plummer, Jan. 17, 1799.*
Georg, and Mary Foulsom, June 12, 1672.
Hannah, and Thomas Folinsby, jr., Jan. 5, 1715-16.*
Hugh, and Dorcas Blackleach, May 29, 1676.
Hugh, and Sarah Moody, Mar. 29, 1683.
Hugh, sr., and Sarah Healy, Dec. 3, 1685.
Ichabod, and Mary Rogers, Mar. 10, 1748. C. R. 2.*
Jacob, and Ruth Bradshaw of Charlestown, at Charlestown, June 24, 1747.*
Jane, and John Newman of Ipswich, Dec. 15, 1720.*
Jane, and William Carpenter, Feb. 12, 1756.*
Jane, and Joseph Holbrook of Newcastle, N. H., Nov. 29, 1770.*
John, and Jemima True, Oct. 1, 1679.
John, and Mrs. Mary Angier of Reading [Watertown. int.], at Reading, Dec. 11, 1700.*
John, jr. [3d. int.], and Mary Smith, Apr. 5, 1723.*
John, Esq., and Mrs. Martha Brown, Mar. 4, 1741-2.*
John, 3d, and Sarah Dole of Salisbury, int. Oct. 23, 1756.
John, 3d, and Sarah Emery, Mar. 5, 1761.*
John C., Rev., and Alice L. Hale, Apr. 23, 1832.*
Joseph, and Abigail March, Jan. 5, 1715-16.*
Joshua, and Martha Merril, Aug. 18. 1726.*
Joshua, jr., and Rebeckah Gerrish, Jan. 1, 1752.*
Judeth, and Elexander Williams of Boston, int. Apr. 14, 1740.
Judith, and Thomas Tharley, Apr. 13, 1670.
Judith, Mrs., and Humphrey Hooke [of Salisbury. int.], July 10, 1700.*
Judith, and Thomas Noyes, 3d, Jan. 3. 1722-3.*
Martha, and James Johnston of Newburyport, July 5, 1772.*
Martha Ann, of Newburyport, and Moses Davison of Salem, Nov. 29, 1832.

*Intention also recorded.

March, Mary, Mrs. [wid. int.], and Joseph Herrick of Salem
   Village, Jan. 29, 1706-7.*
Mary, and Jacob Hook of Salisbury, Apr. 17, 1707.*
Mary [Mrs. int.], and John Emery, Jan. 2, 1723-4. [He takes
.   her without any estate, refusing to pay any debts of her
   former husband, Capt. James March. int.]*
Mary, and Stephen Noyes, Aug. 25, 1725.*
Mary, and Samuel Allen of Gloucester, Jan. 26, 1726-7.*
Mary, of Salisbury, and Jacob Hale, at Salisbury, Jan. 11,
   1738-9.*
Mary, and Giles Harris, Nov. 26, 1747.*
Mary, and Samuel Peirce of Newcastle, N. H., Apr. 23, 1761.*
Mary, and Isaac Bayley, Aug. 23, 1764.*
Mary, and Lewis Gay, both of Newburyport, Mar. 28, 1771.
Mary, and John Smith, May 1, 1788.*
Mary, and Capt. George Campbell of Newburyport, Mar. 9,
   1813.*
Mary, and Ezekiel B. Pulsifer of Rowley, int. June 12, 1830.
Mehetable, and John Rawlings, jr., Nov. 14, 1776.*
Mehitable, and William Follinsbe, Oct. 2, 1733.*
Mercy, and Joseph Wormwell, Apr. 1, 1751.*
Mercy, and Dr. Joseph Goodridge, int. Dec. 19, 1778.
Molly, and Benjamin Sawyer of Byfield Rowley, Apr. 16,
   1761.*
Moses, and Judith Bartlet, Jan. 6, 1777.*
Nathaniel, and Abigail Homes of Ipswich, int. Nov. 11, 1747.
Nathaniell, and Hannah Mors, Mar. 6, 1717-18.
Patience, Mrs., and Joseph Toppan, Aug. 9, 1828.*
Rhoda, and Caleb Tenny, Oct. 17, 1826.*
Robert, and Eunice Moulton, Apr. 8, 1789.*
Ruth, and Moses Bayley, int. July 25, 1761.
Ruth, and Thomas Emery, Oct. 10, 1770.*
Samuel, and [wid. int.] Anne Rolfe, Apr. 29, 1713.*
Samuel, and wid. Hannah Smith, Apr. 14, 1726.*
Samuel, of Salisbury, and Mary Currier, Aug. 23, 1793.*
Sarah [wid. int.], and Archelaus Adams, Mar. 18, 1697-8.*
Sarah, and [Sergt. int.] Humphry Deering, Dec. 25, 1705.*
Sarah, and Daniel Chace [jr. int.], Jan. 2, 1706.*
Sarah, and John Marshall "both Living in Newbury", int.
   Aug. 25, 1781.
Sarah, and George Wilson. Nov. 28, 1841.*
Stephen, of Portsmouth, N. H., and Elisabeth Gerrish, June
   14, 1753.*

*Intention also recorded.

MARCH, Stephen H., a. 34 y., ship carpenter, s. Ichabod and
Mary, and Mary J. Allen, a. 19 y., d. Joseph and Abigail,
Oct. 5, 1845.*
Susanna, Mrs., and Moses Pike, Nov. 11, 1741.*
Tabitha, and Nicholas Pettengaill, Dec. 25, 1718.*
Tabitha, and Mark Pettegrew, int. Jan. 18, 1844.
Truman, and Judeth Morss, Nov. 14, 1727.*

MARQUAND, Daniel, Capt., and Mrs. Mary Brown, Mar. 13,
1739-40.*

MARRIL (see also Merrill), Mary, and Jabez Bradbury, May
16, 1749.*

MARRINER, Adam, of Boston, and Hannah Nessbee, Sept.
23, 1713.*
Hannah, and Richard Kent [jr. int.], Nov. 7; 1734.*

MARROW (see also Merrow), James, of Newburyport, and
Susan C. Bartlett, int. Sept. 12, 1846.

MARSH, Abigail, and John Symoors, int. May 17, 1806.
Abigail, and Joseph Rand, Apr. 18, 1809.*
David, of Haverhill, and Mary Moodey, Aug. 16, 1722.*
Experience, and Tho[ma]s McKeel, both of Gloucester, Apr.
30, 1735. C. R. 7.
Frederick, a. 34 y., seaman, s. Joseph and Betsey, of Newbury-
port, and Olive J. Bradbury, a. 22 y., d. David and Sarah,
Mar. 1, 1846.*
Joseph, and Elizabeth Noyes, Dec. 23, 1806.*
Judith, of Haverhill, and John Boardman, at Haverhill, Nov.
9, 1752.*
Mary, of Haverhill, and Edmund Bartlett, at Haverhill, Oct.
2, 1754.*
Mary N., a. 25 y., d. Joseph and Elizabeth, and George W.
Wyman of Boston, a. 24 y., lighterman, b. Boston, s. Al-
pheus and Mary, of Boston, Oct. 25, 1847.*
Polly, and Joseph Mace, int. Sept. 2, 1809.
Samuel, and Anna Flanders of Amesbury, int. Feb. —, 1789.
Samuel, and Mary Minah, int. Mar. 27, 1790.
Sarah, and James Pike, May 23, 1700.
Sarah, and John Rolfe, jr., Aug. 27, 1767.*

*Intention also recorded.

MARSHAL (see also Marshall), Isaac, and Margaret Cook of Salem, int. June 5, 1801.

MARSHALL (see also Marshal), Abigail, of Ipswich, and Edward Shaw of Hampton, July 2, 1719.

Cyrus Lewis, of Dracut, and Nancy Titcomb, Nov. 8, 1827.*

John, and Sarah March, "both Living in Newbury," int. Aug. 25, 1781.

John, of Nottingham West, N. H., and Elizabeth Noyes, Feb. 27, 1812.*

John, of Frankfort, and Sally Williams, July 12, 1821.

John, and Mary Ann Larkin, July 3, 1822.*

John H., a. 18 y., shoemaker, and Almira D. Bayley, a. 18 y., d. Joseph and Almira, May 20, 1849.*

Mary, of Ipswich, and Caleb Moody Carr, resident in Newbury, int. Oct. 30, 1750.

MARSTON (see also Maston), Isaac, of Newburyport, and Mary Jane Brown, int. Apr. 5, 1834.

Jacob, of Andover, and Mary Brown [at Andover. dup.], Dec. 11, 1718.*

Sam[ue]ll, of Hampton, and Katharine Car, Mar. 17, 1709.*

Stephen W., and Mary White of Newburyport, int. Dec. 7, 1816.

Zachariah, of Portland, and Salley Plummer, Oct. 9, 1800.*

MARTIN, Anne, of Amesbury, and Thomas Sawyer, at Amesbury, Aug. 4, 1793.*

Charles, and Mary Ann Allgreen, int. Aug. 17, 1816.

Deborah, and Theophilus Tilton, Nov. 22, 1813. [1814. c. r. 5.]*

Elizabeth, of Boston, and John Petelle, Oct. 4, 1725. c. r. 7.

Elizabeth, and Greenleaf Tilton, Apr. 4, 1811.*

Hackett, and Abigail Coffin, both of Newburyport, Dec. 5, 1821.

Hannah, of Newburyport, and Samuel Merrill, jr., int. Apr. 25, 1846.

Jacob, and Hannah Moody, int. May 26, 1827.

John, of Andover, and Hannah Bartlett of Bradford, May 7, 1729. c. r. 7.

Jonathan, and Mercy Jackman, May 25, 1756.*

Jonathan, and Miriam Keizer, Dec. 14, 1790.*

*Intention also recorded.

MARTIN, Jonathan, and Priscilla Parker of Newburyport, int.
Nov. 11, 1820.
Joseph, of Andover, and Rachel Noyes, Aug. 5, 1725.*
Mary, and Thomas Slatery, int. Sept. 22, 1792.
Mercy, and Jonathan [John, jr. int.] Danford, Sept. 4, 1766.*
Oliver, and Elisabeth Knight, Mar. 28, 1786.*
Richard, and Mary Low, Feb. 1, 1781.*
Ruth A., of Newburyport, and Benjamin Pierce, int. Jan. 18,
1847.

MASON, Henry, and Nancy Hobson, June 5, 1832.*
Nancy, and Caleb Reed, int. May 27, 1841.
Nathaniel, of Boston, and Ruth Hills, Sept. 1, 1743.*
Nathaniel, of Newburyport, and Mary Casida, int. Aug. 16,
1766.
Sarah E., of Newburyport, and Ezra Thurlo, int. Nov. 27,
1847.

MASSEY, Daniel, of Salem, and Abigail Baker of Beverly,
May 21, 1734. c. r. 7.

MASTON (see also Marston), Symon, of Hampton, N. H.,
and Hanna Carr, int. Jan. 26, 1705-6.

MATHEWS (see also Matthews), Hugh, and Mary Emerson,
Aug. 28, 1683.

MATTHEWS (see also Mathews), Elisabeth, and William
Couch, Jan. 21, 1725-6.*

MAUGRIDGE (see also Morgaridge), Mary, of Portsmouth,
N. H., and Benjamin Coffin, int. July 29, 1821.

MAXFIELD, Joseph, of Salisbury, and Joanna Richardson,
Dec. 17, 1717.

MAXWELL, Albert G., and Harriet M. Flanders, int. Dec.
7, 1833.

MAY, Moses, and Elizabeth Frost, both of Ipswich, July 3,
1734. c. r. 7.
Stephen, and Nancy Parmenter, int. Sept. 3, 1813.

*Intention also recorded.

MAYEW (see also Mayhew), Aquilla [Augustus, of Rye. int.], and Patty Flood, June 17, 1802.*

MAYHEW (see also Mayew), Elijah, and Eunice Sargent, at Gloucester, June 14, 1761.
Patty, and Thomas Noyes, int. Jan. 8, 1803.

MAYLER, Richard, resident in Newbury, and Sarah Jones, int. Dec. 7, 1753.

MAYO, Elisabeth, and William Gerrish, Mar. 20, 1711-12.*
Joseph, and Sarah Short, May 29, 1679.
Joseph, and Mrs. Jane Lunt, sr., int. Oct. 29, 1712.
Sarah, and Maverick Gileman [of Exeter. int.], June 16, 1702.*
Thomasin, and Joseph Greenleaf, Nov. 18, 1707.*

MEAD, Elizabeth C., of Charlestown, and John N. Wills, int. Apr. 21, 1832.
Emily B., of Charlestown, and Charles Wills, int. Sept. 9, 1837.
Susanna, Mrs., and Joshua Pike, May 14, 1739.*

MEANS, Catherine A., and Nehemiah Cleaveland of Brooklyn, N. Y., Nov. 25, 1842.*
Rebecca Wentworth, and Robert Appleton of Boston, int. Dec. 14, 1846.

MENDUM, John S., and Abigail H. Jackman, Jan. 6, 1839.*

MERRICK (see also Mireck. Mirick, Mirrick, Mirricke, Myrick), Abigail, and Steephen Ordway, July 10, 171[8. c. r. 2.]*

MERRIL (see also Merrill), David, and Mary Morse, Dec. 18, 1706.*
Enoch, and Sarah Long, May 17, 1750. c. r. 7.
James, and Hannah Bailey, Oct. 2, 1733. c. r. 7.*
John, and Deborah Hazeltine of Haverhill, int. Aug. 7, 1708. (Forbidden by Penuel Titcomb at the request of Sarah Sawyer, single woman.)
Joseph, and A[nn. int.] Wiggins of Haverhill, Feb. 16, 1707.*

*Intention also recorded.

MERRIL, Martha, and Joshua March, Aug. 18, 1726.*
Nathaniel, and Joan Ninny [Kinny ?], Oct. 15, 1661.
Sam[uel], and Ruth Moss, Aug. —, 1717. c. r. 7.
Sarah, and Richard Pillsbery, Feb. 7, 1750.*
Stevens, and Sarah Chase, Jan. 7, 1752.*

MERRILL (see also Marril, Merril, Merryl), Abel [jr. int.],
    and Ruth Kelly, Dec. 12, 1721.*
Abel, of Falmouth, and Abigail Knight, Nov. 22, 1759.*
Abel, and Anna Emery, Jan. 4, 1776.*
Abel, and Elisabeth Pilsbery, Oct. 18, 1779.*
Abell, and Priscilla Chase, Feb. 10, 1670.
Abell, and Abigael Stephens, June 19, 1694.
Abigail, and John Kent, jr., Jan. 10, 1722-3.*
Abigail, and James Hills, Dec. 26, 1723.*
Abigail, and Joseph Downer, Mar. 6, 1733-4.*
Abigail, and Nathaniel Knight of Plaistow, N. H., Sept. 25,
    1750.*
Abigail, and Zachariah Baker of Falmouth, int. Jan. 10, 1775.
Abigail, and Zachariah Baker of Falmouth, Feb. 23, 1778.*
Abigail, and George Roaf, int. Mar. 15, 1828.
Abraham, and Abigal Webster, Jan. 18, 1660.
Abraham, jr., and Abigael Bartlet, jr., d. Samuel, int. Oct. 7,
    1696.
Abraham, Dea., and wid. Sarah Bond of Salisbury, int. Aug.
    15, 1713.
Abraham, and Rachel Lowell of Amesbury, int. Sept. 17, 1748.
Anna, and Timothy Sweet of Haverhill, Mar. 8, 1753.*
Anna, and Daniel Flanders, Dec. 16, 1784.*
Anna, and William Merrill of Freeport, Oct. 17, 1797.*
Anna, and Siméon Cooper, May 11, 1831.*
Annis, and Lydia Merrill of North Yarmouth, June 10, 1784.*
Asa, and Mrs. Elizabeth Mace, Oct. 24, 1811.*
Asa, of Newburyport, and Keturah M. Gerish, int. July 20,
    1833.
Benjamin, and Elizabeth Dow, Feb. 4, 1739-40.*
Benj[ami]n, and Sarah Stanwood, May 27, 1802.*
Betsey C., and George Bartlet, int. Aug. 16, 1837.
Bettee, and Joseph Little, jr., Apr. 28, 1763.*
Charles, and Mary Stevens, ——, 1808 or 9. [Sept. 23, 1808.
    int.]*

*Intention also recorded.

MERRILL, Charles N., and Antoinette Jackman of Newbury-
port, int. Dec. 8, 1840.
Charlottee, and Robert Griffith, jr. of Newburyport, int. Feb.
7, 1840.
Daniel, and Sara Clough, May 14, 1667.
Daniel, jr., and Sarah Moers, May 20, 1725.*
Daniel, jr., and Thomasin Chase, Nov. 1, 1743.*
Daniel, and Susanna Sanders, Oct. 11, 1753.*
Daniel, jr., and Mary O'Sillaway, Nov. 27, 1759.*
Daniel, and Mrs. Elizabeth Edwards, June 18, 1831.*
Deliverance, and Thomas Williams, jr., May 15, 1739.*
Dorothy, and Jacob Mireck, June 23, 1763.*
Ednah, and John Moulton, Nov. 25, 1790.*
Ednar, and Dr. James Bricket [3d. int.], Oct. 8, 1760.*
Elbridge, and Abigail E. Morse, June 7, 1837.*
Elbridge, of Salisbury, and Mary J. Short of Newburyport,
——, 1839.
Elbridge G., and Ruth G. Savory, Sept. 27, 1833.*
Elisabeth, Mrs., and William Cooch, Mar. 23, 1742-3.*
Elisabeth, and Jonathan Tewksbury, Nov. 26, 1778.*
Eliza Ann, and Sidney S. Young of St. Johns, N. S., int. Sept.
30, 1825.
Elizabeth, and Joseph Emery, Oct. 2, 1693. CT. R.
Elizabeth, of Newburyport, and Sawyer Currier, int. Nov. 23,
1833.
Elizebeth, and Moses Burnham, Mar. 30, 1815.*
Enoch, and Temperance Little, May 31, 1778.*
Enoch, and Mary Morse of Bradford, int. Jan. 4, 1821.
Esther, and Edmund Chase, Nov. 30, 1769.*
Esther S., and Daniel L. Morse, int. Dec. 8, 1842.
Eunice, and Amos Chase, Aug. 2, 1787.*
Ezekiel, and Sarah Emery, June 1, 1773.*
Ezra P., of Newburyport, and Sarah Howard, int. Aug. 6,
1820.
Hanah [d. Abraham. int.], and Shubiel Long, Aug. 26, 1695.*
Hanah, and Samuel Hutchins, both of Haverhill, Jan. 4,
1715-16.
Hanna, d. John, and Steven Swett, May 24 [164-?].
Hannah, and Jonathan Hills, Oct. 25, 1749.*
Hannah, and Ebenezer White of Plaistow, N. H., Apr. 14,
1757.*
Hannah, and Thomas Brown, June 8, 1769.*

*Intention also recorded.

MERRILL, Hannah, and Jonathan Chase, jr., Apr. 22, 1773.*
Hannah, and Moses Hoyt, Apr. 12, 1779.*
Hannah, and Charles Porter, Apr. 1, 1822. [Feb. 22, 1823.
    int.]*
Harriet, of Newburyport, and George W. Wood, int. Mar. 30,
    1839.
Henry, and Mary Peterson, Apr. 2, 1745.*
Henry, and Priscilla Lowell, May 5, 1748.*
Henry, jr., and Rebeckah Moulton, Nov. 25, 1773.*
Henry, 3d, and Lydia Jackman, int. June 16, 1803.
Henry, and Hannah Chase, June 10, 1824.*
Irena, of Salisbury, and Elias Jackman, jr., int. Oct. 27, 1837.
J. William, and Mary S. Grow of East Topsham, Vt., int. Nov.
    27, 1847.
Jacob, and Elisabeth Wyatt, Nov. 21, 1762.*
Jacob, and Mary Dow, Feb. 8, 1778.*
Jacob, jr., and Esther Sumner of Newburyport, int. May 12,
    1810.
Jacob, and Abigail Farrington, May 4, 1835.
James, and Mary Adams, Nov. 23, 1714.*
James, and Ellis Cooper, Nov. 11, 1768.*
James, and Betty French of Tewksbury, int. Oct. 29, 1774.
Jane, and Phineas C. Balch of Bradford, May 17, 1820.*
Jemima, and Joseph Sandors of Amesbury, Aug. 25, 1774.*
Jeremiah, of Freeport, and Lydia Merrill, Nov. 4, 1795.*
John [jr. int.], and Anne Knight, May 15, 1725.*
John, and Margaret Lowel, Apr. —, 1729.*
John [3d. int.], and Ruth Hale, June 1, 1730.*
John, 3d, and Anne Ordway, int. Dec. 19, 1746.
John, and Mary Little, int. Jan. 25, 1771.
John, A. M., and Elizabeth Dodge, Sept. 22, 1814.*
John, jr., and Sally Moulton, int. Apr. 13, 1827.
John A., and Elizabeth A. Garland of Newburyport, int. May
    1, 1847.
Jonathan, and Mary Merrill, Jan. 13, 1757.*
Jonathan, and Salley Penson of Salisbury, Dec. 25, 1799.*
Jonathan, jr., of Methuen, and Susannah Adams, Mar. 29,
    1800.*
Joseph, and Hannah Rogers, Sept. 4, 1797.*
Joseph, and Nancy Raynell of Newburyport, int. Nov. 2, 1813.
Joshua, and Jenny Moors of Haverhill, at Haverhill, Mar. 4,
    1775.*

*Intention also recorded.

MERRILL, Josiah, and Hannah Graves of Salisbury, at Salisbury, Oct. 30, 1746.*

Juba, and Hannah Holland of Exeter, N. H., Aug. 3, 1777.*

Judith, and William Sampson, Jan. 3, 1758.*

Julia Ann [Morril. c. r. 10.], and Charles Hopkinson, Sept. 23, 1824.*

Keturah M., Mrs., and Thomas Pritchard, jr. of Newburyport, Oct. 31, 1837.*

Louise, and Daniel G. Todd of Rowley, int. July 2, 1841.

Love, and James Carr of Newburyport, May 7, 1796.*

Luther, and Elizabeth Ann Chesley of Lee, N. H., int. Sept. 11, 1841.

Lydia, and Moses Davis, Nov. 17, 1759.*

Lydia, and Josiah Baker of Falmouth [in Casco Bay. int.], Nov. 7, 1768.*

Lydia, of North Yarmouth, and Annis Merrill, June 10, 1784.*

Lydia, and Jeremiah Merrill of Freeport, Nov. 4, 1795.*

Lydia, and Dr. Daniel N. Poor, July 3, 1796.*

Lydia, and Henry Moet [Mowat. int.], Mar. 22, 1801.*

Martha, and Richard Dole, 3d, Oct. 16, 1759.*

Martha F., and Sylvanus Merrill of Rowley, June 10, 1829.*

Mary, and Jonathan Tharly, Dec. 22, 1685.

Mary [d. Daniel, deceased. int.], and James Freeze, June 2, 1697.*

Mary, and John Sawyer, Dec. 25, 1700.

Mary, and Jonathan Morss, Oct. 27, 1731.*

Mary, and William [Nathan. int.] Barker of Andover, May 13, 1742.*

Mary, and Jonathan Merrill, Jan. 13, 1757.*

Mary, of Rowley, and Moses Atkinson, at Rowley, May 19, 1757.*

Mary, and Daniel Bayley, Oct. 31, 1779.*

Mary, and Enoch Toppan, Aug. 19, 1797.*

Mary, of Newburyport, and Henry Mowatt, int. Nov. 11, 1803.

Mary, and Joseph Jackman, June 28, 1810.*

Mary, and Wingate Lane, May 2, 1839.*

Mary A., and Ebenezer G. Hayes of Newburyport, int. July 4, 1847.

Mary Ann, and Eliphalet Green. Apr. 19, 1827.*

Mary J., a. 29 y., b. Deerfield. d. Joseph and Nancy, and Newell H. Haynes of Stoneham. a. 30 y., mechanic, b. Epsom, s. Caleb B. and Sarah, Nov. 29. 1849.*

*Intention also recorded.

MERRILL, Mary S[omerby. c. r. 10.], and Albert Brookings,
    Apr. 17, 1830.*
Molly, and Cutting Moulton, May 29, 1773.*
Molly, and Watts Emerson of Hampstead, Apr. 2, 1794.*
Moody, of Amesbury, and Mary Jane Perkins, Dec. 25, 1840.*
Moses [jr. int.], and Mary Plumer [jr. int.], Apr. 5, 1743.*
Moses, and Phebe Coffin, Apr. 7, 1757.*
Moses, and Betsey Russel of Bradford, int. Aug. 28, 1802.
Moses, of Salisbury, and Loruhamah Collins Bartlet, June 24,
    1811.*
Nancy, and Stephen Jackman, June 22, 1828.
Nathan, and Hannah Kent, Sept. 6, 1699.*
Nathan, and Elisabeth Willit, Aug. 18, 1731.*
Nathan, and Ednah Griffen, Dec. 25, 1760.*
Nathan, jr., and Sarah Merrill, Dec. 15, 1785.*
Nathan, 3d, and Mary Carr of Newburyport, int. Nov. 7, 1797.
Nathaniel, and Hannah Stevens of Amesbury, at Amesbury,
    July 28, 1709.*
Nathaniel, of Newburyport, and Eliza Shepherd, int. July 7,
    1809.
Nathaniel K., and Susan M. Knap, July 21, 1825.*
Olive, of Londonderry, N. H., and William French, int. Apr.
    2, 1808.
Olive, and Frederic Haynes, Sept. 6, 1824.*
Orlando B., and Hannah Poor, int. Dec. 10, 1791.
Orlando Bagley, Capt., and Salley Leonard of Newburyport,
    int. Sept. 25, 1802.
Peter, and Sarah Hasletine, Sept. 25, 1717.*
Priscila, and Dr. Ezekel Chase of Groton, May 20, 1729.*
Priscilla, and Nathaniel Noyes, int. June 8, 1704.
Priscilla, and Henry Knight, Dec. 5, 1722.*
Priscilla, and George Knight [jr. int.] of Falmouth, Nov. 16,
    1769.*
Priscilla, and Daniel Bartlet, May 31, 1770.*
Priscilla, and Samuel Chase, Nov. 25, 1779.*
Prudence [d. Dea. Abraham. int.], and John Bartlet, 4th [3d.
    int.], Nov. 25, 1702.*
Rich[ar]d, and Mary Pilsbury, Dec. 24, 1755.*
Roger, and Mary Hale, Mar. 10, 1730-31.*
Roger, and Sarah Johnston of Amesbury, int. Sept. 9, 1774.
Ruth, and John Sanders, jr. of Haverhill [at Haverhill. dup.],
    May 6, 1756.*

*Intention also recorded.

MERRILL, Sally, and Tristram Coffin, jr., Jan. 3, 1792.*

Sally, of Rowley, and Daniel Rogers Currier, int. Dec. 31, 1808.

Sally, and Charles Moody, Esq., of Minot, Me., June 13, 1826.*

Sally, Mrs., and Nathaniel Chase, Feb. 22, 1835.*

Samuel, jr., and Tabitha Flanders, Jan. 1, 1746-7.*

Samuel, jr., and Mary Chase, Apr. 14, 1813.*

Samuel, 3d, and Mary J. Varnum, Oct. 28, 1841.*

Samuel, jr., and Hannah Martin of Newburyport, int. Apr. 25, 1846.

Sarah [d. Daniel. int.], and Willi[am] Morss, May 12, 1696.*

Sarah, d. Abraham, sr., and Joseph Morss, int. Oct. 7, 1696.

Sarah, and Edmund Titcomb, July 29, 1730.*

Sarah, and John Knight of Plaistow, N. H., Nov. 7, 1751.*

Sarah, and Mayo Greenleaf, Dec. 19, 1751.*

Sarah, and Jesse Plumer, Sept. 13, 1763.*

Sarah, and Nathan Woodman, May 26, 1771.*

Sarah, and Obadiah Hills, Jan. 13, 1774.*

Sarah, and Amos Whitmore, Feb. 13, 1780.*

Sarah, and Nathan Merrill, jr., Dec. 15, 1785.*

Sarah, and Moses Bayley, jr., int. Feb. 18, 1803.

Sarah, of Rumney, N. H., and Samuel Chase, jr., int. Jan. 30, 1808.

Sarah, and Stephen Chase of Plaistow, N. H., int. Feb. 5, 1819.

Sarah, and Joseph R. Wells, int. Jan. 26, 1833.

Sarah, a. 24 y., d. Thomas and Abigail, and Otis Delano, a. 24 y., caulker, b. Medford, s. Charles and Bethiah, of Medford, Oct. 8, 1846.*

Sarah Ann, and Samuel C. Currier, int. Oct. 1, 1837.

Sarah J., and David R. Winkley of Newburyport, int. May 10, 1842.

Sarah P., and Frederick Bartlet, int. June 9, 1838.

Stephen, and Elisabeth Bailey, Nov. 4, 1731.*

Stephen, and Mary Bricket, Sept. 25, 1756.*

Stephen, and Anna Bayley of Tewksbury, int. July 13, 1777.

Susan F., a. 26 y., d. Jonathan and Sally, and John P. McQuillen, a. 26 y., shipwright, s. David P. and Sophia, Oct. 5, 1845.*

Susana, and Benjamin Morss, jr., Jan. 28, 1691-2.

Susanna, and John Burbank, Oct. 15, 1663.

MERRILL, Susanna, and Ebenezer Whitmore, Apr. 14, 1784.*
Susanna, and Simeon Welch of Plaistow, May 26, 1799.*
Sylvanus, of Rowley, and Martha F. Merrill, June 10, 1829.*
Thomas, and Judith Kent, Mar. 16, 1704.*
Thomas, and Abigail Bartlet, June 19, 1729.*
Thomas, and Nabby [Abigail. int.] Hale, July —, 1792.*
Thomas, and Abigail Coffin Dutton, Jan. 8, 1809.*
Thomas, of Rowley, and Caroline Saffrodini, Sept. 23, 1829.*
Thomas, jr., and Harriet Currier, Feb. 6, 1833.*
William, of Freeport, and Anna Merrill, Oct. 17, 1797.*
William, and Betsey Coffin, Sept. 30, 1802.*
Will[ia]m, jr., and Rebecca Coffin, Sept. 12, 1813.*
W[illia]m, 3d, and Betsey Edwards of Salisbury, int. Apr. 13, 1827.
William C., and Anna Goodwin, int. Nov. 3, 1845.
William C., widr., of Newburyport, a. 25 y., shipwright, b. Newburyport, s. Jacob and Dorothy S., and Sarah M. Frost of Newburyport, a. 21 y., b. Newburyport, d. Dependance and Jemima L., June 21, 1847.
William C., a. 39 y., shipwright, s. William and Betsy, and Eleanor P. Jackman, a. 39 y., d. Matthias and Abigail, Jan. 13, 1848.*
W[illia]m G., and Eliza A. Pearson of Newburyport, int. Oct. 9, 1847.
William T., of Newburyport, and Lavina Currier, int. Nov. 7, 1846.

MERROW (see also Marrow), James, and Judith E. Reed, int. Sept. 26, 1830.

MERRYL (see also Merrill), Benjamin, and Hannah Bartlet, Feb. 23, 1729-30. C. R. 7.
Deborah, and Thomas Brown, Nov. 14, 1727. C. R. 7.
Judith, and Gideon Downer, Mar. 28, 1729. C. R. 7.
Peter, and Mary Bayley, Feb. 8, 1725-6. C. R. 7.
Peter, and Priscilla Annis, Mar. 10, 1730-31. C. R. 7.
Ruth, of Salisbury, and John Whitton of Arundel, Oct. 21, 1729. C. R. 7.
Ruth, and Christopher Annis, Dec. 3, 1730. C. R. 7.
Sarah, and Seth Bartlet, Nov. 19, 1728. C. R. 7.

*Intention also recorded.

METCALFE, Joseph, jr., of Ipswich, and Deborah Searle of Byfield Rowley, Dec. 4, 1765.

MICHEL (see also Mitchell), Robert, of Newburyport, and Sarah Lunt, int. Sept. 13, 1794.

MICHILL (see also Mitchell), William, and Mary Sayer, Nov. 7, 1648.

MIDLETON, Susanah, and Edmund Chany [jr. int.], Oct. 9, 1740.*

MIGHELL (see also Mighill), Elisabeth, of Rowley, and Daniel Moody, int. Nov. 7, 1799.

MIGHIL (see also Mighill), Dinah, servant of Rev. Christopher Toppan, and Mark Sneling of Boxford, int. Sept. 21, 1745.

MIGHILL (see also Mighell, Mighil, Myghil), Elisabeth, and Samuel Brookins, jr., int. Apr. 5, 1772.
Elizabeth, of Rowley, and Daniel Moody, at Rowley, Nov. 24, 1799.
Ezekiel, and Mrs. Sarah Toppan, Oct. 9, 1735.*
Hannah, of Rowley, and Nathan Little, at Rowley, Nov. 12, 1741.*
Nathaniel, of Rowley, and Judith Dole, int. Aug. 28, 1776.
Sarah, d. Stephen, of Rowley, deceased, and Jonathan Woodman, s. Joshua, int. June 5, 1700.
Sarah, of Rowley, and Parker Noyes, at Rowley, Nov. 7, 1734.*
Sarah, and Samuel True of Salisbury, int. Aug. 27, 1772.

MILBERY, William, Capt., of Newburyport, and Abigail Fowler, Oct. 14, 1792.*

MILES, George W., and Julia Ann Evans, Sept. 27, 1832.*
Noah, Rev., of Temple [N. H. int.], and Jane Pearson, Nov. 16, 1789.*

MILK, Mary, of Falmouth, in Casco Bay, and Moses Little, 3d, Aug. 15, 1757.*

*Intention also recorded.

MILLAR (see also Miller), William, and Lydia Chase, Feb. 7, 1809.*

MILLER (see also Millar), Alice, of Boston, and Arthur Weaver of Tanton, Dean, Eng., now of Boston, woolen manufacturer, Oct. 12, 1726. c. r. 7.
Hannah, Mrs., and Edward Holland, Dec. 17, 1744.*
Hannah J., and John Harmon, int. July 1, 1826.
Lydia, and Thomas Downs, int. Apr. 4, 1821.
Lydia, and Benjamin Jackman, int. Oct. 5, 1822.
Nathaniel [Millerd. c. r. 2.], of Rehoboth, and Ruth Chase, May 29, 1716.*

MILLIKEN, Edward, baker, and Abigail Norman, both of Boston, July 29, 1726. c. r. 7.

MILLWARD (see also Milward), Elizabeth, and Daniell Peirce, Dec. 5, 1660.

MILTIMORE (see also Multimore), Andrew W[illiam. c. r. 10.], Capt., and Sarah B[artlett. c. r. 10.] Wiggin of Strathram, N. H., May 13, 1827.*
Mary L[ane. c. r. 10], and Moses L[ittle. c. r. 10.] Hale of Boston, May 13, 1824.*

MILTON, Hannah, Mrs., and Charles Bartlett, Apr. 15, 1827.*
Henrietta, and Joseph Moulton, int. Feb. 22, 1828.
John, and Hannah Persons, Nov. 9, 1802.*
Sarah P., and Benja[min] P. Floyd, Nov. 13, 1834.*

MILWARD (see also Millward), Anne, and Daniell Peirce, Dec. 26, 1654.

MINAH (see also Miner), Mary, and Samuel Marsh, int. Mar. 27, 1790.

MINER (see also Minah), Mary, of Newburyport, and John Poor, int. Dec. 16, 1809.

MINGO, Rob[er]t, and Eliza Cane, Sept. 27, 1687. ct. r.
Thomas, of Haverhill, and Lydia Tyre, May 4, 1737.*

MINOT, Pamelia, and Parker Bailey, int. Nov. 10, 1832.

*Intention also recorded.

MIRECK (see also Merrick), Anna, and Nath[anie]ll Foster, Jan. 1, 1756.*

Hannah, and Thomas Jillings, Nov. 18, 1725.*

Jacob, and Sarah Stickne of Hampton, int. Dec. 25, 1734.

Jacob, and Dorothy Merrill, June 23, 1763.*

[John. int.], and Ann Macclure, Sept. 2, 1725.*

Joseph, and Lydia Brown, Jan. 6, 1735-6.*

Lydia, and Daniel Richardson, July 27, 1761. [He "takes said Lydia naked, viz., without any of her late husband's Estate." int.]*

Mary, and Samuel Chooke, Apr. 16, 1714. C. R. 7.*

Mary, and Samuel Huse, July 14, 1726.*

Mary, and Nathaniel Knap, jr., June 14, 1757.*

Sarah, and William Stevens, June 12, 1759.*

William, and Elisabeth Hayes, Oct. 15, 1730.*

William, and Mrs. Rachel Anderton, Oct. 31, 1745.*

William, and Elisabeth Bayley, Oct. 24, 1765.*

MIRICK (see also Merrick), Elisabeth, and Eliphalet Noyes, July 7, 1770.*

Isaac, Capt., and Mrs. Martha Trinda of Andover, int. Nov. 24, 1714.

MIRRICK (see also Merrick), Timothy, and Mary Lanchester, d. Joseph, of Amesbury, int. May 9, 1696.

MIRRICKE (see also Merrick), Sara, and John Atkins [Attkinson. CT. R.], Apr. 27, 1664.

MISSILLOWAY (see also Silloway), Daniel, and Anne Chase, sr., June 14, 1672.

MITCHEL (see also Mitchell), Joanna, and George Goodhue, jr. of Newburyport, int. Aug. 27, 1768.

John, and Elizabeth Coker, Mar. 11, 1724-5. C. R. 7.

Lydia, and Benjamin Gage, Dec. 31, 1764.*

Martha, and John Jones of Rochester, Co. Kent, Eng., Mar. 25, 1744. C. R. 7.

Mary, and John Brown, jr., Oct. 15, 1795.*

Phebe, and Daniel Ballard, both of Boston, Apr. 27, 1727. C. R. 7.

Sarah, and Robert Becket [jr. int.] of Gloucester, Dec. 16, 1756.*

Sarah, and William Bradbury of Milford, int. Jan. 16, 1805.

*Intention also recorded.

MITCHEL, Stephen, and Mrs. Katherine Brown, Jan. 4, 1774.
[Said Stephen takes said Katharine naked and so will not
be obliged to pay any of her former husband's debts. int.]*
Susanna [Joanna. c. R. 1.], and George Goodhue, jr. of Newburyport, Sept. 20, 1768.

MITCHELL (see also Michel, Michill, Mitchel, Mitchil,
Mitchill, Mitchel), Jane, and Benjamin Cole, June 18,
1752.*
Joseph, and Rachel Haskell, Feb. 7, 1786.*
Joshua, and Allis Holt, Mar. 10, 1756.*
Robert, and Mary Cross [of Ipswich. int.], Dec 2, 1731.*

MITCHIL (see also Mitchell), Benjamin, and Mehitable Brag-
den of York, int. Jan. 22, 1736-7.
Johannah, and Joseph Goodhue, int. Mar. 1, 1745-6.
John, and Mary Choak, Sept. 18, 1746.*
Joshua, and Esther Swett, int. Jan. 15, 1736-7.
Robert, and Anna Foster of Ipswich, int. June 7, 1746.

MITCHILL (see also Mitchell), Grace [wid. int.], and Mat-
thew Mackanetene [of Haverhill. int.], Feb. 10, 1700.*
John, and Hannah Spaford, May 20, 1680.
John, and Constance Mooers, Nov. 15, 1697.*
Lydia, Mrs., and William Cooch, jr., Nov. 11, 1741.*
Mary, and Robert Savory, Dec. 8, 1656.

MIX, Elizabeth, and John Pearson, at Stonington, Mar. 24,
1714.

MIXER, Mary J., of Newton, and Charles A. Currier, int.
Nov. 18, 1848.

MOAR (see also Moores), Mehittabel, of Andover, and Emery Chase, at Andover, July 25, 1768.*

MOERS (see also Moores), Bethiah, and David Parsons [of
Kingston. int.], Mar. 22, 1750.*
Edmund, jr., and Judith Pilsbury, Jan. 13, 1704.*
Elisabeth, and Thomas Chase [sr. int.], Aug. 2, 1714.*
Jonathan, and Mary Poor, Jan. 7, 1714-15.*
Jonathan, of Newburyport, and Mary Freeze, int. Oct. 18,
1766.
Jonathan, and Dorothy Lunt, Jan. 22, 1771.*

*Intention also recorded.

MOERS, Joseph, and Sarah Davis, int. 'Aug. 12, 1734.
Mark, and Sarah Thirla, May 14, 1712.*
Mary, and John Rolfe, Nov. 2, 1758.*
Mary, and Stephen Jackman, Mar. 30, 1763.*
Peter, and Sarah Noyes, int. Sept. 12, 1713.
Sarah, and Daniel Merrill, jr., May 20, 1725.*
Susanna, and John Follinsbey, Nov. 20, 1760.*

MOET (see also Mowatt), Henry [Mowat. int.], and Lydia˙ Merrill, Mar. 22, 1801.* .

MOGRIDGE (see also Morgaridge), Samuell, and Mary West, May 1, 1724.*

MOLTON (see also Moulton), Lydia, and Nathan Chase, Nov. 24, 1747. c. r. 2.*

MONTGOMERY, Nathaniel, and Mrs. Sarah Moodey, Dec. 15, 1742.*

MOODEY (see also Moody), Abigail, and Josiah Emery, Nov. 25, 1714.*
Abigail, and Isaac Ilsley, Mar. 16, 1720-21.*
Abigail, and Benjamin Greenleaf, Aug. 26, 1726.*
Abigail, Mrs., and Daniel Noyes, Apr. 12, 1739.*
Abigall, of Salisbury, and John Greenlief [jr. int.], at Salisbury, May 7, 1713.*
Ann, and Joseph Knight, Jan. 21, 1747-8.*
Apphia, and Samuel Hale, Aug. 26, 1714.*
Benjamin, and Anne Bradstreet, Nov. 7, 1728.*
Caleb, jr., and Ruth Morse, Dec. 9, 1690.
Caleb [jr. int.], and Tabitha Lunt, Jan. 1, 1722-3.*
Caleb, jr., and Elisabeth Emery, June 15, 1727.*
Cutting, and Judith Little [d. Lt. Joseph. int.], Mar. 25, 1696.*
Cutting, jr., and Martha Smith, Dec. 8, 1742.*
Dorothy, and David Woodman, Nov. 30, 1710.*
Dorothy, and Samuel Toppan, jr., Dec. 5, 1733.*
Edmund, and Mary Jackson of Kittery, int. Mar. 17, 1732.
Elisabeth, and James Smith, Dec. 10, 1719.*
Elisabeth, and John Dow, Jan. 29, 1735-6.*
Elizabeth, and Enoch Titcomb, Jan. 1, 1718-19.*
Ellenor, and James Bridges of Andover, Dec. 28, 1721.*
Ezra, and Martha Greenleaf, Apr. 26, 1716.*
Hannah, and Samuell Tenney of Bradford, Jan. 26, 1709.*

*Intention also recorded.

MOODEY, Hannah, and Thomas Bartlet, Nov. —, 1718.*
Hannah, and Ebenezer Person of Lynn, Sept. 14, 1721.*
Hannah, Mrs., and John Lunt, mariner, of Poolton, parish of
    Wallasy, Cheshire, Eng., Aug. 17, 1747. C. R. 7.
John, and Hannah Dole, May 18, 1692. CT. R.
John, jr., and Hannah Toppan, Apr. 3, 1729.*
Joseph, and Judith Kelly, Nov. 27, 1722.*
Joshua, and Mary Greenleaf, d. Capt. Stephen, sr., deceased,
    int. May 1, 1696.
Joshua, and Mrs. Elizbeth Allin of Salisbury [Hampton. int.],
    at Salisbury, June 23, 1715.*
Joshua, jr., and Abigail Atkinson, Apr. 8, 1725.*
Judeth, and Joshua Greenleaf, Nov. 23, 1736.*
Judeth, Mrs., and Theophilus Bradbury, Mar. 28, 1744.*
Judith, and John Toppan, int. Oct. 25, 1704.
Judith, and Anthoney Morse, int. Apr. 19, 1710.
Judith, and Francis Follinsby, Dec. 15, 1719.*
Lidia, Mrs., and Thomas Clark, Oct. 17, 1705.*
Martha, and Jonathan Gage, Apr. 27, 1730.*
Mary, d. Sergt. Caleb, deceased, and Joseph Hale, int. Dec. 25,
    1699.
Mary, and Peter Ordway, Oct. 29, 1719.*
Mary, and Samuel Greenleaf, Oct. 3. 1721.*
Mary, and David Marsh of Haverhill, Aug. 16, 1722.*
Mary, and Moses Gerrish, jr., Apr. 18; 1728.*
Mary, and Ezekiel Hale, Sept. 6, 1743.*
Mary, and Ephraim Pettingill, int. Oct. 13, 1744.
Mary, Mrs., and Capt. John Brett, Sept. 10, 1747.*
Mehitabel, Mrs., and Enoch Coffin, Jan. 5, 1715-16.*
Mehitable, and Andrew Wiggins of Stratham, Sept. 22, 1743.*
Moses, and Elisabeth Sewall, Sept. 11, 1734.*
Moses, and Rebecca Somerby, Feb. 12, 1735-6.*
Moses, and Elisabeth Jaques, June 12, 1744.*
Oliver, and Martha Noyes, Feb. 28, 1723-4.*
Onner, and Jonathan Rolf, May 21, 1731.*
Ruth, and James Carr, jr., Apr. 25, 1712.*
Samuel, and Mrs. Hanah Sewall, int. July 15, 1698.
Samuel, and Sarah Knight, Apr. 16, 1700.*
Samuel [3d. int.], and Elizabeth Gerrish, Aug. 12, 1739.*
Sarah, and Daniell Greenleaf, Nov. 17, 1710.*
Sarah, and Daniel Sawyer, Apr. 2, 1714.*
Sarah, and John Pike, jr., Feb. 17, 1731-2.*
Sarah, and Nelson Racklyeff of Falmouth. Nov. 27, 1739.*
Sarah, Mrs., and Nathaniel Montgomery, Dec. 15, 1742.*
Steven, and Ann Lunt, May 9, 1734. C. R. 7.

*Intention also recorded.

MOODEY, Tho[mas], and Judeth Hale, Nov. 24, 1692. CT. R.
Thomas [jr. int.], and Rebecka Poor, Oct. 26, 1727.*
William, Dea., and Mrs. Abigail Frier of Berwick, int. Dec.
11, 1714.
William [jr. int.], and Anna Hale, Dec. —, 1728.*
William, jr., and Judeth Poor, Apr. 23, 1741.*

MOODY (see also Moodey), Alice, and William Polleys, Nov.
17, 1787.*
Ann, and John Carr, jr., July 28, 1738.*
Ann M., and Dr. Isaac G. Braman of Georgetown, int. Mar.
5, 1839.
Anna, and Moses Johnson, Apr. 20, 1758.*
Anna, of Newburyport, and Amos Emery, int. Jan. 9, 1784.
Anna, and Richard Bartlet, Sept. 25, 1787.*
Benja[min], jr., and Hannah Glazier, Dec. 1, 1763. c. R. 9.*
Benjamin, sr., and Elisabeth Gould of Dunstable, int. Aug. 28,
1781.
Benja[min], jr., of Newburyport, and Sarah Titcomb, int.
Aug. 13, 1824.
Caleb, and Sara Peirce, Aug. 24, 1659.
Caleb, and Judith Bradbury, Nov. 9, 1665.
Caleb, 3d, and Dorothy Sergeant of Amesbury, int. Nov. 9,
1754.
Caleb, jr., and [Mrs. c. R. 2.] Abigail Bayley, June 3, 1756.*
Charles, and Lydia Atkinson, Nov. 24, 1802.*
Charles, Esq., of Minot, Me., and Sally Merrill, June 13,
1826.*
Cutting, and Dorothy Bartlet, Dec. [15. c. R. 7.], 1737.
Cutting, and Hannah Pilsbury, Dec. 3, 1772.*
Cutting, jr., of Amesbury, and Molly Tenney, int. Apr. 17,
1807.
Daniel, and Elizabeth Mighill of Rowley, at Rowley, Nov. 24,
1799.*
Daniel, and Eunice Boardman of Newburyport, int. Mar. 19,
1807.
Daniell, and Elizabeth Somerby, Mar. 29, 1683.
David, and Mary Johnson, Oct. 13, 1757.*
David, and Emily Corson of Exeter, N. H., ——, 1834. [Dec.
26, 1833. int.]*
Deborah, and Shubael Dummer of Salem, Mar. 1, 1808.*
Dolly, and Lt. Joshua Brown, July 25, 1799.*
Ebenezer, and Lydia Bartlett, Nov. 6, 1784.*
Ebenezer, and Lucy Wood of Bradford, int. Jan. 5, 1810.
Elisabeth, and Parker Titcomb, Jan. 1, 1754.*
Elisabeth, and Nathaniell Knap, Sept. 18, 1754.*

*Intention also recorded.

MOODY, Elisabeth, and Joseph Motey, A. M., [at the Dummer school. int.], Apr. 12, 1780.*

Elisabeth, and Jonathan Stickney, July 28, 1782.*

Eliza, and Joseph Little, Oct. 18, 1820. C. R. 1.

Elizabeth, and Joseph Ridgway, Dec. 22, 1794.*

Elizabeth, and Joseph Little, Oct. 18, 1821.*

Elizabeth T., and Benjamin E. Hoyt of Ipswich, int. Aug. 27, 1836.

Enoch, and Elisabeth Dow, Feb. 26, 1778.*

Enoch [jr. int.], and Ann Kent, Apr. 14, 1798.*

Enoch, 3d, and Salley Pilsbury of Newburyport, int. Apr. 11, 1801.

Enoch, and Mrs. Lydia Whitmore of Newburyport, Mar. 3, 1813.*

Enoch, of Hallowell, and Eunice Balch, Nov. —, 1816.*

Esther, and Michael Sumner of Newburyport, Apr. 7, 1807.*

Eunice B., and Joseph Williams, int. May 12, 1841.

Hannah, and Dr. Enoch Sawyer, jr., Mar. 30, 1758.*

Hannah, and Edmund Sawyer, Nov. 10, 1763.*

Hannah, and John Blydenburgh, M. A., Feb. 26, 1779.*

Hannah, and Amos Little, Nov. 8, 1785.*

Hannah, and Paul P. Downer, Mar. —, 1811.*

Hannah, and Jacob Martin, int. May 26, 1827.

Henry P., and Jane L. Brown, int. Oct. 31, 1846.

Hitty, and Jeremiah Dummer of Hallowell, May 1, 1792.*

Jacob, and Susanna Noyes, Jan. 4, 1784.*

Jane, and Matthew Lunt, int. Feb. 6, 1741-2.

Jane, and Sewal Short, Mar. 21, 1762.*

Jane, and Joseph Kent, Aug. 23, 1768.*

Jane, and [Ens. int.] Samuel Noyes, 3d, Jan. 22, 1795.*

Jemima, and James Hidden of Rowley, at Rowley, Sept. 26, 1748.*

Jeremiah S., a. 26 y., house carpenter, s. Daniel and Jemima. of Newburyport, and Sarah E. Burns, a. 20 y., d. John and Loretta, May 4, 1848.*

John, and Mirriam Emery, Oct. 18, 1750.*

John, and Mary Little, Mar. 9, 1762.*

Joseph, and Elizabeth Moore of York, int. Aug. 24, 1752.

Joseph, of Amesbury, and Anna Tenny. Dec. 8, 1779.*

Joseph. jr., of Amesbury, and Betsey Woodman, int. July 27, 1811.

Joseph, and Hannah M. Goodrich, int. Mar. 6. 1841.

Joshua [jr. int.], and Sarah Dole, May 4, 1758.*

Joshua, of Cornville, Me., and Mrs. Sally Coffin, Jan. 5, 1836.*

Judith, and George Knight, Feb. 3. 1725-6.*

Judith, and John Smith, Apr. 10, 1766.

*Intention also recorded.

MOODY, Judith, of Salisbury, and John Coffin, at Salisbury, July 14, 1799.*
Judith T., and Samuel Moody of New York, int. Oct. 12, 1841.
Lucy, and Thomas Saunders of Gloucester, Nov. 29, 1780.*
Lydia, and Enoch Adams of East Andover, Jan. 30, 1803.*
Martha, and Daniel Dodge, both of Newburyport, Dec. 3, 1769.
Martha, of Salisbury, and Thomas Moody, int. Nov. 26, 1783.
Mary, and Daniel Lunt, June 24, 1679.
Mary, and Henry Somerby, June 26, 1683.
Mary, Mrs., and [Rev. int.] Moses Hale, Sept. 4, 1707.*
Mary, and Bulkley Emerson, July 13, 1752.*
Mary, and John Dane, Oct. 29, 1761.*
Mary, and Jonathan Morss of Newburyport, Aug. 20, 1776.*
Mary, of Newburyport, and Edmund Coffin, int. Sept. 15, 1792.
Mary, and Robert Reed of Litchfield, N. H., Feb. 24, 1820.*
Mary, and Paul Ilsley, jr., Oct. 18, 1821.*
Mary H., of Newburyport, and Edmund Smith, Esq., int. Sept. 26, 1847.
Mary J., and Thomas M. Moody, Dec. 5, 1830.*
Molly, and Nathaniel Moody, May 10, 1794.*
Moses [jr. C. R. 1.], and Hannah Poor, May 28, 1775.*
Moses, 3d, and Elizabeth Elliot of Haverhill, int. Feb. 12, 1780.
Moses, of Newburyport, and Patience Toppan, May 20, 1784.*
Moses, jr., and Betsey Brown of Newburyport, int. Apr. 4, 1806.
Moses S., Capt., and Ruth Ordway, June 4, 1795.*
Moses Sargent, and Susanna Brown, May 15, 1783.*
Moses Sargent [Capt. C. R. 2.], and Sarah Dean, Sept. 15, 1787.*
Nathaniel, and Molly Moody, May 10, 1794.*
Nathaniel, and Rebecca Bartlet of Campton, N. H., int. Mar. 25, 1831.
Oliver, jr., and Sarah Tilton, Mar. 12, 1753.*
Paul, jr., and Susannah Morrill of Amesbury, int. June 25, 1800.
Paul, and Eunice Thurlow, Nov. 30, 1823.*
Rebecca, and Jonathan Boardman, Mar. 12, 1761.*
Ruth, and Moses Pike, Nov. 19, 1767.*
Salley, and Josiah Bartlet, Apr. 23, 1801.*
Sally, and Stephen Pilsbury of Newburyport, May 21, 1801.*
Sally, and Moses Newell, Sept. 21, 1816. [1815. C. R. 2.]*
Sally, and John Dane of Andover, May 6, 1828.*
Samuel, and Mary Cutting, Nov. 30, 1657.
Samuel, jr., and Jane Dole of Salisbury, int. Jan. 11, 1765.

*Intention also recorded.

MOODY, Samuel, Col., and Sarah Cushing of Salisbury, int. May 13, 1779.
Samuel [jr. C. R. 2.], and Hannah Emery, Apr. 25, 1790.*
Samuel, of Hallowell, and Sarah Sawyer, June 17, 1797.*
Samuel, of Newburyport, and Olive Weymouth, Dec. 22, 1831.*
Samuel, of New York, and Judith T. Moody, int. Oct. 12, 1841.
Samuel S., and Emeline Pike of Rowley, int. June 17, 1828.
Sara, and Silvanus Plumer, Jan. 18, 1681.
Sarah, and Hugh March, Mar. 29, 1683.
Sarah, and Benjamin Davis [jr. int.], Mar. 27, 1753.*
Sarah, and Stephen Emery, 3d, Nov. 6, 1760.*
Sarah, and Samuel Tufts, Nov. 24, 1762.*
Sarah, and Asa Strong of Coventry Conn., June 9, 1763.*
Sarah, and Capt. Joseph Huse of Newburyport, Mar. 5, 1776.*
Sarah, and Thomas Huse, Jan. 2, 1777.*
Sarah, and John Plumer, Apr. 24, 1796.*
Sarah, and Samuel Downer, ——, 1808. [Apr. 16. int.]*
Sarah J., of Newburyport, a. 18 y., d. Henry and Jane, of Newburyport, and Sewell B. Noyes, a. 20 y., mason, s. Timothy and Sarah, July 12, 1846.
Sewel, and Judith Longfellow, June 6, 1799.*
Silas, Esq., and Mary Huse of Newburyport, Sept. 5, 1841.*
Somerby, and Luice Patten of Sheepscote, int. July 12, 1755.
Thomas, and Martha Moody of Salisbury, int. Nov. 26, 1783.
Thomas, of Newburyport, and Mrs. Sarah Dole Bray, July 21, 1817.*
Thomas M., and Mary J. Moody, Dec. 5, 1830.*
Timothy, resident in Newbury, and Peach Grenold, servant of Capt. Daniel Marquand, int. Dec. 24, 1749.
William, and Mehatabell Sewall, Nov. 15, 1684.
William, and Sarah Noyes, July 18, 1755.*
William, 4th, and Jane Titcomb, Nov. 13, 1760.*
William, and Abigail Burbank, June 1, 1773.*
William, jr., and Sarah Kimbal of Exeter, Oct. 18, 1787.*
William [jr. int.], and Abigail Titcomb. July 11, 1803.*
William, jr., and Almira Kimball of Boxford, int. Oct. 13, 1825.
William [jr. int.], of Newburyport, and Martha Titcomb, Oct. 4, 1832.*
William, and Rebecca Gray of Rowley, int. Sept. 22, 1835.

MOOERS (see also Moores), Ammi Ruhamah, and Jane Osillaway, July 8, 1751. C. R. 2.*
Constance, and John Mitchill, Nov. 15, 1697.*

*Intention also recorded.

MOOERS, Daniel, and Abigail Springer of Haverhill, at Haverhill, Jan. 4, 1753.*

Francis, Dr., of Cambridge, and Abigail Boylston of Charlestown, Jan. 1, 1733-4. C. R. 7.

Martha, and Thomas Look of Rowley, Feb. 13, 1716-17.

MOOR (see also Moores), Abraham, Rev.. and Sally Hook
[of Salisbury. int.], at Salisbury, May 10, 1796.*

Adams, M. D., of Littleton, N. H., and Maria Little, Aug. 14,
1843.*

Catharine W., of Derry, N. H., and George J. Warner, int.
May 25, 1848.

Margaret, of Kittery, and Epps Greenough, int. Dec. 11,
1730.

Mary, and Sam[ue]ll Gregg, both of Londonderry, Sept. 22,
1731. C. R. 7.

Sarah, and Henry Woodnott, sailor, both of Boston, Oct. 30,
1730. C. R. 7.

MOORCOCK, John, of Boston, and Mary Pike, int. Sept. 27,
1708.

MOORE (see also Moores), Adams, of Littleton, N. H., and
Anna Mary Little, int. May 9, 1829.

Elizabeth, of York, and Joseph Moody, int. Aug. 24, 1752.

Jonathan, and Elizabeth Woodhead of Cambridge, at Cambridge, Aug. 14, 1701.

Laura, of Ipswich, and Aaron Goodwin of Essex, Nov. 27,
1839.

Mathew, and Sara Laroy [Lary. CT. R.], Mar. 27, 1662.

MOORES (see also Moar, Moers, Mooers. Moor, Moore,
Moors. More, Mores), Benjamin, and Hannah Moores,
Feb. 22, 1763.

Dorcas, of Newburyport, and Francis Ellison, Sept. 19, 1810.*

Edmund. and Sarah [Coopper. in pencil. and CT. R.], Jan. 2,
1676.

Edmund. and Abigail Savory. Dec. 24, 1735.*

Greenleaf, and Elizabeth Woodbury, Apr. 14. 1810.*

Hannah. and Benjamin Moores. Feb. 22. 1763.

Jonathan. and Constance Longhorne. abt. May 10. 1670.

Martha. and Joseph Goodridg. Aug. 28, 166[4?].

Mary, and Caleb Boynton, June 24, 1672.

Mary, and Samuel Kenne. Feb. 29, 1711-12.*

Mary, and Thomas Chase. 3d. Sept. 3, 1724.*

Parker. and Mercy Lull of Byfield Rowley. May 20. 1762.

Samuell, and Mary Ilsly. Sept. 12. 1656.

MOORS (see also Moores), Jenny, of Haverhill, and Joshua Merrill, at Haverhill, Mar. 4, 1775.*
Jonathan, jr., and Bethia Bishop, Oct. 16, 1741.*
Lydia, and Enoch Rogers of Newburyport, July 11, 1771.
Mark, jr., and Ruth Greenleaf, July 24, 1735.*
Ruth, and Jonathan Thorla, both of Byfield Rowley, Nov. 16, 1758.
Samuell, and Hanna Plumer, May 3, 1653.

MORE (see also Moores), Mary, of Salem, and Moses Hale, at Salem, Nov. 21, 1763.*

MORES (see also Moores), Abigail, and Joseph Wadley of Hanover, int. Feb. 27, 1802.
Abigail, and Isaac Bartlet, jr., int. Aug. 16, 1804.
Edmund [Morss. int. and c. R. 2.], and Mary Griffin, Jan. 16, 1728-9.*
Greenleaf, and Polly Poor, Nov. 12, 1795.*
Greenleaf, and Hannah Knight of Newburyport, int. Dec. 11, 1802.
Joseph K., and Martha Ordway, Feb. —, 1834.
Lydia, and Samuel Stickney, int. Oct. 2, 1804.
Mark, and Elisabeth March, Dec. 29, 1778.*
Moses, a. 45 y., laborer, s. John and Mary, and Elizabeth A. Stickney, Oct. 11, 1846.
Sally Elliot, and Richard Lurvey, int. May 18, 1822.
Stillman, and Mary Colman, Aug. 11, 1829.

MOREY, Elizebeth, Mrs., and Benjamin Flood, Apr. 22, 1741.*

MORGAN, Robert, resident in Newbury, and Abigail Coffin, July 13, 1727. c. R. 7.

MORGAREDGE (see also Morgaridge), Sarah, and Joseph Woodbridge, Dec. 15, 1746.*

MORGARIDGE (see also Maugridge, Mogridge, Morgaredge), Anna, and Samuel Remick, Oct. 20, 1765.*
Elisabeth, and Nath[anie]ll Knap, Jan. 19, 1763.*
John, and Sarah Pilsbury, Feb. 26, 1778.*
Mary, of Salisbury, and John Butler, int. Aug. 20, 1757.
William, and Abigail Pilsbury, int. May 28, 1771.

MORISON (see also Morrison), Allen, and Hannah Flood, Nov. 13, 1795.*
Daniel, and Mary Folesome of Exeter, int. Mar. 27, 1707.

*Intention also recorded.

MORLAND, Anna, and Stephen Coffin, Aug. 26, 1801.*
Martin [of Newburyport. int.], and Anna Dusten, Nov. 25, 1790.*

MORRIL (see also Morrill), Aphiah, and Joseph Swacey [Sweasy, jr. int.], Dec. 15, 1735. c. r. 7.*

MORRILL (see also Morril), Abigail, of Salisbury, and Henry Lunt, jr., int. Apr. 25, 1741.
Benjamin, and Elisabeth Pike, Mar. 15, 1757.*
Benjamin, of Pittsfield, and Lucy Wells, Feb. 7, 1815.*
Elisabeth, and David Dutson [Duston. int.], Mar. 23, 1743-4.*
Ellen D., of Newburyport, and John Little, int. Jan. 21, 1843.
Hannah, of South Hampton, and John Poor, int. Aug. 20, 1756.
Jacob, Capt., of Salisbury, and wid. Abigail Burbank, Apr. 9, 1771.*
Jemima, of Salisbury, and Joseph Pike, jr., at Salisbury, Jan. 18, 1720-21.
Jemima, Mrs., of Salisbury, and David B. Buffum of Amesbury, Oct. 30, 1839.
Joseph Hobson, of Boscawen, and Lydia Lunt, int. Nov. 19, 1804.
Mary True, and Henry Short, jr., Dec. 10, 1821.*
Orlando W., of Rowley, and Caroline Larkin, int. Oct. 22, 1831.
Peter, of Berwick, s. John and Hannah, both deceased, and Elizabeth Brown, wid. John, Dec. 21, 1782. c. r. 6.
Ruth, Mrs., and Joseph Morse, Jan. 17, 1839.*
Susannah, of Amesbury, and Paul Moody, jr., int. June 25, 1800.

MORRIS, Mary Rolf, of Newburyport, and Sewell Short, int. July 15, 1820.

MORRISON (see also Morison), Abigail, and Roger Chase, Mar. 16, 1725-6.*
Abigail L., of Sanbornton, N. H., and Samuel Lunt, jr., int. Jan. 18, 1828.
Daniel, and Abigail Kimbal of Rowley, int. Nov. 8, 1712.
Ebenezer, and Sarah Nowell, July 29, 1762.*
Ebenezer [jr. int.], of Newburyport, and Jane Somerby, Oct. 18, 1787.*
Elizabeth, Mrs., and Joseph Wilson, both of Newburyport, Dec. 31, 1821.
Emma, and John Lowden, Jan. 1, 1750.*
Hannah, and Moses Woodman, jr., May 29, 1761.*

MORRISON, Mary, and Charls Annis, Oct. 18, 1716.*
Mary, and Benjamin Stickny, both of Rowley, Oct. 2, 1750.
Michael, and Paulina Chipman, both of Newburyport, Oct. 20, 1794.
Spindelo, and Emma Kent, Apr. 3, 1740.*
William, and Mrs. Rachel Rogers, Nov. 21, 1744.*

MORRY (see also Murray), Mary, and Henry Short. [Dec.] —, 1821. c. R. 1.

MORS (see also Morse), Abel, and Grace Parker of Bradford, int. May 1, 1714.
Anthony, and Elizabeth Little, Jan. 21, 1717-18.
Anthony [jr. int.], and Sarah Ilsley, Dec. 22, 1721.*
Benjamin, and Ruth Sawyer, Aug. 27, 1667.
Benjamin, 3d, and Mercy Be[ll. int.], Jan. 22, 1712-13.*
Daniel, and Elisabeth Mors, June 20, 1720.
Daniell, and Sarah Swaine of Reading, at Reading, Aug. 17, 1727.
Elisabeth, and Daniel Mors, June 20, 1720.
Elisabeth, and Joseph Poor, Mar. 25, 1742.*
Hanah, and John Emery, jr., int. Feb. 2, 1704-5.
Hannah, and Nathaniell March, Mar. 6, 1717-18.
Hannah, and John Darling of Kingston, Oct. 18, 1738.*
Joseph [3d. int.], and Rebecca Adams, Dec. 22, 1721.*
Joseph, jr., and Mary Coker, Apr. 2, 1724.*
Joshua, and Prudence Ordway, Aug. 19, 1741.*
Josiah, of Chester, and Mary Chase, Oct. 27, 1743.*
Judeth, Mrs., and Enoch Stickne, Jan. 19, 1743-4.*
Lydia, and John Titcomb, Apr. 17, 1712.*
Mary, and Francis Browne, Dec. 31, 1679.
Mary, and Abner Brown of Salisbury, Sept. 23, 1713.*
Mary, and Nicholas Jackman, May 29, 1718.
Mary, and Nathan Sawyer [Feb. 5. int.], 1745-6.*
Meriam, and Barnabas Bradbury of Haverhill, Jan. 26, 1742-3.*
Moses, jr., and Sarah Chase, Sept. 15, 1743.*
Parker, and Mrs. Hannah Huse, Mar. 14, 1736-7.*
Priscilla, and Nathan[ie]ll Ordway, Aug. 14, 171[8. c. R. 2.].*
Ruth, and Abraham Chase, Nov. 16, 1716.*
Samuel, and Elizabeth March, Feb. 23, 1712-13.*
Sarah [d. Dea. Benjamin. int.], and Caleb Pilsbury, Feb. 11, 1703.*
Sarah [Mary. int.], and Daniel Parker of Bradford, Nov. 26, 1713.*
Sarah, and Jonathan Ilsley, Dec. 13, 1714.*
Sarah, and Stephen Brown, Feb. 26, 1721-2.*

*Intention also recorded.

Mors, Sarah, and Joseph Muzze, Mar. 31, 1724.*
Sarah [wid. c. r. 2.], and John Kent, jr., June 20, 1737.*
Sarah, and George Goodhue, Sept. 28, 1737.*
Sarah, and Josiah Ladd of Exeter, Jan. 3, 1737-8.*
Timoth[y], and Dorothy Pike, Dec. 22, 1721.*

MORSE (see also Mors, Morss, Moss), Abigail, and Joshua
    Bailey, Apr. 23, 1812.*
Abigail E., and Elbridge Merrill, June 7, 1837.*
Amelia, and David Jackman, jr., int. Oct. 21, 1804.
Amos, and Lucretia Dean of Exeter, int. Sept. 15, 1817.
Anna, and Cornelius Felton, June 1, 1806.*
Anne, and Francis Tharlay, Feb. 5, 1654.
Anne, and Soloman Springer of Haverhill [at Haverhill. dup.],
    July 30, 1752. c. r. 2.*
Anthoney, and Judith Moodey, int. Apr. 19, 1710.
Anthony, and Elizabeth Knight, May 8, 1660.
Anthony, and Mary Barnard, Nov. 10, 1669.
Anthony, and Sara Pike, Feb. 4, 1685.
Anthony, jr., and Betty Plats, Mar. 9, 1758.*
Charles C., of Bradford, a. 21 y., shoemaker, b. Bradford, s.
    Benjamin and Abigail, of Bradford, and Sarah A. Jack-
    man, a. 20 y., d. Joseph N. and Mary, June 3, 1846.*
Daniel, and Mary Chase, July 24, 1806.*
Daniel L., and Esther S. Merrill, int. Dec. 8, 1842.
Dolly [Dorothy. int.], and Asa Adams, July 1, 1795.*
Edmund, of Newburyport, and Ruth Hidden, int. Nov. 22,
    1788.
Elisabeth, of Haverhill, N. H., and Enoch Bayley, int. May
    21, 1796.
Elisabeth, and Joseph Niles, int. Oct. 11, 1804.
Esther, and Robert Homes, Feb. 26, 1668.
Ezekiel, and Mary Prescot of Kingstown, int. June 9, 1789.
Hanah, d. Dea. Benj[amin], and Samuel Poer, jr., int. Sept.
    —, 1705.
Hannah, and John Pearson, 3d, Dec. 10, 1747.*
Hannah, of Newburyport, and Joseph Smith, int. Dec. 13,
    1798.
Hannah, and Leonard Sawyer, Feb. —, 1834.
Humphrey, and Sarah Knight, Feb. 11, 1808.*
Isaac, and Jane Lunt, Mar. 22, 1738-9. c. r. 7.
Israel A., of Bradford, a. 21 y., shoemaker, s. Benjamin and
    Abigail, of Bradford, and Caroline P. Ordway, a. 19 y.,
    d. Moses and Eunice, May 18, 1845.*
John, and Mary Woodbury, Sept. 12, 1749.*
John, of Chester, N. H., and Anna Jewett of Byfield Rowley,
    Oct. 15, 1778.

*Intention also recorded.

MORSE, John, jr., and Polly Pingry, int. Aug. 22, 1793.

Jonathan, and Mary Clarke, May 3, 1671.

Jonathan, and Mary Clark of Andover, at Andover, Feb. 14, 1792.*

Jonathan, of Newburyport, and Elisabeth Row, int. Feb. 18, 1803.

Joseph, and Judith Short, Oct. 4, 1788.*

Joseph, and Susannah Pearson, Oct. 9, 1803.*

Joseph, and Olive Morse of Bradford, int. Apr. 19, 1807.

Joseph, and Mrs. Ruth Morrill, Jan. 17, 1839.*

Joseph W., and Elizabeth Tappan of Newburyport, int. Oct. 13, 1846.

Joshua, and Martha Lunt, int. Apr. 11, 1805.

Judith [Mace. int.], and Benjamin Bradley of Canterbury, Dec. 26, 1799.*

Keturah, cf Newburyport, and Paul Gerrish, int. Apr. 20, 1799.

Lidia, and David Fisk, Feb. 20, 1794. C. R. 2.*

Lydia, and Samuel Sawyer, jr., Nov. 26, 1778.*

Lydia, and David W. Jackman, Apr. 7, 1829.*

Martha E[veline. int.], and Benjamin Davis, Nov. 2, 1829.*

Mary, and Phillip Eastman, Aug. 22, 1678.

Mary, and David Merril, Dec. 18, 1706.*

Mary, and Michael Lovel, both of Medfield, May 25, 1726. C. R. 7.

Mary, of Methuen, and Enoch Brown of Haverhill, Jan. 16, 1734-5. C. R. 7.

Mary, of Bradford, and Enoch Merrill, int. Jan. 4, 1821.

Mary, of Newburyport, and John Robinson, int. Nov. 26, 1822.

Mary, and Joshua Stevens, Oct. —, 1833.

Mary, see Noyes, Mary.

Mary O., a. 33 y., d. Joseph, and David Jackman, a. 39 y., farmer, s. David and Amelia, Feb. 20, 1845.*

Moody, and Sally Follansbee of Andover, Sept. 9, 1806.*

Moses, and Rebeckah Bartlet, Nov. 6, 1800.*

Moses, and Susanna Morse, Sept. 19, 1813.*

Nathaniel, and Maria George of Haverhill, int. Sept. 11, 1842.

Olive, of Bradford, and Joseph Morse, int. Apr. 19, 1807.

Philip, and Sarah Pillsbery, Sept. 28, 1749.*

Phillip, and Ma[ry] Brown of Salisbury, Dec. 11, 1707.*

Polly, and Edmund Worth, jr., Oct. 7, 1802.*

Rhoda, and William England, Oct. 31, 1815.*

Robert, and Ann Lewis, Oct. 30, 1654. CT. R.

Robert, of Newburyport, and Mary Adams, int. Mar. 29, 1806.

Ruth, and Caleb Moodey, jr., Dec. 9, 1690.

Sara, and Amos Stickney, June 24, 1663.

Sarah, and Henry Sleeper, Mar. 29, 1749.*

*Intention also recorded.

MORSE, Sarah, and Joseph Manson [Munson. int.] of Scarboro, June 27, 1749.*

Sarah, and Paul Noyes, Jan. 7, 1762.*

Sarah, and Isaiah Short, Nov. 10, 1796.*

Sarah, and Prince Lumbard Downs, int. Sept. 8, 1798.

Susanna, and Moses Morse, Sept. 19, 1813.*

Timo[thy], and Hannah Ilsley, June 21, 1753. C. R. 9.*

Timothy, and Sarah Palmer, Apr. 30, 1788.*

Timothy, jr., of Ipswich, and Ruth Worth, ———, 1809. [Sept. 23. int.]*

MORSS (see also Morse), Abel, jr., and Ednar Hale, Nov. 11, 1736.*

Abigail [Mrs. C. R. 2.], and John Carr, Nov. 23, 1758.*

Abigail, and Daniel Chisemore, Mar. 7, 1759.*

Anne, and Eliphalet Adams of Ipswich, Apr. 16, 1730.*

Anthony, of Newburyport, and Molly Adams, int. Jan. 1, 1768.

Benjamin, jr., and Susana Merrill, Jan. 28, 1691-2.

Benjamin, 3d, and Margaret Bartlet, Oct. 3, 1726.*

Caleb, and Sarah Ordway, Nov. 23, 1732.*

Caleb, and Mary Woodman, Aug. 9, 1770.*

Daniel, and Mary Challis of Kingstown, N. H., int. June 6, 1779.

Daniel T., of Newburyport, and Ann E. Goodwin, int. June 24, 1843.

David, and Abigail Bayley, Sept. 3, 1770.*

Dolly, and John Morss, jr., Jan. 8, 1761.*

Edmund, jr., and Mary Rowell, Dec. 16, 1751.*

Ednah, and Roger Stephens, Sept. 19, 1758.*

Ednar, and Edward Woodman [jr. int.], July 8, 1742.*

Elisabeth, and John Adams, Nov. 2, 1730.*

Elisabeth, and George Lowel, June 28, 1732.*

Elisabeth, and Thomas Noyes, 4th, Jan. 4, 1753.*

Elisabeth, and Joseph Somerby, Jan. 4, 1757.*

Elizabeth, and Nicholas Noyes Short of Newburyport, Mar. 11, 1777.*

Elizabeth, and John Thomas of Newburyport, int. Nov. 13, 1779.

Enoch, and Martha Goodhu of Ipswich, int. Dec. 8, 1738.

Eunice, and Thomas Rogers, Dec. 2, 1761.*

Hannah, and Thomas Rogers, 3d, Sept. 30, 1729.*

Hannah, and John Campbell, Dec. 5, 1754.*

Hannah, and William England, Jan. 15, 1812.*

Hester [d. Dea. Benjamin. int.], and Jonathan Kelly, July 6, 1702.*

James, Rev., of Newburyport, and Mrs. Elizabeth Tyng, int. Dec. 10, 1830.

*Intention also recorded.

MORSS, James Ordway, and Judith Morss, May 4, 1756.*
Joanna, and Nathan Sawyer, int. Apr. 19, 1743. (Certificate
forbidden.)
Joanna [Hanna. int.], and Jonathan Chase, Jan. 24, 1744-5.*
John, and Elisabeth Holdgate [of Haverhill. c. r. 2.], June
20, 1754.*
John, jr., and Dolly Morss, Jan. 8, 1761.*
John, and Hannah Whitmore, Nov. 25, 1767.
John, of Newburyport, and Lydia Clark, int. Nov. 13, 1780.
Jonathan, and Mary Merrill, Oct. 27, 1731.*
Jonathan, of Newburyport, and Mary Moody, Aug. 20, 1776.*
Jonathan, of Newburyport, and Judith Brown, Feb. 18, 1779.*
Jonathan, of Plymouth [N. H. int.], and Abiah Worth, June
8, 1786.*
Joseph, and Sarah Merrill, d. Abraham, sr., int. Oct. 7, 1696.
Joseph, and Joanna Godfree, Apr. 22, 1730.*
Joseph [3d. int.], and Mary Jackman, July 17, 1738.*
Joseph B., and Martha H. Boardman, both of Newburyport,
Jan. 6, 1840.
Joshua, and Hannah Hazzen of Boxford, July 13, 1727.*
Joshua, and Rebecca Patten, Apr. 21, 1765.*
Judeth, and Ephraim Levit of Stratham, int. Sept. 6, 1738.
Judeth, and Truman March, Nov. 14, 1727.*
Judith, and James Ordway Morss, May 4, 1756.*
Judith, and William Rogers, Dec. 6, 1763.*
Katharine, 2d w., and Joseph Smith, [Dec.]—, 1808. c. r. 1.
Lydia, and William Noyes, 3d, Aug. 10, 1742.*
Lydia, and Jonathan Buck of Haverhill [at Haverhill. dup.],
Oct. 19, 1742.*
Lyphe, and Anna [Anne. int.] Rolfe, May 12, 1761.*
Lyphee, and Abigail Pettengell, Mar. 9, 1757.*
Margeret, and Joseph Coffin, July 15, 1725.*
Martha, and Wells Chase [of Amesbury. int.], Aug. 6, 1734.*
Mary, and Joseph Chase [jr. int.], Sept. 7, 1724.*
Mary, and Amos Person, Dec. 8, 1726.*
Mary, and Richard Emerson of Haverhill [at Haverhill.
dup.], Jan. 2, 1738-9.*
Molly, and Ezekiel Goodridge, Dec. 23, 1765.*
Moses, and Mrs. Ann Sawyer, Dec. 16, 1742.*
Moses, and Sarah Brickit, Oct. 25, 1759.*
Nathan, and Hittey Emory, Oct. 20, 1741.*
Nathaniel, and Sophia W. Estabrook of Haverhill, int. May
29, 1847.
Peter, and Thomasin Hale, Mar. 30, 1726.*
Prudence, Mrs., and Dea. Edmund Bayley, Jan. 4, 1758.*
Prudence, and Stephen Chase, Aug. 29, 1769.*
Rebeca, and Nathan Brown, Dec. 24, 1736.*

*Intention also recorded.

MORSS, Robert, of Boston, a. 29 y., accountant, s. Robert and Mary, of Boston, and Abby C. Dow, a. 20 y., d. Daniel and Joanna, Nov. 18, 1846.*

Ruth, and John Carr, jr., May 5, 1763.*

Samuel, and Bethiah Dalton of Andover, at Andover, Sept. 24, 1725.

Samuel, and Betsey Davis, Nov. 20, 1811.*

Sarah, and Jacob Pearly of Boxford, May 28, 1729.*

Sarah, and Josiah Bachelder of Kingston, Jan. 18, 1737-8.*

Sarah, wid., and John Hopkinson, jr. of Bradford, June 18, 1742.*

Sarah, and Nath[anie]ll Atkinson, Apr. 1, 1756.*

Sarah, and Joseph Bartlet, 3d, Oct. 12, 1762.*

Sarah, and Mark Woodman, Dec. 3, 1769.*

Sarah, and Simeon Jackman, int. Sept. 29, 1770.

Stephen, and Elisabeth Worth, July 21, 1725.*

Stephen, jr., and Judeth Carr, Oct. 5, 1749.*

Susanna, and Thomas Perrin of Ipswich, May 24, 1731.*

Susanna, and Moses Brown of North Yarmouth, int. July 19, 1746.

Susannah, and Nathaniel Piper of Ipswich, Mar. 26, 1728.*

Susannah, and Joseph Patten, both of Newburyport, Aug. 10, 1838.

Thomas, and Elisabeth Bartlet, June 30, 1747.*

Timothy, and Mrs. Martha Bayley, Sept. 27, 1769.*

Willi[am], and Sarah Merrill [d. Daniel. int.], May 12, 1696.*

William [jr. int.], and Judith Hale, June 17, 1729.*

MORTON, William, a. 22 y., shipwright, s. James and Elizabeth, and Caroline F. Gurney, a. 19 y., d. Nathaniel and Harriet, Nov. 24, 1847.*

MOSELEY, David C., of Boston, and Elizabeth M. Peirce, Oct. 26, 1817.*

MOSEMORE, Jane, Mrs., of Boston, and Thomas Follinsby, sr., int. Apr. 3, 1713.

MOSER, Lydia, of Hampton, N. H., and Wade Ilsley, int. Mar. 31, 1827.

MOSS (see also Morse), Joseph, and Elizabeth Poor, Jan. 30, 1692-3. CT. R.

Judith. Mrs., and Offin Boardman of Salisbury, at Salisbury, Apr. 24, 1740.*

*Intention also recorded.

Moss, Moody, and Hannah Carlton of Andover, at Andover, May 27, 1741.*

Ruth, and Sam[uel] Merril, Aug. —, 1717. c. r. 7.

MOTEY, Joseph, A. M., [at the Dummer school. int.], and Elisabeth Moody, Apr. 12, 1780.*

MOTHS, Nicholas, and Sarah Potter, int. Aug. 17, 1828.

MOULTON (see also Molton), Abigail, and David Jackman, July 17, 1760.*

Abigail, and Nehemiah Bartlet, Jan. 7, 1791.*

Ann, and Leonard Griffin of Portland, May 6, 1818.*

Anna [Anne. int.], and Aquila Hodgkins, May 29, 1761.*

Anna, and Aquila Chase, jr., July 9, 1780.*

Anne, and Cutting Bartlet, Aug. 27, 1745.*

Batt, and Hannah Sible [Sibly. int.], Dec. 4, 1712.*

Batt, and Jemima George, both of Amesbury, May 29, 1730. c. r. 7.

Cutting, and Molly Merrill, May 29, 1773.*

Cutting, and Judith Emery, Nov. 25, 1784.*

Daniel, and Diedamia Spofford of Rowley, int. Apr. 11, 1818.

Elsey Murray, and Michael Divine, Jan. 11, 1807.*

Eunice, and Thomas Eaton of Salisbury, Oct. 5, 1749.*

Eunice, and Robert March, Apr. 8, 1789.*

Eunice, and John Cheever, jr. of Newburyport, Apr. 19, 1808.*

Eunice Sawyer, and John Davison of Newburyport, int. May 18, 1787.

Ezekiel, of Hampton, and Sarah Moulton, July 4, 1727.*

Harriet, and John N. Kent, Oct. 20, 1835.*

Henrietta, and Joshua Lake of Haverhill, int. June 25, 1830.

Jabez, of Hampton, N. H., and Eunice Peirce, int. Jan. 1, 1767.

John, and Ednah Merrill, Nov. 25, 1790.*

John, jr., and Elizabeth Bartlett, Dec. 2, 1833.*

Jonathan, and Rebecca Chase, Dec. 5, 1716.*

Jonathan, and Elisabeth Barrett, Nov. 29, 1759. c. r. 8.

Joseph, and Mary Noyes, July 25, 1717.*

Joseph, and Anna Boardman, Sept. 5, 1754.*

Joseph, jr., of Newburyport, and Abigail Noyes, int. Sept. 14. 1765.

Joseph, and Henrietta Milton, int. Feb. 22, 1828.

Joseph, and Elizabeth L. Colman, July 12, 1838.*

Lydia, of Hampton, and Daniel Coffin, Jan. 11, 1726-7. c. r. 7.

Mary, and Jonathan Haynes, Jan. 1, 1674.

Mary, and Samuel Pettingell of Salisbury, May 7, 1751. c. r. 2.

Mary, and Thomas Dutton, jr., Nov. 27, 1788.*

Mercy, and Joshua Grant, both of York, June 10, 1736. c. r. 7.

*Intention also recorded.

Moulton, Miriam, and Abraham Lunt, both of York, July 11, 1733. c. r. 7.
Miriam, and Paul Thurston, Aug. 11, 1763. c. r. 9.*
Moses E., of Newburyport, and Ruth Somerby, Nov. 14, 1825.*
Nathan, of Newburyport, and Sarah Thirston, Oct. 10, 1765.*
Rebecca, wid., and Robert Savory of Bradford, Dec. 13, 1722.*
Rebeckah, and Henry Merrill, jr., Nov. 25, 1773.*
Sally, and Ezra Goodwin of Amesbury, at Amesbury, Nov. 30, 1797.*
Sally, and John Merrill, jr., int. Apr. 13, 1827.
Samuel, and Mary Ordway, Nov. 29, 1743.*
Sarah, and Ezekiel Moulton of Hampton, July 4, 1727.*
Sarah, and Samuel Dresor of Ipswich, int. Nov. 17, 1733.
Silas, and Hannah Adams, May 7, 1791.*
Stephen, and Abigall Williams, Aug. 8, 1754.*
Steven, and Rebecca Chase, Dec. 14, 1721.*
William, and Abigail Webster, May 27, 1685.
William, jr., and Ruth Emery, Apr. 24, 1716.*
William, and Lydia Greenleaf, Sept. 16, 1742.*
William, of Newburyport, and Judith Noyes, Oct. 1, 1801.*
William, jr., and Ruth Bartlet, Dec. 25, 1817.*
W[illia]m, and Statira Preble of Newburyport, int. Nov. 5, 1825.

MOUNTFORT, Edmund, and Hannah Caswell, Nov. 1, 1753.*

MOWATT (see also Moet), Henry, and Mary Merrill of Newburyport, int. Nov. 11, 1803.

MO——, Robert, and ——, Oct. 30, 1654.

MUDD, John, widr., shipwright, and Mary Jenkins, wid., both of Boston, Feb. 15, 1727-8. c. r. 7.

MULINCUM (see also Mulliken), Mary, of Bradford, and Samuel Kenne, int. Oct. 29, 1743.

MULLICAM (see also Mulliken), John, of Bradford, and Mary Pore, Nov. 15, 1717.*

MULLICAN (see also Mulliken), Rob[er]t, and Rebecca Savery, Dec. 15, 1687. ct. r.

MULLIKEN (see also Mulincum, Mullicam, Mullican), Hannah G[iles. int.], of Newburyport, and Capt. Micajah Lunt, jr., May 29, 1826.*

*Intention also recorded.

MULLIKEN, Sarah, and Timothy Pike, Aug. 8, 1757.*
Sarah, and Giles P. Stone, both of Newburyport, Oct. 5, 1831.
Susanna, of Bradford, and Caleb Norton, at Bradford, Sept.
—, 1787.

MULLOONE, James, and Anne Harris, Sept. 18, 1722.*

MULTIMORE (see also Miltimore), Dolly, and Capt. Peter
Rousseau of Boston, Mar. 23, 1819.*

MURPHY, James, of Newburyport, and Sally Leatherby, July
31, 1806.*

MURRAY (see also Morry, Murry), Eliza, of Newburyport,
and William Harris, int. Oct. 1, 1822.
Sarah, and Moses Dresser, resident in Newbury, int. Mar. 1,
1781.

MURRY (see also Murray), Polly, and James Cavender, May
17, 1790.*

MUTRY, James, resident in Newburyport, and Elizabeth Pearson, int. July 15, 1780.

MUZZE₁(see also Muzzey), Hannah, and Robert Hunkins [jr.
dup.], of Haverhill [at Haverhill. dup.], Dec. 6, 1738.*
Joseph, and Sarah Mors, Mar. 31, 1724.*
Joseph, jr., and Margarett Pettingill, June 18, 1728.*
Joseph, jr., and Elisabeth Pettingill, Nov. 15, 1737.*
Mary, and Benjamin Lunt [jr. int.], Dec. 15, 1725.*

MUZZEY (see also Muzze, Muzzy), Joanna, and Thomas
Plumer, Mar. 28, 1765.*
Joseph, jr., and Lydia Atkinson, May 26, 1756.*
Mary, and Stephen Knight of Newburyport, int. Aug. 4, 1770.

MUZZY (see also Muzzey), Benjamin, and Mary Pettingell,
Dec. 31, 1751.*
Joseph, and Esther Jackman, Feb. 9, 1670.
Joseph, and Johanah Petengall, int. Nov. 2, 1700.
Samuel, of Boscawen, N. H., and Mehitable Plumer, Sept. 15,
1774.*

MYGHIL (see also Mighill), Mary, and Thomas Stevens, Oct.
13, 1681.

*Intention also recorded.

MYRICK (see also Merrick), Anne, and Samuel Gardner, Nov. 23, 1761.*

Frederick W., of Nantucket, and Mary Ann Cook of Newburyport, July 24, 1839.

Rachel, and William Rogers, Sept. 21, 1749.*

NAISH, George, and Rachel Davis, Aug. 29, 1754. c. R. 8.

NASON, John [resident in Newbury. int.], and Sarah Jenkins, Nov. 20, 1763.*

Maria H., a 27 y., d. Levi, and Mark W. Footman of Somersworth, N. H., a. 28 y., manufacturer, s. Francis, of Durham, N. H., Jan. 1, 1845.*

Samuel, of Newburyport, and Sally Gerrish, Oct. 4, 1796.*

Susan A., a. 21 y., b. Ashland, d. Levi and Sarah, and George L. Dearborn, of Somersworth, N. H., a. 25 y., physician, b. Wakefield, s. Lewis, of Somersworth, Nov. 29, 1849.*

NEAL (see also Neil), Salley [Mary. int.], of Newburyport, and Nathan Chase [jr. int.], Feb. 18, 1800.

NECK, Thomas, of Dover, and Abigail Bricket, Nov. 5, 1705.

NEIL (see also Neal), Lawrence O., and Catherine Ross of Newburyport, int. May 23, 1846.

NELSON, Ann [of Rowley. int.], and John Smith [jr. int.], Dec. 9, 1709.*

Anne, and Moses Hoyt, Sept. 13, 1758. [Said Hoyt takes said Anne naked and so will not be obliged to pay any of her former husband's debts. int.]*

Benjamin, of Rowley, and Polley Dressor, int. Feb. 20, 1802.

Daniel, and Betsey Taylor, Dec. —, 1835.*

Daniel P., of Rowley, and Mary P. Hoyt, [Nov. 14. int.], 1840.*

Elisabeth, and William Perkins of Topsfield, Apr. 18, 1734.*

Elisabeth, of Newburyport, and William Haskel, int. Feb. 2, 1788.

Hannah, and Joseph Gardner of Charlestown, July 24, 1706.

Jacob, and Catherine Ward, Sept. 12, 1805. c. R. 5.

Jane, of Rowley, and William Chandler, at Rowley, Feb. 11, 1752.*

Jeremiah, Hon., and Mary Balch, Apr. 11, 1831.*

John B., of Newburyport, a. 30 y., merchant tailor, b. Newburyport, s. Samuel and Sarah, of Newburyport, and Clara M. Feltch, a. 32 y., b. Kensington, d. Jacob and Hannah, July 18, 1849.*

*Intention also recorded.

NELSON, Mary, of Byfield Rowley, and Thomas Prime of Rowley, Jan. 1, 1778.
Mary Jane, of Rowley, and Philip K. Rogers, int. Mar. 17, 1827.
Phillip, and Elizabeth Lowell [Lowle. dup.], d. John, at Rowley, Nov. 1, 1666. [Jan. 1, 1666. dup.]
Samuel, and Elisabeth Bradbury, Oct. 28, 1762.*

NESBE (see also Nessbee), Sarah, and Joseph Pidgeon of Southampton, Great Britain, Apr. 29, 1718.*

NESSBEE (see also Nesbe), Hannah, and Adam Marriner of Boston, Sept. 23, 1713.*

NEWCOMB, Hannah D., of Boston, and Joseph A. Woodwell, int. Nov. 4, 1848.
Joanna, and Timothy Kelly, Dec. 28, 1783.*
Margaret M[uzzey. int.], and Josiah Burleigh, jr. of Newmarket, N. H., Jan. 13, 1813.*

NEWELL (see also Nowell), Joseph, and Anna March, June 10, 1790.*
Lydia, and John Osgood, Dec. 3, 1778.*
Moses, and Sally Moody, Sept. 21, 1816. [1815. c. R. 2.]*
Rebecca, and Richard Heath, Oct. 15, 1812.*

NEWHALL, Asa Tarbell, of Lynn, and Judith Little, int. Sept. 12, 1807.
Elezer, and Mary Fowler of Ipswich, int. July 21, 1738.
Mary, of Newburyport, and Ebenezer Coffin, int. Sept. 25, 1793.
Mercy, and Samuel Lane [jr. int.] of Gloucester, Jan. 28, 1762.*

NEWMAN, Abigail, and David S. Caldwell of Dunbarton, N. H., Dec. 5, 1827.*
Elisabeth, and David Noyes [of Falmouth. int.], resident in Newbury, Mar. 26, 1761.*
Elizabeth S., and Nathaniel S. Osgood of Newburyport, int. Feb. 9, 1828.
Esther, and Capt. Benjamin Hopkins of Wellfleet, Jan. 19, 1800.*
Hannah, of Newburyport, and Jeremiah Johnson, int. Sept. 8, 1821.
Hannah O., and Eleazer W. Pettingell, int. Mar. 29, 1848.
Jacob, and Susanna Goodwin, Oct. 12, 1749.*
Jacob, of Newburyport, and Rebekah Knight, Sept. 27, 1819.*

*Intention also recorded.

NEWMAN, John, of Ipswich, and Jane March, Dec. 15, 1720.*
John [jr. int.], and Mary Toppan, Dec. 5, 1734.*
John, 3d, and Abigail Noyes, Mar. 16, 1763.*
John, and Rhoda [Rebecca. int.] B. Danforth, Sept. —, 1833.*
John, Capt., and Henrietta Woodbury of Gloucester, int. Nov.
   1, 1841.
Judith, and Moses Rolfe, Nov. 29, 1759.*
Mary, Mrs., and John Pettingill [jr. int.], Aug. 25, 1743.*
Mary, of Newburyport, and Joseph Cooch, int. Nov. 24, 1769.
Mary, of Newburyport, and Amos Coffin, int. Aug. 29, 1846.
Mary Hale, and Stephen Plumer, jr., May 24, 1838.*
Nathaniel, jr., and Martha Sweet of Ipswich, int. Nov. 13,
   1742.
Rebecca K., and Albert Cheever, int. Oct. 5, 1844.
Sally, and Thomas Lord of Newburyport, May 3, 1801.*
Sally, and Charles Loyd of Newburyport, Jan. 7, 1802.*
Samuel, of Newburyport, and Phebe Hale, int. May 2, 1801.
Sarah, and Thomas Smith, jr., Sept. 4, 1746.*
Sarah, and Joseph Edwards, Nov. 12, 1753.*
Susanna, and Francis Holliday, July 31, 1754.*

NEWMARSH, Elisabeth, of Ipswich, and John Sweasy, int.
   Sept. 16, 1752.

NEWTON, Elizabeth Ann D., and Benja[min] W. Robinson,
   Oct. 22, 1826.*
Hannah, Mrs., of Boston, and John Lyle, late of Belfast, Ire-.
   land, now of Boston, June 29, 1731. c. r. 7.

NICHOLS (see also Nicols), Elisabeth, and John Short, jr.,
   int. Nov. 17, 1764.
Harriet, of Haverhill, and William Stephens, int. Mar. 27,
   1816.
Jane, and John Courser, jr., Nov. 24, 1742.*
Joseph, of Amesbury, and Rebecca Chase, Feb. 1, 1732-3.*
Mary, of Amesbury, and Steven Rogers, June 29, 1744. c. r. 7.
Mary, and Joseph Willet, jr., Apr. 13, 1758.*
Mary (should be Sarah), of Newburyport, and David E. Cary,
   int. July 31, 1847.
Mehetable, and Nath[anie]ll Willet, June 4. 1754.*
Phebe, and Joseph G. Pearson, June 30. 1836.
Sally, of Newburyport, and Joseph Piper. Mar. 11, 1809.*
Thomas, of Amesbury, and Judith Hoag. 24: 3 m: 1720(?)
   c. r. 6. [int. 20: 2 m: 1721.]*
William, of Londonderry, and Anne Coffrin. Oct. 18. 1724.*

*Intention also recorded.

NICOLS (see also Nichols), Edmund, and Sarah Downer of Newburyport, int. Apr. 17, 1802.
Moses, of Amesbury, and Abigail Worth, int. May 19, 1790.

NILES, Anna, and Joseph Bayley, Nov. 2, 1800.*
Hannah M., of Georgetown, d. W[illia]m and Hannah, and Isaac G. Hagat of Georgetown, a. 23 y., shoemaker, s. Stephen and Catharine, Oct. 26, 1848.
Joseph, and Elisabeth Morse, int. Oct. 11, 1804.
Thomas, Rev., of Rumney, N. H., and Anna Woodman, Feb. 1, 1774.*

NINNY, Joan [Kinny?], and Nathaniel Merril, Oct. 15, 1661.

NISBIT, W[illia]m, and Mrs. Hanah Woodman, June 5, 1690.

NOICE (see also Noyes), Deborah, and Jacob Knight, Oct. 17, 1734. C. R. 7.
Jonathan, and Lidia Bancroft of Reading, at Reading, Aug. 24, 1742.*

NOONAN, Nathaniel Cornelius, and Martha Greenleaf Hale, Sept. 14, 1788.*

NORMAN, Abigail, and Edward Milliken, baker, both of Boston, July 29, 1726. C. R. 7.

NORRIS, Sarah [of Exeter, N. H. int.], and Benjamin Hoag, June 23, 1702.*

NORTHEND, Dorothy, of Byfield Rowley, and William Dummer, June 2, 1761.*
Elizabeth, of Byfield Rowley, and Jacob Jewett, jr., of Rowley, Nov. 19, 1771.
Elizabeth, and John Saffredini, int. Mar. 18, 1809.
Elizabeth, and John Kent, Sept. 14, 1823.*
Hannah, of Rowley, and Richard Dummer, at Rowley, June 21, 1785.
John, and Nancy Titcomb, Mar. 30, 1809.*
Mary, of Byfield Rowley, and Joseph Hale, jr., Nov. 19, 1765.*
Mary Ann, and Moses Tenny, Apr. 6, 1831.*
Samuel, and Harriet Perley, Sept. 6, 1838.*
Samuel, and Mary H. Currier of Newburyport, int. Nov. 11, 1841.
Sara, and Thomas Hale, May 16, 1682.

*Intention also recorded.

NORTON, Adar, of Newburyport, and Theodore P. Huse, int. Aug. 16, 1840.

Amos, and Mrs. Hannah Ross, Sept. 14, 1828.*

Benjamin, and Margeret Richardson, June 14, 1722.*

Benjamin, and Mary Shute, Dec. 5, 1744.*

Caleb, and Susanna Mulliken of Bradford, at Bradford, Sept. —, 1787.

Daniel, of Newburyport, and Mary Carr, int. Feb. 16, 1822.

Elizabeth, of Manchester, and John Woodbridge, Feb. 24, 1706.*

John, and Mehitebal Richardson, July 14, 1725.*

Jonathan, and Mary Couch, Aug. 11, 1743.*

Joseph R., of Newburyport, and Mary H. Robbins, int. Oct. 16, 1842.

Joshua, and Lydia Bishop, Jan. 14, 1752.*

Judeth, Mrs., and Enoch Swett, July 5, 1743.*

Lydia, of Newburyport, and George Rogers, int. Mar. 17, 1815.

Martha, of Newburyport, and John Mace, Oct. 29, 1812.*

Sarah, of Newburyport, and Benjamin Dutton, Oct. 2, 1808.*

Sarah, a. 48 y., d. Amos and Sarah, and Paul Floyd, widr., a. 59 y., farmer, s. John and Polly [Elizabeth. dup.], Jan. 21, 1845.*

NORWOOD, Jonathan, and Elizabeth Davis, both of Gloucester, Mar. 26, 1734. c. r. 7.

Nancy, and Joseph Edmonds Barrett, Feb. 2, 9 or 16, 1812.*

Thomas, of Newburyport, and Judith Little, Jan. 7, 1783.*

NOWELL (see also Newell), George [Newell. int.], and Hannah Chase, Sept. 14, 1786.*

John, and Mary Cross, Aug. 6, 1753. c. r. 9.*

Mary, and Henry Chipman, Feb. 5, 1755.*

Paul, and Mary Nutting, both of Cambridge, June 25, 1734. c. r. 7.

Samuel, and Elizabeth Favor, July 16, 1747. c. r. 2.*

Sarah, and Ebenezer Morrison, July 29, 1762.*

Zacheriah, and Mary Carr, Nov. 27, 1735.*

Zecheriah, and Mary York of Ipswich, at Ipswich, Aug. 8, 1732.

NOYCE (see also Noyes), Sam[ue]ll, and Martha Smith of Reading, at Reading, Sept. 26, 1734.*

NOYES (see also Noice, Noyce, Noys, Noyse), Abigail, Mrs., and Simon French of Salisbury, May 8, 1707.*

Abigail, and John Newman, 3d, Mar. 16, 1763.*

*Intention also recorded.

NOYES, Abigail, and Joseph Moulton, jr., of Newburyport, int. Sept. 14, 1765.
Abigail, and David Little, Mar. 24, 1785.*
Abigail, and Moses Carr, jr., Oct. 23, 1800.*
Abigail, and Samuel Cater of Danvers, Nov. 12, 1836.*
Allen F., and Hannah T. Rogers, May 24, 1843.*
Amelia, and Abraham Dodge of Newburyport, Sept. 16, 1783.*
Amos, jr., and Nancy [Anna. c. R. 1.] Hazelton of Newburyport, Nov. 26, 1807.*
Anne, and Samuel Bailey [jr. int.], Mar. 19, 1748.*
Anne, and Thomas Hart of Portsmouth, N. H., Nov. 14, 1762.*
Bathsheba, and Cutting Pettingill, Nov. 24, 1714.*
Benjamin, and Mary Poor, Jan. 19, 1726-7.*
Benjamin, and Tamzen Greenfield of Salisbury, int. Aug. 29, 1761.
Benjamin H., a. 24 y., trader, s. Amos and Nancy, and Ellen C. Bragdon, a. 19 y., b. York, d. James and Alice, of York, Me., Oct. 2, 1845.*
Bethyah, and Joseph Danford, Dec. 13, 1717.
Caroline, of Newburyport, and Rev. Leonard Withington, May 29, 1827.*
Caroline, and Richard T. Jaques, Aug. 20, 1837.*
Caroline, of Newburyport, and William Thurlow, int. May 1, 1844.
Catharine, and Zecheriah Dodge, Dec. 15, 1804.*
Charles, and Margaret M. Clark of Newburyport, int. Nov. 12, 1842.
Crissia Hunt, and William Coker, Aug. 29, 1822.*
Cutting, and Elizabeth Knight, Feb. 25, 1673.
Cutting, and Elizabeth Toppan, Jan. 8, 1702.*
Cutting, jr., and Elisabeth Gerish, Dec. 22, 1709.*
Cutting, 3d, and Mary Woodman, Apr. 15, 1724.*
Daniel, and Judith Knight, Dec. 29, 1702.*
Daniel, and Abigail Toppan, Feb. 14, 1727-8.*
Daniel, and Mrs. Abigail Moodey, Apr. 12. 1739.*
Daniel [3d. int.], and Mrs. Ann Chase of Haverhill, at Haverhill, Oct. 3, 1745.*
Daniel, of Ipswich, and Mary Hale Parish, June 23, 1818.*
Daniel [David. c. R. 10.], and Sarah Pearson, Oct. 16, 1826.*
Daniel P., and Jane N. Davis, int. Oct. 6, 1849.
David, and Hephzibah Knight, Nov. 9, 1756.*
David [of Falmouth. int.], resident in Newbury, and Elisabeth Newman, Mar. 26, 1761.*
Dolly, and David Knight, May 18, 1793.*
Dorcas, and Silas Noyes, Oct. —, 1792.*
Dorcas, and James Ferguson, May 19, 1825.*

*Intention also recorded.

NOYES, Dorothy, and Samuel Little, Feb. 18, 1735-6.*

Ebenezer, of Haverhill district, and Elizabeth Greenleaf, Jan. 7, 1748. C. R. 2.*

Ebenezer [Dr. int.], of Dover, N. H., and Hannah Chase, Nov. 29, 1764.*

Edmund, of Newburyport, and Anne Brown, int. Sept. 22, 1770.

Edna, and Daniel Adams [jr. int.], Nov. 26, 1788.*

Ednah, and John Emery, jr., Apr. 7, 1756.*

Ednah, and Daniel Adams, Oct. 26, 1758.*

Eleanor, and Amos Stickney, int. Feb. 2, 1792.

Elijah P., a. 25 y., farmer, s. Daniel and Mary H., and Martha R. Wiggins, a. 28 y., d. John and Margaret, of Newburyport, Nov. 17, 1848.*

Eliphalet, and Judeth Gains of Ipswich, int. Oct. 3, 1746.

Eliphalet, and Christian Hunt, July 20, 1760.*

Eliphalet, and Elisabeth Mirick, July 7, 1770.*

Eliphalet, and Martha Handson, int. Dec. 12, 1809.

Elisabeth, d. Col. Tho[ma]s, Esq., and Thomas Woodbridg, int. Jan. 21, 1703-4.

Elisabeth, and Williams Adams of Rowley, Apr. 22, 1728.*

Elisabeth, and Nathaniel Dole, Nov. 26, 1730.*

Elisabeth, and John Hopkinson, Mar. 9, 1737-8.*

Elisabeth, and Benjamin Jackman of Rowley, Nov. 20, 1745.*

Elisabeth, and James Smith, 3d, Jan. 12, 1748.*

Elisabeth, and Moses Short, Oct. 16, 1750.*

Elisabeth, and Stephen Ilsley, Oct. 27, 1757.*

Elisabeth, and Joseph Ames [resident in Newbury. int.], Mar. 5, 1765.*

Eliza, of Newburyport, and Josiah Thing, jr., int. Oct. 4, 1823.

Elizabeth, and John Adams, Jan. 22, 1707.*

Elizabeth, and Samuel Pettingale, jr., Jan. 3, 1709.*

Elizabeth, and Joseph Marsh, Dec. 23, 1806.*

Elizabeth, and John Marshall of Nottingham West, N. H., Feb. 27, 1812.*

Elizabeth, of Newburyport, and Joseph Rappell, int. Aug. 26, 1834.

Elsy, and Richard Smith, 3d, May 22, 1808.*

Enice [Eunice. int.], and Joseph Perkins, ——, 1804. C. R. 1.*

Enoch, and Lucy Dickinson of Rowley, at Rowley, July 4, 1739.*

Enoch, and Elisabeth Chewte of Rowley, Feb. 24, 1746-7.*

Enoch, and Sarah Emery, Oct. 30, 1765.

Enoch, jr., and Salley Chase, June 16, 1803.*

Enos, and Betty Pearson of Rowley, int. Feb. 24, 1777.

Ephraim, and Prudence Stickny, Dec. 27, 1722.*

NOYES, Ephraim, and Elisabeth Wiet of Newburyport, int. Oct. 5, 1789.

Ephraim, jr., and Polly Brown of Rowley, int. Aug. 9, 1792.

Eunice, and Nathaniel Lunt, Jan. 14, 1741-2.*

Eunice, and Samuel Dummer, May 16, 1765.*

Eunice, and Simeon Hale, June 18, 1771.*

Eunice, and James Knight, jr., Feb. 8, 1785.*

Folansbe, jr., and Rebeckah Richardson of Bradford, int. Sept. 20, 1805.

Friend, and Elisabeth Knight, Oct. 17, 1785.*

Friend, and Abigail Ilsley of New Bradford, N. H., int. Mar. 17, 1792.

Giles A., and Susan F. Fairweather, int. Oct. 6, 1849.

Hanna, and Peter Cheny, May 14, 1663.

Hannah, and Benjamin Lunt, Jan. 16, 1712-13.*

Hannah, of Tamworth, and James Lunt, jr., int. May 28, 1743.

Hannah, and Nicholas Short, Jan. 17, 1743-4.*

Hannah, and Hezekiah Hutchins, July 5, 1750.*

Hannah, and Caleb Kimbal, jr., Nov. 25, 1766.*

Hannah, and John Little, Oct. 27, 1767.*

Hannah [wid. int.], and Joseph Richardson, jr. of Bradford, Feb. 7, 1782.*

Henry, and Mille Hale, Nov. 5. 1761.*

Horace P., a. 25 y., farmer, s. Silas, and Helen M. Horton, a. 16 y., d. James, of Newburyport, July 23, 1844.*

Huldah, and William Noyes, June 15, 1789.*

Huldah, and David Wallis of Hamilton. Jan. 1, 1795. C. R. 2.*

Humphery, and Elisabeth Little, Nov. 22, 1743.*

Isaac, and Jane Sommerby, Jan. 24, 1716-17.*

Isaac, and Sarah Pettingill, Nov. 24, 1743.*

Isaac P., and Abigail K. Stevens, Dec. 10, 1843.*

Jacob, and Jane Titcomb, Nov. 2, 1726.*

Jacob, and Betsey Wiley, Jan. 2, 1812.*

Jacob C., of West Newbury, and Lydia K. Smith, June 14, 1833.*

James, and Hannah Knight, Mar. 31, 1684.

James, jr., and Sarah Coffin, int. May 13, 1713.

James, jr., and Sarah Little, May 30, 1729.*

James, and Eleanor Jaques, May 7, 1747.*

James, and Jane Noyes, July 2, 1761.*

James, a. 21 y., farmer. s. Noah J. and Mehitable, and Elizabeth Brown, a. 18 y.. d. Daniel and Betsey. June 7, 1845.*

Jane, and Benjamin Person, jr., June 23, 1720.*

Jane, and David Person of Rowley, Oct. 31, 1722.*

Jane, Mrs., and John Studley. Jan. 12, 1741-2.*

Jane, and Ephraim Lunt, Apr. 10. 1744.*

Jane, and Jonathan Dole, jr., Jan. 4, 1749-50.*

*Intention also recorded.

Noyes, Jane, and Richard Little, Sept. 19, 1754.*
Jane, and James Noyes, July 2, 1761.*
Jean, and Capt. John Pearson, jr., Feb. 13, 1787.*
Joanna, and Richard Carr, jr. of Salisbury, Nov. 16, 1770.*
John, and Mary Poore, Nov. 23, 1668.
John, and Mary Noyes, d. John, deceased, int. Apr. 6, 1700.
John [jr. int.], and Mary Thurlo, Jan. 5, 1703.*
John [3d. int.], and [Mrs. int.] Tabitha Dole, Nov. 17, 1715.*
John, 3d, and Sarah Johnson, Nov. 18, 1729.*
John, and Ann Woodbridge, Oct. 23, 1735.*
John, 5th, and Mary Wyat of Newburyport, int. Oct. 24, 1767.
John, and Bethiah Dodge of Rowley, at Rowley, Feb. 29, 1768.
John, jr., and [wid. int.] Edna Adams, May 4, 1777.*
John, 5th, and Mary Pierce of Newburyport, June 15, 1777.*
John [4th. int.], and Elisabeth Pilsbery, Oct. 27, 1782.*
John, jr., and Sarah Knight, Feb. 24, 1812.*
John, jr., and Ann Silloway of Newburyport, int. Apr. 7, 1813.
John J., a. 23 y., farmer, s. John and Sarah, and Augusta C.
    Lander, a. 20 y., d. Henry and Lydia, Apr. 13, 1847.*
John James, and Elizabeth Lamphrey of Hampton, N. H.,
    June 3, 1838.*
Jonathan, and Mary Willet, Sept. 26, 1749.*
Joseph [s. Capt. James. int.], and Joannah Hale ["sometime
    since of Beverly." int.], Feb. 15, 1710.*
Joseph, and Jane Dole, Aug. 17, 1711.*
Joseph, jr., and Mrs. Hannah Wadleigh of Exeter, int. Mar.
    26, 1715.
Joseph [sr. int.], and [Mrs. int.] Martha Clarke, Nov. 10,
    1715.*
Joseph, 4th, and Elisabeth Woodman, Nov. 10, 1726.*
Joseph [jr. int.], and Mary Noyes, Apr. 21, 1738.*
Joseph, jr., and Hannah Knap, Jan. 14, 1761.*
Joseph, jr., and Abigail Bayley, June 12, 1766.*
Joseph, and Bethiah Dodge of Rowley, int. Jan. 1, 1768.
Joseph H. W., a. 24 y., shoemaker, s. Timothy K. and Sarah.
    and Ednah A. Russell, a. 18 y., d. Joseph and Eliza A.,
    Dec. 17, 1846.*
Joseph P., and Louisa F. Lambord of Ludlow, int. June 4,
    1842.
Joshua, and Sarah Hale, Apr. 7, 1730.*
Joshua, and Eunice Jewit of Rowley, int. Apr. 5, 1797.
Joshua, of Georgetown, and Alice Larkin, int. May 3, 1843.
Josiah, and Mary Lunt, Mar. 2, 1737-8.*
Josiah P., widr., a. 48 y., baker, b. Newburyport, s. Timothy
    and Elizabeth, of Newburyport, and Elizabeth M. Mace
    of Newburyport, a. 34 y., b. Newburyport, d. John and
    Martha, June 12, 1848.*

NOYES, Josiah Plummer of Newburyport, and Patience Thur-
lo, Nov. 22, 1820.*
Judeth, wid., and Eliphalet Coffin of Exeter, int. Feb. 3, 1710.
Judeth, and Thomas Pike, May 12, 1721.*
Judeth, and Benjamin Poor, Feb. 14, 1748.*
Judith, Mrs., and Richard Jaques, jr., Feb. 19, 1722-3.*
Judith, and Samuel Fisk of Boxford, Feb. 1, 1737-8.*
Judith, and Thomas Webster of Kingston, Oct. 12, 1738.*
Judith, and Nathaniel Dole, Jan. 15, 1761.*
Judith, and Benjamin Jaques [jr. int.], Mar. 4, 1762.*
Judith, and Reuben Peasly of Newton, N. H., June 14, 1770.*
Judith, and Nicolas Noyes, jr., Nov. 29, 1788.*
Judith, and William Moulton of Newburyport, Oct. 1, 1801.*
Justin, a. 28 y., farmer, s. John and Sarah, and Myra E. Lunt,
a. 20 y., d. Daniel A. and Elizabeth, Nov. 27, 1849.*
Katharine, and Benjamin Beel, June 7, 1772.*
Lemuel [Ens. int.], and Sarah Brown of Salem, at Salem, Nov.
3, 1781.*
Lidya, and Joseph Dole, Feb. 1, 1716-17.*
Lois, and Benjamin Pearson, jr., May 6, 1823.*
Louisa, a. 20 y., d. John and Sarah, and Elisha Bean, jr., a.
23 y., shoemaker, s. Elisha and Margaret, June 28, 1848.*
Lucinda, and Thomas Carleton, Jan. 31, 1811.*
Lydia, and Isaiah Dole, May 10, 1770.*
Lydia, and John Hopkinson of Bradford, Oct. 21, 1800.*
Lydia, and Samuel Folansbe, Nov. 26, 1800.*
Lydia, and Samuel Coffin [jr. int.], Apr. 25, 1803.*
Lydia, and Jacob Emery, int. Nov. 5, 1804.
Maria, and Increase Sumner Chase, May 14, 1818.*
Martha, and Joseph Lunt, Dec. 29, 1702.*
Martha, and Thomas Smith, Mar. 29, 1715.*
Martha, and Oliver Moodey, Feb. 28, 1723-4.*
Martha, and John Swett, Apr. 21, 1726.*
Martha, of Newburyport, and Capt. Gideon Woodwell, int.
Nov. 21, 1772.
Martha, and Enoch Dole, jr., May 31, 1808.*
Martha, and Harry Wyman of Beverly, int. Mar. 9, 1816.
Mary, d. John, deceased, and John Noyes, int. Apr. 6, 1700.
Mary, and Moses Gerrish, Nov. 12, 1714.*
Mary, and Joseph Moulton, July 25, 1717.*
Mary, and Isaac Fits of Ipswich, June 5, 1723.*
Mary, and Abial Somerby, jr., Apr. 20, 1724.*
Mary, and Benjamin Jaques, Dec. 5, 1727.*
Mary, and Joseph Hale, jr., int. May 1, 1736.
Mary, and Joseph Noyes [jr. int.], Apr. 21, 1738.*
Mary, and Joseph Cooch, Oct. 23, 1740.*
Mary, and Samuel Jaques, May 8, 1750.*

*Intention also recorded.

Noyes, Mary, and John Pettengell, Feb. 14, 1758.*
Mary, and John Willet, Nov. 1, 1759.*
Mary, of New Marblehead, and Jeremiah Dalton, int. May 6, 1761.
Mary, and Thomas Bricket, Aug. 27, 1766.*
Mary [Morse. int.], and Joshua Hills, Nov. 13, 1766.*
Mary, and Webster Bayley, Aug. 24, 1773.*
Mary, and Moses Chase of Plaistow, Apr. 17, 1788.*
Mary, and Theodore Atkinson, Feb. 13, 1796.*
Mary, and Jonathan Hunkins, Nov. 19, 1799.*
Mary, and Jacob Kent of Amesbury, Mar. 14, 1812.*
Mary, and John Pearson, jr. of Newburyport, Nov. 18, 1824.*
Mary Pilsbury, and Walter Bailey, July 10, 1816.*
Mary R., of Newburyport, and Zaccheus P. Thurlow, June 20, 1831.*
Molly, and Nath[anie]l Howard of Newburyport, May 12, 1784.*
Molly, and Simeon Copps, Dec. 24, 1794. c. r. 2.*
Moses, and Hannah Smith, Feb. 28, 1723-4.*
Moses [jr. int.], and Susanah Jaques, May 21, 1738.*
Moses, 3d, and Mrs. Margaret Woodbridge, Feb. 17, 1741-2.*
Moses, jr., and Abigail Savoury, Jan. 5, 1758.*
Moses, and Eunice Pilsbury, Apr. 2, 1795.*
Moses, and Martha Baker, both of Rowley, Mar. 14, 1816. c. r. 5.
Nancy, and Edward Rogers, July 4, 1838.*
Nathan, and Sarah Clark, June 3, 1714.*
Nathan, and Mary Greenleaf, Dec. 27, 1725.*
Nathaniel, and Priscilla Merrill, int. June 8, 1704.
Nathaniel, Rev., of South Hampton, N. H., and Mrs. Sarah Hale, Nov. 12, 1765.*
Nathaniel, Rev., of South Hampton, N. H., and Sarah Noyes, Feb. 8, 1774.*
Nathaniel, of Salisbury, N. H., and Sarah Emery, ——, 1808 or 9. [Nov. 25, 1808. int.]*
Nathaniel, jr., of Newburyport, and Mary Coffin, Nov. 12, 1815.*
Nehemiah, and Anne Stickne, May 16, 1732.*
Nicholas, jr., and Sarah Lunt, d. Daniel, int. July 17, 1695.
Nicholas, and Judeth Pike, Jan. 1, 1716-17.*
Nicolas, jr., and Judith Noyes, Nov. 29, 1788.*
Noah J[ohnson. int.], and Mehetable Foster, ——, 1807. c. r. 1. [Sept. 26. int.]*
Parker, and Judeth Coffin, Dec. 11, 1707.*
Parker, and Sarah Mighill of Rowley, at Rowley, Nov. 7, 1734.*
Parker, and Rebecca Bailey, int. Aug. 8, 1807.

*Intention also recorded.

Noyes, Parker, of West Newbury, and Sarah E. Wilson of
  Newburyport, Dec. 15, 1842.

Patience, and Daniel Carr of Newburyport, int. Oct. 28, 1825.

Patty, and Thomas Gray Chase, int. Nov. 3, 1807.

Paul, and Sarah Morse, Jan. 7, 1762.*

Pike, and Elizabeth Knight, Feb. 18, 1819.*

Priscilla, and Joseph Tompson, Nov. 7, 1727.*

Prudence, and Jacob Bayley, Oct. 16, 1745.*

Prudence, and John Serls, Dec. 24, 1786.*

Rachel, and Joseph Martin of Andover, Aug. 5, 1725.*

Rachel, and Stephen Corser of Boscawen, N. H., Mar. 1,
  1795.*

Rebecca, and John Knight, Jan. 1, 1671.

Rebecca, and Joseph Knight, jr., Apr. 29, 1708.*

Rebeckah [Mrs. int.], and Joseph Ilsly [3d. int.], Nov. 28,
  1717.*

Salley, and John Torry, Mar. 29, 1798.*

Sally, and John Brown, Sept. 5, 1795.*

Sally, and Jonathan Boardman of Newburyport, Feb. 15,
  1820.*

Samuel, and Hannah Poor, Dec. 1, 1714.

Samuel [3d. int.], and Rebecca Wheeler of Newburyport,
  Mar. 21, 1764.*

Samuel, of Portland, and Betty Palmer, Sept. 30, 1787.*

Samuel, jr., of Newburyport, and Mary Tompson, int. Nov.
  16, 1791.

Samuel, 3d [Ens. int.], and Jane Moody, Jan. 22, 1795.*

Samuel, 3d, and Hannah Stickney, Jan. 16, 1805.*

Samuel, of Haverhill, and Harriet Dutton, Dec. 3, 1835.*

Samuel M., jr., and Betsey Ann Rogers, int. Aug. 9, 1849.

Samuel M[oody. int.], and Elizabeth N[oyes. c. r. 5.] Tenney
  of Rowley, May 15, 1823.*

Sam[ue]ll [jr. int.], and Mary Bradbury, Nov. 17, 1757.*

Sara, and Matthew Pettingall, Apr. 13, 1674.

Sara, Mrs., and John Hale of Beverly [at Beverly. dup.],
  Mar. 31, 1684.

Sarah, and John French, Jan. 6, 1708.*

Sarah, and Peter Moers, int. Sept. 12, 1713.

Sarah, and Henry Gardner of Charlestown, Jan. 27, 1731-2.*

Sarah, and Richard Adams, jr., Jan. 21, 1755.*

Sarah, and William Moody, July 18, 1755.*

Sarah, and Thomas Parsons, int. Apr. 1, 1758.

Sarah, and Moses Ilsley, Mar. 21, 1764.

Sarah, and Rev. Nathaniel Noyes of South Hampton, N. H.,
  Feb. 8, 1774.*

Sarah, and Daniel Bailey, jr., Sept. 17, 1806.*

Sarah, and Stephen Kent, jr., Mar. 17, 1808.*

*Intention also recorded.

Noyes, Sarah, Mrs., and William Pilsbury, Nov. 11, 1817.*
Sarah Ann, and Charles Bradstreet of Newburyport, Mar. 7,
 1830.*
Sarah Jane, and John Divine, Aug. 22, 1831.
Sarah Jane, and John C. Adams, June 20, 1838.*
Sarah L., and Zaccheus Brown of Hampton, N. H., int. Nov.
 6, 1842.
Sarah Putnam, and Moses Rolf, Dec. 29, 1808.*
Seusanah, and Stephen Dole, Nov. 29, 1716.*
Sewell B., a. 20 y., mason, s. Timothy and Sarah, and Sarah
 J. Moody of Newburyport, a. 18 y., d. Henry and Jane,
 of Newburyport, July 12, 1846.
Silas, and Dorcas Bradford, at Boston, Feb. 4, 1790.
Silas, and Dorcas Noyes, Oct. —, 1792.*
Simeon B., and [Mary. int.] Ann Goodwin, Nov. 26, 1826.*
Simon, and Elisabeth Eaton, Dec. 10, 1754.*
Statira M., and William H. Lambert of Newburyport, int.
 May 4, 1847.
Stephen, and Mary March, Aug. 25, 1725.*
Stephen, jr., and Susanna Chase, June 15, 1756.*
Stephen, jr., and Betty Chase, Mar. 23, 1758.*
Stephen, 3d, and Sarah Pearson, July 8, 1772.*
Stephen, and Jane Little Knight, ——, 1804. c. r. 1. [int. Apr.
 3.]*
Stephen, and Ruth Ayer of Haverhill, int. Feb. 7, 1818.
Susan R., and William Darrah, ——, 1833. [int. Dec. 14.]*
Susanna, Mrs., and Richard Dole, jr., Jan. 14, 1745-6.*
Susanna, and Nathan Emery, int. Aug. 5, 1777.
Susanna, and Jacob Moody, Jan. 4, 1784.*
Tabitha, and James Greenough, June 30, 1790.*
Thomas, and Martha Peirce, Dec. 28, 1669.
Thomas, and Elizabeth [Greenleaf. c. c. and ct. r.], Sept. 24,
 1677.
Thomas, and Sarah Knight, Nov. 16, 1686. ct. r.
Thomas, 3d, and Judith March, Jan. 3, 1722-3.*
Thomas, Ens. [jr. int.], and Mary Emery, Jan. 5, 1726-7.*
Thomas, Capt., and Mrs. Elisabeth Ilsley, July 24, 1740.*
Thomas, 3d, and Ann Follinsbe, June 30, 1743.*
Thomas, of Haverhill, N. H., and Elisabeth Pettingill, Jan. 1,
 1746-7.*
Thomas, 4th, and Elisabeth Morss, Jan. 4, 1753.*
Thomas, 3d, and Rachel Clement, int. Jan. 29, 1757.
Thomas, 4th, and Sarah Bennet, Jan. 20, 1784.*
Thomas, Maj., and Sarah Chase, Dec. 9, 1798.*
Thomas, and Patty Mayhew, int. Jan. 8, 1803.
Thomas, and Mary Brown, ——, 1812. [Oct. 10. int.]*

*Intention also recorded.

NOYES, Thuda L. [Thulalinda. int.], and Abiel T. Lovejoy, Mar. 10, 1814.*

Timothy, and Mary Knight, Jan. 13, 1680.

Timothy, and Lydiah Plumer, Mar. 18, 1717-18.

Timothy, and Sarah Richards, June 9, 1735.*

Timothy, and Betty Dean, Jan. 10, 1770.*

Timothy, and Lydia Davis of Sandown, N. H., int. Dec. 21, 1784.

Wadleigh, and Hannah Smith, Nov. 29, 1768.*

Wadleigh, and Ann Boardman, Dec. 30, 1809.*

Wadley, and Hannah Savery of Bradford, int. Jan. 23, 1801.

William, and Mrs. Sara Cogsall, Nov. 6, 1685.

William [jr. int.], and Mrs. Anne Presbury, Aug. 26, 1741.*

William, 3d, and Lydia Morss, Aug. 10, 1742.*

William, and Hannah Stevens, Dec. 24, 1750.*

William, and Mary Pike of Salisbury, int. Nov. 2, 1753.

William, and Huldah Noyes, June 15, 1789.*

Will[ia]m, and Sally Green of Haverhill, Sept. 17, 1800.*

William, and Patty Horton Brown, Nov. 22, 1809.*

William, Capt., of Georgetown, Columbia, and Mary Hunt, Mar. 17, 1812.*

William P., and Frances S. Towle of Newburyport, int. Nov. 4, 1843.

NOYS (see also Noyes), Susanna, and Stephen Knight, Nov. 16, 1752.*

NOYSE (see also Noyes), Joseph, jr., and Ruth Peaslee of Plaistow, int. Oct. 16, 1776.

Mary, and John Hale, Sept. 14, 1732. c. r. 7.

NUTE, Elizabeth C., of Newburyport, and Solomon P. Felker, int. July 7, 1849.

NUTTING, Lydia S., of Newburyport, a. 18 y., d. Gay and China, of Newburyport, and William I. Lunt of Newburyport, a. 25 y., pilot, s. Jeremiah and Lois P., of Newburyport, Oct. 8, 1846.

Mary, and Paul Nowell, both of Cambridge, June 25, 1734. c. r. 7.

Solomon D., a. 22 y., farmer, b. Lisbon, Me., s. Abner and Rebecca, and Marinda Perkins, a. 18 y., d. Benjamin and Sally, Oct. 24, 1847.*

OAKS, Thomas, of Medford, and Elisabeth Greenleaf, Aug. 2, 1716.*

*Intention also recorded.

OBRIAN (see also Obrien), Thomas, and Mary Mace, Sept. 7, 1755.*

OBRIEN (see also Obrian, Obrine), Mary, and Robert Dunning of Brunswick, int. Dec. 11, 1802.

OBRINE (see also Obrien), Marcia S., and Rev. Jeremiah Chaplain of Danvers, Apr. 16, 1806.*

O'CONNELL, Michael, and Catherine Laughran of Newburyport, Sept. 17, 1843.

ODIORNE, John, of Newburyport, and Susan Greenleaf Boardman, ——, 1810. [Sept. 21. int.]*

O'DONOVAN, William, of Boston, and Polly White, int. Mar. 1, 1783.

OGDEN, James, of West Newbury, a. 23 y., farmer, b. Lincolnshire, and Hannah M. Dawkins, a. 18 y., b. England, d. William and Charlotte, Dec. 11, 1847.*

OLIVER (see also Olliver), Mary, and Samuel Apleton, Dec. 8, 1656.
Susannah, and Andrew Johonnot, both of Boston, May 21, 1730. C. R. 7.

OLLIVER (see also Oliver), Joanna, wid. John, and William Gerrish, Apr. 17, 16[45. T. C.].

OLMSTEAD, Charles A., a. 28 y., shipwright, b. Perry, Me., s. Eliphalet, of Perry, Me., and Elizabeth C. Hilliard, a. 35 y., d. William and Betsy Currier, May 17, 1849.*

ORANGE, Hannah, and Francis Bullard, mariner, both of Boston, July 4, 1733. C. R. 7.
Mary, of Boston, and Capt. James Brown of Waterford, Ire., Nov. 19, 1725. C. R. 7.

ORDEWAY (see also Ordway), John, and Margeret Alline of Reading, at Reading, Aug. 18, 1726.

ORDIWAY (see also Ordway), Jeane, and Joshua Richardson. Jan. 4, 1687-8. CT. R.

*Intention also recorded.

ORDWAY (see also Ardway, Ordeway, Ordiway), Abigail, and Samuel Savory, July 24, 1724.*

Abigail, and Abel Sawyer, Apr. 24, 1744.*

Abigail, and Jonathan Carlton, Jan. 3, 1784.*

Abigail, and Oliver Rogers, Nov. 1, 1795.*

Alfred, of West Newbury, and Rebecca L. Scribner, Mar. 31, 1835.*

Ann, and Abial Rogers, June 26, 1746.*

Ann M., a. 24 y., tailoress, d. John, and John S. Holt of Cambridge, a. 26 y., mason, s. Thomas, of Cambridge, Sept. 1, 1844.*

Anne, and John Merrill, 3d, int. Dec. 19, 1746.

Benjamin, and Rebecca Carr of South Hampton, int. Oct. 3, 1746.

Benjamin, and Susanna Davis, Dec. 25, 1775.*

Benjamin, and Ann Davis of Newburyport, Dec. 27, 1829.*

Caroline P., a. 19 y., d. Moses and Eunice, and Israel A. Morse of Bradford, a. 21 y., shoemaker, s. Benjamin and Abigail, of Bradford, May 18, 1845.*

David, and Lois Patten, Apr. 16, 1767.*

David, jr., and Mary Emery, Aug. 9, 1802.*

David, and Catharine G. Coker, both of West Newbury, Sept. 7, 1836.

Edward, and Mary Wood, Dec. 12, 1678.

Edward, jr., of Haverhill, and Elisabeth Eaton, at Haverhill [bef. 1780].

Eliphalet, and Sukey Rogers, Sept. 22, 1799.*

Eliphalet, of Sanbornton, N. H., and Rebekah Bartlett, June 18, 1822.*

Elisabeth, and Evan Jones of Salisbury, Mar. 20, 1721-2.*

Elisabeth, and Eliphalet Knight, June 6, 1745.*

Elisabeth, and Nathaniel Hills, int. Mar. 16, 1771.

Elisabeth, and Caleb Rogers, Oct. 27, 1799.*

Enoch, and Elizabeth Rogers, Sept. 25, 1783.*

Enoch, and Dorothy Verny, Apr. 5, 1787.*

Esther, and John Rogers, int. Mar. 14, 1712-13.

Eunice, and Sergeant Smith, Nov. 9, 1736.*

Francis, a. 21 y., ship carpenter, s. Nathaniel and Polly, and Emily Fitts of Salisbury, a. 19 y., d. William and Priscilla, of Salisbury, Oct. 29, 1845.*

Hannah, and Willet Peterson, Feb. 19, 1746-7. c. r. 2.*

Hannah, and Charles Hardy of Hampton Falls, N. H., Apr. 14, 1839.*

Hannaniah, and Rebecca Smith, Mar. 12, 1711.*

Hanson, of West Newbury, and Mary Ann Lunt, Jan. 14, 1830.*

Isaac, and Sarah Coker, Dec. 1, 1814.*

*Intention also recorded.

ORDWAY, James, and Johana Corley, Oct. 4, 1687. CT. R.
James [jr. int.], and Sarah Clark [d. John. int.] of Rowley, at Rowley, June 19, 1696.*
James [3d. int.], and Judeth Bailey, Nov. 28, 1711.*
James, and Hannah Sumnah, Nov. 3, 1799.*
James [jr. int.], and Judith Chase, Apr. 28, 1836.*
Jane, and Aron Patten of Amesbury, Dec. 6, 1739.*
Jane, and Joshua Greenleaf, jr., Oct. 21, 1789.*
Joanna, and William Titcomb [jr. int.], Jan. 26, 1714-15.*
John, and Mary Godfry, Dec. 5, 1681.
John, jr., and Hannah Bartlet, Dec. 18, 1706.*
John, and Polly Chase, Oct. 2, 1783.*
John, and Sarah Rogers, Jan. 5, 1786.*
John, and Anna Chase, Mar. 25, 1807.*
John, jr., and Elizabeth S. Chase, Nov. 21, 1831.*
John, and Hannah Chase of West Newbury, Mar. 29, 1837.*
Joseph, and Abigail Bailey, Sept. 4, 1796.*
Joshua, and Sarah Downer, Oct. 9, 1759.*
Joshua, jr., and Mary Chase, Nov. 25, 1800.*
Judith, and Stephen Sergent of Amesbury, Oct. 22, 1730.*
Louisa M., a. 26 y., d. Richard and Elizabeth, and William G. Sampson, a. 27 y., ship joiner, b. Boston, s. William and Mary, Nov. 12, 1848.*
Lowis, and Thomas Chase, June 12, 1800.*
Luther, and Lydia Page, int. July 18, 1846.
Lydia, and Evan Jones, May 13, 1726.*
Martha, and Joseph K. Mores, Feb. —, 1834.
Mary, and Daniel Goodridg, int. Nov. 16, 1698.
Mary, and John Bartlet, 3d, Nov. 18, 1702.*
Mary, and Jonathan Blake, May 18, 1721.*
Mary, and Enos Bartlet, Jan. 28, 1730.*
Mary, Mrs., and Josiah Sawyer, Dec. 25, 1735. C. R. 7.
Mary, and Moses Bayley, July 10, 1739.*
Mary, and Samuel Moulton, Nov. 29, 1743.*
Mary, and Moses Chase, 3d, Aug. 14, 1777.*
Matthew [Adams, jr. int.], and Hannah Rawlins, May 17, 1744.*
Moody, and Rebecca B. Davis, both of West Newbury, Sept. 30, 1836.
Moses, and Hanna Hadle, inc. Nov. 29, 1735.
Moses, and Polley Dennis of Newburyport, int. Aug. 25, 1804.
Moses, and Eunice Chase, May 9, 1822.*
Nathan, and Hannah Rogers, Jan. 7, 1724-5.*
Nathan, and Sarah Brown, Mar. —, 1726-7.*
Nathan, and Sarah Brown, Dec. 29, 1748.*
Nathan, and Dorothy Annis, July 12, 1768.*
Nathaniel, and Sarah Hale, Apr. 13, 1736.*

*Intention also recorded.

ORDWAY, Nathaniel, and Martha Bartlet, Nov. 27, 1800.*
Nathaniel, and Ann Bolton, both of West Newbury, Aug. 25, 1825.
Nathaniel L., and Mary Bennett, int. Mar. 10, 1823.
Nathan[ie]ll, and Priscilla Mors, Aug. 14, 171[8. c. r. 2.].*
Parsons, and Rebecca S. Clement of Newburyport, int. Sept. 16, 1843.
Peter, and Mary Moodey, Oct. 29, 1719.*
Peter, and Jemima Chase, Nov. 3, 1721.*
Peter, and Hannah Rawlings, June 5, 1754.*
Peter, and Elisabeth Poor, May 23, 1758.*
Peter, and Mary Jackman, July 24, 1783.*
Peter, jr., Capt., and Martha Smith, Apr. 9, 1815.*
Prudence, and Joshua Mors, Aug. 19, 1741.*
Prudence, and Josiah Bartlet, jr., June 1, 1773.*
Rebecah, and Seth Bartlet, Jan. 22, 1754.
Rebecca, and Benjamin Hills, Nov. 7, 1709.*
Richard, and Elizabeth March of Newburyport, int. Apr. 29, 1820.
Ruth, and Capt. Moses S. Moody, June 4, 1795.*
Sally, and Emanuel Roberts, Apr. 15, 1818.*
Sally, of Newburyport, and Samuel Colleyer, int. Mar. 26, 1825.
Samuel, and Sarah Ordway, d. James, abt. Feb. 25, 1692.
Samuel, of Haverhill, and Catherine Kinrick, Apr. 19, 1813.*
Samuel S., and Elizabeth Sawyer, May 4, 1836.*
Sara, and Richard Fitts, Oct. 8, 1654.
Sarah, d. James, and Samuel Ordway, abt. Feb. 25, 1692.
Sarah, and Caleb Morss, Nov. 23, 1732.*
Sarah, and Dudley Currier of Salem, N. H., May 11, 1780.*
Sarah, and William Wade, int. [Feb.] 22, 1806.
Sarah E., a. 20 y., d. John, and George White Remick of Newburyport, a. 23 y., mariner, s. William C., Oct. 13, 1844.
Steephen, and Abigaill Merrick, July 10, 171[8. c. r. 2.]*.
Stephen, jr., and Abigail Hadlock, Mar. 28, 1750.*
Stephen, jr., and Rebekah Chase, Nov. 29, 1784.*
Susan Davis, and Sprague Chase, Nov. 8, 1832.*
Thomas, and Phebe Sawyer, Feb. 24, 1800.*
Thomas, and Lydia Hanson, Nov. 15, 1807.*
Thomas S., and Elizabeth M. Dutton, both of West Newbury, Dec. 27, 1824.
Walter, of West Newbury, and Salome B. Wentworth, Feb. 13, 1835.*
William, and Abigail Bartlet, Nov. 8, 1801.*

ORMES, Richard, and Rebeckah Rawlince, Nov. 5, 1700.*

*Intention also recorded.

ORNE, Harriet, of Newburyport, and Solomon Haskell, jr., int. Jan. 5, 1830.

OSBORN, Alice, of Newburyport, and Cutting Lunt, int. Oct. 4, 1806.
Augustus K., of Boston, widr., a. 44 y., trader, s. Sylvester and Elizabeth, of Danvers, and Jane C. Stickney, a. 34 y., d. Benjamin and Ann, May 26, 1845.*

OSGOOD (see also Ossgood), Bradley, and Mehitabel Wood of Bradford, Aug. 1, 1811.*
John, and Lydia Newell, Dec. 3, 1778.*
Joseph, of Salisbury, and Apphia Pilsbury, Sept. 15, 1719.*
Joseph, of Salisbury, and Lydia Clemment, Dec. 15, 1774.*
Mary, of Amesbury, and William Adams, int. Apr. 3, 1843.
Mary N., of Newburyport, and Anthony Ilsley, int. Dec. 7, 1844.
Nathaniel S., of Newburyport, and Elizabeth S. Newman, int. Feb. 9, 1828.
Oliver, jr., and Ruth Pearson, both of Salisbury, June 9, 1822.
Sarah, Mrs., of Andover, and Joseph Lunt [jr. int.], at Andover, Nov. 24, 1738.*
Timothy, of Salisbury, and Mehettebel Chase, Nov. 29, 1715.*
Timothy, jr., of Salisbury, and Eunice Varnum, Oct. 8, 1827.*
Wyatt, of Salisbury, and Sarah M. Bailey, July 29, 1832.*

OSHULAWAY (see also Silloway), John, and Abigail Thurla, int. Apr. 24, 1714.

OSILIWAY (see also Silloway), Amos, and Elisabeth Baretue, at Amesbury, Jan. 5, 1737-8.*
Daniel, and Sarah Stevens of Amesbury, at Amesbury, Dec. 30, 1714.*
John, and Mary Pressy of Amesbury, at Amesbury, Mar. 30, 1715.*

OSILLAWAY (see also Silloway), Jane, and Ammi Ruhamah Mooers, July 8, 1751. c. R. 2.*

O'SILLAWAY (see also Silloway), Mary, and Daniel Merrill, jr., Nov. 27, 1759.*

OSSGOOD (see also Osgood), Anna, of Salisbury, and Oliver Titcomb, int. Sept. 23, 1752.

OTIS, James Frederick, of Portland. Me., and Susan Higginson of Newburyport, int. Sept. 24, 1832.

*Intention also recorded.

OWEN, Deliverance, and Thomas Thorla, jr., Aug. 4, 1774.*

PADDLEFORD, Elijah, and Margaret Randall of Newbury-port, int. Jan. 12, 1811.

PAGE (see also Paige), Cornelius, of Haverhill, and Mary Cooper, Dec. 9, 1729.*
David P[erkins. int.], and Susan M. Lunt of Newburyport, Dec. 16, 1832.*
Henry, and Elisabeth Homes, int. Aug. 4, 1804.
Joanna, of Billerica, and Benjamin Farley of Bedford, Jan. 19, 1732-3. C. R. 7.
John, of Newburyport, and Ruth Caldwell, int. Feb. 4, 1809.
Lewis, of Haverhill, and Lydia Griffin, Feb. 11, 1735 or 6.*
Lucy M., of Newburyport, and William A. Felch, Dec. 19, 1844.*
Lydia, and Luther Ordway, int. July 18, 1846.
Nathan, and Elisabeth Foster of Ipswich [of Chebacco. int.], at Chebacco parish, Ipswich, Apr. 19, 1758.*
Onesiphorus, of South Hampton, N. H., and Mehetabel Duty, Apr. 28, 1767.*
Ruben, of Newburyport, and Eliza Jane Chase, Mar. 22, 1804.*
Ruth, of Rowley, and Stephen Gerrish, int. Nov. 21, 1772.
Susanah, and John Swett, jr., int. June 4, 1698.

PAIGE (see also Page), Nathan, s. Theophilus and Hannah, of Kensington, N. H., and Mary Brown, d. Stephen, deceased, and Sarah, Oct. 23, 1765. C. R. 6.

PALKE, Joseph, and Mrs. Margeret Woodbridge, int. Mar. 14, 1716.

PALMER (see also Parmer), [Ann. T. C.], wid., and Francis Plumer, Mar. 21, 164[9. T. C.].
Betty, and Samuel Noyes of Portland, Sept. 30, 1787.*
Elisabeth, and Elkanah Lunt, jr., Apr. 5, 1759.*
Joanna, of Bradford, and Jonathan Chace, int. July 11, 1702.
Joseph, and Sara Jackman, Mar. 1, 1664.
Mary, and John Coffin of Newburyport, Nov. 18, 1781.*
Mehitable, of Rowley, and John Smith, at Rowley, Oct. 3, 1754.*
Ruth, and Moses Adams, Feb. 6, 1760.*
Samuel, of Rowley, and Ann Evins, int. July 3, 1738.
Samuel, and Elisabeth Shaw, Oct. 25, 1787.*
Sarah, of Bradford, and Richard Cauley of Stratham, July 15, 1728. C. R. 7.
Sarah, and Timothy Morse, Apr. 30, 1788.*

*Intention also recorded.

PARDEE, Fanny M., of Newburyport, and William E. Currier, int. Feb. 22, 1834.

PARISH, Amelia, and Rev. Ebenezer Perkins of Royalston, June 8, 1819.*
Elijah, Rev., and Mary Hale, Nov. 7, 1796.*
Mary Hale, and Daniel Noyes of Ipswich, June 23, 1818.*
Moses P., of Newburyport, and Mary S. Sawyer, Sept. 12, 1829.*

PARK, Esther, and John Flanders of Newburyport, int. Mar. 13, 1830.

PARKER, Abraham, jr., of Bradford, and Hannah Chase, Dec. 14, 1738.*
Caroline, and Nathaniel Hills, both of Newburyport, Mar. 12, 1839.
Daniel, of Bradford, and Sarah [Mary. int.] Mors, Nov. 26, 1713.*
Enoch, and Abigail Jackson, both of Newtown, July 14, 1736. c. R. 7.
Grace, of Bradford, and Abel Mors, int. May 1, 1714.
James, and Hannah Taylor of Amesbury, int. Mar. 20, 1827.
Joseph, and Ann Coker, Oct. 31, 1734.*
Joseph, and Elisabeth Lowell, Aug. 9, 1762. [He "takes the said Elisabeth naked, without any of her former husband's estate." int.]*
Josiah, and Nancy Bailey, Nov. 25, 1802.*
Mary, and Joshua Richardson, Jan. 31, 1678.
Mary, and Sam[ue]ll Buckman, Nov. 25, 171[7. c. R. 2.].
Mary, and Moses Pilsbury, jr., Aug. 6, 1728.*
[N. 7. c.]athan, and Susanna Short, Nov. 20, 1648.
Nathan, and Mary Browne, Dec. 15, 1675.
Nathaniel, of Bradford, and Rachel Sargent, Mar. 29, 1739.*
Nathaniel, Lt., of Bradford, and Ruth Bayley, Sept. 22, 1782.*
Priscilla, of Newburyport, and Jonathan Martin, int. Nov. 11, 1820.
Sarah, wid., and Josiah Chandler, both of Andover, July 1, 1735. c. R. 7.
Zerviah, and Samuel Winch, Aug. 28, 1732.*

PARKHURST, Jemima, of Weston, and Benjamin Bartlett, at Weston, Apr. 20, 1738.*
Mary, of Weston, and Edmund Bailey, at Weston, Aug. 20, 1731.

PARMENTER, Nancy, and Stephen May, int. Sept. 3, 1813.

*Intention also recorded.

PARMER (see also Palmer), Samuel, and Abigail Badger, June 23, 1785.*

PARSONS, David [of Kingston. int.], and Bethiah Moers, Mar. 22, 1750.*
David, and Mary Dutton, Nov. 22, 1812.*
John, and Charlotte M. Burrill, int. July 3, 1839.
Jonathan, jr., and Hannah Giles, Aug. 26, 1756.*
Mary G[riffin. int.], and Amos Jackman, July 31, 1823.*
Nancy, and Reuben Lane, May 4, 1813.*
Sarah, Mrs., and Rev. Eli Forbes of Gloucester, Sept. 13, 1781.*
Sarah [Mrs. c. R. 10.], and Enoch Peirce, Jan. 30, 1814.*
Susanna, and Capt. James Gray of Epsom, N. H., Mar. 20, 1777.*
Thomas, and Sarah Noyes, int. Apr. 1, 1758.
Thomas, and Sarah Sawyer, July 18, 1762.*
William, of Gloucester, and Abigail Beck, Feb. 8, 1753.*

PATTEE, Sophia, of Amesbury, and Josiah Cooper, int. July 13, 1815.

PATTEN (see also Pattin), Aron, of Amesbury, and Jane Ordway, Dec. 6, 1739.*
George P., and Mary Jane Green, July 29, 1834.*
Harriet, of Amesbury, and William Wigglesworth, int. Mar. 14, 1834.
Joseph, and Susannah Morss, both of Newburyport, Aug. 10, 1838.
Lois, and David Ordway, Apr. 16, 1767.*
Luice, of Sheepscote, and Somerby Moody, int. July 12, 1755.
Mary, of Kensington, and Nath[anie]l Coffin. Nov. 24, 1814.*
Nathaniel, of Windham, Conn, and Mary Hill of Billerica, June 22, 1734. c. R. 7.
Rebecca, and Joshua Morss, Apr. 21, 1765.*
Thomas B., and Emeline Green, Nov. 7, 1833.*
Thomas B., and Laura H. Loring, July 4, 1841.*

PATTERSON, George, and Anne Goodhue, Feb. 14, 1758.*

PATTIN (see also Patten), Hannah, and Benjamin Balch of Newburyport. Sept. 8, 1786.*

PAUL, Andrew M., of Newmarket, N. H., a. 24 y., iron moulder, b. Newmarket, N. H., s. Nathaniel and Mary, of Newmarket, and Sophia B. Greenleaf, a. 21 y., d. Abner and Sophia B., Nov. 4, 1845.*
Love, of Exeter, and John Sawyer, int. Oct. 8, 1796.

*Intention also recorded.